JCMS Annual Review of the European Union in 2011

Edited by

Nathaniel Copsey
and
Tim Haughton

General Editors: Michelle Cini and Amy Verdun

This edition first published 2012

Blackwell Publishing was acquired by John Wiley & Sons in February 2007. Blackwell's publishing program has been merged with Wiley's global Scientific, Technical and Medical business to form Wiley-Blackwell.

Registered Office
John Wiley & Sons Ltd, The Atrium, Southern Gate, Chichester, West Sussex, PO19 8SQ, United Kingdom

Editorial Offices
350 Main Street, Malden, MA 02148-5020, USA
9600 Garsington Road, Oxford, OX4 2DQ, UK
The Atrium, Southern Gate, Chichester, West Sussex, PO19 8SQ, UK

For details of our global editorial offices, for customer services, and for information about how to apply for permission to reuse the copyright material in this book please see our website at www.wiley.com/wiley-blackwell.

ISBN 978-1-4443-6699-0
ISSN 0021-9886 (print) 1468-5965 (online)

Set in 11/12.5 Pt Times by Toppan Best-set Premedia Limited
Printed in Singapore

2012

CONTENTS

Editorial: Desperate, but not Serious – The EU in 2011 1
NATHANIEL COPSEY AND TIM HAUGHTON

The ECB as Lender of Last Resort 6
WILLEM BUITER AND EBRAHIM RAHBARI

On the Stability of Public Debt in a Monetary Union 36
DANIEL GROS

1989: The Missed Opportunity 49
DOUGLAS HURD

The JCMS Annual Review Lecture 53
ERIK JONES

The Hungarian Rhapsodies 68
ATTILA ÁGH

Poland in the Driving Seat 76
KAROLINA POMORSKA AND SOPHIE VANHOONACKER

Governance and Institutions 85
DESMOND DINAN

Internal Market 99
JAMES BUCKLEY, DAVID HOWARTH AND LUCIA QUAGLIA

Justice and Home Affairs 116
JÖRG MONAR

Legal Developments 132
FABIAN AMTENBRINK

The Arab Spring, the Eurozone Crisis and the Neighbourhood 147
RICHARD G. WHITMAN AND ANA E. JUNCOS

Relations with the Rest of the World 162
DAVID ALLEN AND MICHAEL SMITH

The Eurozone in 2011 178
Dermot Hodson

Economies of Member States Outside the Eurozone 195
Richard Connolly

Chronology: The European Union in 2011 210
Fabian Guy Neuner

Index 217

JCMS 2012 Volume 50 Annual Review pp. 1–5 DOI: 10.1111/j.1468-5965.2012.02280.x

Editorial: Desperate, but not Serious – The EU in 2011*

NATHANIEL COPSEY[1] and TIM HAUGHTON[2]
[1] Aston University. [2] University of Birmingham

Two themes dominated the European headlines in 2011. At home, the news was relentlessly gloomy as economic stagnation persisted across much of the continent and Europe's leaders lurched from one emergency summit to another. Governments fell, austerity measures were promised, new rescue packages were agreed and yet the mighty bond markets remained implacable. The euro's imminent demise was regularly announced, particularly in the British press, yet last-minute bail-outs prevented sovereign default in the peripheral economies and held the 17-strong group together. The bonds of European solidarity were severely tested for the first time in 2011. For the moment, they have held fast, but the crisis remains very far from resolution. Indeed, crisis appears to be the new normal state of affairs in the European Union.

Yet from abroad came good news: a series of revolutions on Europe's southern flank in North Africa and the Middle East toppled four long-serving Arab strongmen: Tunisia's Ben Ali (in office since 1987); Egypt's Mubarak (in office since 1981); Yemen's Salah (in power since 1978 in North Yemen and all of Yemen since 1990); and the comedic arch-villain of Arab politics, Libya's Gaddafi, who had clocked up an impressive 42 years as leader since 1969. Civil uprisings also took place in Bahrain and Syria, with major protests in Algeria, Iraq, Jordan, Kuwait and Morocco. The Arab Spring took Europe completely by surprise, and first reactions were at best muted, or at worst wildly inappropriate. Failing to capture the public mood, in the first weeks of the Tunisian revolution, France's foreign minister, Michèle Aliot-Marie, for instance, embarrassingly offered to send French security forces to Tunis to help restore order.

As the revolutions progressed, however, the Europeans changed tack and mobilized much-needed air cover in support of the Libyan rebels, which proved decisive in turning the tide against Gaddafi by the summer. Although the Libyan campaign was not all plain sailing, it did demonstrate that Europe – albeit not explicitly the EU – still had the potential to be a force on the world stage. The Libyan campaign was the first joint Anglo–French mission undertaken without active American military engagement since the ill-fated Suez campaign of 1956, and the first European military intervention in North Africa since the end of French rule in Algeria in 1962. These historical memories are an invaluable aid in illustrating the problems that the EU will face in attempting to support the process of transformation across the Middle East and North Africa. In brief, Europe does not begin with a clean slate in North Africa and this, combined with the severe economic and political problems back home, will make for a complex relationship with the new Arab regimes.

* Tim Haughton co-edited this year's *Annual Review* whilst holding an Austrian Marshall Plan Foundation Fellowship at Johns Hopkins University's School of Advanced International Studies. Grateful thanks are extended to the Foundation for financial support and the Center for Transatlantic Relations for providing such a congenial location to edit the publication.

The year 2011 was an important one for the European External Action Service (EEAS), which 'after an uncertain and prolonged birth finally got down to work in January' as David Allen and Michael Smith put it in their contribution to this issue. Nonetheless, the EEAS was bedevilled not just by institutional turf wars and the teething problems of appointing personnel to key posts, but also by the fact that the head of EEAS, Catherine Ashton, was the subject of much open criticism from foreign ministers and the media, not to mention sniping from within her own institution. We noted in last year's editorial that 2011 was 'intended to be the year when the EEAS would be up and running and could be measured against its results' (Copsey and Haughton, 2011, p. 4). Whilst critics ought to acknowledge both the flaws in the institutional design and the ongoing crisis in the eurozone, so far even supporters of the EEAS recognize the results have been underwhelming. Nonetheless, even in what sometimes felt like the dark days of 2011, there were glimmers of hope. Overshadowed by the euro crisis and David Cameron's decision to block any new treaty, Croatia's EU accession treaty was signed at the December European Council, reminding us of both the long and difficult path followed by Croatia in the two decades since its declaration of independence and the impact of the prospect of enlargement, which is sometimes dubbed the EU's most powerful foreign policy tool.

There can be no doubt that the political consequences of the economic crisis of the past few years have shaken the European integration project to its core. Throughout 2011, the EU's leadership seemed to find itself continually on the back foot, reacting to events, rather than shaping them. This lumbering from crisis to crisis was at least partly due to the deliberative method of decision-making in the Union. Bringing resolution to the eurozone crisis involves too many veto players with frequently diverging interests. The good news for European integration was that all parties agreed that the euro must be saved. The bad news was that they differed widely in their approach to fixing the problem. An unfortunate consequence was that the failure to agree on decisive joint action gave the impression that Europe's leaders were fiddling whilst Rome burned – or in the Viennese expression, that the situation was desperate, but not serious. This cost Europe dearly in credibility.

As the year wore on, a long-term solution to the eurozone's problems began to take shape in the form of the Commission's so-called 'Six Pack' of reforms to the Stability and Growth Pact which entered into force in December, and the German-inspired Fiscal Compact which was also proposed in that same month. In combination, the reforms are designed to prevent macroeconomic imbalances from building up. Both measures have the potential to go a long way to do more than just paper over the cracks, but they raise deep and profound questions not just about the construction of the single currency project, but about the focus, direction and purpose of European integration.

Moments of crisis offer dangers, but also opportunities. The very weaknesses and vulnerabilities of Europe exposed by the eurozone crisis are also the reasons why individual European states need to integrate and show solidarity. In an era of frayed trust between Member States and economic hardship for ordinary citizens, the ease with which voters can be mobilized by banging a populist and nationalist drum is all too apparent, especially in cases like Italy and Greece where elected politicians were replaced by technocrats who seemed to be following an externally determined agenda. The year also marked the tenth anniversary of the Laeken Declaration with its clarion call to bring the EU closer to its citizens. This is a message as relevant – if not more relevant – today than a decade ago.

***

This is our fourth issue of the *JCMS AR* as editors and we have continued our policy of commissioning contributions from practitioners and commentators from outside the academic world. Given the prominence of the eurozone's woes in 2011, we commissioned articles from two of Europe's most astute economists. Willem Buiter, Chief Economist at Citigroup and a former member of the Bank of England's monetary policy committee, explains, together with Ebrahim Rahbari, how and why the European Central Bank should become lender of last resort to the eurozone's sovereigns. Nonetheless, they emphasize that a technically efficient lender of last resort should not be created at the expense of other objectives – not least the need to have in place the 'right incentives for banks and sovereigns to behave prudently, to avoid a repeat of the fiscal bacchanalia and irresponsible bank lending, investing and funding of the decade before 2008'. Moreover, they argue that any changes need to be constructed in such a way as to strengthen – or at the very least not weaken – the linkages of accountability between citizens and decision-makers.

Debt is central to what one of the contributors to last year's *Annual Review* described as the single currency's 'saga of Wagnerian intensity' (Marsh, 2011, p. 45). Our second commissioned article on the euro is written by Daniel Gros, Director of the Brussels-based Centre for European Policy Studies. He focuses on a simple but fundamental question which not only feeds into contemporary debates, but also touches on deeper questions concerning the construction of the single currency: is a high level of public debt inherently more dangerous within a monetary union? He reminds us that many commentators were asserting that only by entering EMU could economies like Italy and Spain protect themselves from the high interest rates they had to pay on public debt. Membership of EMU, this view suggested, would convince financial markets that these countries would not inflate away the value of their debt. Today, however, the very same countries are forced to pay a high-risk premium because they have 'lost the option to use the printing press and could thus be forced into default if interest rates are too high'. His article draws some instructive, if uncomfortable, conclusions, underlining that highly indebted countries only have unpleasant choices within or outside a monetary union.

Although the euro crisis dominated the headlines with the constant question marks over whether some members would remain in the club, the completion of negotiations and the signing of the accession treaty with Croatia whilst the rotating EU Presidency was held by Hungary and Poland remind us of some of the great achievements of the EU, particularly the big-bang enlargement of 2004 and 2007 which united west and east, transcending the cold war division of Europe. It is worth stepping back from the mood of doom and gloom to recall that Estonia, which joined the eurozone on 1 January 2011, was still a constituent part of the Soviet Union just 20 years earlier.

Nevertheless, just as the seemingly unremitting battery of bad news about the single currency can cloud our judgements and lead us to forget some of the great achievements of European integration, we should also remember that making mistakes is not the exclusive preserve of the current generation of European leaders. Following our three previous issues of the *Annual Review* in which we commissioned State of the Union articles from leading figures in contemporary EU institutions (Barroso, 2009; Trichet, 2010; and Buzek, 2011), we turned this year to one of Europe's elder statesmen, former British Foreign Secretary, Douglas Hurd, for his reflections on the legacy of 1989. His conclusion that 1989 was a wasted opportunity unlikely to be repeated is frank, even gloomy, yet it provides a good starting point for Europe and the United States to develop a new grand strategy to tackle the foreign policy challenges of the 21st century. Indeed, it is striking that another elder statesman on the other side of the Atlantic, Zbigniew Brzeziński (2012), also sees 1989–91 in a similar light.

In this year of shocks and adjustments, the *JCMS AR* lecture delivered in Washington, DC by Erik Jones argues that crisis is nothing new in the history of European integration. In every decade since the end of World War II Europe has experienced moments that have much in common with the current malaise affecting the EU. Each time the European project has emerged stronger as a consequence. This time, however, according to Jones, it *is* different. Europe faces ever-tightening constraints on the possibilities for further integration and its political leadership faces an existential crisis not just for the EU, but for the notion of 'Europe' as a whole. Central to Jones' diagnosis of the woes facing the EU is his notion of solidarity. 'Solidarity', for him, is both a useful concept for understanding why countries choose to participate in the European project and for explaining the resilience of Europe writ large. In the crisis of trust facing the European project in which finger-pointing and the blame game are rife, the message needs to be conveyed that European solidarity exists in many different patterns across many different domains of integration.

The *Annual Review* lecture not only provides a prominent scholar of European integration with the opportunity to comment on the big picture of European integration, but to offer some fresh thinking on the challenges facing policy-makers. Following in the footsteps of the previous three lectures given by Vivien Schmidt (2009), Kalypso Nicolaïdis (2010) and Loukas Tsoukalis (2011), Jones sketches out some prescriptions for the EU, highlighting the importance of maintaining and deepening the notions of solidarity. The process of rising to those challenges he notes, however, will be 'deliberative, consensual, complicated and, during the implementation at least, will be inefficient'.

We would like to thank all the contributors to this issue of the *JCMS AR* for their efforts and efficiency in rising to the challenges we set them by producing such excellent copy on time. We would also like to thank Michelle Cini and Amy Verdun for their continued support over the past year as *JCMS* editors, and hope our relationship will continue to be as congenial and productive in the future.

References

Barroso, J. (2009) 'State of the Union: Delivering a "Europe of Results" in a Harsh Economic Climate'. *JCMS*, Vol. 47, No. S1, pp. 7–16.

Brzezinski, Z. (2012) *Strategic Vision: America and the Crisis of Global Power* (New York: Basic Books).

Buzek, J. (2011) 'State of the Union: Three Cheers for the Lisbon Treaty and Two Warnings for Political Parties'. *JCMS*, Vol. 49, No. S1, pp. 7–18.

Copsey, N. and Haughton, T. (2011) 'Editorial: 2010, Kill or Cure for the Euro?' *JCMS*, Vol. 49, No. S1, pp. 1–6.

Marsh, D. (2011) 'Faltering Ambitions and Unrequited Hopes: The Battle for the Euro Intensifies'. *JCMS*, Vol. 49, No. S1, pp. 45–55.

Nicolaïdis, K. (2010) 'The JCMS Annual Review Lecture – Sustainable Integration: Towards EU 2.0?' *JCMS*, Vol. 48, No. S1, pp. 21–54.

Schmidt, V. (2009) 'Re-envisioning the European Union: Identity, Democracy, Economy'. *JCMS*, Vol. 47, No. S1, pp. 17–42.

Trichet, J.-C. (2010) 'State of the Union: The Financial Crisis and the ECB's Response between 2007 and 2009'. *JCMS*, Vol. 48, No. S1, pp. 7–19.

Tsoukalis, L. (2011) 'The JCMS Annual Review Lecture: The Shattering of Illusions – and What Next?' *JCMS*, Vol. 49, No. S1, pp. 19–44.

JCMS 2012 Volume 50 Annual Review pp. 6–35 DOI: 10.1111/j.1468-5965.2012.02275.x

The European Central Bank as Lender of Last Resort for Sovereigns in the Eurozone

WILLEM BUITER and EBRAHIM RAHBARI
Citigroup, London

Introduction

This article argues that the European Central Bank (ECB) has been acting as lender of last resort (LoLR) for the sovereigns of the eurozone since it first started its outright purchases of eurozone periphery sovereign debt under the Securities Markets Programme (SMP) in May 2010 (see De Grauwe, 2011b; Wyplosz, 2011, 2012; Buiter and Rahbari, 2012a). The scale of its interventions as LoLR for sovereigns has grown steadily since then and its range of instruments has expanded. We interpret the longer-term refinancing operations (LTROs) of December 2011 and February 2012 as being as much about acting, indirectly, as LoLR for the Spanish and Italian sovereigns by facilitating the purchase of their debt by domestic banks in the primary issue markets, as about dealing with a liquidity crunch for eurozone banks. A future third LoLR instrument will be indirect lending by the eurozone to periphery sovereigns. This will be achieved through national central banks lending to the International Monetary Fund (IMF) and the IMF lending to the Spanish and Italian sovereigns, once these sovereigns have come under suitable troika (that is, IMF, European Commission and ECB) programmes. If and when the European Stability Mechanism (ESM) gets a banking licence (becomes an eligible counterparty of the eurozone for the purpose of repos or other forms of collateralized borrowing), the ECB will have a fourth mechanism through which it can act as LoLR for sovereigns.

The ECB denies acting as LoLR for sovereigns, presumably because this would open it up to the criticism that it is in violation of Article 123 of the Treaty on the Functioning of the European Union (TFEU, henceforth 'the Treaty'). This forbids (direct) funding of the eurozone sovereigns by the ECB and the national central banks of the eurozone. The ECB rationalizes its SMP purchases as being motivated by the desire to maintain or restore orderly sovereign debt markets, which are necessary for the proper functioning of the monetary transmission mechanism – through interest rates. It characterizes its LTROs as addressing banking sector liquidity problems.

We disagree that this is the complete story of what the ECB intended to do through either its SMP purchases or through its LTROs, or of what these interventions actually achieved. We establish in this article that sovereigns, like banks, need a LoLR. We argue that the ECB is the only credible and effective LoLR from within the eurozone. Because of institutional and policy failures in the eurozone, the ECB has been forced to take on material sovereign credit risk on top of the growing counterparty risk and credit risk it is assuming through its repos and other collateralized lending operations with the eurozone banking sector and through its outright purchases of private securities. We argue that, in a rationally designed economic and monetary union (EMU), joint and several guarantees by the eurozone Member States could, should and would have been used to protect the ECB and the national central banks (NCBs) from taking on avoidable sovereign credit risk and, indeed, any credit risk higher than that implied by a joint and several guarantee from all eurozone Member States. With disorderly markets, however, and with financial panics leading to a potentially self-fulfilling fear-of-default-driven withdrawal of private funding from the markets, even joint and several guarantees by the 17 eurozone sovereigns may not be sufficient to restore market liquidity and funding liquidity. Among the eurozone policy actors, only the ECB can provide unconditional euro liquidity in any amount and without notice.

It is possible that a global LoLR like the IMF could have been an adequate source of ultimate liquidity for troubled eurozone sovereigns. However, there was no consensus among the global political leadership on the extent to which the IMF should play this role. The United States and Canada, for instance, refused to make any financial contribution to the fund-raising efforts of the IMF since the middle of 2011 that were aimed at providing additional financial resources – beyond the US$380 billion of loanable funds remaining at the disposal of the IMF at the time of the IMF–World Bank Spring Meetings in April 2012. The US$430 billion finally pledged to the IMF fell well short of the US$600 billion Managing Director Lagarde had requested. It is also quite inadequate for the IMF, alone or jointly with the eurozone fiscally backed facilities (the European Financial Stability Facility [EFSF] and/or the ESM), to act as a credible LoLR for the eurozone. The ECB will still be needed to provide the true sovereign LoLR firepower; it is the only credible liquidity back-stop.

We show that, as a result of the failure of the European and wider global political authorities to provide adequate liquidity support and solvency support (including the resources required to permit the orderly restructuring of the debt of insolvent eurozone sovereigns and banks), the ECB has in fact acted not only as LoLR for sovereigns and banks (and continues to do so on a steadily expanding scale) but has gone well beyond that: it has provided financial support to manifestly insolvent banks and sovereigns to prevent disorderly defaults of sovereigns and of systemically important banks and to create a window for orderly sovereign debt restructuring and for orderly bank debt restructuring and bank recapitalization instead.

We argue that the ECB should exit from the quasi-fiscal role that has been forced upon it by the inability of the eurozone political leadership to create legitimate fiscally backed institutions for dealing with sovereign illiquidity, sovereign insolvency and bank insolvency. Changes are required in the Treaty to allow the ECB/eurozone to provide liquidity directly to sovereigns in the primary sovereign debt markets and through direct lending to the sovereigns. To ensure that liquidity support by the ECB to sovereigns and banks does not turn into quasi-fiscal transfers from the ECB to these sovereigns and banks should they turn out to be insolvent as well as illiquid, all sovereign debt exposure of the ECB – whether through outright purchases of eurozone sovereign debt, through loans to sovereigns or through lending secured against financial instrument issued or guaranteed by eurozone sovereigns – should be backed with the full joint and several guarantees of all the eurozone Member States. To prevent this from turning into a one-way road to Weimar-style inflation, all ECB lender-of-last-resort interventions, like all other decisions affecting the size and composition of the balance sheet and off-balance sheet assets and liabilities of the ECB/eurozone, should be at the sole discretion of the ECB, and sufficiently strong incentives must be provided for sovereigns to adhere to fiscal discipline.

Finally, as a further safeguard against opening the floodgates to excessive credit expansion, the substantive accountability of the ECB should be materially enhanced. For example, the remuneration of the members of the Governing Council could be tied to the medium-term performance of inflation relative to the (more clearly defined than currently) numerical inflation target. Even if members of the Governing Council are motivated in part (or even exclusively) by non-pecuniary considerations, having pay related to performance will provide another natural focal point for accountability through media scrutiny and the associated risk of embarrassment. Additional transparency requirements should be introduced for disclosing the details of operational decisions, including the size and composition of the ECB's and NCBs' balance sheets, the terms on which financial transactions are conducted and the identities of the counterparties. The European Parliament should be able to dismiss the Executive Board (collectively) for incompetence.

I. Why Sovereigns Need a Lender of Last Resort

An LoLR provides funding liquidity to solvent but illiquid counterparties. In the classical Bagehot approach, this liquidity is provided against good collateral and at a penalty rate (Bagehot (1999 [1873])). The Bagehot approach is, however, too restrictive in our view and we shall use the term 'lender of last resort' in the sense of a lender to illiquid but most likely solvent counterparties on whatever terms. We recognize that illiquidity is almost always the product of fear of insolvency and that in practice it may be very difficult to determine whether an illiquid entity is indeed most likely solvent provided the illiquidity is remedied by providing the illiquid counterparty with liquidity on terms that are appropriate for a solvent borrower.

It has long been recognized that, because of liquidity and maturity mismatch among their assets and liabilities, banks need a LoLR (see Friedman and Schwartz, 1961; Goodhart and Illing, 2002). It is less well appreciated that sovereigns are in a similar position to banks. Like banks, a sovereign that does not have full control over its central bank is prone to liquidity and maturity mismatch between its assets and liabilities, broadly defined, even when these liabilities are domestic-currency-denominated. The sovereign is at risk of the equivalent of a bank run or bank funding strike – a sovereign debt roll-over strike, sovereign funding strike or 'sudden stop'. Of course, control of the Treasury over the central bank (fiscal dominance) only solves the sudden-stop problem for domestic-currency-denominated funding. It does not help when the sovereign faces a foreign currency funding gap (for related aspects, see Eichengreen *et al.*, 2005). The main assets of the sovereign are intangible, implicit and illiquid ones – notably the net present discounted value of future taxes. Clearly, the net present discounted value of future public spending is an intangible, implicit and highly illiquid liability.

The sovereign clearly needs a source of unconditional liquidity: there are strict technical and political limits on the ability of the authorities to securitize future tax receipts and thus turn their net present discounted value (NPV) into a liquid asset that can be used to meet immediate liquidity needs. *A fortiori*, when a sovereign has trouble rolling over maturing debt or funding new deficits, it is hard, if only because of credibility and commitment problems, to turn a political commitment today to cut future public spending (whose NPV represents a reduction in an illiquid sovereign liability) into the capacity to increase the issuance of liquid liabilities (new debt). There are, regrettably, no markets for the net present discounted value of primary (non-interest) government budget surpluses.

Among the revenue sources of the Treasury are the payments made to the Treasury by the central bank – the Treasury's share of the central bank's seigniorage profits (the profits derived by the central bank from its monopoly of the issuance of legal tender). The NPV of these future 'taxes' paid by the central bank to the Treasury is, however, also an intangible and illiquid asset of the Treasury. A related intangible asset of the central bank is the NPV of its future seigniorage. How much seigniorage can be extracted in the future by the central bank, if it is committed to a price stability target or a low inflation target is a key question, the answer to which determines whether or to what extent the central bank can act as LoLR to the sovereign without compromising its price stability mandate. How the NPV of this future seigniorage can be mobilized today to deal with sovereign liquidity problems is another key issue.

To motivate and focus the discussion we will start from the basic accounting identities of the general government sector (central, state and local government plus the social security funds, but excluding the central bank) and of the central bank. We shall refer in what follows to the general government as the Treasury. We will use these budget identities and the relevant no-Ponzi finance boundary conditions to generate the intertemporal budget constraints of the Treasury and the central bank. Finally, we will recast the intertemporal budget constraints as 'comprehensive balance sheets' and contrast them with the conventional balance sheets of tangible real assets and financial assets and liabilities. With these building blocks we then tackle the LoLR issues that can plague the sovereign.

II. A Stylized Set of Accounts for the Treasury and the Central Bank

The central bank has as liabilities the monetary base $M \geq 0$ and non-monetary liabilities (term deposits or central bank bills and bonds) N. The monetary base consists of coin and currency, with a zero nominal interest rate, and overnight deposits held with the central bank by commercial banks and other eligible counterparties – commercial bank reserves with the central bank: both required reserves and excess reserves. The interest rate on these reserves is set by the central bank. The average nominal interest rate on the monetary base is denoted i^M. For simplicity, all non-monetary debt instruments issued by both the central bank and the Treasury are assumed to be one-period maturity, domestic-currency-denominated safe nominal bonds with a nominal interest rate i.

As assets, the central bank holds the stock of gold and international foreign exchange reserves, R^f, in foreign currency, earning a risk-free one-period nominal interest rate in terms of foreign currency, i^f, and the stock of domestic credit, which consists of central bank holdings of nominal, interest-bearing Treasury bills, B^{cb}, earning a risk-free domestic-currency nominal interest rate, i, and central bank claims on the private sector, L, with domestic-currency nominal interest rate, i^L. The stock of Treasury debt (all assumed to be denominated in domestic currency) held by the public outside the central bank is denoted B^p. It pays the risk-free nominal interest rate, i; T^p is the nominal value of the tax payments by the domestic private sector to the Treasury – it is a choice variable of the Treasury and can be positive or negative; T^{cb} is the nominal value of payments made by the central bank to the Treasury – it is a choice variable of the Treasury and can be positive or negative.

H is the nominal value of the transfer payments made by the central bank to the private sector (a 'helicopter drop of money' if the counterpart of an increase in H is an increase in the monetary base). We can have helicopter money in this set-up if we assume H to be a choice variable of the central bank. In most countries, the central bank is not a fiscal principal and can neither tax nor make explicit transfer payments. If the central bank does not have the power to tax, then $H \geq 0$, but we can still have transfers by the central bank to the private sector – that is, helicopter money.

We leave H in the central bank's budget constraint for two didactic purposes. First, even though in the real world only the Treasury can make explicit transfer payments to the private sector (that is, $H \equiv 0$) and the central bank cannot engage in helicopter money, the Treasury and the central bank together can engage in a joint policy action equivalent to helicopter money. This would be a tax cut or increase in transfer payments by the Treasury (a reduction in T^p) with a matching increase in 'taxes' paid by the central bank to the Treasury (an increase in T^{cb} that keeps $T^p + T^{cb}$ constant, which the central bank finances with an increase in the monetary base). The second reason for introducing helicopter money is because it highlights the feature that, even when we set $H \equiv 0$ and thus rule out any explicit (quasi-fiscal) tax transfer actions by the central bank, the central bank can (and in practice often does) engage in a variety of implicit quasi-fiscal actions by lending to private (and sometimes public) counterparties at rates different from the appropriate risk-adjusted opportunity cost rate of return. The central bank frequently subsidizes, and occasionally taxes, its private counterparties, and it tends to do so in ways that are less than transparent.

Total taxes net of transfer payments received by the consolidated Treasury and central bank are $\tilde{T} = T^p - H$; e is the value of the spot nominal exchange rate (the domestic currency price of foreign exchange); $C \geq 0$ is the nominal value of Treasury spending on current goods and services; and $C^{cb} \geq 0$ the nominal value of central bank spending on current goods and services. Total current spending by the consolidated Treasury and central bank is $\tilde{C} \equiv C + C^{cb}$. The central bank is not assumed to hold real assets, but the general government/Treasury can. The stock of real assets held by the Treasury is denoted K, the money price of a unit of this real asset is P^K, each unit of physical capital earns a rental rate, ρ, in nominal terms and depreciates at a constant proportional rate, δ. The time subscripts on asset stocks refer to the end of the period in question, or the beginning of the subsequent period. For simplicity we assume that only the central banks holds foreign assets (the official gold and foreign exchange reserves) and that neither the Treasury nor the central bank issue foreign-currency-denominated liabilities.

Equation 1 is the single-period budget constraint of the Treasury and Equation 2 that of the central bank:

$$B_t^p + B_t^{cb} - P_t^K K_t \equiv C_t - T_t^p - T_t^{cb} + (1+i_t)\left(B_{t-1}^p + B_{t-1}^{cb}\right) - \left(\rho_t + P_t^K(1-\delta)\right)K_{t-1} \qquad (1)$$

$$M_t + N_t - B_t^{cb} - L_t - e_t R_t^f \equiv C_t^{cb} + T_t^{cb} + H_t + (1 + i_t^M) M_{t-1} + (1 + i_t)(N_{t-1} - B_{t-1}^{cb}) - (1 + i_t^L) L_{t-1} - (1 + i_t^f) e_t R_{t-1}^f \quad (2)$$

Before we can proceed with the substantive economic analysis, one more bit of notation is required: I_{t_1,t_0} is the nominal stochastic discount factor between periods t_1 and t_0, defined recursively by

$$\begin{aligned} I_{t_1,t_0} &= \prod_{k=t_0+1}^{t_1} I_{k,k-1} \quad \text{for} \quad t_1 > t_0 \\ &= 1 \qquad\qquad\qquad \text{for} \quad t_1 = t_0 \end{aligned} \quad (3)$$

The interpretation of I_{t_1,t_0} is the price in terms of period, t_0, money of one unit of money in period $t_1 \geq t_0$. There will in general be many possible states in period t_1, and period t_1 money has a period t_0 (forward) price for each state. Let E_t be the mathematical expectation operator conditional on information available at the beginning of period t. Provided earlier dated information sets do not contain more information than later dated information sets, these stochastic discount factors satisfy the recursion property

$$E_{t_0}\left(I_{t_1,t_0} E_{t_1} I_{t_2,t_1}\right) = E_{t_0} I_{t_2,t_0} \quad \text{for } t_2 \geq t_1 \geq t_0 \quad (4)$$

Finally, the risk-free nominal interest rate in period t, i_t (that is, the money price in period t of one unit of money in every state of the world in period $t + 1$) is defined by

$$\frac{1}{1 + i_t} = E_t I_{t+1,t} \quad (5)$$

The solvency constraint of the Treasury is the familiar no-Ponzi finance condition that the present discounted value (NPV) of the terminal stock of net financial liabilities minus tangible assets be non-positive:

$$\lim_{F \to \infty} E_t I_{F,t-1}\left(B_F^p + B_F^{cb} - P_F^K K_F\right) \leq 0 \quad (6)$$

The solvency constraint of the central bank is that the present discounted value of its terminal stock of net *non-monetary* financial liabilities be non-positive:

$$\lim_{F \to \infty} E_t I_{F,t-1}\left(N_F - B_F^{cb} - L_F - e_F R_F^f\right) \leq 0 \quad (7)$$

The reason monetary liabilities are not included in the solvency constraint of the central bank is that currency is irredeemable: the holder cannot demand, at any time, its exchange from the issuer for anything else. We extend this irredeemability property to the other component of the monetary base, commercial bank reserves with the central bank.

These solvency constraints and the single-period budget constraints of the Treasury and central bank imply the following intertemporal budget constraints for the Treasury and the central bank:

$$P^K_{t-1}K_{t-1} - \left(B^p_{t-1} + B^{cb}_{t-1}\right) \geq E_t \sum_{j=t}^{\infty} I_{j,t-1}\left(C_j - \left(T^p_j + T^{cb}_j\right) + S_j\right)^1 \tag{8}$$

$$B^{cb}_{t-1} + L_{t-1} + e_{t-1}R^f_{t-1} - N_{t-1} \geq E_t \sum_{j=t}^{\infty} I_{j,t-1}\left(C^{cb}_j + T^{cb}_j + H_j + S^{cb}_j - \left(M_j - \left(1+i^M_j\right)M_{j-1}\right)\right) \tag{9}$$

where

$$S_j = \left(1 + i_j - \left(\frac{\rho_j}{P^K_{j-1}} + (1-\delta)\frac{P^K_j}{P^K_{j-1}}\right)\right)P^K_{j-1}K_{j-1} \tag{10}$$

and

$$S^{cb}_j = \left(i_j - i^L_j\right)L_{j-1} + \left(1 + i_j - \left(1+i^f_j\right)\frac{e_j}{e_{j-1}}\right)e_{j-1}R^f_{j-1} \tag{11}$$

are the (implicit) losses (profits if negative) incurred by the Treasury on its real assets (in Equation 10) and the implicit quasi-fiscal losses (profits if negative) incurred by the central bank (in Equation 11) by getting a return on its loans to the private sector and on its foreign exchange reserves below the opportunity cost – the safe rate of interest. Total implicit losses of the consolidated Treasury and central bank on its portfolio are denoted $\tilde{S} \equiv S + S^{cb}$.

We also define the following notation: For any stream of nominal payments X_j, $j = 1, 2, \ldots$ the net present discounted value at the beginning of period t is defined as $V_{t-1}(X) \equiv E_t \sum_{j=t}^{\infty} I_{j,t-1}X_j$. We omit the time subscript of the net present discounted value operator when this can cause no confusion.

Two useful measures of the current revenue obtained by the central bank from its issuance of base money are:

$$\begin{aligned}\omega^1_t &\equiv M_t - \left(1+i^M_t\right)M_{t-1} \\ &= \Delta M_t \quad \text{if } i^M = 0\end{aligned} \tag{12}$$

and

$$\omega^2_t \equiv \left(i_t - i^M_t\right)M_{t-1} \tag{13}$$

The first measure, ω^1, measures the command over real resources achieved in period t by the issuance of base money. When the nominal interest rate on base money is zero (as it is for its currency component), ω^1 is just the change in the monetary base (see also Buiter, 2007). The second measures the interest saved in a period by having borrowed through the

[1] Note that $E_t E_{t-1} I_{t,t-1} = E_{t-1} I_{t,t-1} = \dfrac{1}{1+i_t}$.

issuance of base money liabilities rather than through the issuance of non-monetary debt. It can be shown by brute force that the two measures are related as follows:

$$E_t \sum_{j=t}^{\infty} I_{j,t-1}\left(M_j - (1+i_j^M)M_{j-1}\right) \equiv E_t \sum_{j=t}^{\infty} I_{j+1,t-1}\left(i_{j+1} - i_{j+1}^M\right)M_j - \left(\frac{1+i_t^M}{1+i_t}\right)M_{t-1} + \lim_{N\to\infty} E_t I_{N,t-1} M_N \tag{14}$$

It follows that if we assume that the NPV of the terminal base money stock is zero in the long run, then

$$V_{t-1}(\omega^1) = V_{t-1}(\omega^2) - \left(\frac{1+i_t^M}{1+i_t}\right)M_{t-1} \tag{15}$$

We can therefore rewrite Equation 9 as:

$$\begin{aligned} &B_{t-1}^{cb} + L_{t-1} + e_{t-1}R_{t-1}^f - M_{t-1} - N_{t-1} \\ &\geq E_t \sum_{j=t}^{\infty} I_{j,t-1}\left(C_j^{cb} + T_j^{cb} + H_j + S_j^{cb} - (i_j - i_j^M)M_{j-1}\right) \end{aligned} \tag{16}$$

The single-period budget constraint of the consolidated general government/Treasury and central bank is

$$\begin{aligned} M_t + N_t + B_t^p - L_t - e_tR_t^f - P_t^K K_t \equiv\ & \tilde{C}_t - \tilde{T}_t + (1+i_t^M)M_{t-1} + (1+i_t)(N_{t-1} + B_{t-1}^p) \\ & - (1+i_t^L)L_{t-1} - (1+i_t^f)e_tR_{t-1}^f - (\rho_t + P_t^K(1-\delta))K_{t-1} \end{aligned} \tag{17}$$

The intertemporal budget constraint of the consolidated general government/Treasury and central bank is

$$P_{t-1}^K K_{t-1} + L_{t-1} + e_{t-1}R_{t-1}^f - N_{t-1} - B_{t-1}^p \geq E_t \sum_{j=t}^{\infty} I_{j,t-1}\left(\tilde{C}_j - \tilde{T}_j + \tilde{S}_j - \left(M_j - (1+i_j^M)M_{j-1}\right)\right) \tag{18}$$

or equivalently

$$P_{t-1}^K K_{t-1} + L_{t-1} + e_{t-1}R_{t-1}^f - M_{t-1} - N_{t-1} - B_{t-1}^p \geq E_t \sum_{j=t}^{\infty} I_{j,t-1}\left(\tilde{C}_j - \tilde{T}_j + \tilde{S}_j - (i_j - i_j^M)M_{j-1}\right) \tag{19}$$

Finally, using the less cluttered net present discounted value operator notation, we can rewrite the intertemporal budget constraints: (I) For the Treasury:

$$P_{t-1}^K K_{t-1} + V_{t-1}(T^p) + V_{t-1}(T^{cb}) \geq B_{t-1}^p + B_{t-1}^{cb} + V_{t-1}(C) + V_{t-1}(S) \tag{20}$$

(II) for the central bank: either

$$B_{t-1}^{cb} + L_{t-1} + e_{t-1}R_{t-1}^f + V_{t-1}(\omega^1) \geq N_{t-1} + V_{t-1}(C^{cb}) + V_{t-1}(T^{cb}) + V_{t-1}(H) + V_{t-1}(S^{cb}) \tag{21}$$

or, equivalently,

$$B^{cb}_{t-1} + L_{t-1} + e_{t-1}R^{f}_{t-1} + V_{t-1}(\omega^2) \geq M_{t-1} + N_{t-1} + V_{t-1}(C^{cb}) + V_{t-1}(T^{cb}) + V_{t-1}(H) + V_{t-1}(S^{cb}) \tag{22}$$

(III) for the consolidated Treasury and central bank: either

$$P^{K}_{t-1}K_{t-1} + L_{t-1} + e_{t-1}R^{f}_{t-1} + V_{t-1}(\tilde{T}) + V_{t-1}(\omega^1) \geq N_{t-1} + B^{p}_{t-1} + V_{t-1}(\tilde{C}) + V_{t-1}(\tilde{S}) \tag{23}$$

or, equivalently,

$$P^{K}_{t-1}K_{t-1} + L_{t-1} + e_{t-1}R^{f}_{t-1} + V_{t-1}(\tilde{T}) + V_{t-1}(\omega^2) \geq M_{t-1} + N_{t-1} + B^{p}_{t-1} + V_{t-1}(\tilde{C}) + V_{t-1}(\tilde{S}) \tag{24}$$

Figures 1, 2, 3 and 4 help to illustrate why sovereigns also require a LOLR. Figure 1 presents a stylized general government (Treasury) conventional balance sheet and Figure 2 the stylized central bank conventional balance sheet. On the asset side of Figure 1, we find marketable (and often relatively liquid) assets, including in principle (but omitted here for simplicity) general government holdings of gold, foreign exchange and other foreign investments, equity in partially or wholly publicly owned firms, and real assets, including land, structures and real estate, but also natural resource rights, from subsoil minerals, oil and gas to band spectrum. All this equity and real assets is captured by $P^{K}_{t-1}K_{t-1}$. On the liability side, there is marketable and non-marketable public debt, $B^{p}_{t-1} + B^{cb}_{t-1}$. Conventional general government/Treasury net worth, W_{t-1}, is the difference between the value of the tangible assets plus the financial assets and the financial liabilities.

Figure 1: Stylized General Government (Treasury) Conventional Balance Sheet

Assets		Liabilities	
$P^{K}_{t-1}K_{t-1}$	Value (at actual sale or purchase prices) of land, real estate, structures, mineral assets and other real assets, equity in public enterprises and other financial assets	Marketable and non-marketable general government debt	$B^{p}_{t-1} + B^{cb}_{t-1}$
		General government financial net worth	W_{t-1}

Source: Authors' own data.

Figure 2: Stylized Central Bank Conventional Balance Sheet

Assets		Liabilities	
$e_{t-1}R^{f}_{t-1}$	Gold and foreign exchange holdings and other investments	Base money	M_{t-1}
B^{cb}_{t-1}	Treasury debt	Non-monetary liabilities	N_{t-1}
L	Private sector debt and loans to the private sector	Central bank financial net worth	W^{cb}_{t-1}

Source: Authors' own data.

Figure 3: Stylized General Government Comprehensive Balance Sheet

Assets		Liabilities	
$P^K_{t-1}K_{t-1} - V_{t-1}(S)$	Fair value of land, real estate, structures, mineral assets and other real assets, equity in public enterprises and other financial assets	Marketable and non-marketable general government debt	$B^p_{t-1} + B^{cb}_{t-1}$
$V_{t-1}(T^p)$	Net present value of taxes, levies and social security contributions	Net present value of general government primary current expenditure	$V_{t-1}(C)$
$V_{t-1}(T^{cb})$	$V_{t-1}(S^{cb})$ Net present value of payments made by the central bank to the Treasury		
		Comprehensive general government net worth	$\hat{W}_{t-1}$

Source: Authors' own data.

Figure 4: Stylized Central Bank Comprehensive Balance Sheet

Assets		Liabilities	
$e_{t-1}R^f_{t-1}$	Gold and foreign exchange holdings and other investments	Non-monetary liabilities	N_{t-1}
B^{cb}_{t-1}	Treasury debt	Net present value of current primary expenditure by central bank	$V_{t-1}(C^{cb})$
L_{t-1}	Private sector debt and loans to the private sector	Net present value of payments made by the central bank to the Treasury	$V_{t-1}(T^{cb})$
$V_{t-1}(\omega^1)$	Net present value of future base money issuance by the central bank	Net present value of transfer payments by the central bank to the private sector (helicopter money drops)	$V_{t-1}(H)$
		Net present value of implicit subsidies paid by the central bank	$V_{t-1}(S^{cb})$
		Central bank comprehensive net worth	$\hat{W}^{cb}_{t-1}$

Source: Authors' own data.

Figure 2 has the financial assets of the central bank, $B^{cb}_{t-1} + L_{t-1} + e_{t-1}R^f_{t-1}$, the financial liabilities of the central bank (monetary, M_{t-1} and non-monetary, N_{t-1}) and the financial net worth of the central bank, W^{cb}.

Figure 3 presents the general government or Treasury comprehensive balance sheet, which also features the intangible assets and liabilities that are omitted from the published financial or conventional balance sheets (see also Buiter, 2010). The comprehensive balance sheet of the general government *is* its intertemporal budget constraint (Equation

Figure 5: Alternative, but Equivalent, Stylized Central Bank Comprehensive Balance Sheet

Assets		Liabilities	
$e_{t-1}R^f_{t-1}$	Gold and foreign exchange holdings and other investments	Base money	M_{t-1}
B^{cb}_{t-1}	Treasury debt	Non-monetary liabilities	N_{t-1}
L_{t-1}	Private sector debt and loans to the private sector	Net present value of current primary expenditure by central bank	$V_{t-1}(C^{cb})$
$V_{t-1}(\omega^2)$	Net present value of interest saved by the central bank through its issuance of base money	Net present value of payments made by the central bank to the Treasury	$V_{t-1}(T^{cb})$
		Net present value of transfer payments by the central bank to the private sector (helicopter money drops)	$V_{t-1}(H)$
		Net present value of implicit subsidies paid by the central bank on the financial assets it holds	$V_{t-1}(S^{cb})$
		Central bank comprehensive net worth	$\hat{W}^{cb}_{t-1}$

Source: Authors' own data.

20), with the familiar no-Ponzi finance terminal condition imposed: the net present discounted value of the terminal conventional net worth of the general government must be non-negative.

Figures 4 and 5 present two equivalent versions of the central bank's comprehensive balance sheet, corresponding, respectively, to Equations 21 and 22, the two equivalent representations of the intertemporal budget constraint of the central bank.

The most important intangible asset in Figure 3 is the present value of taxes, levies and social security contributions, $V_{t-1}(T^p)$. We also single out for future reference one particular stream of general government revenues: the share of central bank profits paid to the general government, generally to the central government Treasury, $V_{t-1}(T^{cb})$. The present value of transfers, entitlement spending and exhaustive general government primary current expenditure, $V_{t-1}(C)$, appears on the liability side. We could have entered $V_{t-1}(S)$, the present value of the subsidies paid by the general government on its real assets as a liability on the right-hand side of Figure 3. Instead, we subtract it from the market value of the real assets (the price at which these assets can be bought from or sold to the private sector) to get the fair value of the assets were they to remain in the public sector: $P^K_{t-1}K_{t-1} - V_{t-1}(S)$.

The comprehensive balance sheet of the central bank also includes an intangible asset and several intangible liabilities not included in its conventional financial balance sheet. Consider, for instance, Figure 5 and contrast it with Figure 2. The additional asset of the central bank is the NPV of future interest saved by having borrowed through the issuance of base money rather than through the issuance of non-monetary debt instruments,

$V_{t-1}(\omega^2)$. The additional liabilities of the central bank are: (1) the NPV of the payments made by the central bank to the Treasury, $V_{t-1}(T^{cb})$, which we encountered as an asset of the Treasury in Figure 3; (2) the NPV of the helicopter money drops made by the central bank, $V_{t-1}(H)$ (zero in most real-world economies); and (3) the NPV of the implicit, quasi-fiscal subsidies made by the central bank on its financial assets, $V_{t-1}(S^{cb})$.

Even when central banks cannot engage in helicopter money drops (that is, even if $V_{t-1}(H) \equiv 0$), they can provide implicit subsidies/transfers to private counterparties through subsidized lending rates through the term $V_{t-1}(S^{cb})$ in Figure 5. Take the two three-year LTROs of the ECB in December 2011 and February 2012. These loans were made at an interest rate linked to the official policy rate – the refi rate. This stands currently at 1.00 per cent, but is expected by us to come down to 0.50 per cent by the end of the year and to remain at that level over the life of the LTRO. Over the three years of the LTRO, the bank's cost of borrowing could therefore be as little as 60 basis points. In addition, collateral requirements for the loans were weakened dramatically. There can be little doubt that these LTROs involved a significant subsidy from the ECB to the borrowing banks – in our view, at least 3.00 per cent per year. With just over €1 trillion worth of LTROs undertaken, the annual subsidy would be €30 billion; over three years, the NPV of the subsidy would be around €85.6 billion, using a 4 per cent discount rate for the NPV calculations.

As noted earlier, the main asset of the sovereign is highly illiquid: the NPV of future taxes, levies and social security contributions – denoted $V_{t-1}(T^p)$. It may be possible to securitize some future tax flows and thus turn the NPV of such taxes into tradable instruments, but this has only been attempted on a limited scale and the resulting financial instruments have not been widely traded in liquid markets. Among the revenue streams of the central bank are the bulk of its distributed profits, $V_{t-1}(T^{cb})$. Typically, the national Treasury is the beneficial owner (and in some cases, as in the United Kingdom, the legal owner) of the central bank, and the non-retained part of central bank profits are paid out as a form of dividends to the national Treasury. The equity in the central bank, even in those cases where the central bank is formally a joint stock company, is usually not traded, however, so the Treasury, even where it holds most or all of the central bank's equity, cannot realize the NPV of future central bank profits by selling the equity. The actual stream of payments made by the central bank to the Treasury in any given period need bear little relationship to economic profits earned in that period. The value of T^{cb} in one or more periods and even of $V_{t-1}(T^{cb})$ could be negative if the Treasury makes transfers to the central bank, say to recapitalize it.

Another key future stream of resources for the sovereign comes from *forgone* public spending – that is, a reduction in $V_{t-1}(C)$. The NPV of primary (non-interest) general government current spending is a key intangible liability. If it were possible to turn commitments to future cuts in public spending – a reduction in an illiquid liability – into a matching capacity to issue new liquid liabilities, one would have achieved a financial engineering miracle: the *de facto* securitization of future public spending cuts. This may be possible when optimism, confidence and trust in the government are high, but when pessimism rules, confidence has vanished and trust is weak, the government may be unable to translate promises of future public spending cuts or of future tax increases into a present ability to fund itself in the markets. Even during normal times, the bulk of the intangible assets of the sovereign is illiquid and of long maturity, and even a determined attempt to reduce the intangible liabilities of the government need not translate into any significant increase in its ability to borrow today.

In addition to holding significant amounts of illiquid intangible assets and liabilities, many sovereigns have non-trivial financial deficits and/or a sizeable stock of sovereign debt, part of which matures and requires refinancing each period. Most governments therefore have regular, recurrent funding needs. Like banks, sovereigns therefore suffer from maturity and liquidity mismatch among their assets and liabilities. So even if the sovereign is solvent – provided it can get funded at yields that reflect the market's belief that the sovereign *is* solvent – this sovereign could be tripped into a fundamentally unwarranted payments default should the market instead adopt the 'self-fulfilling fear equilibrium belief' that the government is (most likely) not solvent. A lender of last resort capable of issuing an unquestionably liquid instrument (for instance, base money) in any amount, may well be necessary to trump the 'fear equilibrium' or 'sovereign debt run equilibrium' that always threatens the sovereign, just as the lender of last resort is necessary to prevent solvent but illiquid banks from succumbing to a bank run (see also Kopf, 2011). The truth of this proposition has been underlined several times since 2010 in the case of the eurozone where a single central bank faces 17 sovereigns. It is equally true, however, in the case of the United States, where a single sovereign faces the central bank (see also De Grauwe, 2011a; Gros and Mayer, 2010).

The economic logic of the intertemporal budget constraints implies that the Treasury is solvent if and only if its comprehensive net worth is non-negative, $\hat{W}_{t-1} \geq 0$. Likewise, the central bank is solvent if and only if its comprehensive net worth is non-negative, $\hat{W}_{t-1}^{cb} \geq 0$. These solvency conditions are, of course, quite consistent with the conventionally defined financial net worth of the Treasury, W, and/or the conventionally defined financial net worth of the central bank, W^{cb}, being negative. This can be seen by noting that:

$$\hat{W} \equiv W + V(T^{p}) + V(T^{cb}) - V(S) - V(C) \tag{25}$$

and that

$$\hat{W}^{cb} \equiv W^{cb} + V(\omega^{2}) - V(C^{cb}) - V(T^{cb}) - V(H) - V(S^{cb}) \tag{26}$$

In the case of the central bank, for instance, even if its conventional financial net worth (regulatory net worth or regulatory capital) were negative, comprehensive net worth could be positive if the NPV of future interest saved because of the central bank's monopoly of the issuance of domestic base money exceeds the NPV of its future running costs, $V(C^{cb})$, its future payments to the Treasury, $V(T^{cb})$, its future helicopter money drops, $V(H)$, and its future quasi-fiscal subsidies on its lending and other assets, $V(S^{cb})$.

Finally, Figure 6 presents the conventional balance sheet of the consolidated general government (Treasury) and central bank, and Figures 7 and 8 present two equivalent representations of the comprehensive budget constraint of the consolidated general government (Treasury) and central bank, corresponding to Equations 23 and 24, respectively. Note that the comprehensive net worth of the consolidated Treasury and central bank, $\hat{\tilde{W}}_{t-1}$, can be positive even when either the financial net worth of the Treasury or the financial net worth of the central bank, or both, are negative. This follows from

Figure 6: Conventional Balance Sheet of Consolidated Treasury and Central Bank

Assets		Liabilities	
$P^K_{t-1}K_{t-1}$	Market value of land, real estate, structures, mineral assets and other real assets, equity in public enterprises and other financial assets	Base money	M_{t-1}
		Non-monetary liabilities of the central bank	N_{t-1}
		Marketable and non-marketable Treasury debt held by public	B^p_{t-1}
		Consolidated Treasury and central bank conventional or financial net worth	$\widetilde{W}_{t-1} = W_{t-1} + W^{cb}_{t-1}$

Source: Authors' own data.

Figure 7: Comprehensive Balance Sheet of Consolidated Treasury and Central Bank

Assets		Liabilities	
$P^K_{t-1}K_{t-1} - V_{t-1}(S)$	Fair value of land, real estate, structures, mineral assets and other real assets, equity in public enterprises and other financial assets	Non-monetary liabilities of the central bank	N_{t-1}
$V_{t-1}(T^p)$	Net present value of taxes, levies and social security contributions	Marketable and non-marketable general government debt	B^p_{t-1}
$V_{t-1}(\omega^1)$	Net present value of future base money issuance	Net present value of consolidated Treasury and central bank primary current expenditure	$V_{t-1}(\widetilde{C})$
		Net present value of transfer payments by the central bank to the private sector (helicopter money drops)	$V_{t-1}(H)$
		Net present value of implicit subsidies paid by the central bank on the financial assets it holds	$V_{t-1}(S^{cb})$
		Comprehensive consolidated Treasury and central bank net worth	$\hat{\tilde{W}}_{t-1}$

Source: Authors' own data.

Figure 8: Alternative, but Equivalent, Comprehensive Balance Sheet of Consolidated Treasury and Central Bank

Assets		Liabilities	
$P^K_{t-1}K_{t-1} - V_{t-1}(S)$	Fair value of land, real estate, structures, mineral assets and other real assets, equity in public enterprises and other financial assets	Base money	M_{t-1}
$V_{t-1}(T^p)$	Net present value of taxes, levies and social security contributions	Non-monetary liabilities of the central bank	N_{t-1}
$V_{t-1}(\omega^2)$	Net present value of future base money issuance	Marketable and non-marketable general government debt	B^p_{t-1}
		Net present value of consolidated Treasury and central bank primary current expenditure	$V_{t-1}(\tilde{C})$
		Net present value of transfer payments by the central bank to the private sector (helicopter money drops)	$V_{t-1}(H)$
		Net present value of implicit subsidies paid by the central bank on the financial assets it holds	$V_{t-1}(S^{cb})$
		Comprehensive consolidated Treasury and central bank net worth	$\hat{\tilde{W}}_{t-1}$

Source: Authors' own data.

$$
\begin{aligned}
\hat{\tilde{W}} &\equiv \tilde{W} + V(T^p) + V(\omega^2) - V(\tilde{C}) - V(H) - V(\tilde{S}) \\
&= W + W^{cb} + V(T^p) + V(\omega^2) - V(\tilde{C}) - V(H) - V(\tilde{S})
\end{aligned} \tag{27}
$$

The comprehensive balance sheet of the consolidated Treasury and central bank adds the intangible assets and the intangible liabilities of each of them to the conventional or financial balance sheet of the consolidated Treasury and central bank. Of particular importance for our purposes are the differences between the conventional and comprehensive balance sheets of the Treasury alone (Figures 1 and 3, respectively) and their consolidated counterparts, given in Figures 6 and 8, respectively. Contrast Figures 3 and 8. The additional NPV of the resources the central bank brings to the consolidated Treasury and central bank balance sheet is the NPV of current and future seigniorage, where 'seigniorage' is defined as interest saved by borrowing through the issuance of base money rather than through the issuance of non-monetary debt instruments. Base money consists of coin and currency, which bear a zero nominal interest rate, and overnight deposits or demand deposits held by commercial banks and other eligible counterparties with the central bank – also referred to as 'commercial bank reserves with the central bank'. These reserves carry a remuneration rate determined by the central bank. However, the contribution of the central bank to the asset side of Figure 8 is not the only significant contribution it makes to the public finances. On the liability side of Figure 8 (and indeed of Figure 6) appears the stock of base money. Since the central bank has the ability to issue this unquestionably liquid liability at will, the consolidated general government should never face a potential *domestic currency* illiquidity problem, unlike the conventional general government, whose financial liabilities held by the public, B^P, can become illiquid.

III. Other Potential Lenders of Last Resort for Eurozone Sovereigns

In principle, the domestic central bank is not the only possible lender of last resort for sovereigns. Sovereigns could also rely on some form of self-insurance (for instance, by amassing a large stock of liquid financial assets) or an external institution, such as the IMF, could play the role of lender of last resort. Both of these alternative sources of emergency liquidity are likely to be useful (and are in fact used) in the eurozone, but are simply not large enough to replace the central bank as the primary lender of last resort for domestic currency liquidity for eurozone sovereigns and banks. The insufficient size of the facilities available to these other potential lenders of last resort is not dictated by the laws of nature or of economics; it is a consequence of unwillingness/political inability of the political leadership in the eurozone and in the wider global community to create facilities of sufficient size.

As noted above, a truly credible LoLR needs to be able to issue unquestionably liquid instruments in any amount and on demand – that is, without delay. At a minimum, a credible LoLR should be able to cover the plausible liquidity needs of the agents that are potentially vulnerable to a funding strike by private investors. In the eurozone, one way to make the latter requirement operational is to estimate the total financing requirements of eurozone sovereigns over, say, the next two or three years. These are presented in Table 1, which shows the gross financing requirements of the eurozone periphery (Greece, Cyprus,

Table 1: Selected Eurozone Countries: Gross Financing Requirements, 2012–14 (€ billion)

Country/group	*2012*	*2013*	*2014*	*2012–14 Q2*
Austria	26.7	24.9	31.5	56.7
Belgium	81.0	43.4	31.3	117.5
Cyprus	4.1	2.5	0.9	6.0
Finland	18.9	7.9	7.7	21.7
Greece	44.9	25.1	23.7	76.5
Ireland	21.7	19.5	20.7	50.2
Italy	388.6	211.1	162.5	567.1
Spain	201.3	156.0	95.2	386.4
Portugal	29.7	19.2	18.0	53.3
France	429.2	225.9	158.3	634.5
Germany	281.9	224.9	178.9	519.4
Netherlands	91.4	56.6	46.0	157.0
GR + IR + PO	100.5	66.3	63.3	186.0
CY + GR + IR + PO + SP + IT	726.3	451.7	328.6	1180.6
Total	1619.4	1016.9	774.6	2646.4

Source: Bloomberg, IMF and Citi Investment Research and Analysis.
Notes: Redemptions are bond and bill redemptions due in the respective years. Government agency debt is not included. Budget deficit forecasts are IMF forecasts for Austria, Finland, Cyprus and the Netherlands, and CIRA forecasts for all of the others.

Table 2: EFSF: Financial Capacity (€ billions)

Effective size	*440.0*
Irish (€17.7 billion) and Portuguese (€26 billion) programmes	–43.7
EFSF contribution to 1st Greek programme	–27.0
2nd Greek programme	–109.1
Theoretical maximum remaining capacity	259.2

Sources: EFSF and CIRA.

Table 3: EFSM: Financial Capacity (€ billions)

Effective size	*60.0*
Irish (€22.5 billion) and Portuguese (€26 billion) programmes	–48.5
Maximum remaining capacity	11.5

Sources: Commission and CIRA.

Ireland, Italy, Portugal and Spain), estimated as maturing general government bonds and bills plus estimates for the general government deficit, and for the eurozone 'soft core' (Austria, Belgium, France, Netherlands) exceed €1 trillion in 2012 alone. For the eurozone as a whole, gross financing requirements for the general governments are closer to €1.5 trillion for 2012 alone. If we assume that the LoLR should be able to cover at least two years' worth of funding for all eurozone sovereigns, its minimum funding capacity better not fall short of €3 trillion.

In the eurozone, self-insurance could be carried out at the national level or by some or all eurozone countries joining together to create a common liquidity facility (through a eurozone/EU-wide facility or based on an intergovernmental agreement). The EFSF and the ESM, as well as their smaller relative, the EFSM, belong to the latter category (Tables 2 and 3). The EFSF was created in June 2010 to provide nominally up to €440 billion in loans (even though its lending capacity compatible with a desired AAA-rating was much smaller at around €255 billion at most) to eurozone countries in need. Subsequently, its size has been raised to provide an effective lending ceiling of €440 billion and its mandate widened to include not only loans to sovereigns, but interventions in primary and secondary eurozone sovereign markets, precautionary facilities, support for eurozone banks (even though this would still need to be routed through the sovereign) and credit enhancements for sovereign bonds. In June 2011, the notional size of the EFSF was increased to €780 billion so as to increase its effective size to €440 billion.[2] The EFSF is backed by guarantees from eurozone Member States and funds itself in the market. Until October 2011, it was only able (by statute) to issue debt to meet its near-term lending commitments. Since October 2011, the EFSF can do a limited amount of pre-funding, but now as before there are no plans to pre-fund a significant portion of the EFSF's lending capacity. The Member State guarantees, furthermore, are not joint and several, but pro rata, with each contributing country's share based on its equity share in the ECB.

[2] The nominal or notional size of the EFSF is larger than its effective size or its lending capacity because the eurozone heads of state and heads of government (HoSHoGs) wanted the facility to be rated triple A, which was much higher than the average sovereign rating in the eurozone, and because countries that are themselves on a Troika programme are not asked to contribute to the EFSF lending to other eurozone Member States.

The successor facility of the EFSF, the ESM, is supposed to become operational on 1 July 2012. It has the same mandate as the EFSF, but unlike the EFSF, it is supposed to be permanent, and it is partly backed by paid-in capital. It is also expected to have senior creditor status *vis-à-vis* all creditors other than the IMF, and includes a sovereign debt restructuring mechanism, partly contractual or market-based (through mandatory collective action clauses [CACs] for eurozone sovereign debt issues from 2013) and partly statutory.

After the 31 March 2012 decision to allow the ESM to run side-by-side with the EFSF, the maximum liquidity that the EFSF/ESM can provide is €700 billion (including the almost €200 billion that have already been committed to the Irish, Portuguese and Greek programmes with EFSF participation). This is a substantial amount, but still falls far short of the plausible liquidity needs pointed out above. What is more, the €700 billion are largely a theoretical funding capacity – as noted, the EFSF/ESM are only pre-funded to a very limited degree and do not have the ability to issue unquestionably liquid instruments at short notice without the support of the ECB. The limit on the size of the EFSF/ESM was a political decision of the eurozone political authorities (the HoSHoGs and their ministers of finance). Another political decision, even though it was likely also driven by legal concerns, was not to make the link between the eurozone rescue facilities and the ECB official – for example, by providing the EFSF/ESM with a banking licence that would have made it an eligible counterparty of the eurozone central banks for repos and other collateralized loans. Without access to ECB liquidity, even a much larger nominal funding ceiling for the EFSF/ESM is unlikely to enable these facilities, severally or running in tandem, to play the role of a truly credible lender of last resort for eurozone sovereigns. Truly self-insuring during a crisis is not an option.

Liquid gold and hard-currency foreign exchange reserves, including IMF quotas, are in principle part of the stock of available foreign assets. However, part of the eurozone stock of gold and foreign exchange reserves is held by the ECB and much of the rest by the NCBs. Unlike Japan, the United Kingdom and the United States, where the Treasury is the owner of the gold and foreign exchange reserves, with the central banks only acting as agents for their national Treasuries in the foreign exchange markets, the ownership and control of the eurozone gold and foreign exchange reserves is rather opaque. The Bundesbank in 2011 effectively vetoed German government plans for using the German IMF quotas to supplement the resources of the EFSF, and the German contribution to the IMF's fund-raising campaign for the eurozone (supposed to be around €50 billion) also appears to require the consent of the Bundesbank.

A second alternative to the ECB as LoLR for eurozone sovereigns would be for an external institution (probably the IMF) to play the role of a LoLR. This LoLR support could take the form of sufficiently large credit lines or overdraft facilities that provide guaranteed and unconditional access to credit under all circumstances, or they could take the form of sufficiently large discretionary lending arrangements, potentially on terms and conditions (henceforth conditionality) regarding fiscal-financial austerity and structural reform.

Of course, the IMF is already involved in the Irish, Greek and Portuguese troika programmes to the tune of almost €100 billion, even though it is at the very least debatable that these operations meet the definition of lending to illiquid rather than insolvent institutions (in the case of Greece, the sovereign default of March–April 2012 could, in

Table 4: IMF: Financial Resources, as of End-February 2012

	US$ billion	*% change from 2010*
I. Total resources	841.4	34.7
Members' currencies	408.3	13.8
SDR holdings	15.9	174.1
Gold holdings	4.9	0.0
Other assets	21.5	110.8
Available under NAB activation*	314.0	n/a
Other borrowing arrangements	76.9	–68.6
II. Less: Non-usable resources	224.8	44.9
Of which: Credit outstanding	137.7	60.7
III. Equals: Usable resources	616.6	31.4
IV. Less: Undrawn balances under GRA arrangements	176.0	10.1
V. Equals: Uncommitted usable resources	440.6	42.4
VI. Plus: Repurchases one-year forward	19.2	540.0
VII. Less: Repayments of borrowing due one-year forward	1.1	n/a
VIII. Less: Prudential balance**	61.7	–43.4
IX. Equals: Forward commitment capacity (FCC)	397.7	95.4

Sources: IMF and Citi Investment Research and Analysis.
Notes: * Reflects second activation of the enlarged NAB on 1 October 2011 (SDR189 billion) and undrawn committed resources from the first enlarged NAB activation. ** As of 1 April 2011, amounts available under Fund bilateral borrowing and note purchase agreements of NAB participants needed to cover financing of undrawn balances under pre-NAB approved Fund arrangements based on the current 1:1 bilateral borrowed to quota resources financing ratio and undrawn balances under bilateral agreements of non-NAB participants fully available to finance both pre- and post-NAB commitments.

our view, have been anticipated when the IMF joined the first troika programme for that country in May 2010). The IMF is also likely to be involved in efforts to provide funding to other illiquid eurozone sovereigns in the future – most likely Spain and Italy – but the scope of its own funding contribution will be limited for two reasons. First, its membership is deeply divided on the issue of substantially increasing IMF exposure to the eurozone. Among the G7, the United States, the United Kingdom and Canada are sceptical. Many emerging markets perceive the IMF to be unduly lenient with its European debtors, compared to the severe conditions many emerging market countries had to satisfy to obtain IMF support in the past. Second, the financial resources of the IMF are, in any case, limited (Table 4). In February 2012, the IMF's forward commitment capacity stood at US$398 billion. At the G20 meeting in Washington, DC, IMF Managing Director Lagarde announced that she had obtained commitments to increase the IMF's resources by at least US$430 billion.[3] A substantial share of the resource increase would come from the eurozone countries themselves which pledged €150 billion that is expected to be contributed by the NCBs of the eurozone. Even if the resource increase comes through as planned and even if most of it were to be available for LoLR funding to eurozone sovereigns, it would still fall short of the minimum size required for a credible LoLR.

IMF resources of various shapes – be it as funding provided through a precautionary programme or a full-blown programme (Stand-by Agreement) – could be a useful addition to the combined LoLR facility for the eurozone Member States, but are likely to play no more than a supporting role in keeping the eurozone sovereigns funded.

[3] See «http://www.imf.org/external/np/sec/pr/2012/pr12144.htm».

IV. Four Instruments through which the ECB Can Act as Lender of Last Resort for Sovereigns

The ECB has thus far intervened as lender of last resort for the Spanish and Italian sovereigns using two instruments – outright purchases of sovereign debt in the secondary markets under the SMP and the provision of subsidized funding to eurozone banks that are eligible counterparties for repo operations. Financial repression by the national authorities in periphery countries where the sovereign continues to have market access (for example, Spain and Italy) ensures that at least part of this very cheap ECB credit to banks ends up being invested by these banks in national sovereign debt in amounts higher than and at yields lower than those that would prevail without official pressure on the banks. We expect the ECB to use a third instrument before long: loans by NCBs to the IMF, which will be on-lent by the IMF to the sovereigns of Spain and Italy at low rates reflecting the IMF's preferred creditor status, as soon as these countries have accepted IMF or troika programmes and the associated conditionality. Unlike the EFSF and the ESM, which can make loans directly to governments and can purchase sovereign debt in both the primary and secondary markets, the ECB can only buy sovereign debt outright in the secondary markets. A fourth instrument, giving the ESM a banking licence (making it an eligible counterparty for the ECB for repos and other forms of collateralized borrowing) may follow in due course.

Direct Outright Purchases in the Secondary Markets under the Securities Market Programme

The first, direct, instrument is the outright purchases of government securities in secondary markets under the SMP. The creation of the SMP was announced on 10 May 2010, and in principle covers the outright purchases of both private and public debt securities.[4] On 13 April 2012, eurozone periphery sovereign debt worth €214 billion was outstanding under the SMP. The ECB does not publish data on the composition of its purchases, but it is widely assumed that so far the ECB has purchased Greek, Portuguese, Irish, Spanish and Italian government debt securities under the SMP. The flow of new sovereign debt purchases under the SMP has declined markedly recently and has been effectively zero since February 2012.

There is little doubt that the ECB's SMP purchases prevented major financial turmoil that could have resulted in a chain of defaults of likely solvent eurozone banks and sovereigns – notably in May 2010 and again in August 2012 and October and November 2011. However, purchases in the secondary markets are an ineffective instrument for

[4] 'In view of the current exceptional circumstances prevailing in the market, the Governing Council decided: 1. to conduct interventions in the euro area public and private debt securities markets (Securities Markets Programme) to ensure depth and liquidity in those market segments which are dysfunctional. The objective of this programme is to address the malfunctioning of securities markets and restore an appropriate monetary policy transmission mechanism. The scope of the interventions will be determined by the Governing Council. In making this decision we have taken note of the statement of the euro area governments that they "*will take all measures needed to meet [their] fiscal targets this year and the years ahead in line with excessive deficit procedures*" and of the precise additional commitments taken by some euro area governments to accelerate fiscal consolidation and ensure the sustainability of their public finances. In order to sterilise the impact of the above interventions, specific operations will be conducted to re-absorb the liquidity injected through the Securities Markets Programme. This will ensure that the monetary policy stance will not be affected' («http://www.consilium.europa.eu/uedocs/cmsUpload/ECB_press_releases.pdf»; emphasis added).

ensuring that the new funding needs of a sovereign (the sum of its financial deficit and the maturing debt) are met at a sustainable rate of interest for that sovereign. Unless the purchaser (in this case, the ECB) is known to have deep pockets and to be willing and politically able to use all the resources it has at its disposal to cap the yield/set a floor under the price in the secondary markets, there is a risk that the purchaser ends up owning much of the outstanding stock of debt without doing much to save the sovereign from default by purchasing the gross new debt issuance. Since the ECB does not use rhetoric to support and leverage its purchases of sovereign debt in the secondary markets, even if it focuses its interventions around the dates of primary market issuance and auctions it would likely have to spend much more to achieve the same impact on market yields (and on the sovereign's marginal funding cost) than it would have to spend if it did put its mouth where its money is, or if it focused on primary market purchases.

The reason the SMP is restricted to secondary market purchases is legal. Article 123.1 of the Consolidated Version of the Treaty on the Functioning of the European Union reads:

> Overdraft facilities or any other type of credit facility with the European Central Bank or with the Central Banks of the Member States (hereinafter referred to as 'national central banks') in favour of Union institutions, bodies, offices or agencies, central governments, regional, local or other public authorities, other bodies governed by public law, or public undertakings of Member States shall be prohibited, as shall the purchase directly from them by the European Central Bank or national central banks of debt instruments.

Lending to governments or primary market purchases are thus currently simply not on the agenda for the ECB. Secondary market purchases are less effective, but at least they are legal in the sense of not forbidden by the Treaty.

The SMP route to provide LoLR support suffers from a serious shortcoming in our view by being limited to secondary market interventions. It is also subject to another shortcoming – namely that it lacks a mechanism for reinforcing the ability of sovereigns at the receiving end of LoLR support to validate the presumption of solvency. SMP support does not come with explicit fiscal or structural reform conditionality, nor is an explicit debt sustainability analysis a prerequisite for SMP support. In the absence of such a commitment mechanism, the availability of LoLR support has the potential to weaken incentives for fiscal discipline that could, *ad extremum*, turn an illiquidity problem into an insolvency problem.

Of course, conventional LoLR support to banks is granted to illiquid but solvent institutions only, but is in principle provided without conditionality. Instead, the borrower from the LoLR is supposed to provide good collateral, or rather, collateral that would be good under orderly market conditions. The distinction between illiquidity and insolvency is especially hard to make when the beneficiary/borrower does not offer collateral (as is typically the case for sovereign LoLR operations). Establishing the solvency of the beneficiary is also especially hard in the case of sovereigns, for three reasons. First, as noted above, the main assets of governments are intangible – the present value of taxes, levies and social security contributions – and correspondingly hard to value. Second, and more importantly in the case of eurozone sovereigns, the incentives of sovereigns to repay can sometimes be very uncertain. In the eurozone, sovereign insolvency is in general a 'won't pay', not a 'can't pay' issue. Third, enforcement actions against sovereigns are notoriously difficult, especially when much of the outstanding government debt was issued under domestic law (and is therefore subject to legal transformation initiated by the country's legislative branch of government). Even when the debt was issued under foreign law (most often under New York or English law), the principle of sovereign immunity or simply diplomatic niceties prevent effective cross-border enforcement of rulings against governments. And gunboat diplomacy as a means of sovereign contract enforcement is not what it used to be. In the absence of a credible commitment mechanism for sovereigns, it should therefore come as no surprise that the ECB shies away from putting its mouth where its money is – that is, it does not provide rhetorical support for its SMP LoLR operations.

A third potential shortcoming is that SMP purchases could, instead of carrying an illiquid but likely solvent sovereign through a period of temporary loss of market access, cause persistent damage to the prospects of the sovereign returning to being funded in the private markets. This can happen if the sovereign is, as a result of the SMP purchases, left with an 'overhang' of effectively senior creditors, including not only the ECB, but also potentially the IMF and the EFSF/ESM. In our view, the problem of 'seniority overhang' is a real one in the case of the troika programmes for Greece, Ireland and Portugal, but this is because these were not truly LoLR operations as the borrowing sovereigns were not likely solvent even when the first SMP operations and troika programmes in their support were put together. For solvent but illiquid sovereigns, the creation, through SMP purchases or through EFSF/ESM and IMF loans, of a class of senior creditors would be only of secondary concern. Even if we discount the potential issue of seniority overhang, it is clear that the SMP is not fit for the purpose of providing credible and efficient LoLR support for eurozone sovereigns.

Indirect Outright Purchases of Eurozone Periphery Sovereign Debt in the Primary Markets through Banks

A second, indirect instrument is outright purchases of sovereign debt in the primary issue markets. The ECB and the NCBs are prohibited from doing this by the Treaty.[5] They provide half of the required mechanism by making very cheap, heavily subsidized, credit available to banks, currently under the three-year full-allotment LTROs, the first of which was implemented to the tune of €489 billion on 22 December 2011, and the second of which amounted to €529.5 billion allotted on 29 February 2012. The terms on which this funding is provided are very attractive. The interest rate is tied to the refi rate, which was 100 basis points in April 2012 but could be down to 50 basis points before the end of 2012. Over the three-year life of the LTRO, the average cost of funding could end up at as little as 60 basis points. Collateral standards were also relaxed at the same time that the three-year LTROs were announced:

> [T]he Governing Council has decided [. . .] to increase collateral availability by (i) reducing the rating threshold for certain asset-backed securities (ABS), and (ii) allowing national Central Banks (NCBs), as a temporary solution, to accept as collateral additional performing credit claims (i.e. bank loans) that satisfy specific eligibility criteria.[6]

[5] See Note 4.
[6] ECB Press Release, 8 December 2011.

Table 5: Selected Eurozone Countries: MFI Holdings of Domestic Sovereign Debt, as of End-February 2012

Country	*€ billion*	*% of total stock of outstanding marketable sovereign debt*	*% of MFI capital and reserves*	*% MFIs balance sheet size*
Greece	42.4	15.5	94.5	8.7
Ireland	14.6	12.1	11.6	2.4
Italy	295.4	17.9	75.3	7.1
Portugal	26.4	20.9	61.5	4.5
Spain	238.2	30.8	62.7	6.5

Sources: National Central Banks and Citi Investment Research and Analysis.
Note: Holdings of domestic credit institutions only for Ireland.

The other half of the mechanism is financial repression by the periphery authorities, which forces periphery banks and other regulated entities (such as pension funds and insurance companies) to purchase, often in the primary markets, more of their own sovereign's debt and at lower yields than they would voluntarily in the absence of moral suasion, arm-twisting, friendly or not-so-friendly persuasion and other forms of pressure by the authorities. Arm-twisting of banks by the national authorities and NCBs can apply not just to the amount of national sovereign debt purchased by the banks at the sovereign debt auctions in the primary markets and to the terms on which this is bought, but also to the amount of uptake by the banks of the longer-term financing offered by the ECB.

The ECB/eurozone acts as the 'nice cop' in the financial repression policy by making available funding at highly subsidized rates, thus permitting banks that are forced to use part of their LTRO borrowing to purchase additional debt issued by their own sovereign to do so while still making an attractive return despite the financial repression. There is no serious downside for the banks that are subject to financial repression. The likely outcome is their sovereign not defaulting on its debt. Thanks to the subsidized LTRO funding, even government debt purchased at higher than fair prices in the primary issue markets offers an acceptable carry trade. In the unlikely event the sovereign defaults, those banks were already so heavily exposed to their own sovereigns (explicitly through holdings of government bonds or lending to the government, implicitly through the ripple effect that a sovereign default has on other bank exposures and on the banks' own funding conditions) that insolvency of the banks would likely have resulted even without the additional sovereign debt purchased as a result of financial repression (Table 5). And by announcing that there will be no bank stress test in 2012, the European Banking Authority (EBA) has effectively taken away the threat that falling prices of government securities could lead to extra capital requirements in the near term.

This second route has three advantages over the SMP route of providing LoLR support. First, banks can, unlike the ECB, lend to governments and purchase sovereign debt in primary markets, and therefore provide more effective LoLR support than through the ECB's SMP purchases. Second, since it is the banks that purchase the government debt, the problem of effectively senior officially held debt subordinating private creditors would not arise. Third, again, as it would be the banks that would be lending to eurozone sovereigns or purchasing their debt, not even German law professors may be likely to mount a legal challenge against this version of LoLR support on the basis of Article 123 of the Treaty.[7]

However, in our view, the combination of subsidized bank funding and financial repression still has two big shortcomings that make it unattractive as more than a stop-gap LoLR for eurozone sovereigns. First, just as with SMP purchases, there are no commitment mechanisms binding sovereigns to fiscally responsible actions. Second, the subsidized funding that is provided to eurozone banks is not explicitly tied to liquidity support for deserving sovereigns. Indeed, only a relatively small share of the LTROs has gone to purchases of Spanish and Italian sovereign debt. By suppressing borrowing costs and otherwise loosening borrowing terms and conditions, such actions risk keeping alive fundamentally insolvent *banks* and encourage imprudent lending by all banks, creating medium-term risks for financial stability and likely making it harder to restore conditions for sustainable growth.

Indirect Lending to Eurozone Periphery Sovereigns through the IMF

The third instrument – not yet used – for the ECB to act as a LoLR is another indirect one, and is also aimed at getting around the Treaty's prohibition of direct funding by the ECB and the NCBs of the sovereigns. Importantly, this third route would also likely improve on the second route in terms of its implications for medium-term financial stability and sovereign incentives for engaging in responsible fiscal budgeting. This third approach has the NCBs lending to the IMF which then lends, on favourable terms reflecting its preferred creditor status, to eurozone sovereigns, once these sovereigns are subject to IMF/Troika programmes, including an IMF Stand-by Programme or a substantively similar arrangement of subsidized loans in exchange for fiscal, financial and structural reform conditionality. Just like banks, the IMF *can* lend to eurozone sovereigns (indeed, like the EFSF and the ESM, the IMF can *only* fund sovereigns). And as long as the NCB lending to the IMF does not occur explicitly to support eurozone sovereigns – for example, by creating a separate account for eurozone support at the IMF – this route also appears to be consistent with the Treaty, though we regard it as likely to be challenged in either the European Court of Justice or in one of the national constitutional courts.

Financial and structural reform conditionality are likely to be key for an effective LoLR regime based on NCB lending to the IMF and through the IMF to the fiscally weak sovereigns. Fiscal and structural reform conditionality and a debt sustainability analysis are also standard ingredients for IMF programmes. This set-up therefore offers a much improved channel for LoLR support, compared to the first two options. Two concerns remain. First, the political obstacles to using the IMF to provide significantly enhanced support to the eurozone will likely remain, potentially impeding the IMF's ability to act fast and on the necessary scale. It is also not clear to what extent the programme conditionality will be effective in providing incentives for sovereigns to be fiscally responsible, and whether the debt sustainability analysis is sufficiently discriminating to

[7] However, even this route is not completely free of legal risk. German law professor Bernd Schuenemann has recently sued the Executive Board of the Bundesbank for incurring great risks on behalf of the German taxpayer, while lacking the legitimacy to do so. This lawsuit does not directly refer to LoLR support for eurozone sovereigns channelled through banks, but is concerned with the total size of the exposure, of which LoLR actions to sovereigns and banks, of course, account for a substantial part.

ensure that only illiquid sovereigns are offered LoLR support and that insolvent sovereigns are required to restructure their debt so as to ensure future sustainability as a precondition for access to programme funding. The example of Greece, where the troika provided funding to the sovereign despite the manifest insolvency of the sovereign does not inspire confidence. Nor do the troika programmes for Ireland and Portugal, where funding was provided to the two sovereigns despite a high likelihood that both were insolvent. We hope and expect that when Portugal and Ireland apply for a second troika programme (or for an extension of their current programmes) the issue of sovereign debt restructuring as a precondition for future funding of the sovereign by the troika will be revisited.

Giving the ESM a Banking Licence

A fourth instrument is also indirect and has also not yet been used. It is to make the ESM an eligible counterparty of the eurozone so that it can access the eurozone's liquidity facilities using its claims on eurozone sovereigns as collateral. The ESM would then on-lend the funds, on favourable terms reflecting the ESM's preferred creditor status, to eurozone sovereigns. The ESM's funding would always be accompanied by a 'programme', but since the ESM also has the option of offering precautionary access to funding, fiscal and structural reform conditionality imposed as part of the programme can range from non-existent to substantial.

Many of the characteristics of this LoLR set-up are similar to the third one. This includes the possibility to engage in primary market interventions and the option to impose fiscal and structural reform conditionality and to make debt sustainability a condition for obtaining funding by the ESM. However, it still is subject to the risk that this regime will be ineffective in providing the right fiscal incentives. On the plus side, because the ESM is a European institution – and would, in this configuration, be endowed with a European funding back-stop through its access to the eurozone's collateralized lending facilities – this route also helps to create the impression that at long last the eurozone is capable of coming up with a sustainable and durable institutional LoLR set-up of its own, rather than engaging in the rather unseemly process of having a rich region ask, through the IMF, for financial support from much poorer emerging markets.

However, there are still political and potential legal hurdles to taking this route. This is first that, because of the need to respect Article 123 of the Treaty, courts have to confirm that they see the ESM as a credit institution rather than a state agency; if this is not possible, Article 123 will have to be amended or scrapped, and Treaty revisions take time even if they are not controversial. Materially altering Article 123 would be highly controversial. A second challenge concerns whether the size and/or the duration of the ESM's potential LoLR exposure violates constitutional requirements for budgetary sovereignty of national parliaments, including but not limited to the German parliament.

V. Remaining Issues

How to Sharpen Incentives for Fiscal Discipline

As noted above, true LoLR support is granted to illiquid but solvent institutions only against good collateral (or collateral that would be good in normal times) but in principle without further conditions attached to accessing the support. Since the distinction between illiquidity and insolvency for sovereigns is particularly tricky and since *ex post* enforcement actions aimed at sovereigns are particularly difficult (a problem aggravated by the inability of most sovereigns to offer adequate collateral for any financial support they receive), additional safeguards to ensure that the presence of a LoLR does not weaken incentives for fiscal discipline seem merited. Among these could be statutory fiscal rules, such as those that are part of the amended Stability and Growth Pact (SGP), and the Fiscal Compact. Regular debt sustainability analyses should be carried out and a positive verdict should be a precondition for obtaining LoLR support. These are mostly meant to reduce the likelihood that eurozone sovereigns would run into solvency problems. Fiscal and structural reform programme conditionality is also likely to be required for LoLR access. However, all of these together are unlikely to be sufficient.

For the regime to be effective in the long term, sovereigns would likely have to be allowed to fail. Sovereigns must be allowed to fail (that is, to restructure their debt by imposing losses on creditors), and not only the small and not systemically important sovereigns, and not only after months or years of procrastination and bickering. For that, it is possible that a sovereign debt restructuring mechanism (SDRM) may be necessary. The ESM contains the outline of such an SDRM, but only the contractual or market-based component is spelled out clearly through the requirement that all sovereign debt in the eurozone issued from 1 January 2013 have collective action clauses (CACs) that permit a qualified majority of the debt holders to accept a debt restructuring offer from the sovereign. The elimination of the unanimity requirement for approving a sovereign debt restructuring proposal reduces the problem of hold-outs and vulture funds delaying restructuring. We believe that a statutory dimension, too, will have to be given to any effective eurozone SDRM.

A key lesson of the ongoing eurozone crisis is that it is essential to decouple national sovereigns from the banks in their jurisdictions. We have witnessed an insolvent sovereign dragging its national banking sector (which apart from its exposure to the sovereign was most likely solvent) into insolvency (Greece). We may well witness an insolvent banking sector deemed too big too fail turn out to be too big to save and dragging its sovereign into insolvency (Ireland). Our conclusion is that, in order to survive, the eurozone does not need an ambitious fiscal union, but rather a eurozone banking union with a minimal and capped fiscal component.

This banking union has five key dimensions: (1) a eurozone-wide regulator and supervisor for banks and other systemically important financial institutions (sifis); (2) a eurozone-wide resolution and bail-in regime for banks and other sifis; (3) a eurozone-wide bank recapitalization facility (Eurotarp); (4) a eurozone-wide facility for guaranteeing new unsecured term borrowing by banks; and (5) a eurozone-wide deposit insurance regime and insurance fund. Features (3), (4) and (5) require limited, capped fiscal facilities – say, €400 billion for the Eurotarp, €400 billion for the unsecured term borrowing guarantee facility (UTBGF) and a temporary €500 billion fiscal deposit insurance fund, which would over time be replaced by a banking-industry-funded facility. The unsecured term borrowing guarantee facility is necessary if, as we fear, there will be significant unsecured bank debt restructuring during the years to come in the eurozone. It is likely that not only subordinate unsecured debt holders but senior unsecured bank debt holders too will find themselves transformed into bank shareholders as part of the unavoidable deleveraging, restructuring, recapitalization and consolidation of the eurozone banking sector.

The three fiscal 'pots' required for eurozone banking union could, even under the existing treaties, be funded with debt issued under joint and several guarantees by the new Eurotarp, Euro UTBGF and euro deposit insurance fund, as they can be described as 'projects'. A nice symbolic acknowledgement of eurozone banking union would be to require all eurozone banks and other sifis to incorporate as 'Societates Europeae' – that is, not under national statutes, but under European statute. It would also be desirable to ensure that the ECB/eurozone's role in the LoLR processes for sovereigns and for banks be limited to the provision of liquidity support and not of solvency support. The straightforward way to do this would be to require that any assets held by the ECB and the NCBs (acting as part of the eurozone) that are not of the highest credit quality (defined as the rating attached to an instrument jointly and severally guaranteed by all the eurozone Member State governments) be jointly and severally guaranteed by the eurozone Member State governments. This would put an end to the non-transparent and unaccountable quasi-fiscal role of the ECB.

This would mean joint and several guarantees by all eurozone Member States of SMP purchases of sovereign or private debt and of lending by the eurozone against collateral issued or guaranteed by lowly rated sovereigns. Borrowing by the ESM from the eurozone (should the ESM get banking licence) would also be jointly and severally guaranteed by the eurozone Member States. Bank borrowing from the eurozone secured against risky private financial instruments would likewise have to be jointly and severally guaranteed by the Member States. This would turn the asset side of the eurozone's balance sheet into what is sometimes called a 'Treasuries only' configuration (ignoring foreign exchange reserves to simplify the argument), where 'Treasuries' is shorthand for the highest credit rating available in the eurozone area – that is, the credit rating attached to a jointly and severally guaranteed instrument. It would not solve the problem of finding some effective commitment mechanism for the national sovereigns to ensure fiscal sustainability. Indeed, with the ECB and the NCBs benefiting from a joint and several guarantee from the eurozone sovereigns, the eurozone itself would be incentivized to engage in imprudent lending to national sovereigns and to banks. Clearly, as regards the national sovereigns, the *quid pro quo* would have to be reduced for fiscal and wider economic sovereignty of beneficiary governments, at least for the duration of the financial support programmes. For banks, a more effective eurozone regulator/supervisor and a credible eurozone-wide special resolution regime for banks, which are not captured (cognitively or otherwise) by bank executives, shareholders and unsecured bank creditors, are essential.

How Much Credible LoLR Support Can the ECB Provide?

The ECB/eurozone has deep pockets. Of course, if we don't impose an inflation constraint, the domestic-currency pockets of the ECB/eurozone are infinitely deep – they print the stuff (euro currency) and create it electronically by crediting overnight deposit accounts with the eurozone for eligible banks. We believe the ECB takes its price stability mandate seriously and will not depart from it. We have therefore, conservatively, estimated its non-inflationary loss absorbing capacity (NILAC), and come up with a central estimate of about €3.4 trillion (see Buiter and Rahbari, 2012b). This is the sum of two components. The first consists of about €80 billion of conventional capital and reserves and about €394 billion of loss-absorbing capacity in the eurozone's revaluation accounts (realizable capital gains on gold reserves and other assets). This corresponds to W^{cb} above. The second, larger component is about €2.9 trillion for the net present discounted value of future non-inflationary seigniorage (narrowly defined as interest saved as a result of zero-interest currency issuance – that is, $V(\omega^2)$), assuming a 2 per cent inflation rate, a 1 per cent growth rate for real gross domestic product and a nominal discount rate of 4 per cent. This means that the ECB/eurozone has the non-inflationary resources to provide the 'Big Bazooka' firewall/ring fence to safeguard the eurozone banks and sovereigns and indeed the eurozone as a whole.

Will the European Treaties Need to be Changed?

In our view, substantial Treaty change is likely to be unavoidable if the eurozone is to come up with a robust LoLR set-up. For this purpose, we propose the following changes:

1. Get rid of Article 123 (politically very difficult, but necessary for a rational solution). This would permit the ECB, at its discretion, to act as lender of last resort to eurozone sovereigns through sovereign debt purchases in primary and secondary markets, by lending to the sovereigns directly (with or without collateral) and by engaging in collateralized lending to the banking licence-enhanced ESM.
2. Restrict the ability of the ECB/eurozone to purchase sovereign debt in primary and secondary markets, to purchases that benefit from a full joint and several guarantee from all eurozone governments.
3. Restrict the ability of the ECB/eurozone to lend to sovereigns directly, to loans either secured against against 'good' collateral or benefiting from a full joint and several guarantee.
4. Stipulate that outright purchases of sovereign debt by the ECB/eurozone or loans to sovereigns (financial operations under 2 and 3) can occur only at the discretion of the ECB. The ECB cannot be instructed or forced to engage in such operations.
5. Any countries benefiting from 2 or 3 should be subject to tough conditionality under ESM or troika programmes that involve a material surrender of national fiscal and wider economic policy sovereignty for the duration of the programme.

Alternatively, the ESM with banking licence could do 2 and 3, but would have to be fully joint and severally guaranteed to avoid quasi-fiscal credit risk exposure for the ECB/eurozone. In this case, 4 and 5 would continue to apply.

Conclusions

The search for a suitable policy regime and institutional arrangement to provide LoLR support for sovereigns of the eurozone continues. Routes that are limited to secondary market interventions (like the SMP operations of the ECB) are a non-starter beyond the immediate present, where legal and/or political impediments prevent the national and supranational decision-makers from coming up in a timely manner with a more efficient regime to ensure that fundamentally unwarranted sovereign default is avoided. Relying on subsidized funding for banks (provided by the ECB through the LTROs) and on financial repression (provided by the national authorities in those periphery countries like Italy and Spain, where the sovereign still funds itself in the markets but at increasingly painful and ultimately unsustainable yields) is also inherently undesirable as this route blunts incentives for both banks and sovereigns to exercise financial prudence. We expect that ECB/eurozone lending to periphery sovereigns under troika programmes will fill part of the sovereign funding gap for the larger periphery countries like Spain and Italy during the years to come. And we consider it possible (and desirable) that the ESM will be given a banking licence in due course.

The creation of a technically efficient LoLR for sovereigns (capable of mobilizing large amounts of resources at short notice) should not come at the expense of two other equally important objectives. The first is to take the ECB/eurozone out of the quasi-fiscal game. It is simply unacceptable in a democracy that unelected technocrats are put in a position where they have to rule on the allocation and distribution of multiple trillions of euros without any legitimizing accountability. Our proposal addresses that issue. The second is to create the right incentives for banks and sovereigns to behave prudently, to avoid a repeat of the fiscal bacchanalia and irresponsible bank lending, investing and funding of the decade before 2008. In a number of countries, financial instability reached critical levels because of the behaviour of households and non-financial corporations (always of course deeply entangled with the banking sector). This requires strengthening both the preventive arm of the eurozone fiscal and wider macroeconomic and financial stability regime, and the remedial or corrective arm. The constantly evolving complex network of institutions and procedures through which prevention and cure are supposed to be administered remains incomprehensible and probably ineffective despite (or perhaps because of) the creation of a new alphabet soup of treaties, arrangements, procedures and pacts: the reinforced SGP, the Excessive Deficit Procedure (EDP), the Excessive Imbalance Procedure (EIP), the Macroeconomic Imbalance Procedure (MIP) and the associated Alert Mechanism Report (AMR); the country-specific medium-term budgetary objectives (MTO); the European Semester for co-ordination of economic and fiscal policy planning; the Euro+ Pact; the Fiscal Compact (aka Treaty on Stability, Co-ordination and Governance); the ESM Treaty; the EFSF; the EFSM; the Six Pack and the Two Pack. These function alongside the European System Risk Board (ESRB), the EBA, the European Securities and Markets Authority (ESMA), the European Insurance and Occupational Pensions Authority (EIOPA), the national financial sector supervisors and regulators, the Directorate-General Economic and Financial Affairs, and the Directorate-General Internal Market.

With instruments and institutions in such chaos and disarray, it is actually surprising that things are not worse than they are, given the Rube Goldberg Machine that the national political and European leaderships have concocted to pursue fiscal and financial stability. It is therefore not surprising that most of the heavy lifting to prevent disorderly sovereign defaults, disorderly collapses of systemically important financial institutions and the disintegration of the eurozone has been done by the ECB, lender of last resort of sovereigns and banks, and the protagonist of quasi-fiscal union in the eurozone.

References

Bagehot, W. (1999 [1873]) *Lombard Street: A Description of the Money Market* (London: Wiley).

Buiter, W.H. (2007) 'Seigniorage'. *Economics: The Open-Access, Open-Assessment e-Journal*, Vol. 2007–10. Available at: «http://www.economics-ejournal.org/economics/journalarticles/2007-10».

Buiter, W.H. (2010) 'Games of "Chicken" between Monetary and Fiscal Authority: Who Will Control the Deep Pockets of the Central Bank?' *Citi Global Economics View*, 21 July.

Buiter, W.H. and Rahbari, E. (2012a) 'Why does the ECB Not Put Its Mouth Where Its Money Is? The ECB as Lender of Last Resort for Euro Area Sovereigns and Banks'. *Citi Global Economics View*, 27 February.

Buiter, W.H. and Rahbari, E. (2012b) 'Looking into the Deep Pockets of the ECB. *Citi Global Economics View*, 27 February.

De Grauwe, P. (2011a) 'The Governance of a Fragile Eurozone'. CEPS Working Document 346. Available at: «http://www.ceps.eu/ceps/download/5523/».

De Grauwe, P. (2011b) 'Why the ECB Refuses to be a Lender of Last Resort'. *VoxEU*, 28 November. Available at: «http://www.voxeu.org/index.php?q=node/7352».

Eichengreen, B., Hausmann, R. and Panizza, U. (2005) 'The Pain of Original Sin'. In Eichengreen, B. and Hausmann, R. (eds) *Other People's Money: Debt Denomination and Financial Instability in Emerging Market Economies* (Chicago, IL: University of Chicago Press).

Friedman, M. and Schwartz, A. (1961) *A Monetary History of the United States, 1867–1960* (Princeton, NJ: Princeton University Press).

Goodhart, C. and Illing, G. (eds) (2002), *Financial Crises, Contagion and the Lender of Last Resort: A Reader* (Oxford: Oxford University Press).

Gros, D. and Mayer, T. (2010) 'Towards a European Monetary Fund'. CEPS Policy Brief 202. Available at: «http://www.ceps.eu/book/towards-european-monetary-fund».

Kopf, C. (2011) 'Restoring Financial Stability in the Eurozone'. CEPS Policy Brief 237. Available at: «http://www.ceps.eu/book/restoring-financial-stability-euro-area».

Wyplosz, C. (2011) 'An Open Letter to Dr Jens Weidmann'. *VoxEU*, 18 November. Available at: «http://voxeu.org/index.php?q=node/7296».

Wyplosz, C. (2012) 'The ECB's Trillion Euro Bet'. *VoxEU*, 13 February. Available at: «http://voxeu.org/index.php?q=node/7617».

JCMS 2012 Volume 50 Annual Review pp. 36–48 DOI: 10.1111/j.1468-5965.2012.02273.x

On the Stability of Public Debt in a Monetary Union*

DANIEL GROS
Centre for European Policy Studies

Introduction

During the first half of the 1990s Europe faced a series of financial crises. Countries like Italy and Spain had to deal with the combination of a plunging currency, high-risk premiums on their public debt and a sharp fall in growth. These problems in the end strengthened the drive for economic and monetary union (EMU) as it seemed that the high-risk premiums had arisen because investors expected these countries to return to a regime characterized by high inflation and continuous depreciation. The only way out of this trap was, it was argued then, for Spain and Italy to enter EMU, which would make their commitment to low inflation instantaneously credible. Interest rates on Italian and Spanish government debt did indeed fall quickly once these countries started to prepare for EMU, and during the first decade of EMU (1999–2009) interest rate differentials remained very small, seemingly validating the thesis that membership in EMU facilitated the financing of public debt. The euro crisis is now leading many to exactly the opposite conclusion. It is now argued that financing a high public debt in a monetary union is particularly difficult, or at least unstable, because a government that loses the confidence of investors has no other option left than to default. Paul de Grauwe (2011) calls this the 'inherent fragility' of a monetary union.

This raises a fundamental question: is it inherently more difficult to finance a large public debt in a monetary union than outside? In addressing the question, this contribution starts by discussing developments during 2011, which were widely interpreted as proof of the hypothesis of the 'fragility' of EMU. It then describes the key role of the European Central Bank (ECB) in restoring, at least temporarily, financial stability. With this background, the article sets out the main analytical issue, and then turns to the experience of Italy during the 1990s and asks what makes the crisis of 2011 different. The article subsequently concludes with the hypothesis that the nature and strength of the liquidity support for the banking system play a key role in the stability of high public levels.

I. Background

During 2011 the 'euro' crisis continued and even worsened as attention switched from the three smaller countries which had been 'bailed out' earlier (Greece, Ireland and Portugal, henceforth 'the GIPs') to Spain and Italy. While it could have been argued that Greece and Ireland had only themselves to blame for losing access to financial markets – Greece by

* The author would like to thank Cinzia Alcidi, Paul de Grauwe and Christian Kopf as well as the editors of the *JCMS Annual Review*, Nathaniel Copsey and Tim Haughton, for very useful comments and discussions.

the overspending of its government and Ireland by trying to save its banks after an extraordinary construction bubble – Spain and Italy were widely seen as fundamentally solvent. Moreover, these two countries were by common consent systemic in the sense that their failure would endanger the existence of the euro and thus were 'too big to fail'. However, once governments and market participants tallied up the numbers, it became pretty clear that both were also 'too big to be saved'. The financing needs of these two countries would have been far larger than the funding that could have been mobilized via the euro rescue fund (then the European Financial Stability Fund [EFSF], now the European Stability Mechanism [ESM]) (Giovannini and Gros, 2012).

The year 2011 also showed the key role of the ECB, whose support for government debt markets becomes crucial when investors simply refuse to refinance levels of public debt which are perceived as unsustainable in the long run. It is widely assumed that without the intervention of the ECB in the Italian and Spanish government bond market during the summer of 2011, when it bought over €100 billion in government bonds of these two countries under its 'Securities Markets Programme' (SMP), the crisis might have escalated further. The absence of a central bank systematically ready to support the government debt market thus came to be seen as the Achilles heel of the euro.

The Maastricht Treaty explicitly ruled out any form of 'monetary financing' for governments.[1] This was done to safeguard the independence of the ECB, and thus ensure that governments would be forced to follow sound fiscal policies. However, this prohibition of financing deficits via the printing press creates a problem when risk aversion increases so much that even solvent borrowers can no longer roll over their debt. The year 2011 showed that in such a situation access to liquidity becomes crucial, both for the sovereign and the banking system.

The core of the problem for public debt is a classic maturity mismatch: a government has long-term assets (the flow of tax revenues), but liabilities of a much shorter duration. A simple numerical example illustrates the nature of the problem: imagine a country with a balanced budget, which would normally be considered solvent even if the debt-to-GDP ratio is above 100 per cent because with a balanced budget the debt-to-GDP ratio will decline towards zero as long as GDP grows in nominal terms. However, even if the average maturity of government debt is eight years (rather conservative and close to the case for Italy), the same country has to refinance every year old debt worth more than 12.5 per cent of GDP; much above what even the strongest government could hope to finance out of a surplus. This implies that any government could become immediately insolvent if investors refuse to roll over the debt due for repayment or refinancing. This is exactly the same mechanism as in a bank run. A bank has typically long-term assets (loans) but short-term liabilities (deposits). If all depositors want their money back at the same time, the bank will not be able to liquidate immediately its loan portfolio (Diamond and Dybwig, 1983). This potential for bank runs, which did occur on a large scale during the 1930s, was the main reason why modern central banks became the lender of last resort for banks.

[1] Buying government debt on the secondary market does not formally constitute 'monetary financing' as the ECB in this way only allows other (private) investors to exit their holdings of bonds without any fresh money being provided to the government. However, it is clear that indirectly the ECB will be providing governments with easier access to financial markets if investors know that after a short while they will be able to sell any new government debt they buy to the ECB.

The danger of a run on the government does not exist for the local currency debt of a country with its own national currency because in that case the national central bank can provide the liquidity needed to keep the sovereign solvent in the short run even in the case of a total investors' strike. However, within the eurozone, the central bank is forbidden to provide liquidity back-up for sovereigns (see Gros and Mayer (2011, forthcoming) on how the problem could be addressed).

The problem created by the absence of a lender of last resort for the sovereign became particularly acute after the July 2011 European Council, which was supposed to end the crisis by settling the Greek case with a mixture of generous long-term financing at low interest rates and some private sector rescheduling and restructuring. However, the result of this summit was the opposite of what it set out to achieve. Indeed, the crisis entered an even more acute phase because the official announcement that private investors would be forced to accept losses on their holdings of Greek government bonds opened up a Pandora's box.

The *de facto* default announced for Greece in July 2011 (it was only implemented in March 2012) was a first for any advanced country and forced investors to ask themselves whether other countries with high debt levels might end up in a similar situation. This opened the potential for vicious, feedback loops starting to operate for other countries. The mechanism is quite simple: even a rather high level of public debt would be sustainable if the government had to pay only a low interest rate, say, close to the compensation required on a riskless investment. However, the same level of debt might become unsustainable if the borrowing cost is much higher. Hence many authors (most persuasively, De Grauwe, 2011) have argued that there might be multiple equilibria: if the market thinks the government can pay it will be able to pay because its borrowing cost will be low. However, if the market thinks the government cannot pay, in practice it will not be able to pay because the high-risk premium requested will make the debt service so expensive that it will not be able to find the necessary resources. Doubts about the ability of a government to service its debt could thus become self-fulfilling. Once these doubts materialized during the second half of 2011, the absence of a lender of last resort became a serious problem, as described above. This is due to the fact that even a fundamentally sound country like Italy with a deficit below the eurozone average was in danger of becoming immediately insolvent as the market refused to roll over the existing stock of debt.

The ECB tried at first to deal with this situation by buying large amounts (over €100 billion in less than two months) of Italian and Spanish debt on the secondary market. However, this created an immediate outcry in Germany where the Bundesbank and the general public saw this as a clear violation of the prohibition for the ECB to finance governments enshrined in the Treaty on the Functioning of the European Union.[2] The resignation of the German member of the ECB's Executive Board added to the perceived political tension. The ECB was thus not able to stabilize markets via more purchases of Italian and Spanish bonds because it was not clear for how long it could continue to buy the debt of peripheral countries without risking a serious political backlash.

[2] Technically this was not the case since the ECB was not providing any direct financing to the Italian government as it was not buying any new debt, but only bought existing debt on the secondary market from other investors. A judgment of the Federal Constitutional Court in Germany confirmed this interpretation of the Treaty.

II. Enter the 'Deus ex Machina'

The crisis of 2011 also illustrated the tight link between the market for public debt and the state of financial markets in general. This became apparent in particular for banks whose fate is linked to that of the sovereign. The main reason is that banks hold large amounts of government debt.[3] In all the peripheral countries (including Spain and Italy), banks hold government bonds of their own government amounting to over 100 per cent of their capital. This implies that any increase in the risk premium, which is equivalent to a fall in the market value of the bonds of their own government, will impact the capital of the banks. As a consequence, even strong banks with a fundamentally sound business (that is, banks without doubtful assets on their balances sheet) will see their own share prices falling and credit-default spreads widening and will react by refusing to provide the other banks with inter-bank liquidity. The breakdown in the inter-bank market, in turn, leads to a breakdown of the credit circuit, which in turn worsens the situation.

This 'sovereign-banks' downwards spiral was broken only when the ECB addressed the problem in the banking sector by announcing in December 2011 that it would offer potentially unlimited amounts of three-year loans (called 'longer term refinancing operation', LTRO). At the same time, it also announced more generous rules regarding the type of collateral it would require. The LTRO thus addressed the two key issues which had been at the root of the acute crisis of late 2011 (see Gros, 2011a). It is thus no surprise that the LTRO operations led initially to a quick reduction of the tensions in financial markets. In two instalments the ECB provided banks with close to €1 trillion of three-year funding. Although for about a half of this sum banks simply substituted shorter-term funding with the newly available three-year credits from the ECB, this represented still a considerable improvement for the eurozone banking system. In particular, banks in southern Europe benefited because the new collateral rules allowed them to mobilize hundreds of billions of additional funding.

The availability of the LTRO ensured that no bank would face a liquidity squeeze for the next three years. This lowered immediately the funding cost of banks and allowed the inter-bank market to start functioning again. Moreover, banks were fully expected to use at least part of the funding from the ECB to buy government debt. As a result, the negative feedback loop between banks and sovereigns was at least temporarily broken. The LTRO did not, of course, solve the underlying longer-term problems behind the euro crisis. The LTRO was instituted when the financial system was close to collapse, as evidenced by the fact that short-term rates had gone above longer-term ones. In financial markets this so-called 'inversion' of the yield curve is taken as an indicator of imminent default. The LTRO was meant to stave off this expectation of immediate collapse. This aim was achieved in the sense that in most countries under market pressure (Spain, Italy, etc.) interest rates fell quickly. Short-term rates fell considerably more (relative to longer-term), thus re-establishing a normal yield curve (short-term rates below long-term ones). This remained the case even when market turbulences returned in early April 2012. While longer-term rates (and risk premiums relative to

[3] Another, more technical reason is that the credit of banks rating usually falls along with that of their own sovereign. The reason is simple: in any financial crisis only the government can save a bank. The impact can be quite severe. When a major rating agency lowered the rating of Italy in 2011, it also lowered that of Italian banks. This led to an immediate increase in the funding cost for the entire banking system.

Germany) rose in Spain and Italy to the crisis levels experienced in late 2011, shorter-term rates remained much lower.

This more durable impact of the ECB's action on shorter rates is not surprising. Banks hold shorter-term bonds for the simple reason that their supervisors require them to approximately match the maturity for their funding and their portfolio investments. Given that banks have mostly shorter-term funding (typically of maturity of up to about three years), this implies that prior to the LTRO banks could at most acquire government bonds of three years' maturity. The much shorter-term funding the ECB had been offering beforehand (typically three months, at most one year) was only of limited usefulness for banks because this short-term funding could not be used to finance government bonds of more than a year's maturity. It was only the three-year LTRO which allowed the banks to buy or simply continue to hold on to their bonds. Moreover, the LTRO also made it easier for banks to at least roll over existing medium-term credit to the private sector, which they otherwise might have had to cancel. The LTRO thus probably prevented a sharp credit crunch.

In reality, the LTRO is unlikely to have led directly to a large increase in the aggregate eurozone's banks' holdings of government debt because most of the funding banks received via the LTRO returned to the ECB via increased deposits. What seems to have happened is that northern European investors reduced their holdings of southern bonds (and increased their deposits at the ECB by the amount of their disinvestment), whereas the southern European banks used part of the additional funding from the ECB to buy more of their own government bonds. Whether the net aggregate demand for Italian and Spanish government bonds increased significantly is thus difficult to determine. The large impact of the LTRO came probably from the availability of longer-term funding for banks (which for regulatory reasons is essential for banks, but was no longer available in the market) and the loosening of the collateral requirements, which allowed banks in Italy and Spain a much larger share of their assets for funding operation with the ECB.

III. The Analytical Issue: Instability of High Public Debt within and outside a Monetary Union

The euro crisis begs a simple question: is a high level of public debt inherently more dangerous within a monetary union? During the 1990s it was often argued that only by entering EMU could Italy (and Spain) protect itself from the high interest rates it had to pay then on its public debt because only then could it convince financial markets that it would not inflate away the value of its debt. A prominent paper of the period when plans for EMU were taking shape encapsulated this insight in the title: 'The Advantage of Tying One's Hands' (see Giavazzi and Pagano, 1988).Today, however, it is argued that Italy and Spain are forced to pay a high-risk premium because they have lost the option to use the printing press and could thus be forced into default if interest rates are too high (De Grauwe, 2011).

During the late 1990s economists noticed that the southern European countries had somehow achieved the low inflation credibility and thus lower nominal interest rates that had eluded Latin American countries for decades. The conclusion then was that membership in the euro should make it easier to service a high public debt. Today the relevant comparison is between Spain and the United Kingdom. Kopf (2011) – then also taken up and popularized by De Grauwe (2011) – was the first to notice that if one compared the United Kingdom and Spain, the latter appeared to have a stronger fiscal position. In spite of this, Spain (with a debt-to-GDP ratio of less than 70 per cent) experiences difficulties in refinancing its public debt, paying a high-risk premium over German rates while the British government can issue long-term debt at rock-bottom rates despite a debt-to-GDP ratio close to 100 per cent. The conclusion seems to be obvious: it is easier to service a high public debt by keeping a national central bank and one's national currency.

As noted above, it is commonplace by now to argue that a high level of public debt can lead to vicious, feedback loops and even multiple equilibria in a monetary union. The argument is quite simple: even a rather high level of public debt would be sustainable if the government had to pay only a low interest rate, say, close to the compensation required on a riskless investment. However, the same level of debt might become unsustainable, forcing a country into default, if the borrowing cost is much higher. Hence many authors (most persuasively, De Grauwe, 2011) have argued that there might be multiple equilibria: if the market thinks the government can pay, it will be able to pay because its borrowing cost will be low. However, if the market thinks the government cannot pay, in practice it will not be able to pay because the high-risk premium requested will make the debt service so expensive that it will not be able to find the necessary resources. Doubts about the ability of a government to service its debt could thus become self-fulfilling. This line of reasoning has been used to justify central banks' interventions in the market such as the bond purchase programme of the ECB.

Many economists seem to forget that during the 1990s a similar argument was used to justify the creation of the EMU with an independent central bank. The reasoning was again quite simple:

> [A] fixed exchange rate regime can experience a self-fulfilling crisis if a high risk premium leads to high domestic interest rates that depress domestic activity, and thus make it more likely that the government will actually abandon the system. Depending on the parameter configuration, two equilibria might exist. One is characterized by low interest rates and a low (possibly zero) probability that the exchange rate commitment will be abandoned; the other is characterized by high interest rates and a high probability that the exchange rate commitment will be abandoned. (Adrian and Gros, 1999, p. 129)[4]

Countries with a high level of debt thus seem to have only bad choices: if they enter a monetary union, a speculative attack can force them to default; but if they keep monetary autonomy, investors might buy government debt only if the interest rate is high enough to pay for the risk of inflationary surprises. The intermediate regime with fixed exchange rates is also vulnerable to speculative attacks which can force them into high inflation. Calvo (1988) confirms this: he considers both the case of a country with monetary autonomy and the case when it does not. He finds that multiple equilibria can arise in both cases. He also finds that in both cases the high interest rate equilibrium is Pareto inferior.

This type of result is not surprising since from the point of view of investors it should not really matter whether the government defaults on its obligations (and imposes a

[4] A number of other authors arrived at similar conclusions. See, for example, Obstfeld (1986, 1995). Note that this quote refers to the analysis of a country under a fixed exchange regime; however it applies also to the case of free-floating exchange rate. The debt burden in both cases would be reduced through inflation; the difference is that under the fixed regime there is first a currency crisis and the exit from the exchange rate regime.

haircut on investors) or whether it is forced into high inflation, which then reduces the real value of the debt securities they hold, even without a formal default. Assume, for instance, that within a monetary union the probability of a default of a member country is one in five and that the haircut in case of default is 20 per cent. This would justify an interest rate premium (over the riskless rate) of four percentage points. If the country had kept its own currency, the risk of abandoning the hard currency policy might also be one in five and the inflation rate, in case the hard currency option is abandoned, might be also 20 per cent. This would also require, for a risk-neutral investor, an additional compensation (risk premium) of four percentage points. The risk (and thus its price) should be the same under both circumstances: being part of a monetary area or having one's own currency.

A first step towards resolving this seeming contradiction is to notice that the nature of the risk differs: during the 1990s the risk was that Italy or Spain would devalue their public debt via depreciation and inflation. Today the risk is that their governments might default on their debt – that is, the risk is that one day the Italian government might simply not have the euros required to pay interest and amount borrowed (the principal) in full. As in the case of Greece, private investors might then be forced to accept a 'voluntary haircut'. *A priori* one could argue that default and inflation should be two equivalent ways to reduce the burden of a high public debt and, similarly, two equivalent types of risk to which an investor who lends funds to a government is exposed (this is of course not a novel point of view). The key question that remains at the analytical level is thus whether there are other mechanisms which make a formal default with a haircut different from debt monetization (and hence inflation) which reduces the real value of government debt, and hence the purchasing power for investors, by the same amount.

Inflation and default should be equivalent from the point of a risk neutral investor. However, in reality, risk neutrality might not hold and then the high probability of a low impact event (a bit of inflation) is not equivalent to the low probability of a high impact event (default). Inflation tends to be a gradual process (unless it spirals into hyperinflation) whose effects on the purchasing power of different agents is also gradual and predictable. By contrast, a formal default is an abrupt event, with, *ex ante*, unpredictable consequences for different classes of investors (see also Sims, 2012).

One could of course argue that, at least for an EU member country, the cost of defaulting on government debt is much higher than the cost of exiting a fixed exchange rate regime and permitting inflation to increase to double digit figures. However, the same models used to justify a 'conservative central banker'[5] would then also imply that, given the much higher cost of defaulting, the credibility of the government not to default should be much higher and consequently the likelihood of multiple equilibria much lower.

IV. Evidence: The Case of Italy, Pre-euro versus Post-euro

The case of Italy is instructive. Italy's debt-to-GDP ratio is today about 120 per cent – very close to the value of the early 1990s. At that time Italy was also in difficulties, with a much higher deficit than today, and it had to pay much higher interest rates than today. The key parameter for the government debt sustainability is the difference between the borrowing cost and the growth rate of GDP, which is often also called the 'snowball factor'. If the

[5] This literature started with Barro and Gordon (1983).

Figure 1: Italy – Snowball Factor

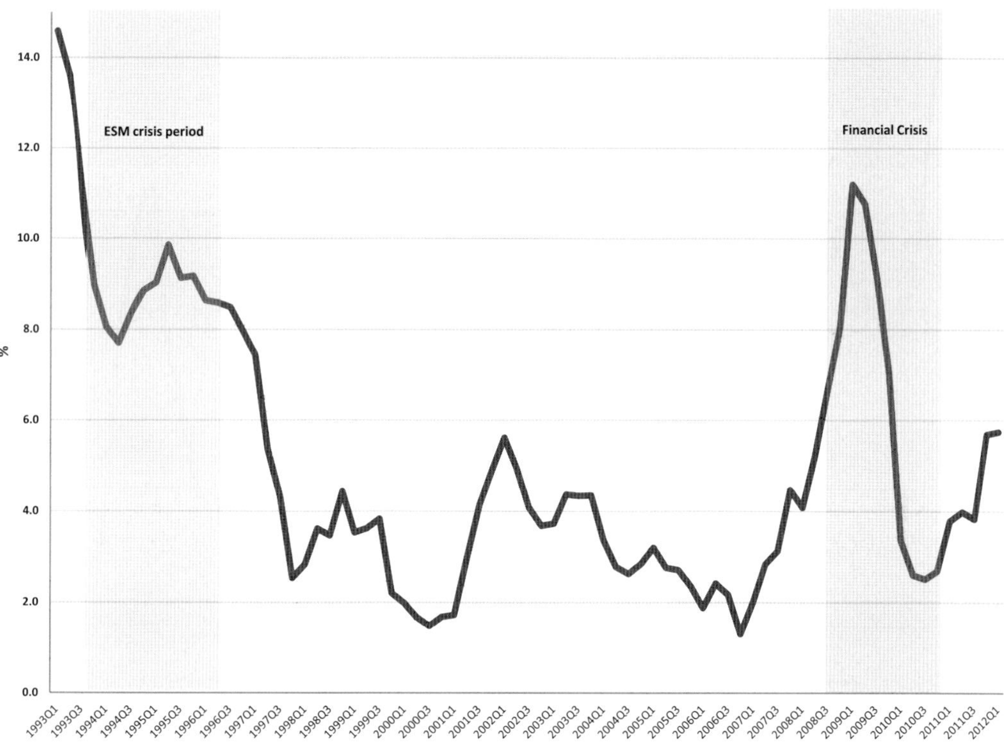

Source: Own calculation on ECB data.

interest rate is higher than the growth rate, the debt-to-GDP ratio will continue to grow and eventually explode unless the country runs continuously a primary surplus. In the case of Italy, the evolution of the snowball factor depends crucially on the 'risk premium' – that is, the difference between the risk-free rate and Italy's effective borrowing cost, since nominal GDP growth rates have not varied that much over time (2008/09 provides the only exception).

Figure 1 thus shows the difference between the long-term interest rate on Italian government debt and the growth rate of nominal GDP (of Italy, realized over the preceding 12 months which is usually taken as the best predictor for the near future). It is apparent that the country was under extreme stress during the wave of speculative 'attacks' of the early 1990s. In 1993, when the authorities were still defending the peg within the European Monetary System (EMS) the difference between the (nominal) interest rate and the growth rate of (nominal) GDP was over ten percentage points. This did decline somewhat after the country left the EMS, but the snowball factor remained in the region of 8–9 per cent during the following few years during which the exchange rate fluctuated widely and tensions in financial markets remained high. At the time, the average maturity of public debt was rather low so that the higher nominal interest rates quickly resulted in higher government expenditure on interest, which rose to over 11 per cent of GDP.[6]

[6] Data from the European Commission services, Ameco database.

Figure 2: Italy – Snowball Factor and Government Deficit

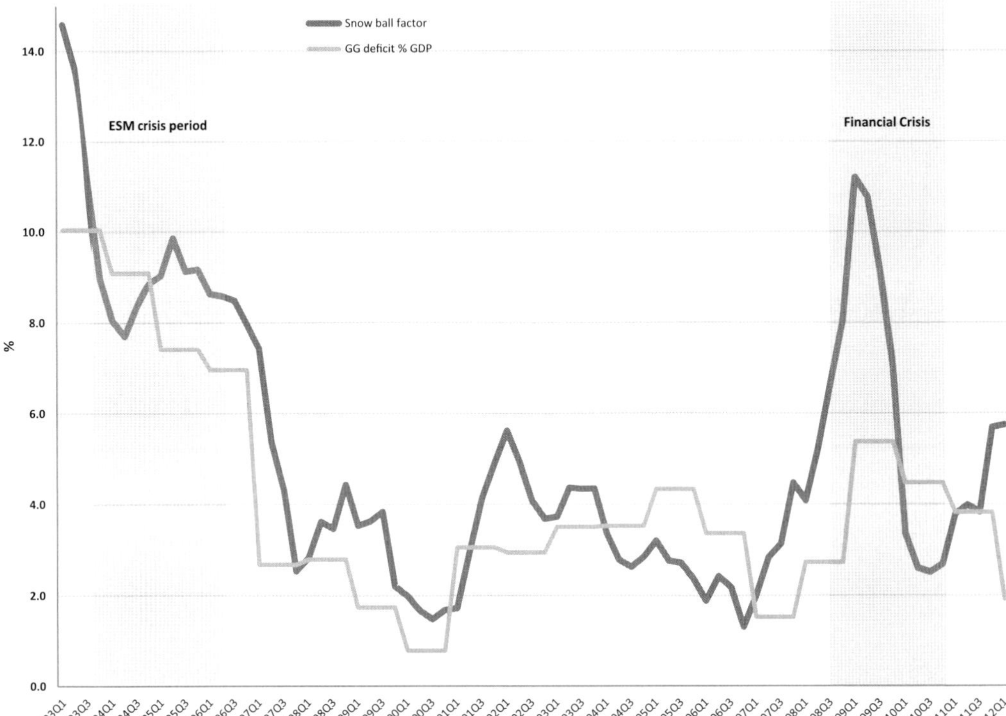

Source: Own calculation on ECB and European Commission Services (Ameco) data.

Compared to this period of *de facto* flexible exchange rates,[7] today's fiscal position of Italy should not be so dire: the snowball factor remains, at around four percentage points, much below the level of over eight percentage points of the early 1990s. The spread on German government securities (the benchmark risk-free rate) would have to double for the snowball effect to reach the same level of tension as 15 years ago. Moreover, interest on public debt now accounts for only a little over 5 per cent of GDP, again less than one-half of that during the 1990s and it would take several years of interest rates at high levels before this would translate into materially higher interest expenditure for the government.

Figure 1 also suggests that the sharp fall in nominal GDP right after the Lehman collapse induced a short-lived spike in the snowball effect, which was apparently discounted by the financial markets because of its temporary nature. What caused the rather rapid decline in the snowball factor (and the risk premium) after 1996? It is difficult, even *ex post*, to disentangle the different factors that may have determined the adjustment. It is sometimes argued that the perspective of EMU membership was decisive, but Figure 2 suggests that the very determined fiscal adjustment undertaken over this period must have been in the end decisive. Indeed, it is apparent that falls in the fiscal deficit (of

[7] At the time Italy was formally in the European Rate Mechanism, but as this permitted fluctuation bounds had been increased to +/– 15 per cent the lira was *de facto* floating.

general government) precede in general the large reductions in the snowball factor which materialized until the start of EMU. Towards the end of the period, the interest rates paid on public debt declined rapidly, thus reinforcing the fiscal adjustment. However, this came after a series of primary surplus of more than 4 per cent of GDP which the country achieved between 1995 and 1999 – again much more than in 2011, when the country barely reached primary balance.

The Italian experience of the 1990s also provides important evidence about the link between fiscal policy and growth. In 2011 and 2012, it was often argued that the problem of Italy (and other countries) is growth and that too much 'austerity' would be self-defeating. In Italy, the sharp fiscal adjustment of the mid- to late 1990s did not seem to have depressed growth enough to prevent these reductions in the snowball factor, which already incorporates any negative effects of a fiscal adjustment on growth. Today's discussion is much more about the risk premium of Italian bonds relative to German ones, but with German rates rock bottom the risk premium alone is not very informative.

All in all the experience of the 1990s suggests that Italy's public finances cannot be said to be unsustainable at interest rates of 5–6 per cent and thus an interest rate/growth rate differential of four to five percentage points (contrary to what is being asserted by many commentators). The experience of Italy of the 1990s also illustrates that the argument that a cut in expenditure (or an increase in taxes) is self-defeating because it reduces demand and hence GDP is at least not always true. At any rate if it were true, it would follow that tax cuts would actually lead to lower deficits because they would more than self-finance themselves through higher growth. Gros (2011b) provides a further discussion of the thesis that austerity could be 'self-defeating'.

However, the very strong reaction of financial markets during the summer of 2011 suggests that the level of interest rates alone does not seem to represent the best measure of the severity of the crisis. The flashpoint for financial markets seems to have been the banking system. Even though the absolute level of the yield on Italian government debt remained low by the standards of the 1990s, the shares of Italian banks have plunged to multi-year lows, and these banks are no longer able to refinance themselves on the inter-bank market.

The difficulties of Italian banks resulted, of course, from the general liquidity squeeze described above. Another contribution to this liquidity squeeze might have come from the informal 'red lining' of all Italian (and indeed generally southern European) exposure by risk managers and supervisory authorities, especially in savings-rich northern Europe, and beyond.[8] The perception of a pervasive 'counterparty risk' was also the main reason why the inter-bank market froze after the bankruptcy of Lehman Brothers in September 2008. Until recently, sovereign risk was not recognized at all within the eurozone. It seems that now some supervisors (mostly in the creditor countries) make the crisis worse by going to the opposite extreme: all exposure to a country whose public debt trades at a risk premium is suddenly considered risky.

The behaviour of the risk premium on Italy's foreign currency debt shows another interesting difference between today and the 1990s. Throughout the period when Italy experienced sustained speculative attacks on its currency the risk premium on its foreign

[8] Other anecdotal evidence is a Bloomberg report of 10 October 2011 that ATP, Denmark's biggest pension fund, ruled out accepting Italian or even French bonds as collateral.

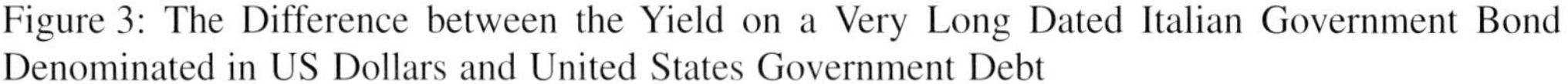

Figure 3: The Difference between the Yield on a Very Long Dated Italian Government Bond Denominated in US Dollars and United States Government Debt

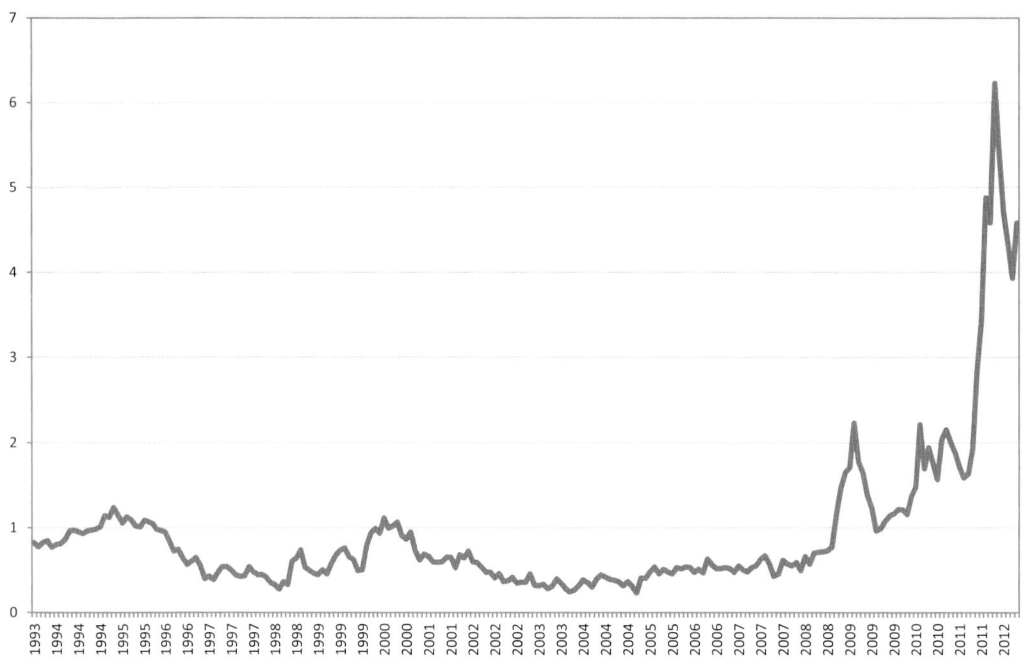

Source: Bloomberg Finance.

currency debt remained most of the time below 100 basis points as shown in Figure 3, which shows the difference between the yield on a very long dated Italian government bond denominated in US dollars and United States government debt. It is only in the summer of 2011 that the risk premium rose to over 300 basis points (about the same magnitude as that on euro debt relative to Bunds).

Concluding Considerations

The idea that within a monetary union high levels of public debt lead inherently to more instability because financial markets could force a government into default by simply refusing to lend at low interest rates is intellectually very appealing and seems to have been validated by the extension of the euro crisis to Italy and Spain. Yet before one accepts this hypothesis, two issues would need further investigation. At the conceptual level two important analytical issues overlooked in the literature are uncertainty and risk aversion.

To begin with uncertainty: the models underlying the view that high public debt is inherently unstable in a monetary union usually assume a binary decision rule for the government. In other words, if interest rates are too high it defaults, but if interest rates are low enough it does not. Thus there is no uncertainty once a threshold interest has been passed. However, in reality this is not the case. Even once the interest rate threshold has been set, a lot of uncertainty persists about whether there will be default or not. One key reason why this happens is that the future contains many sub-periods during which many important changes can take place. Many things could happen between the time the interest rate is identified and the time the decision on default is taken. One particularly important aspect is the political process. In reality at least one, possibly several elections, are likely to be held between the period in which interest rates are set in the market and the final period when the government decides whether to default and what haircut to impose on creditors. Different parties will compete and might have different views on default (or inflation). Some of them might oppose default on non-economic grounds, or because they have a different view of the cost of defaulting (inflation). There is thus a large range of interest rates over which there is some likelihood of a default (or inflation) and lowers the range over which multiple equilibria might exist. Adrian and Gros (1999, p. 129) also find that: 'An increase in the uncertainty of the shocks hitting the economy reduces the parameter range in which multiple equilibria can arise'.

The second issue is risk aversion, which might play a key role. Simply put, under risk aversion the high probability of a low-impact event (inflation) is not the same as the low probability of a high-impact event (default). This aspect deserves more research. First of all, it is analytically difficult to determine why a formal default of a sovereign is – or should be – such a high-impact event. From a purely political point of view it makes, of course, a world of a difference whether a country declares itself bankrupt, or whether it merely produces a few points of more inflation which over time reduces the real burden on its public debt. However, this real-world difference is difficult to capture in formal models (except through the standard ad hoc assumption of bankruptcy costs).

All in all it appears that the fundamental problem for the eurozone at present is the sudden disappearance of liquidity, both for the sovereign and the banking system and the immeasurable costs of bankruptcy for both the sovereign and banks. If this problem is so apparent today, one must wonder why it was not anticipated when the plans for EMU were made. However, during the late 1980s and early 1990s the main problem appeared to be how to decisively defeat inflation. The previous decade had seen an increasing divergence between the performance of Germany, which had generally lower inflation (and lower fiscal deficits) and most of southern Europe, which had had much higher inflation and higher deficits. Financial stability appeared at the time not to be a serious problem per se given that Germany had not experienced any systemic financial crisis during its post-war 'hard currency' regime. Some academic economists and some observers at international financial institutions argued already in the 1990s that the ECB should also play a greater role in safeguarding financial stability and that a common currency area also required a common financial supervisor. However, this was not taken seriously in Europe where the German experience was taken as proof that an independent central bank and price stability would be a sufficient condition for financial stability. Moreover, interventions to maintain financial stability in a crisis always involve fiscal issues – who pays for the banks? – and a key element of the Maastricht framework was that fiscal policy should remain a national responsibility with transfers among Member States categorically excluded. This neglect of the planning for a financial crisis proved to be a mistake.

Systemic financial crises are rare events; they often do not occur for decades. Yet when they arrive, typically unexpectedly, they require quick decisions on fundamental issues. This is exactly the situation in which the eurozone finds itself today.

References

Adrian, T. and Gros, D. (1999) 'A Stochastic Model of Self-Fulfilling Crises in Fixed Exchange Rate Systems'. *International Journal of Finance and Economics*, Vol. 4, No. 2, pp. 129–46.

Barro, J. and Gordon, D. (1983) 'A Positive Theory of Monetary Policy in a Natural Rate Model'. *Journal of Political Economy*, Vol. 91, No. 4, pp. 589–610.

Calvo, G. (1988) 'Servicing the Public Debt: The Role of Expectations'. *American Economic Review*, Vol. 78, No. 4, pp. 647–61.

De Grauwe, P. (2011) 'Governance of a Fragile Eurozone'. CEPS Working Document WD 34. Available at: «http://www.ceps.eu/book/governance-fragile-eurozone».

Diamond, D.W. and Dybvig, P.H. (1983) 'Bank Runs, Deposit Insurance and Liquidity'. *Journal of Political Economy*, Vol. 91, No. 3, pp. 401–19.

Giavazzi, F. and Pagano, M. (1988) 'The Advantage of Tying One's Hands: EMS Discipline and Central Bank Credibility'. *European Economic Review*, Vol. 32, No. 5, pp. 1055–75.

Giovannini A. and Gros, D. (2012) 'How High the Firewall? Potential Financing Needs for the Periphery'. *CEPS Commentary*, March.

Gros, D. (2011a) 'Speculative Attacks within or outside a Monetary Union: Default versus Inflation (What to do Today)'. CEPS Policy Brief 257. Available at: «http://www.ceps.eu/book/speculative-attacks-within-or-outside-monetary-union-default-versus-inflation-what-do-today».

Gros, D. (2011b) 'Can Austerity be Self-Defeating?' *Voxeu*, 29 November. Available at: «http://voxeu.org/index.php?q=node/7360».

Gros, D. and Mayer, T. (2011) 'Debt Reduction without Default'. CEPS Policy Brief 233, February.

Gros, D. and Mayer, T. (forthcoming) 'Refinancing the EFSF through the ECB'. CEPS Policy Brief.

Kopf, C. (2011) 'Restoring Financial Stability in the Euro Area'. CEPS Policy Brief 237, March. Available at: «http://www.ceps.eu/book/restoring-financial-stability-euro-area».

Obstfeld, M. (1986) 'Capital Mobility in the World Economy: Theory and Measurement'. *Carnegie Rochester Conference Series on Public Policy*, No. 24, pp. 55–104.

Obstfeld, M. (1995) 'International Capital Mobility in the 1990s'. In Kenen, P. (ed.) *Understanding Interdependence* (Princeton, NJ: Princeton University Press).

Sims, C. (2012) 'Gaps in the Institutional Structure of the Euro Area'. *Banque de France Financial Stability Review*, No. 16, pp. 217–23.

JCMS 2012 Volume 50 Annual Review pp. 49–52 DOI: 10.1111/j.1468-5965.2012.02269.x

1989: The Missed Opportunity

DOUGLAS HURD
House of Lords

'There is a tide in the affairs of men . . .', but the whole thrust of Shakespeare's advice is that the tide must be taken at the flood. If lost, the result is misery. There have arguably been three such tides in human affairs, by which I mean those occasions during which the international community exerted itself to create a set of rules and institutions which would reduce to a minimum the danger of war between states. The opportunities presented themselves in 1815, 1919 and 1945. Each time the effort followed a disastrous war. Each time the effort failed.

Admittedly I am looking at the world from a European angle. That is certainly a limitation, but not necessarily a fatal one. Only out of Europe in the period I am covering could a war which started in one continent spill over to engulf other continents. Only out of Europe could a war which began on the borders of Poland extend within months to convulse parts of Asia, Africa, America and the Middle East. On each occasion the belligerent powers emerged from conflict determined to organize their relationships so that no such war could happen again. Three times they failed and now in 2012 the same task confronts us again in a different form. We are not this time short of international institutions. They have multiplied to a formidable extent. They hold hundreds of meetings, yet no one can seriously argue that they cover our needs and are fit for purpose.

The first of the three attempts at a settled international order was made after the defeat of Napoleon and was negotiated in 1814 and 1815 under the guidance of the British Foreign Secretary Castlereagh, the French Minister Talleyrand and Emperor Alexander of Russia. These countries had lived through a terrifying experience. They had seen a revolutionary movement erupt violently in France and spread across much of Europe, culminating in the imperial despotism of Napoleon. They brought Europe back to a somewhat tremulous stability by restoring its ancient dynasties and providing through the Congress system a mechanism by which leading powers would confer to find the best means to deal with any outbreak of trouble. This Vienna Settlement resolved competently along traditional lines the questions left outstanding at the end of hostilities; it settled the boundaries of France, Poland and of the different German states with due regard to the verdicts of the battlefields. It left out one factor which turned out to be crucial in the 19th and 20th centuries – namely the desire of countries to determine their own future. So in 1919 the victorious allied powers were forced back to the drawing board. They composed a new map which in theory responded to the appetite for self-determination. But the Versailles settlement produced answers which though in theory more equitable in practice proved unacceptable, indeed dangerous and indecisive. A marked failing of the Versailles settlement was its refusal to take account of the actual balance of power as it had emerged from World War I. That is why their effort – the San Francisco Settlement of 1945 –

swallowed its misgivings of principle and accepted in the Security Council of the United Nations a system of great power vetoes which was an attempt to bring the post-war arrangement more or less into line with the weight of armies on the ground, dividing Germany into four zones of occupation and allowing the Soviet Union in practice a wide area of influence over the whole of eastern Europe.

In 1989 there was a fleeting chance to do better. Once again war and revolution had wiped the slate clean. In that year the Soviet Union's control over eastern Europe collapsed and with it the deadlock which had in practice provided a new balance of power between east and west. An early result of this was the unification of Germany, which had always been favoured by the United States and its allies and in 1991 actually happened. There seemed in 1989 and 1990 no limit to the reach of the only superpower – the United States. Was there then an opportunity for the United States and Europe to come together and create a set of institutions which would this time last the course? Again, as in 1945, the victorious powers declared their absolute determination to exclude the possibility of war.

Yet in 2012 we are acutely conscious hour by hour of fresh examples of bloodshed and institutional breakdown. Yet again we find ourselves with a new set of dangers, different from those of the 19th and 20th centuries but no less virulent. There are again quarrels between states, but this time the spotlight has been on the breakdown of states into civil conflict, in some cases excited by the partisanship of external powers. These powers – for example, in Iraq and Afghanistan – find themselves tempted, they would say compelled, to intervene forcibly in disputes and arguments with which until recently they have had no part. The doctrine of RTP (the responsibility to protect) has evolved within the UN to justify the kind of intervention which on the face of it requires a renunciation of Article 2(7) of the UN Charter which was drafted to prevent the organization intervening in disputes which are essentially within the domestic jurisdiction of member states.

This time there is no prospect of unanimity. On the contrary, a number of states, including crucial players such as China and Russia, strongly challenge what amounts to an extension of the reach of the UN. The result is institutional strain within the UN which could lead to a breakdown.

Sometimes no international institution has come to birth even though the need for it is clear beyond doubt. There is fierce argument within and between individual countries about the effect of climate change, with the result that we are not yet in sight of arrangements under which individual states would pledge themselves to specific undertakings which in the view of most scientists are necessary to save our planet from degradation or event destruction.

These gaps and imperfections in our present system are clear enough. I believe that there was a fleeting opportunity at least to begin the work of repair, but this opportunity has now passed us by. A crucial component of any new or revised international system must be the declared willingness of every major power to abide by the rules or limitations which have been discussed internationally and broadly agreed. To reach this happy state of affairs, two conditions seem necessary. First, there must be dominance by one country or one group of countries which is not seriously challenged by others. Second, that country or group of countries must be willing to forgo the advantages of superiority and accept the same restrictions on its own freedom of action as it expects other countries to accept, even though those other countries are, by definition, weaker.

In practice I believe that the initiative in this matter must be taken by the president of the United States as the only country to which these two conditions apply now or in the conceivable future. Are those conditions in any way practicable? I became foreign secretary in the autumn of 1989 and worked closely with President George W. Bush Sr, developing a high regard for his integrity and common sense. He and his Secretary of State James Baker gave the world the calm unhurried leadership which we needed at that time and need now again. His experience and sound judgement were admirable assets. But he was not, as he acknowledged himself, a man of vision. He could look round the next corner, but not the corner after that. He was neither a second Woodrow Wilson nor a second Franklin D. Roosevelt. He was suspicious of rhetoric and preferred his own style, which was down to earth, even prosaic.

In 2008 the American people elected a very different kind of president. We need have no doubt about Barak Obama's intelligence or integrity, but it is far too early to make a judgement of him. Even if he had the aptitude for this task of ambitious construction, the events of our century have already rendered it impossible. It is no longer conceivable, as it was briefly in 1989, to imagine that the United States could use its world supremacy to modernize the world's institutions and bring them up to date. The world has in effect once more changed its shape. The concept of a superpower able to guide the international community by a mixture of power and wisdom is no longer close to reality. The United States is fast losing its absolute primacy and is already having to content itself with the role of first among equals. Other countries, notably China, dispute even that claim and by rapid economic and military development mount a formidable challenge. Certainly China will reject any attempt by the United States to reshape the world on what we in the west regard as modern needs. Nor will the Chinese lack followers in repudiating what they see as the legacy of western imperialism.

In the past, the European nations have not challenged the role of the United States as first among equals. Even General de Gaulle, when it came to the crunch, was content to follow an American lead. Since then there has been a sharp decline in the quality of European policy-making. Gone are the hopes of a European foreign policy acting as a necessary complement to America, acting on the whole as a force for caution but occasionally as a stimulus for action which would otherwise not be taken. At the moment western Europe is sluggishly contemplating mechanisms for united action, but the common will for such action was never strong and is rapidly shrinking. The enlargement of the EU is after all, as some feared, in danger of resulting in collective enfeeblement rather than greater strength. The Libyan crisis showed France and Britain proving our willingness to act together by ourselves, but also underlined the relative feebleness of such action unless underpinned by American power. There is no sign in any European country of a willingness to support American determination to reshape the world.

The newcomers have on the whole been content to follow the lead set by the long-standing members, with the important exception that they are markedly more suspicious of Russian policy. Unless they feel directly threatened from the east, it seems unlikely that the new European members will be galvanized into a more dynamic common foreign policy.

These conclusions seem to me inescapable. We need to give up our previous ambitions, and accept that the most we can hope for is incremental improvement. The opportunity of

1989 has been missed and will not recur. It does not follow that we are faced with a new Armageddon. The penalties of conflict are greater than ever before. This time there is no reason why rivalry which is inevitable should end in conflict. The price of peace and the penalties of war are greater than ever before. We are likely to fail if we set our sights too high. The case for limited peaceful coexistence between states is overwhelming. This may not be the highest aim of statesmanship, but it could be the most compelling.

JCMS 2012 Volume 50 Annual Review pp. 53–67 DOI: 10.1111/j.1468-5965.2012.02272.x

The JCMS Annual Review Lecture European Crisis, European Solidarity*

ERIK JONES
Johns Hopkins University/SAIS

Introduction

The past four years have challenged the process of European integration fundamentally. The succession of *JCMS Annual Review* lectures reflect that fact. Vivien Schmidt (2009) focused on the interaction between identity, democracy and economy. Her goal was to assess how well the European Union (EU) could cope with the challenges it confronted. Her conclusion was that European institutions must adopt more flexible decision-making procedures (and a more flexible identity) if they are to traverse this period of uncertainty with their legitimacy intact. Writing a year later, Kalypso Nicolaïdis reinforced the call for sustainable integration. Her vision of a new European Union (EU 2.0) is one that accepts a 'narrative diversity' that goes even beyond the flexibility advocated by Schmidt (Nicolaïdis, 2010, p. 47). Like Schmidt, Nicolaïdis called for fundamental reform and decisive action. Finally, Loukas Tsoukalis returned to a question he has wrestled with for many years about 'the kind of Europe' Europeans should aspire to live in. He recommended a new division of labour between European institutions and the individual Member States. He warned that 'we risk losing some of the things that we used to take for granted after many years of integration in Europe' if our politicians do not rise up to the necessity for decisive action (Tsoukalis, 2011, p. 41).

The problems those observers confronted have not gone away. On the contrary, the turmoil in European sovereign debt markets has renewed speculation about a crisis in European integration. Some, like German Christian Social Union general secretary Alexander Dobrindt, argue that Greece should either embrace reform or exit from the euro;[1] others, like European Council President Herman Van Rompuy, warn that the exit of one country could mean that 'the euro zone would fall apart. Then the whole union would fall apart'.[2] Van Rompuy was referring to the Netherlands rather than to Greece, but the principle remains the same. If national exchange rates within the euro are not irrevocably fixed, then the eurozone is not a single currency but a fixed exchange rate regime. And if Europe cannot maintain its commitment to the euro, then how can it shore up other core elements of the integration project?

* Many thanks to Tim Haughton, Nathaniel Copsey and Valeria Calderoni for their excellent comments and suggestions. The usual disclaimer applies. The material in this article was originally developed in the mid-2000s together with my good friend and graduate student Frederick Hood. We originally planned to expand the argument into a book. Unfortunately Fred passed away in a tragic skiing accident on Christmas Eve of 2008. This article is dedicated to his memory.

[1] *RP online*, 1 February 2012. Available at: «http://www.rp-online.de/politik/eu/csu-general-raet-griechen-zu-euro-aus-1.2693270».

[2] *Reuters*, 4 March 2012. Available at: «http://www.reuters.com/article/2012/03/04/us-eurozone-crisis-vanrompuy-idUSTRE8230B020120304».

Then again, this is hardly the first time that voices have expressed concern about the viability of the EU. Indeed, the process of European integration has been under strain since the mid-1990s, when a sharp reversal in economic performance sapped popular enthusiasm and triggered more than a decade of contentious institutional reform debates (Hix, 2008). The EU continued to make progress nonetheless. The introduction of the single currency, the consolidation of the Schengen Area, the enlargement of membership to the countries of central and eastern Europe, and the elaboration of common foreign, security and defence policies are all historic achievements. Enthusiasts may lament that Europe has not gone far enough and critics may complain that it has gone too far; no one can deny, however, that the EU has moved forward since the negotiation of the Maastricht Treaty despite considerable adversity. This is not the first time either. Every decade since the end of World War II has experienced moments that are similar in many respects. Each time, however, the European project has emerged stronger as a consequence. Why should this time be any different?

The question is obvious, at least for those who have been around in Europe for a while, and yet the answer is not. At least part of the problem is that – in contrast to previous decades – there seems to be little room left for the EU to develop. There is no new frontier to bring into the Union and no new project to capture the imagination. Geographically, the existing Member States appear reluctant to expand much beyond the Western Balkans and even there it will be difficult to manage enlargement to Albania, Bosnia, Kosovo and Macedonia – albeit for different reasons. Institutionally, the Member States show little enthusiasm for revisiting the existing treaties or elaborating new frameworks for co-operation. Economically, the Union has few new projects to offer and quite a number of challenges shoring up the single currency and the internal market. Politically, there is more concern with fending off the anti-European agendas of the new radical right than with fostering a common European identity.

This is not to suggest that European integration has reached some sort of stasis or equilibrium. The simmering tensions in Europe's sovereign debt markets and the conflict over macroeconomic policy co-ordination together form the most dramatic illustration of the need for some kind of resolution. The linked challenges of immigration and national border controls are a close second. Enlargements past, present and future – including the Turkish application for membership – offer a third. The EU is not some bicycle that must keep moving to avoid falling over, but Europe's political leaders cannot afford to leave such contentious issues unaddressed either. If progress is defined as problem solving, then Europe's leaders must ultimately choose to drive integration forward or accept that it will move in reverse.

The argument in this article is that this time is different. Europe faces ever-tightening constraints on the possibilities for further integration as a consequence. In that sense, I echo the calls made in this same forum by my immediate predecessors (Schmidt, 2009; Nicolaïdis, 2010; Tsoukalis, 2011). Europe's political leadership faces an existential crisis not just for the EU, but for the notion of 'Europe' as a whole. Moreover, for Europe's political leaders to respond effectively to the problems they confront, they will have to give new meaning to the European project.

The article has five sections. The first looks at past moments of tension to show how they were surmounted indirectly rather than head-on. The second uses that experience to develop the notion of solidarity as a concept for bracketing why countries choose to participate in the European project and for explaining the resilience of Europe writ large. The third describes how European solidarity can break down. The fourth suggests why it may be happening now. The fifth shows that Europe's problems will not go away on their own and so offers some suggestions for a more decisive response.

I. Progress

When the French parliament voted to table ratification of the European Defence Community in August 1954, Raymond Aron and Daniel Lerner (1956, p. 209) announced the end of the European project. The logic of their argument was compelling. Now that France had turned its back on supranationalism and on the Franco–German relationship, there was little foundation upon which to construct a united Europe. That logic also turned out to be incomplete. Even before Aron and Lerner had the chance to submit their edited volume to the publishers, Europe's leaders were meeting in Messina. Paul-Henri Spaak's report on the common market coincided with the French edition of the book (Aron and Lerner, 1956); the English language edition came alongside the Treaty of Rome (Lerner and Aron, 1957). What is even more ironic is the possibility that the original proposal to form a common market may have been designed to sabotage the European Defence Community (Griffiths and Milward, 1986). If true, then European failure and success were all part of the same game plan.

The 1950s was not the only time that the death of European integration was announced prematurely. The challenge posed by General De Gaulle in the early to mid-1960s is another good illustration. The Fouchet Plan, the British veto and the 'empty chair' each pointed to the reassertion of national primacy against the threat posed by supranational institutions or norms (Hoffmann, 1968). Yet it was premature to discount supranationalism entirely (Parsons, 2003). The early 1960s were also a period of consolidation for the European Court of Justice (ECJ) and a whole new pattern of European jurisprudence (Weiler, 1999). Given how important the ECJ has become over time, it is easier to look back on the Gaullist period as a useful corrective than as a fundamental challenge.

The collapse of the Werner Plan for monetary union in the 1970s is a further illustration. The plan was designed to promote the irrevocable fixing of national exchange rates by the end of the decade. Almost before it began, however, it ran into trouble. Turmoil in the wider Bretton Woods system of fixed but adjustable exchange rates caused the Europeans to accelerate their efforts at monetary integration. Inadvertently, this pre-empted the argument between those who believed countries should have similar economies before forming a common currency and those who believed that having irrevocably fixed exchange rates would force economies to be more similar. Europe's political leaders decided to try to manage their internal exchange rates despite their obvious differences and failed spectacularly. The veteran French diplomat Robert Marjolin (1975, p. 1) commented in surveying the wreckage of their efforts that Europe's economies had never been farther apart. His diagnosis was accurate, but not fatal. Soon thereafter, Europe's leaders pushed for the creation of a more effective exchange rate mechanism which in turn underpinned a more stable European Monetary System.

The pattern of failure either leading or accompanying success can be found in the 1980s and 1990s as well. The fierce debates about the British budgetary question gave way to the 1992 project to complete the single market. The exchange rate crises of the early

1990s were followed by renewed efforts to construct a single currency. German insistence on tightening fiscal discipline with a stability pact soon merged with efforts to promote growth and reduce unemployment through the European employment strategy. Today it is hard to think about Europe without thinking about the internal market and the euro, and it is even harder to imagine that European institutions would not be implicated in the struggle to create jobs and growth.

If there is a deeper structure to this pattern of intertwining success and failure, it is that each time the Member States have arrived at an impasse with one another in one area of integration, they seem to have found some other area where they could promote progress. This is a weak correlation and not a strong causal argument. Whether successful integration breeds further success despite the occasional failure, as in the transactionalist view; or successful integration is necessary to correct failure as in the neofunctionalist approach; or success is essential because the only alternative to integration is failure, as in the European rescue of the nation-state, remains indeterminate. The theories of Karl Deutsch (Deutsch *et al.*, 1957), Ernst Haas (1958) and Alan Milward (1992) are all relevant and different causal mechanisms may operate at different times. The point is simply that integration seems to flow around substantive controversies, leaving some standing and washing others away.

A similar point applies to the composition of membership for different ventures. Although it would be convenient to imagine the Member States moving together in lockstep, they have often responded to conflict by creating exceptions or derogations rather than allow the requirements for consensus or unanimity to act as an obstacle or constraint. Hence the West European Union, the European Monetary System and the Schengen agreement all started outside the formal institutional framework for European integration, they incorporated different countries under different rules, and yet they evolved into the foundations for the common policies toward security, currency and immigration at the core of the European project today. As with the substantive controversies, some of the exceptions to membership remain standing and others have eroded over time.

The resilience of European integration derives from this sub-surface complexity. For there to be a real crisis in European integration, it would not be enough for one or more countries, or one or more projects to come into conflict. Van Rompuy is probably wrong to suggest that a single country exiting the euro would bring down the eurozone or to argue that a collapse of the euro would bring down the EU altogether.[3] Past experience suggests that membership controversies and substantive controversies can be resolved given time. Therefore, something would have to overwhelm the capacity of Europeans to respond flexibly by making exceptions to existing rules or by developing new institutions and relationships. Either countries – meaning, more precisely, national politicians and their electorates – would have to refuse to participate in the complex and adaptive European arrangement or they would have to reject the complex adaptations that make the arrangement attractive to, or viable for, other participants. The bottom line is that the European project will continue so long as Europeans want to participate.

[3] *Reuters*, 4 March 2012. Available at: «http://www.reuters.com/article/2012/03/04/us-eurozone-crisis-vanrompuy-idUSTRE8230B020120304».

II. Solidarity

That last sentence sounds like a bromide but it actually constitutes a significant challenge for analysis. Theories of European integration do not have strong accounts of this underlying 'willingness to participate'. The transactionalists point to cross-cultural affinity; the neofunctionalists have welfare-maximizing rationality; the intergovernmentalists have exogenous, intermediated national interests; the legalists have dispute resolution; and the constructivists have norms and ideas. Each of these accounts holds some measure of the underlying motivation behind why people and governments choose to participate in European projects or to accept the guidance of European institutions. Yet proponents of each theoretical tradition also strive for some measure of supremacy over the rest in explaining the broad pattern of events.

This struggle for supremacy is unfortunate because it means that competing assumptions about the willingness to participate in Europe are confirmed by testing their logical entailments rather than being examined directly. The conflict between neofunctionalism and liberal intergovernmentalism at the start of the 1990s is one illustration; the constructivist assault on liberal intergovernmentalism in the late 1990s and early 2000s is another. For the theorists involved the debate has been absorbing; for others it held only fleeting interest. Hence, the reaction among those analysts with few stakes in the theoretical competition has been to borrow eclectically from different traditions as they move from one problem to the next (Peterson, 2001; Verdun, 2003).

Meanwhile attempts to study the 'willingness to participate' directly have been subsumed within the wider debate about European identity. Unfortunately, there is no obvious mapping from identification with Europe to a willingness to participate in specific European projects. It is possible to reveal correlations between expressions of support or priority for different policy areas or for integration as a whole and assertions of European identity. However, it is more challenging to pin down a causal connection between the different sets of attitudes, to assess its strength and stability, and to rule out the existence of some prior causal influence. In other words, just because people say they support integration and identify themselves as European does not mean that one thing leads to another or that either or both opinions might not suddenly change. Hence some of the best work on identity has tried to isolate individuals or groups most able to experience European integration directly or to map the emergence of a truly European public space (Fligstein, 2008; Risse, 2010). Such arguments build on the logic that individuals with more exposure to Europe should be more willing to participate in European ventures – often following Deutsch's transactionalist tradition – but they do not test that causal link explicitly.

An alternative perspective would start with the logic of participation and then work backward to the willingness of the participants, rather than starting with the identity of the participants and building up to Europe. Such a perspective would necessarily incorporate elements of affinity, rationality, self-interest, dispute resolution, norms and ideas. However, because it would place more emphasis on the nature of the project than on the identity of the participants, it would be easier to build in the possibility that the willingness to participate could vary within the same group of participants from one aspect of integration to the next. In this way, it would be easier to capture why different areas of integration have different exceptions, derogations or patterns of membership.

'Solidarity' is a term that could bracket this alternative perspective on the willingness to participate without stretching the concept beyond its conventional use (Jones, 2005). The dictionary definition includes the existence of shared or complementary interests. That definition obviously touches on notions of 'affinity', 'rationality', 'norms' and all the rest. Concepts like 'sharing', 'complementarity' and 'interests' are all socially constructed even if they rest on objective or material requirements (Searle, 1997). More important, solidarity is functionally specific. The pattern of sharing or complementarity of interests that governments or individuals find in any one domain of integration does not need to resemble the patterns they confront in other aspects of the European project. Hence the composition of acceptable partners could be functionally specific as well.

The kind of solidarity expressed in wartime is a good illustration. The most important interest shared by Great Britain, the Soviet Union and the United States was the need to defeat Nazi Germany. To a lesser extent they also shared an interest in containing Japan. Once the conflict was over, however, this wartime solidarity proved to be a wasting asset. Having vanquished their common enemies, the victorious powers did not share an interest in either economic or political integration. Quite the opposite was in fact the case, and efforts to promote economic integration in Europe led to conflict between the Soviet Union and the west.

Market solidarity has an altogether different logic from the-enemy-of-my-enemy-is-my-friend thinking that gave structure to alliances in World War II. Instead of standing up to a common adversary, everyone has to agree to abide by the same rules for competition. This is not as easy as it sounds. As Karl Polanyi (1957) explained, the rules for market competition contain a wealth of other norms and values. Markets are embedded in a rich social environment and market institutions embody conceptions of 'fairness', 'equity', 'priority' and 'status'. This means that as different societies institutionalize markets domestically, they inadvertently create obstacles or barriers to market competition internationally (Myrdal, 1956). This explains why market solidarity is different at different levels of aggregation, being greater within countries than between them. Acceptance of this reality by the architects of the post-World War II international economic system is essentially what John Gerard Ruggie (1982) described as 'the compromise of embedded liberalism'.

Of course Ruggie was interested in welfare state formation as well as market integration. In that sense, he focused on redistribution as well as competition. Here again, the logic of solidarity is different. Redistributive institutions do not require everyone to abide by the same rules; instead they tend to privilege one part of society at the expense of another. Participants must be willing to accept to play their assigned roles knowing that they may never get as much out of the system as they put into it (Baldwin, 1990). Solidarity in this context hews to subtly different notions of equity, fairness or justice. Hence even countries with very similar market institutions may have very different welfare states, with different notions of inclusiveness, financial underpinnings and expectations in terms of outcomes (Esping-Andersen, 1999).

Once the analysis focuses on the willingness to participate directly, it is easier to understand why the European project is so complicated and how it has proven so resilient. The breakdown of solidarity in any given endeavour need not entail the collapse of solidarity in another. On the contrary, the same countries might decide they do not need a common army after the end of the Korean conflict and after the death of Stalin, but would be willing to participate in a common market. The fact that these countries all come from Europe does not mean that the two projects are essentially 'European' and it does not mean that European integration hinges on their success or failure either. If anything the two projects are essentially different and neither is more European than the other. The history of European integration includes both. It also includes the Council of Europe, the North Atlantic Treaty Organization (Nato), the Organisation for Economic Co-operation and Development (OECD) and the Organization for Security and Co-operation in Europe (OSCE).

III. Contagion

By focusing directly on the willingness to participate it is also possible to identify what would constitute a crisis for European integration. The failure of one or more projects by itself is not sufficient. As has often been the case, occasional setbacks either run alongside or anticipate offsetting successes. Instead a crisis of integration requires that otherwise discrete problems spread from one European project to the next. The Gaullist episode provides a good illustration of this dynamic. De Gaulle wanted a common agricultural policy and some measure of foreign policy independence. He also wanted to hold the supranational Commission in check. His success in any or all of these endeavours was not the problem. The real challenge to integration came from the threat his tactics posed to the other activities of the European Economic Community. By pulling his representatives from the Council of Ministers he generalized the conflict. That constituted a real crisis – which the Luxembourg Compromise resolved by giving every country the right to exercise a veto over matters of national interest. In effect, the Luxembourg Compromise eliminated the generalized crisis by ensuring that most future conflicts would be specific (Nicoll, 1984).

The Gaullist institutional challenge is unlikely to be repeated. Although the Luxembourg Compromise no longer operates as it did in the 1960s and 1970s, the norms of consensus that it fostered still dominate deliberations in the Council of the EU (Peterson and Bomberg, 1999, pp. 31–59). This does not eliminate the possibility that conflicts would spill over from one European project to the next. Contagion does not have to be formal or institutional to generate a crisis of integration.

Consider the case of Ireland in the early 2000s. The story starts with a commitment from the Irish government to raise the country's surplus as part of the EU's agreed 'broad economic policy guidelines'. However, the Irish government reneged on that pledge in December 2000 because it was heading toward elections the following March. The Council of Economics and Finance Ministers (Ecofin Council) responded by reprimanding the Irish government in February 2001, sparking a public quarrel between the Council and Irish Taoiseach Bertie Ahern as he headed to the polls. Unfortunately, this spat also coincided with the campaign leading up to the June 2001 Irish referendum on the Nice Treaty – from which Ahern's government was notably absent. When the referendum resulted in a veto, commentators across Europe opined that the Irish resented losing subsidies as a consequence of enlargement and European Commission President Romano Prodi suggested that perhaps the Irish did not understand the referendum question. Neither accusation had merit; both helped poison the debate (Jones, 2002).

It would be possible to extend the Irish example to run from the December 2001 Laeken Declaration to the failed 2005 referendums on the European Constitutional Treaty in France and the Netherlands, but that would give too much responsibility to the Irish. A more realistic claim is that there were a number of episodes in the early 2000s where conflicts cascaded from one area of integration to another. The epicentre might be the divisions over the war in Iraq, the excessive deficit procedure or the completion of the internal market for services, but the consequences would be felt in terms of EU finances, enlargement, welfare state reform or the ratification of the European Constitutional Treaty (Jones, 2005). A few analysts, like Jeremy Rifkin (2004) or Mark Leonard (2006), chose the moment to write books about how Europe would emerge as a future superpower; many more expressed concern about the depths of the EU's malaise (Hix, 2008; Menon, 2008; Taylor, 2008).

This notion of contagion is what makes the situation in the EU so worrying today. Consider the sovereign debt crisis. The problem is not that Greece is insolvent or that it has defaulted on its debts. Greece is a relatively small country and its total outstanding debt could be financed with common resources that are already available. The real crisis comes from the failure to understand how Greece got that way and to appreciate what are the implications for the rest of Europe if Greece is left to its own fate.

Here it is worth laying out a few threads of the tangled series of events as they unfolded since 2008. The story begins in March when the European Commission noted anomalies in Greek fiscal accounts. This triggered a sudden capital outflow as investors sought to lower their exposure to Greek government debt. A second outflow started in October 2008 as the European Commission required the Greek government to announce a modest upward revision to its deficit figures. Then in January 2009, Standard and Poor's downgraded Greece, citing concern about the quality of the government's accounting practices. This outflow suddenly ended in February at about the same time that German finance minister Peer Steinbrück announced to a group of German businessmen that no eurozone Member State would be allowed to go bankrupt. By May 2009, significant flows of capital started to return and Greek government bond yields moved below those for Ireland. The situation remained stable up to the following October. Once again, the Greek government revised its deficit data upward. This time, however, it did so not once but twice, and in much greater magnitudes than the year prior. The market reaction was counter-intuitive: the yield differential between Greek and German government bonds did not change significantly in October and November; meanwhile capital flowed into Greece, not out (Merler and Pisani-Ferry, 2012).

There are many ways to interpret the market reactions to Greece's October 2009 fiscal revisions. Market actors may have been relieved to put a number on a problem they already knew existed; Greek banks may have sought to repatriate assets held abroad; or the European Central Bank (ECB) may have responded proactively by providing generous access to liquidity for the Greek banking system. Indeed each of these elements may have played a role. What is certain is that investors in Greek sovereign debt markets did not stage a rout. That only happened in the spring of 2010, with the most significant capital outflows following the March European Council summit. Up until then, Greek government bond auctions were hugely oversubscribed. Once Angela Merkel made it clear that Greece could go bankrupt, however, private sector investors in Greek government securities began to look for some way to escape from that exposure. The story ends with the first Greek bail-out in May 2010 (Jones, 2010b).

This narrative is important because it shows the breakdown of solidarity in European sovereign debt markets. In February 2009, the German finance minister was willing to reassure markets that Greece would not go bankrupt; by March 2010, the German chancellor was not. The design of the first Greek bail-out suggests that Europe's political leaders believed the problems could be contained within Greece. If so, the illusion passed quickly. The potential for contagion to spread across other sovereign debt markets was almost immediately apparent and so the Ecofin Council and the ECB introduced the first elements of a more generalized bail-out.

At this point it is easy to narrate the European sovereign debt crisis as a problem that spread from one country to the next – starting with Greece and then progressing to Ireland, Portugal, Spain and Italy. The more important dynamic, however, is how the crisis spread from sovereign debt markets to banks to government finances. This is the link from Greece to Ireland. Irish sovereign debt was under strain throughout the summer of 2010. However, it was only after the French and the Germans agreed that private sector investors in Greece should absorb some of the costs associated with the Greek sovereign debt bail-out that the pressure on Ireland became unsustainable (BIS, 2010, p. 11). The Irish government was already having difficulty meeting its commitment to bail out the country's larger domestic banks. However, the ECB refused to allow that country to involve the private sector in any losses. Instead, private sector investors in Irish banking securities had to be made whole. This meant that the Irish government had to issue increasing volumes of promissory notes for use as capital in its struggling banks – extending the government's liabilities beyond the point at which the private sector lost confidence in the Irish state (Whelen, 2012, p. 25).

The close interdependence between national governments and national banks played a crucial role in the other countries most affected by the crisis as well. Here the case of Italy is particularly dramatic. Throughout 2010 Italy was a net recipient of capital and a net creditor in the Target2 system that moves liquidity across the eurozone from one country to another (Merler and Pisani-Ferry, 2012, p. 9). Moreover, while Italy's public debt was high its deficit net of debt servicing – the 'primary balance' – showed a higher surplus than any other EU Member State and its conservative banking system seemed less exposed to losses in the United States and elsewhere (Rovelli, 2010). When Europe's leaders began to negotiate a second Greek bail-out in the late spring of 2011 with higher levels of private sector involvement, investors in Italian government debt securities suddenly lost confidence. Given that Italy has the world's third largest sovereign debt market with more than €2 trillion in obligations, even a small risk of insolvency could translate into significant losses. The large exposure of Italian banks to their own government's securities meant they were vulnerable as well. Once money started to flow out of the country, the higher interest rates on government bonds and loss of deposits for domestic banks transformed investors' fears into a self-fulfilling prophecy. Both the Italian government and the major Italian banks experienced successive downgrades, bringing the country to the brink of crisis and leading to the collapse of the centre-right government of Silvio Berlusconi (Jones, 2012).

As Europe's sovereign debt crisis has engulfed ever-larger countries, it has touched on an ever-wider array of European institutions and triggered deep divisions between the Member States. Sometimes the arguments are very technical, like the debate about financial imbalances between central banks in the eurozone that emerged at the height of the Italian crisis only to explode onto the front pages of the financial newspapers in March 2012 at a time when many hoped that the crisis might already have been resolved. Sometimes they are more straightforward, like the conflict between the British government and its European counterparts over the restriction on sovereignty implied by the fiscal compact or the conflict between the Spanish government and the European Commission over the requirement to meet strict fiscal deficit targets. And sometimes they give the impression that history is repeating itself, like the conflict between the Irish government and the ECB over the re-profiling of Irish promissory notes – which unfortunately took place during the run-up to a popular referendum in Ireland to ratify the fiscal compact.

So far the contagion has spread across countries and institutions. It looks likely to spread across policy domains as well. In part this is due to the centrality of taxing and spending to all European activities. In part it is also due to persistent difference in national interests and priorities. As governments embrace austerity, they will give more protection to some programmes than to others. This creates a significant free-rider problem. The Schengen border controls are a good example. Tunisian migrants that flow into Italy are more likely to speak French than Italian. Hence an Italian government has little interest to throw such migrants into expensive detention centres and considerable interest in helping them cross the Italian peninsula in order to make their way into France. This was true when French President Nicolas Sarkozy confronted Italian Prime Minister Silvio Berlusconi during the early months of 2011, as the political transformation of Tunisia sparked a surge in cross-border migrants, overwhelming the small Italian island of Lampedusa (see Monar in this issue). Both leaders called on their European counterparts for greater assistance. When those calls fell on deaf ears, France temporarily suspended free movement across its Italian border. Less than a year later, Sarkozy threatened to pull France out of Schengen altogether.[4]

IV. Timing

The argument that the current crisis threatens to spread across the whole range of European activities is fairly easy to make, although in fairness there are some areas that seem less affected than others. The European employment strategy and the wider Europe 2020 reform process may not stand out as overwhelming achievements, but they continue to rack up important successes at helping to put Europeans back to work and shaping more sustainable welfare state institutions and labour markets. The internal market provides an essential framework for the cross-border trade in goods and services. Educational exchange programmes continue to offer cross-cultural opportunities, albeit perhaps with diminished support. European troops are deployed on large numbers of peacekeeping operations. European diplomats continue to provide post-conflict assistance in Bosnia and Kosovo. And the EU remains a formidable power in global trade negotiations and in efforts to protect the global environment. Hence even if we accept that Europe is facing a real crisis of integration, there are many avenues where Europeans could continue to make progress in solving problems collectively until the crisis passes.

This is where more general measures of popular attitudes toward Europe become important. The basic claim is that where the people are indifferent toward Europe and where they tend not to have trust in European institutions, they will have little motivation to support participation in European projects. Hence it will be up to national political elites to mobilize support for participation in Europe or, at a minimum, to inspire enough confidence to ensure that voters will not reject European policies when given the chance

[4] «http://online.wsj.com/article/SB10001424052702304450004577275313803633368.html».

to express their opinion at elections to the European Parliament or in national referendums on European questions.

The aggregate data are not reassuring. To begin with, responses to questions about whether membership in the EU is a good thing for the respondent's country and about whether the respondent believes their country benefits from membership point in opposite directions, with fewer respondents saying membership is a 'good thing' for their country than saying that their country benefits from membership. The data for trust in European institutions is less ambiguous. More respondents tend not to trust specific institutions like the European Commission, the European Parliament and the ECB, than tend to trust them, and the gap between those who tend not to trust and those who tend to trust the EU as a whole is larger than for any of the component parts (Eurobarometer, 2011, pp. 19, 21 and annexes).

Of course some of these indicators are overly influenced by the economic context. When economies contract and unemployment rises, the people naturally look for someone to blame – even if only to blame them for not making matters better more quickly. The problem for Europe is that it is so heavily dependent upon its performance for legitimation (Scharpf, 1999). Hence when Europeans experience a worsening of their economic situation, it chips away at their confidence in the EU as well as support for their national governments (Jones, 2009).

The fact that national governments, parliaments and political parties do even worse in public opinion surveys than European institutions is not reassuring either. National political elites need to mobilize support for European institutions or policies. If they lack the confidence of the electorate, then they are likely to invest little effort in driving a distinctly European agenda. Indeed, this seems to be the pattern for public communication about Europe. National politicians take credit for any successes and then displace the blame for effort or failure to the European level (Menon, 2008, p. 224). Silvio Berlusconi's attempts to blame the euro for Italy's sovereign debt crisis are a good example. While Berlusconi walked back his comments in the face of general outrage that he would say something potentially so destabilizing for the markets, it was only a short while before he came back to reassert that the crisis was not his fault but Europe's (Jones, 2012, pp. 100–1).

The point here is not that national political elites are always abusive of European integration. Rather it is that they lack credibility in general and so it is no wonder that they lack credibility when making the case for Europe. Here it is important to separate out three different dynamics, related to the audience, the messengers and the message. The challenge with the European audience is easy to anticipate. Since the late 1950s, political scientists have noted how much more independent and less strongly connected European voters are to their politicians. The process of political transformation was uneven across countries and it had different implications for different electoral and party systems. But by the start of the 21st century it was probably safe to conclude that the challenges facing politicians in turning out and influencing the voters were everywhere greater than they had been in the past. The politicians themselves were also different. They came from different social groups and equipped with different party apparatuses. They also had to deal with different types of media and a much faster pattern of communication. Again, the process has been uneven. Again it is clear that the situation everywhere has changed.

These first two points are easily grasped because they play prominent roles in any introduction to a comparative politics course. The transformation of the message is also not difficult to anticipate. As the EU has become more prominent, more varied and more expansive, it has also become much harder to explain (Menon, 2008). The winners and losers from integration have become more difficult to identify and compensate (Tsoukalis, 2005). And the old slogans for selling the project have ceased to bear much relation to the underlying reality (Jones, 2010a).

The three factors come together in the recent growth in popularity of new radical right-wing parties. The variety of such movements is impressive (Mudde, 2007). Newer movements like the True Finns, the Sweden Democrats or the Dutch Party of Freedom have little enough in common with each other, let alone with more established groups like the Austrian Freedom Party, the French National Front or the Italian Northern League. Yet all such parties draw strength from widespread voter disaffection with traditional governing elites and they share a general scepticism toward European integration and toward globalization more generally. Moreover, the leaders of these new radical right-wing parties are willing to make use of Europe as a political issue if that is likely to bring them more votes at the polls. As they gain in national importance either by participating in governing coalitions or propping up minority governments, they change the tenor of relations across Member States as well as between the Member States and the institutions of Europe.

Even where new radical right-wing parties do not gain power, they influence the debate by pulling otherwise mainstream parties toward political positions more sceptical of European integration. This is as true in the newer Member States as it is in the older ones. The point is not that European issues will always dominate in domestic politics. In the 2011 parliamentary elections in Slovenia, for instance, European issues were notably absent (Haughton and Krašovec, forthcoming). Nevertheless, given the fluidity of politics in central and eastern Europe, the emergence of new radical right-wing populists may prove to be increasingly important.

The combination of these factors goes a long way to explain the timing of the current crisis in integration. The collapse of the bubble in American sub-prime mortgage markets created the disturbance, but the EU was already fragile. European integration has been struggling off and on since the early 1990s, when the Danish veto of the Maastricht Treaty and the narrowly fought French referendum first punctured the euphoria surrounding the process. It almost faltered during the final stages of the intergovernmental conference that produced the European Constitutional Treaty and then again when the French and the Dutch overwhelmingly rejected ratification of the Treaty document. The question is whether Europe retains enough resilience to weather this most recent shock.

V. Prospects

The economic data do not suggest that Europe's problems will go away quickly. On the contrary, recent estimates point to a long period of slow growth alongside a sharp divergence in performance between those countries on the periphery that have been most adversely affected by the crisis and Germany (OECD, 2012). There are a few relatively bright patches in Poland and Scandinavia, but there are also dark clouds over the United Kingdom, Hungary and the eastern Balkans (see the contributions by Hodson and Connolly in this issue). Such uneven growth is not going to promote greater solidarity in Europe, whether distributive, competitive or otherwise. Instead it is likely to underscore the real differences between countries both in terms of their national interests and in relation to the EU as a whole. These are the conditions that promote disintegration and not integration (Myrdal, 1956).

The collapse of the Soviet bloc provides a cautionary illustration. The point here is not to imply that the EU and the Soviet empire are moral or political equivalents, but only that the dynamics of Soviet disintegration are suggestive. During a long period of economic stagnation, the different countries in the empire each sought to maximize its net benefits within the system in order to position itself more favourably *vis-à-vis* the outside world. Indeed, they continued to negotiate over subsidies even as communism collapsed around them (Stone, 1996). Meanwhile, elites at the core of the Soviet system sought to escape from constraining inefficiencies. They began to challenge the fundamental tenets of communism. And they looked for points of leverage. Allowing the countries of central and eastern Europe to leave the Soviet bloc was the first major step in this process. Extracting Russia from the Soviet Union was the last (Kotkin and Gross, 2009). In the denouement, however, something curious happened. Some countries fled the former Soviet Union, some countries vacillated and others sought to recapture at least something of what they had lost. What is interesting here is that the situation was not more obvious. Whatever the evils of Soviet communism as an ideology of empire, some countries remained willing to participate in post-Soviet forms of integration (Abdelal, 2001).

It goes without saying that the EU should be what the Soviet bloc was not. It should be open, efficient, prosperous and representative. It also goes without saying that the EU tries to do all these things. Although it cannot enlarge indefinitely, it has engaged in an ambitious programme to increase membership. It has emphasized market efficiency from the start. It has contributed substantially to Member State growth. And – whether through the Member States or via the European Parliament – it is representative. There is, however, one further point of difference that deserves more emphasis. Where the Soviet Union gained its top-down legitimacy through the promotion of communist ideology, the EU should strive to be less monolithic. That is what the campaign for 'unity with diversity' was supposed to be about. That message needs to be strengthened.

If the EU is going to survive the current crisis it will need to stop its officials from insisting that a problem in any one aspect of European integration is potentially fatal for the whole. On the contrary, it should put out the message that European solidarity exists in many different patterns across many different domains of integration. And it should strengthen the norms and institutions that prevent problems in one area from spilling over into all the others. This will be challenging because it will call for action in many different directions. It will require some acceptance of spillover and some intergovernmental bargaining; there will be new rules, norms and policy frameworks as well. It will be deliberative, consensual, complicated and, during the implementation at least, it will be inefficient.

This conception of Europe will be hard to sell – for the messengers and not for the audience. European officials will have to give up their monopoly over and ideological commitment to the notion of a monolithic 'Europe' (Schmidt, 2009; Nicolaïdis, 2010). Instead, they will have to admit that Europe means different things to different participants in different projects. Moreover, they will have to extend that European identity to projects outside the formal boundaries of the EU itself. Again, organizations like the Council of Europe, Nato, the OECD and the OSCE are a part of Europe as well. Meanwhile, national officials will have to take responsibility for their participation in specific projects rather than hiding behind or deflecting blame on the EU as a whole. This will be a challenge of a different sort. Where European officials must surrender their cherished commitment, national officials will have to show courage.

The alternative is not that the EU will veer into disaster. So far as European crises go, this one is still too early to tell. Moreover, the European project has a tremendous track record for resilience even under the worst circumstances. We can recognize that it faces a crisis at the moment, but that is no reason to discount it altogether. Still it is worth bearing in mind that European integration is not an inevitable process. Despite its long record of success, the EU can also fail. Europe's leaders will have to do something to prevent that from happening. Nathaniel Copsey and Tim Haughton (2011, p. 4) argued in their editorial to the 2010 *Annual Review* that the essential ingredient is 'political will'. That remains true. This crisis will not resolve itself.

References

Abdelal, R. (2001) *National Purpose in the World Economy: Post-Soviet States in Comparative Perspective* (Ithaca, NY: Cornell University Press).

Aron, R. and Lerner, D. (eds) (1956) *La Querelle de la C.E.D.* (Paris: Armand Colin).

Baldwin, P. (1990) *The Politics of Social Solidarity: Class Bases of the European Welfare State, 1875–1975* (Cambridge: Cambridge University Press).

Bank for International Settlements (BIS) (2010) *Quarterly Review* (December) (Basel: BIS).

Copsey, N. and Haughton, T. (2011) 'Editorial: 2010, Kill or Cure for the Euro?' *JCMS*, Vol. 49, No. S1, pp. 1–6.

Deutsch, K. *et al.* (1957) *Political Community and the North Atlantic Area: International Organization in Light of Historical Experience* (Princeton, NJ: Princeton University Press).

Esping-Andersen, G. (1999) *Social Foundations of Postindustrial Economies* (Oxford: Oxford University Press).

Eurobarometer (2011) *Standard Eurobarometer 76: First Results* (Brussels: European Commission).

Fligstein, N. (2008) *Euro-Clash: The EU, European Identity and the Future of Europe* (Oxford: Oxford University Press).

Griffiths, R. and Milward, A. (1986) 'The Beyen Plan and the European Political Community.' In Maihofer, W. (ed.) *Noi si mura* (Florence: European University Institute).

Haas, E. (1958) *The Uniting of Europe: Political, Social and Economic Forces, 1950–1957* (New York: Stevens & Sons).

Haughton, T. and Krašovec, A. (forthcoming) 'The 2011 Parliamentary Elections in Slovenia'. *Electoral Studies*.

Hix, S. (2008) *What's Wrong with the European Union and How to Fix It* (Cambridge: Polity Press).

Hoffmann, S. (1968) 'Obstinate or Obsolete? The Fate of the Nation-State and the Case of Western Europe.' In Hoffmann, S. (ed.) *Conditions of World Order* (Boston, MA: Houghton Mifflin).

Jones, E. (2002) 'The Politics of Europe 2001: Adversity and Persistence'. *Industrial Relations Journal*, Vol. 33, No. 5, pp. 377–91.

Jones, E. (2005) 'The Politics of Europe 2004: Solidarity and Integration'. *Industrial Relations Journal*, Vol. 36, No. 6, pp. 436–55.

Jones, E. (2009) 'Output Legitimacy and the Global Financial Crisis: Perceptions Matter'. *JCMS*, Vol. 47, No. 5, pp. 1085–106.

Jones, E. (2010a) 'The Economic Mythology of European Integration'. *JCMS*, Vol. 48, No. 1, pp. 89–110.

Jones, E. (2010b) 'Merkel's Folly'. *Survival*, Vol. 52, No. 3, pp. 21–38.

Jones, E. (2012) 'Italy's Sovereign Debt Crisis'. *Survival*, Vol. 54, No. 1, pp. 83–110.

Kotkin, S. and Gross, J. (2009) *Uncivil Society: 1989 and the Implosion of the Communist Establishment* (New York: Random House).

Leonard, M. (2006) *Why Europe Will Run the 21st Century* (New York: Public Affairs).

Lerner, D. and Aron, R. (eds) (1957) *France Defeats the EDC* (New York: Frederick A. Praeger).

Marjolin, R. (1975) 'Report of the Study Group "Economic and Monetary Union 1980"'. Brussels: Commission of the European Communities, II/673/3/74, 8 March.

Menon, A. (2008) *Europe: The State of the Union* (London: Atlantic Books).

Merler, S. and Pisani-Ferry, J. (2012) *Sudden Stops in the Euro Area* (Brussels: Bruegel Policy Contribution).

Milward, A. (1992) *The European Rescue of the Nation State* (London: Routledge).

Mudde, C. (2007) *Populist Radical Right Parties in Europe* (Cambridge: Cambridge University Press).

Myrdal, G. (1956) *An International Economy: Problems and Prospects* (New York: Harper & Brothers).

Nicolaïdis, K. (2010) 'Sustainable Integration: Towards EU 2.0?' *JCMS*, Vol. 48, No. S1, pp. 21–54.

Nicoll, W. (1984) 'The Luxembourg Compromise'. *JCMS*, Vol. 23, No. 1, pp. 35–43.

Organisation for Economic Co-operation and Development (OECD) (2012) *Economic Surveys: European Union* (Paris: OECD).

Parsons, C. (2003) *A Certain Idea of Europe* (Ithaca, NY: Cornell University Press).

Peterson, J. (2001) 'The Choice for EU Theorists: Establishing a Common Framework for Analysis'. *European Journal of Political Research*, Vol. 39, pp. 289–318.

Peterson, J. and Bomberg, E. (1999) *Decision-Making in the European Union* (Basingstoke: Palgrave Macmillan).

Polanyi, K. (1957) *The Great Transformation: The Political and Economic Origins of Our Time* (Boston, MA: Beacon Press).

Rifkin, J. (2004) *The European Dream* (New York: Tarcher).

Risse, T. (2010) *A Community of Europeans? Transnational Identities and Public Spheres* (Ithaca, NY: Cornell University Press).

Rovelli, R. (2010) 'Economic Policy in a Global Crisis: Did Italy Get It Right?' In Giuliani, M. and Jones, E. (eds) *Italian Politics 2009: Managing Uncertainty* (New York: Berghahn).

Ruggie, J. (1982) 'International Regimes, Transactions and Change: Embedded Liberalism in the Postwar Economic Order'. *International Organization*, Vol. 36, No. 2, pp. 379–415.

Scharpf, F. (1999) *Governing in Europe: Effective and Democratic?* (Oxford: Oxford University Press).

Schmidt, V.A. (2009) 'Re-envisioning the European Union: Identity, Democracy, Economy'. *JCMS*, Vol. 47, No. S1, pp. 17–42.

Searle, J. (1997) *The Construction of Social Reality* (New York: Free Press).

Stone, R. (1996) *Satellites and Commissars: Strategy and Conflict in the Politics of Soviet-Bloc Trade* (Princeton, NJ: Princeton University Press).

Taylor, P. (2008) *The End of European Integration: Anti-Europeanism Examined* (London: Routledge).

Tsoukalis, L. (2005) *What Kind of Europe?* (Oxford: Oxford University Press).

Tsoukalis, L. (2011) 'The Shattering of Illusions – and What Next?' *JCMS*, Vol. 49, No. S1, pp. 19–44.

Verdun, A. (2003) 'An American/European Divide in European Integration Studies: Bridging the Gap with International Political Economy'. *Journal of European Public Policy*, Vol. 10, No. 1, pp. 84–101.

Weiler, J. (1999) *The Constitution of Europe* (Cambridge: Cambridge University Press).

Whelen, K. (2012) *Briefing Paper on the IBRC, ELA and Promissory Notes* (Dublin: University College Dublin).

JCMS 2012 Volume 50 Annual Review pp. 68–75 DOI: 10.1111/j.1468-5965.2012.02254.x

The Hungarian Rhapsodies: The Conflict of Adventurism and Professionalism in the European Union Presidency

ATTILA ÁGH
Budapest Corvinus University

Introduction

The Hungarian Presidency of the European Union (EU) in the first half of 2011 was the third in the Spanish–Belgian–Hungarian (SBH) team Presidency. There have always been many good arguments for a given rotating Presidency to claim that it has taken place in the most difficult period in EU history. The Hungarian Presidency was no exception, but as the first of the new Member States to hold the position under the new Lisbon rules and coming at the time of the ongoing global crisis, there was considerable justification for such a claim. There is no doubt, however, that the Hungarian Presidency was dominated by the conflict between domestic and EU policies, and a deeper conflict between the political adventurism of the government and the professionalism of experts and the state administration.

Both the team Presidency preparations of the common programme and the Hungarian domestic preparations to ensure administrative capacity was up to speed began in earnest early in 2007 in a mood of so far, so good. The SBH team Presidency drafted some original priorities and established a good co-operation framework that could be structured into four themes: the implementation of the Lisbon Treaty with a changing role for the team/rotating Presidencies; the elaboration of the Europe 2020 Strategy with the extension of cohesion policy to territorial cohesion and with the inclusion of new policies such as energy security, global climate change and the 'innovation triangle'; the contribution to the preparations for the next multi-annual financial perspectives and to the reform of budgeting in the spirit of a 'policy-driven budget'; and a globalization-cum-regionalization policy created by strengthening both the global role of the EU and the European Neighbourhood Policy (ENP) with the promotion of the pre-accession process in the Western Balkan region and the intensification of the Eastern Partnership (EaP) (see Council of the European Union, 2009). These priorities were accepted as general outlines and discussed in a series of trilateral negotiations and conferences. The State Secretaries of European Affairs met regularly and built up a strong intergovernmental co-ordination mechanism. In this optimistic preparatory period the three countries concerned cherished the idea that the SBH would be the first *real*, well prepared and co-operatively working team Presidency.[1]

The institutional changes introduced by the Lisbon Treaty (LT) radically transformed the role of the team Presidencies. However, the drastic change for the SBH team

[1] The expert preparations for the team Presidency began on 7–9 September 2007 in Lillafüred in Hungary. By 2011, six volumes had been published (see Ágh *et al.*, 2008–10). I have analyzed Hungarian EU policies at length in Ágh (2011a).

Presidency came in late 2009 not with the predictable transformations in the institutional architecture, including the entry into force of the Permanent President of the European Council, but with the shift in EU priorities towards economic crisis management. Thus, the original programme was abandoned and economic governance dominated the agenda.

The first half of 2011 was a particularly stormy period in EU history. Hungary took over the Presidency at the moment that a new wave of crisis crashed onto the European ship of state, with many more to follow during Hungary's time at the helm. This sense of deepening crisis pervaded the Hungarian Presidency, also feeding into its domestically driven turning points. Accordingly, attention shifted from the original programme to tackling the economic crisis. Altogether, this was a very eventful, turbulent six-month period, in which firm EU political leadership was needed to react quickly to the newly emerging substantive issues. Hungary could only be an active junior partner and a helping hand for the European Council.

The collapse of original priorities and the marginalization of the team/rotating Presidencies first became clear at the February 2010 informal summit where the Greek crisis was high on the agenda. It became evident that the problems of economic crisis management could only be solved at the European Council level, which the big powers (the revived Franco-German engine) dominated and the new President of the European Council, Herman van Rompuy, showed real political leadership. Actually, due to the dual effect of the global crisis and the EU institutional reforms, the former priorities were marginalized or downgraded. Given the tremendous burden of crisis management mostly orchestrated by the European Council and the major powers, the challenge of evaluating the Hungarian Presidency requires us to separate the achievements and failures of the EU in general during this period from the actions by, or the special performance of, the Hungarian Presidency.

I. The Changing Hungarian Priorities and the Slogan of Strong Europe

In fact, the deep change in the team Presidency's profile was also caused by the deterioration of the domestic situation in all three countries concerned – first of all in Spain right at the beginning of the SBH team Presidency (Heywood, 2011). The finalization of the Hungarian Presidency programme was delayed until December 2010 since the need for a radical modification of the agenda was seen already at the end of the Belgian Presidency (Drieskens, 2011). The Hungarian government realized that the most important EU priorities were the protection of the euro and the elaboration of the rules for new economic governance. Thus, the Hungarian Presidency focused on crisis management and economic governance – that is, shifting the focus to the Commission's proposal for a six-pack of economic regulation and the ensuing key issues of the reinforcement of economic policy co-ordination. This top priority demanded the softening up, scaling down or emptying out of former priorities, revising the original design of the 18-month programme beyond recognition. Although the Hungarian priorities reflected verbally the original ones to a great extent, after a careful review of the basic policy areas Hungary had to abandon a great deal of related issues. So finally, the Hungarian Presidency indicated the following four priorities for the first half of 2011 as summarized by the Minister of Foreign Affairs, János Martonyi:

> The Presidency Program is built on four priorities, with the human factor – Europe in service of its citizens – as the common link. The four priority areas are: 1) Promoting growth by strengthening economic governance and concentrating on job creation and social inclusion; 2) Strengthening our common policies by making them more efficient and competitive, while preserving underlying fundamental values to enhance cohesion in Europe; 3) Bringing Europe closer to its citizens; and 4) Moving forward with the enlargement process in a credible and responsible manner. Our overall aim as we assume the Presidency is to help create an economically, socially, politically and institutionally stronger and more viable Europe. 'Strong Europe' – this is our motto. (Martonyi, 2011; see in detail HMFA, 2010, 2011)[2]

Actually, the real Hungarian top priority was the maintenance of cohesion policy in general and the promotion of the Danube Strategy (DRS) in particular. The renewed cohesion policy as a real priority was well suited to general Hungarian preferences in the EU and it received strong support from the other new Member States as well. The DRS was accepted on 13 April 2011 by the General Affairs Council with relative ease. Finally, the June 2011 summit endorsed this initiative, although it remains to be seen how it can be promoted in practice. Given the fact that the early drivers were the southern provinces of Germany and Austria, which are still strong supporters of this project, it may have a good chance of being implemented. The support for DRS fitted well to the two Hungarian vital sub-priorities of its enlargement/widening portfolio: West Balkans and EaP, especially to conclude the accession talks with Croatia. It is true that in 'the globalization-cum-regionalization' programme establishing strategic partnerships for better global governance is a task more suitable for the European Council, whereas the team Presidencies can cope more with the problems of regionalizing the EU neighbourhood.[3]

II. The Deep Conflict between the Political and Administrative Roles

The SBH team Presidency proves that there is close relationship in each rotating Presidency between domestic developments and Presidency performance. Even earlier, as Beneš and Karlas (2010, p. 71) have noted in the Czech case: 'The bleak domestic context undermined the whole Presidency'. Indeed, the performance of the Hungarian Presidency can only be understood in its domestic context. The new Fidesz government, which took office in May 2010 with a large, two-thirds majority, followed a domestic programme of 'strong government'. Thus, the 'Strong Europe' slogan of the Hungarian Presidency was imported from home and indicated the dominance of its domestic policy over EU policies. In fact, it was much more a message to the Hungarian audience than to the EU population.

This attitude of the Hungarian government provoked a series of conflicts and controversies in the EU. The core issue was, as the former foreign minister noted, that 'Prime Minister Orbán could not decide whether the EU was a friend or an enemy' (Balázs, 2011, p. 9). At the annual conference of Hungarian ambassadors at the end of August 2010

[2] The slogan of the Hungarian Presidency was 'Strong Europe with a Human Touch', but only the 'Strong Europe' part was used in the EU and in Hungary. This priority has been closely connected to the support of Hungarian minorities living in the neighbouring countries. See also the final adoption of the Roma programme by EUCO in June 2011 (Vizi, 2011, pp. 126–9).

[3] The globalization-cum-regionalization is my wording (Ágh, 2011b), but this scenario was formulated in the Bruegel Institute's proposal for *Europe's Economic Priorities* (see Sapir, 2009, p. 6). As to territorial cohesion, the TA2020, *Territorial Agenda of the European Union 2020* agreed on 19 May 2011 was a significant achievement.

Orbán did not mention the forthcoming EU Presidency, and on 15 March in his speech commemorating the 1848 revolution, he 'compared the influence of the EU to the oppression of the Habsburg Empire and Soviet dictatorship' (Balázs, 2011, p. 9). The EU flag was missing at his public performances and at those of government in general. The two stormy visits of Orbán to the European Parliament (EP) on 19 January and 5 July 2011 highlighted the controversial character of the EU profile of the Fidesz government.[4]

The Hungarian Presidency endured a rough start because of the efforts of the Hungarian government in establishing its *strong state* by weakening the checks and balances system of democratic institutions. On 20 December 2010 a new media law was passed, which led to a collision with many European actors, including the Commission, who thought it was a threat to press freedom. Despite subsequently passing small amendments, the media law was condemned in an EP resolution on 10 March. Its compatibility with European regulations and values was discussed in both EU and domestic circles, and this debate led to a questioning of the democratic credentials of the government. As the foreign minister formulated it in soft terms with real understatement: 'Criticism about the Media Law has made the government's work more difficult' (Martonyi, 2011). In fact, the European press covered Hungarian developments extensively with an avalanche of criticism: 'Opinions on the form or substance of the law var[ied], but there is a broad agreement that the backlash that followed was a distraction to the Hungarian Presidency's agenda' (Armitage *et al.*, 2011, pp. 34–5).[5]

Similarly, the other steps taken by the government to weaken the democratic system of institutions, particularly reducing the competences of the Constitutional Court, provoked negative reactions in EU circles. Moreover, the new Constitution was passed in April 2011 in the face of heavy criticism from EU partners and the Venice Commission. Altogether, the Presidency was overshadowed by international concerns in general over the efforts of the Hungarian government through the new constitution to curb the system of checks and balances and in particular to restrict media freedom.

However, 'Making Europe Work' is still the main job of the Presidencies, and Hungary performed well in the role of the honest broker in administering EU affairs. Thus, there was a big contrast between the political activities of the government and the professional activities of the administration: whilst the general view in Brussels and other EU capitals gave a positive evaluation of Hungarian experts, there was 'quite a different judgment about the performance of the Government of Hungary' (Balázs, 2011, pp. 5, 7). Indeed, the Hungarian team of experts did a good job in the routine work of crisis management from the back seat and it managed well the rolling and incoming issues. Of course, the government's activities were in the limelight and they gave a generally negative impression, but it would be one-sided to evaluate the performance of the Hungarian Presidency only from this aspect. The Hungarian Presidency took place seven years after entry, so the fact that Hungary was a new Member State holding the Presidency for the first time was

[4] Fidesz belongs to the EPP family and the EPP resisted calls to condemn the Orbán government several times in the EP. Finally, however, in early 2012 when the legislation process for the 'strong state' came to an end and the Commission initiated a large-scale process to investigate the conflict between the EU norms and the Fidesz legislation, the EPP leaders changed their minds (see Martens and Daul, 2012).

[5] The Hungarian Presidency provoked significant media reaction, but unlike the other Presidencies there were very few academic analyses (see, for example, Kaczynski, 2011). There is no doubt that these heated debates left their marks on the Hungarian Presidency (see Romsics, 2011).

not important in this regard since it had already enough experience and expertise in the EU with a good administrative capacity to support the Presidency team.

The acid test for EU Presidencies is crisis management of unexpected events. Two major sudden events disturbed the Hungarian Presidency with their severe and durable spillovers: first, the earthquake followed by tsunamis in Japan; and second, the Arab uprisings culminating in the civil war in Libya. The first event provoked debates on the sensitive issue of nuclear power stations in EU energy policy, but did not concern the main line of the Presidency. However, the second event generated a huge migration wave, which proved to be a real stress test for the Schengen system. This contributed to the crisis of Schengen as a whole and the goal of enlargement to Bulgaria and Romania consequently suffered a major setback. This caused a serious problem for the Hungarian Presidency since the entry of Bulgaria and Romania was an important issue for Hungary. In December 2010 the German and French governments announced their reservations on extending Schengen to Bulgaria and Romania, but the Hungarian government neglected these warnings, which proved that political considerations, again, prevailed over expert views.

In several ways this deep conflict between the political and administrative roles characterized the entire Presidency. It has been echoed many times by analysts because they have considered that the Hungarian Presidency was 'a professionally administered Presidency', but this success in managing the EU policies contrasts with the 'parochial domestic politics' (Armitage *et al.*, 2011, pp. 34–5). On one side, 'Budapest conducted its first EU presidency with quite professionalism and effectiveness, focussing on strengthening EU economic governance (the Six-Pack legislation), Roma inclusion and finalizing accession negotiations with Croatia' (Armitage *et al.*, 2011, p. 51), but on the other side it neglected the European values that culminated in the media legislation and the new 'octroi'-type constitution as dangerous deviations from democratic norms. In the last analysis, in 2011 'Hungary was backsliding', which produced finally 'Hungary's illiberal, managed democracy' (Gati, 2012, pp. 66, 71). Thus, during the Presidency and afterwards the Hungarian government was under pressure from growing international criticism due to this deep conflict between the political and administrative roles. The Hungarian authorities, however, refused the separation of political and administrative roles in the evaluation of the Hungarian Presidency and declared that it was successful in both respects. The prime minister in his final comments concluded that Hungary did a good job in both, and accomplished all the tasks of the Presidency (Orbán, 2011).

Conclusions: The Year of Central Europe?

The year 2011 was that of the two central European Presidencies: Hungary and Poland. Some analysts have argued that it was an important time for pushing common regional interests. They have referred to the 'growing importance of the V4' (Visegrad Four) as 'a significant tool of advancing Central European aspirations within the EU', since all countries concerned have 'a vested interest in sustaining a strong European Cohesion Policy' (Kron, 2011, pp. 1, 3). However, other analysts such as Armitage and his co-authors have stated that although they were not able to exert a lasting impact on EU policy in general, these countries were rather successful in particular policies like fostering West Balkan integration with the accession of Croatia and promoting the EU Roma integration strategy. For the central European region as a whole, the Danube Strategy matters first of all, and its adoption was indeed a big success for the Hungarian Presidency (Armitage *et al.*, 2011).

Thus, the 'Presidency effect' (Haughton, 2010, pp. 18, 21) on the central European region must have been slightly positive, primarily because of the Polish Presidency,[6] but on Hungary it was at least ambiguous. For the Hungarian government, the effect was clearly negative since it came at the worst time when the government wanted to consolidate its rule for a long time by changing the whole constitutional set-up of Hungary to a more restricted, guided democracy. The government had a two-thirds majority at home and made all steps to entrench its powers, to capture the state and to weaken the checks and balances system. Therefore, it perceived the EU mostly as an obstacle to the big manoeuvre of consolidating its power and responded to all EU warnings with irritation ('leave us alone – no interference in domestic affairs'). Thus, given the primacy of domestic transformation, for the Hungarian government the EU was only a disturbing factor. In general, the increased international attention, both from politicians and the press, coming together with the Presidency role being confronted with the strong domestic position of government, showed only its external vulnerability.

For the Hungarian population the Presidency was not so important: right before it started the majority of people in Hungary did not know about the Presidency and it was not until just at the end that they realized what it entailed. The main reason is that the Presidency period was dominated by wide ranging socio-economic and political processes that I have termed 'post-accession crisis'. In the late 2000s the Hungarians were frustrated by the problems of the last 20 years, so they therefore supported the populist Fidesz with a large (53 per cent) majority which resulted in a two-thirds parliamentary majority. However, when the Orbán government weakened both democracy and economy, people became even more frustrated and turned more and more against the government, with 80 per cent considering that 'things are going in the wrong direction'. Paradoxically, the EU became important later for the increasing opposition confronting the government. The recurring mass manifestations referred to the EU warnings and chanted pro-EU slogans against the government. The end result of the Hungarian Presidency was an extreme polarization between the pro-EU democratic opposition and the Eurosceptic (in some cases, anti-EU) government that was further deepened.[7]

The SBH Presidency wanted to be the first real team Presidency, working in close co-operation, but failed due to external reasons and domestic processes. The 'Strong Europe' slogan of the Hungarian Presidency might have suited an EU coping with crisis management, but contrasted to a great extent with the low capacity of the Hungarian government to contribute to this goal during its Presidency. The performance of the Presidency was more controversial than usual, so thus it needs to be assessed in its complexity, taking the split between the political and administrative roles into account. This complexity has been formulated in the final evaluation of the former foreign minister:

> As far as Brussels was concerned, leaders of EU institutions and Member States felt better that a Presidency of an unpredictable and sometimes surprising government in the chair

[6] See Pomorska and Vanhoonaker in this issue.

[7] Some 55 per cent of Hungarians had not been aware of the Presidency in December 2010, while at the end of the Presidency, 80 per cent knew about it. In general, Hungarians were not so much interested in the Presidency since they were occupied with the worsening socio-economic and political situation, and the government's *Kulturkampf* (see «http://www.policysolutions.hu/userfiles/file/Hungarian%20Politics%20In-Depth_2011_Week27.pdf»).

> of the Council was coming to an end. [. . .] [I]n spite of the good professional work of the experts, Hungary has not been a real player at top level decisions concerning the stabilization of the Euro-zone. [. . .] This historical occasion was missed and the general image of Hungary in the outside world is worse after the EU Presidency than it used to be before. (Balázs, 2011, pp. 4, 5, 10)

Correspondence:
Attila Ágh
Department of Political Science
Budapest Corvinus University
Budapest IX
Fővám tér 8
H-1093, Hungary
email attila.agh@uni-corvinus.hu

References

Ágh, A. (2011a) 'The Complexity of a Communitarian Europe: *Leitbilder* for the Enlarged European Union in Hungary'. In Brincker, G.-S. and Jopp, M. (eds), *Leitbilder for the Future of the European Union* (Baden-Baden: Nomos).

Ágh, A. (2011b) 'Regionalising the EU's Neighbourhood: Planning the Global Role for the Trio Presidency'. In Fabry, E. (ed.), *Think Global – Act European, Vol. III* (Paris: Notre Europe Institute).

Ágh, A. *et al.* (eds) (2008–10) *Six Volumes on the SBH Rotating Presidencies*. Available at: «http://www.koft.hu/index.php?page=tanulmanyok».

Armitage, D., Zaborowski, M. and Mitchell, W. (2011) *Translating Opportunity into Impact: Central Europe in the European Union, 2010–2020* (Washington, DC: Center for European Policy Analysis). Available at: «http://www.cepa.org/publications/view.aspx?record_id=178».

Balázs, P. (2011) 'The First Hungarian EU Council Presidency'. In Achievements of the First Hungarian EU Council Presidency, Policy Paper 8, *EU Frontiers* (Budapest: Central European University).

Beneš, V. and Karlas, J. (2010) 'The Czech Presidency'. *JCMS*, Vol. 48, No. s1, pp. 69–80.

Council of the European Union (2009) 'The future Spanish, Belgian and Hungarian Presidencies: Draft 18 month programme of the Council', Brussels, 27 November, 16771/09, POLGEN 219.

Drieskens, E. (2011) '*Ceci n'est pas une présidence*: The 2010 Belgian Presidency of the EU'. *JCMS* , Vol. 49, No. s1, pp. 91–102.

Gati, C. (2012) 'Hungarian Rhapsodies'. *The American Interest*, Winter, pp. 65–71.

Haughton, T. (2010) 'Vulnerabilities, Accession Hangovers and the Presidency Role: Explaining New EU Member States' Choices for Europe'. Harvard University Center for European Studies Central and Eastern Europe, Working Paper Series 68. Available at: «http://www.ces.fas.harvard.edu/publications/docs/pdfs/CEE_WP_68.pdf».

Heywood, P. (2011) 'Spain's EU Presidency: Ambitions beyond Capacity'. *JCMS*, Vol. 49, No. s1, pp. 77–89.

Hungarian Ministry of Foreign Affairs (HMFA) (2010) *The Programme of the Hungarian Presidency of the Council of the European Union, 1 January–30 June 2011: Strong Europe*. Available at: «http://www.eu2011.hu/files/bveu/documents/HU_PRES_STRONG_EUROPE_EN_3.pdf».

Hungarian Ministry of Foreign Affairs (HMFA) (2011) *Six Months in the Service of a Stronger Europe: Overview of the Hungarian Presidency of the Council of the European Union,*

January–June 2011. Available at: «http://www.eu2011.hu/files/bveu/documents/HUPRES_EREDMENYEK_EN.pdf».

Kaczynski, P.M. (2011) 'How to Assess a Rotating Presidency of the Council under New Lisbon Rules: The Case of Hungary'. CEPS Policy Brief 232. Available at: «http://www.ceps.eu/book/how-assess-rotating-presidency-council-under-lisbon-rules».

Kron, R. (2011) 'From Visegrád Group to the Weimar Triangle: Central Europe's Growing Toolbox'. Center for European Policy Analysis, Issue Brief 116. Available at: «http://www.cepa.org/programs/view.aspx?record_id=9».

Martens, W. and Daul, J. (2012) 'The EPP will back the Commission's Recommendations that will ensure Hungary's Full Compliance with EU Law'. Press release, 6 January. Available at: «http://www.noodls.com/viewNoodl/12677012/epp-group/martens-and-daul-quotthe-epp-will-back-the-commission82».

Martonyi, J. (2011) 'Interview with the Hungarian Minister of Foreign Affairs'. *Central European Digest*, 1 February. Available at: «http://www.cepa.org/ced/view.aspx?record_id=288».

Orbán, V. (2011) 'Hungary Accomplished Presidency Objectives', 6 July. Available at: «http://www.eu2011.hu/news/orban-hungary-accomplished-presidency-objectives».

Romsics, G. (2011) *An Interim Review of the 2011 Hungarian Presidency: Finding a New Niche for the Rotating Presidency in Times of Storm and Stress* (Stockholm: Swedish Institute for European Policy Studies). Available at: «http://www.sieps.se/sv/publikationer/an-interim-review-of-the-2011-hungarian-presidency-20111op».

Sapir, A. (ed.) (2009) *Europe's Economic Priorities, 2010–2015: Memos to the New Commission* (Brussels: Bruegel).

Vizi, B. (2011) 'The Hungarian Presidency of the Council of the European Union: Focus on the Neighbourhood and on a European Roma Strategy'. *Journal on Ethnopolitics and Minority Issues in Europe*, Vol. 10, No. 1, pp. 123–34.

JCMS 2012 Volume 50 Annual Review pp. 76–84 DOI: 10.1111/j.1468-5965.2012.02276.x

Poland in the Driving Seat: A Mature Presidency in Turbulent Times

KAROLINA POMORSKA and SOPHIE VANHOONACKER
University of Maastricht

Introduction

In the second half of 2011, Poland held the rotating Presidency of the Council of the European Union for the first time. It took over from Hungary (see Ágh's contribution to this issue), another relative newcomer to the EU, and was part of the trio team together with its successors Denmark and Cyprus. Poland's high ambitions matched the self-perception of belonging to the 'big' Member States and the full commitment among the administrative and political elites to make their period at the helm a success. The financial means made available were considerable, as the budget amounted to around €100 million – two or three times more than some of the previous and subsequent Presidencies. Nonetheless, the forthcoming Presidency raised some eyebrows in Brussels as the memories of Poland as a troublemaker were still alive. The frequently unconstructive position during the Law and Justice (PiS)-led government (2005–07) (see Copsey and Pomorska, 2010) or the veto on reduction of CO_2 emissions in June 2011 gave reasons for concern about potentially unpredictable behaviour.

Poland, however, proved to be a quick learner in the EU. In spite of the euro crisis, its economy was performing well (see Connolly in this issue), and was frequently compared in the media to a 'green island' of growth in Europe.[1] Yet, some doubts persisted as to whether the high ambition would not stand in the way of achieving consensus and final success. Although the pro-European liberal conservative Civic Platform (PO) led the government, the prospect of parliamentary elections in the midst of the Presidency and a possible return to power of the Eurosceptic PiS loomed in the background. The Presidency posed some serious challenges for the administration and the government – among others were those related to the logistical capacity to manage responsibilities on such a scale, act as a broker and, in the words of a high-level official, 'to think beyond one's national interest'.[2]

The institutional set-up after Lisbon has also limited the roles and potential impact of the country at the helm of the Council (Dinan, 2010). The prime minister is no longer in the chair of the European Council, which now has its own permanent President. Thus, the media shots from the meeting of heads of state and government in December 2011 featured predominantly Herman Van Rompuy and the leaders of the 'Big Three', with the Polish prime minister, Donald Tusk, somewhat in the background. In terms of the financial crisis, as a non-member of the single currency Poland had not managed to secure

[1] Apparently, the term was coined after one of the prime minister's speeches was accompanied by a map of economic growth in Europe with most of the countries in red and Poland in green. See, for example, *New York Times*, 6 December 2010; *The Observer*, 19 February 2012; Świeboda, 2010.
[2] Interview at the Ministry of Foreign Affairs, Warsaw, 20 December 2011

the right to participate in the meetings of the Eurogroup. In addition, a great share of the foreign policy work was shifted to the High Representative for Foreign Affairs and Security Policy (HR) and the European External Action Service (EEAS). Under Lisbon, it was no longer the rotating Presidency but HR Catherine Ashton and her EEAS staff who chaired the common foreign and security policy (CFSP) meetings and represented the Union (see, for example, Missiroli, 2010; Vanhoonacker *et al.*, 2010, 2012).

Still, the arrival of Van Rompuy and Ashton does not mean that the rotating Presidency has become irrelevant. One can even argue that it has become more pivotal than ever for the smooth running of the EU legislative machine. The further extension of co-decision and the Presidency's central role in interacting with an increasingly assertive European Parliament (EP) means that it continues to carry salient responsibilities in the day-to-day EU policy-making process as organizer, broker and even political leader (Schout and Vanhoonacker, 2006). In a union of 27 Member States and with the EP playing its co-legislative role to the full, the broker role of forging compromises and building bridges is more important than ever. Providing leadership post-Lisbon undoubtedly becomes more difficult, especially in the area of foreign affairs. However, as we will show in this article, this does not mean that the rotating Presidency no longer has the scope to prioritize dossiers or to try to steer the Union in a certain direction.

The article analyzes and evaluates the achievements of the Polish Presidency. It starts by presenting its priorities and examines its major accomplishments. Special attention is given to how the Polish Presidency dealt with crisis situations such as the economic, financial and sovereign debt crisis. The last section evaluates the Presidency's main achievements and investigates its performance with regard to its three key roles of organizer, broker and political leader. We will argue that even though the Poles performed quite well, despite the unfavourable circumstances, their success has gone largely unnoticed by the international public.

I. From Financial Crisis to the Crisis of Trust

An important test for the performance of the Presidency is its capacity to handle crisis situations (Dehousse and Menon, 2009). Very often the source of the crisis is external, but in the case of Poland the challenges came from within the EU itself. The financial, economic and sovereign debt crisis not only threatened Europe's economic well-being, but also raised challenges for the future of the EU. Commission President Barroso spoke of the 'most difficult period since European integration started',[3] and Polish Prime Minister Donald Tusk proclaimed a 'crisis of trust' (Tusk, 2011b). Among the hotly debated topics was solidarity between the Member States, the (un)desirability of big Member States acting as the sole leaders in the integration processes and the more general aims of the integration, including possible closer union.

Although it was handicapped by its non-membership of the eurozone, Poland nevertheless managed to play a meaningful role. The co-ordination between the European Council, the Eurogroup and Ecofin went smoothly – not least thanks to the efforts and good personal contacts of the Finance Minister Jacek Rostowski. Poland contributed positively to finalizing the Six Pack negotiations on financial regulations by forging an

[3] *EUobserver*, 14 December 2011.

agreement on some of the most sensitive issues. It managed to put the crisis in a broader perspective and made it very clear that the response was not less, but 'more Europe', as outlined in the inaugural speech of Prime Minister Tusk in the EP (Tusk, 2011a).

The message was echoed in a rather dramatic speech of Foreign Minister Sikorski in November 2011 in Berlin (Sikorski, 2011). Arguably, this was the only moment when the Presidency attracted wide media attention and sparked debate. Referring to the successful examples of the United States and Switzerland, Sikorski pleaded for nothing less than a European federation, based on a further strengthening of the European institutions, including a merger of the posts of the Presidents of the European Council and the European Commission. He advocated even the direct election of the President by the European demos. Warning that Europe was standing at the brink of a disaster, he spoke strongly in favour of active leadership of its western neighbour: 'I will probably be first Polish foreign minister in history to say so, but here it is: *I fear German power less than I am beginning to fear German inactivity*' (Sikorski, 2011).[4] The speech was a clear expression of the Polish desire to be part of the European core and also an illustration of how Poland, since its accession in 2004, has increasingly been turning towards the EU rather than the United States, with Germany becoming its major partner. The declaration did not go unnoticed at home, where despite general praise it received some fierce criticism from PiS politicians.

Unfortunately, the ambitions expressed by Sikorski contrasted strongly with the reality on the ground. The players who really mattered in the negotiations with Greece and in the development of new and more stringent fiscal rules were German Chancellor Merkel and French President Sarkozy. As a non-member of the eurozone, there were clear limits to the scope of action by the Polish chair.

II. Presidency Priorities

Officially, the Polish Presidency announced three general priorities: European integration as a source of growth, a 'Secure Europe' and 'Europe Benefiting from Openness' (MFA, 2011a). Within these goals, there was strong emphasis on the further development of the Eastern Partnership (EaP) – a flagship initiative and potential source of prestige for the Foreign Ministry under Sikorski, who is a heavyweight in the Polish government. Since it is impossible to give a full account of the many dossiers covered, we limit ourselves to some of the most important ones, including economic growth, external relations, and climate, energy and defence.

Economic Growth

Every Presidency has the responsibility to press forward towards the achievement of the EU 2020 growth agenda. In the face of the financial crisis, the Polish Presidency decided to focus on negotiations over the new financial perspective (2014–20) and deepening the internal market. In the negotiations over the first issue, the Presidency played a minor role as the most important part of the process only took off after the Presidency finished. The fact that the European Commission proposal was kept intact as the basis for negotiations

[4] He added quickly that Polish support was nonetheless conditioned upon Poland being included in the decision-making process.

was generally considered a success (Tokarski and Toporowski, 2012). Poland was also praised for the smooth and timely adoption of the yearly EU budget (Nowak, 2012, p. 12). It was the first time since the entry into force of the new Treaty that the Council and the EP reached an agreement on the annual budget within the time provided by law (MFA, 2011c). Polish officials are also proud of the adoption of the so-called 'Six Pack' – a bundle of six legislative measures aimed at bringing more discipline to the finances of the Member States. It is often mentioned as one of the greatest achievements of the Presidency, but a large part of the work was conducted already by the Hungarians (see Ágh in this issue). A better example of where the Polish Presidency mattered, with the invaluable support of the Polish EP President Buzek, is the agreement with the EP on the so-called 'correlation tables'. Even though a great success, it was met with little publicity. The agreement aims at facilitating the implementation of EU legislation by providing links between the provisions in EU directives and the corresponding rules in the Member States. Poland also managed to finalize eight second-reading agreements,[5] including two of high importance: the so-called 'WEEE dossier' on electronic waste and electrical equipment,[6] and one on biocidal products.[7]

On a less positive note, Poland presented a report entitled *Towards a European Consensus on Growth* (MFA, 2011b), which was criticized for its disappointing analytical angle and lack of innovative ideas, but praised as a political instrument to encourage politicians to think long term (Łada and Kucharczyk, 2012). With regard to the internal market, the main achievement was settling a 30-year long dispute and securing agreement over the single EU Patent, with the creation of the Unitary Patent Court and a system of patent protection. The lack of an intergovernmental agreement over the location of the central patent court (with London, Paris and Munich in the running) added a bitter note to the celebrations and meant that the process was brought to a halt. At the time of writing, the EP had not voted on its position and the Council had not yet adopted the necessary texts.

External Relations

As mentioned above, in the area of external relations, Poland had been stripped of most of the previous Presidencies' prerogatives that were now given to the High Representative Ashton and the EEAS. While possible clashes between an ambitious foreign minister and the HR were to be expected, Sikorski was quick to kill these concerns by announcing that he would be Ashton's 'loyal deputy'.[8] Indeed, the two soon found a common language and agreed on a division of representative duties. Sikorski, for example, represented the EU in Libya, the Foreign Affairs Committee in the EP, and at a meeting with Uzbekistan. The relations with the EEAS gradually took shape, with Polish officials reporting an increase in trust and co-operation as the Presidency proceeded. Polish embassies represented the EU in 12 third countries without EU delegations. Tensions emerged, however, in places where the Presidency coexisted with the EU delegations, especially regarding consular affairs and the lack of the exact division of competences on the ground.

[5] This included three second-reading agreements and five early second-reading agreements.

[6] Proposal for a Directive of the European Parliament and of the Council on waste electrical and electronic equipment (WEEE) (recast) (2008/0241 COD).

[7] Proposal for a regulation of the European Parliament and of the Council concerning the placing on the market and use of biocidal products (2009/0076 COD).

[8] *EUobserver*, 2 July 2011.

An interesting novelty for the Polish Presidency was the fact that for the first time there were several cases of co-decision in the realm of external relations. It concerned the establishment of financing instruments for development co-operation, promotion of democratic and human rights, and for co-operation with industrialized countries. Poland, and especially the chair of the Committee of Permanent Representatives (Coreper II), played a positive role here, investing time and efforts into establishing good relations with the EP.

While the most visible events in the international media were the ongoing revolutions in North Africa, Warsaw devoted most of its efforts and attention to the development of the EaP initiative. Since becoming a member of the EU in 2004, Poland has continuously lobbied within the Council for establishing a more proactive policy towards the EU's eastern neighbours. Supported by Sweden, these efforts were finally rewarded with the inauguration of the EaP in 2009. However, by the time Poland took over the Presidency, the initiative was being criticized for lacking substance and tangible results. In addition, the political situation in the targeted countries was deteriorating in terms of democratic standards. In response, Poland called for the establishment of the European Endowment for Democracy (finalized with a declaration in December) as an instrument to support civil society, media and even political actors in third countries. At the same time, efforts were made to mark the Polish presence in North Africa – for example, with the declarations to share lessons learned from Poland's experience of transition to democracy.

A further landmark event was the EaP summit organized at the end of September in Warsaw. The main results included a long-term commitment to waiving the visas of the partnership countries and the establishment of the Eastern Partnership Academy in Warsaw (European Council, 2011a). Unfortunately, the summit ended with disunity between the Member States and the neighbouring countries regarding the final declaration condemning the political situation in Belarus. Some internal commentators even called it the biggest failure of the Presidency and the *de facto* breakdown of the EU's eastern policy, 'as evidenced by Poland and the Union's helplessness towards the Lukashenko regime in Belarus and the Yulia Tymoshenko show-trial in Ukraine'.[9]

The end of the Presidency was marked by the signing of the Accession Treaty with Croatia and a summit with Ukraine. The arrest of Yulia Tymoshenko made it difficult for Poland to champion the Ukrainian case within the EU, but the substantive part of the negotiations over the Association Agreement were completed, including the establishment of the Deep and Comprehensive Free Trade Area (DCFTA). Nonetheless, the Union postponed the initialling of the agreement until spring 2012, and the signing and eventual ratification of the agreement until after the Ukrainian elections scheduled for autumn 2012. The Council also agreed on negotiation mandates on the visa facilitation and readmission agreements with Armenia and Azerbaijan.

Energy Security, Climate and Defence

The third section of the Presidency programme on European security included areas as diverse as food, energy and defence. It was no surprise to find the external energy policy of the Union, including a new energy strategy, among the priorities of the Presidency. This had been a sensitive topic for Poland, especially in the context of the EU's relations with

[9] *Presseurop*, 15 December 2011.

Russia. Equally unsurprising was the absence of climate policy, which has a significant impact on Polish energy policy and as Poland opposes raising the 2020 emission reduction targets (for more, see Spencer *et al.*, 2011). The Polish veto with regards to the limiting of CO_2 emissions in June 2011 was not the best start to the Presidency. Subsequently, Polish performance during the climate conference in Durban (November–December 2011) prompted some unfavourable comments, including the reminder that Polish diplomats 'ought to speak in the voice of Europe, not Poland' (Karaczun, 2012). Overall, in the realm of energy security, the results were mixed. On the positive side, Poland managed to push for the Council Conclusions of November 2011 to focus on external energy security (European Council, 2011b). In addition, the European Commission was given a mandate to negotiate an agreement with Turkmenistan and Azerbaijan on the legal framework for the Trans-Caspian Gas Pipeline System. On the negative side, the Commission was not granted control over the external security deals.

In the field of internal security, the scale of ambitions was trimmed down as the Presidency drew closer. In the end, it was 'just' border protection and homeland security that found their way into the official Presidency programme. One of the main achievements in this domain was securing agreement over the European Protection Order (EPO), which lays down that victims of crime that have been granted protection from their aggressors in one EU Member State will also get such protection in another EU country.

When it comes to CSDP which was scaled down on the list of priorities, Poland did not manage to strike any groundbreaking deals. Ideological divisions between the Member States were too wide to be bridged. Some small steps were achieved, such as installing a Brussels-based EU Civil–Military Operations Centre for the Horn of Africa. The European Defence Agency agreed to start 12 so-called 'pooling and sharing projects', including, for example, helicopter pilot training, maritime surveillance network, naval training and logistics, air-to-air fuelling and smart munitions. Overall, however, no substantial progress was achieved in this area.

III. Evaluating the Polish Presidency in Its Different Roles

Following the overview of the Presidency aims and the principal dossiers on the agenda, we will now assess the Polish performance through the lenses of the different roles of organizer, broker and political leader. As mentioned before, the Lisbon Treaty has affected these roles, and in the case of political leadership, reduced the Presidency's room for manoeuvre. Still, we argue that there remains sufficient scope for fulfilling each of them.

As chair of all Council formations with the exception of the Foreign Affairs Council (FAC), the Presidency continued to face important logistical challenges, which it fulfilled in close co-operation with the Council General Secretariat. Broadly speaking, Poland did very well in its capacity of an organizer. The administration was overall well-prepared to carry the everyday burdens of the Presidency. Preparations were ongoing for three-and-a-half years, including language courses for the government officials.[10] In the absence of previous experience, lessons had to be learned from others and Polish officials were particularly grateful for the help they received from their Swedish colleagues. Prior to their period at the helm, the informal Presidency Team 'task force' toured the Member

[10] Interview at the Ministry of Foreign Affairs, Warsaw, 20 December 2011.

States in search of the best institutional arrangements. The Permanent Representation in Brussels was reinforced and hosted approximately 300 officials and in total 452 meetings were organized. Besides the careful preparations and the investment in human and material resources, the smooth organization was furthermore fostered by the close co-operation with the Council General Secretariat. Contrary to some other (often big) Member States, Poland did not make the mistake of reinventing the logistical wheel, but rather relied on the highly experienced Secretariat for the organization of the multiple meetings and diffusion of documents.

Second, Poland performed well, but not outstandingly, as a broker. The Presidency not only managed to strike numerous deals within the Council, but was also successful in its interactions with the other institutions, especially with the EP. One has to remember that when Poland took over the Presidency, there was a lot of tension between the Council and the Parliament, now further empowered by the Lisbon Treaty. Some of the biggest successes were the agreement on the correlation tables, the Six Pack, the single EU patent and the EPO. As often is the case, all of these initiatives were already ongoing under previous Presidencies, allowing Poland to build on earlier breakthroughs. The fact that Jerzy Buzek, a Polish national, was the President of the EP was an asset for a Presidency so highly dependent on its co-legislator to achieve results.

One shadow hanging over the Polish mediating role was that the scope for scoring was curtailed due to the high number of dossiers already concluded under its Hungarian predecessor. According to some, this led to the Presidency in Coreper I 'to pull' dossiers from the lower levels, unnecessarily discussing technicalities and departing from the mostly political negotiations at this level.[11] Finally, the small Member States may have felt at times excluded from the Presidency's consultations and the information loop. Despite its efforts, Poland did not manage to achieve agreement regarding Bulgaria and Romania joining the Schengen zone. This was in the first place due to the intransigence of Finland as well as the Dutch government, held hostage by the Freedom Party of Wilders. The EU Affairs Minister called this the 'biggest disappointment of the Presidency'.[12]

Finally, we come to the political leadership question. It is clear that as a non-member of the eurozone, there was little room for a Polish leadership role in the sovereign debt crisis. Here, the initiative was taken by the French President Sarkozy and the German Chancellor Merkel, supported by Herman Van Rompuy as chair of the European Council. As said before, the role of Poland was more of a co-ordinating nature. As a non-eurozone Presidency, it can, however, claim credit for selling the case for a generalization of fiscal discipline beyond the eurozone and making the fiscal treaty as inclusive as possible.

The dossier where Poland was the most active in steering the EU in a particular direction is the boost it gave to the Eastern Partnership initiative. It could do so thanks to its long-standing expertise in the field and co-operation with other partners such as Sweden. The efforts led to concrete results such as the European Endowment for Democracy and the Eastern Partnership Academy. At the same time, the case also illustrates the limits of what a rotating Presidency can do in a period of six months. The political crisis in Belarus and the arrest of Tymoshenko in Ukraine prevented Poland from fully realizing its ambitions.

[11] Interview by the authors, May 2012.
[12] *EurActiv*, 16 December 2011.

Conclusions

The Polish Presidency was well organized and, in most cases, proved that it could think beyond its own national interest. In addition, it took the opportunity to further shape its profile as exporter of democracy to the east and to the south. Not surprisingly, Poland received multiple compliments for its performance both from its peers as well as from the press. Pointing to Poland's high level of professionalism in very turbulent times, the leader of the centre-left Socialists and Democrats in the EP Martin Schultz went as far as praising the conservative Prime Minister Tusk for leading what was 'without a doubt one of the very best presidencies we have ever had'.[13] Poland was clearly no longer the inexperienced and sometimes unreliable partner of the early years. It had developed from a country well-known for its Atlanticist predilections to a player that wanted to fully assume its responsibilities at the core of the EU. Still, except for those involved, the Polish performance passed largely unnoticed. While in the past it was at times of crisis when the Presidency used to catch the public eye, now it was exactly because of the crisis that the Poles remained in the shadows.

The period of the second half of 2011 was not only instructive about the changing Polish position in the EU, it was also illustrative of the altering role of the rotating Presidency. Poland was the fourth country at the helm under the new Lisbon regime. It was clear that while in the legislative processes the workload and responsibilities increased, not only within the Council but also *vis-à-vis* the EP, in other domains the Presidency's room for manoeuvre has been considerably reduced. Any action in the field of foreign policy requires careful co-ordination with the HR, while at the level of the European Council it is now clearly the big Member States, in interaction with Van Rompuy, who set the tone. The Poles themselves seem to be rather conscious of the limits of the rotating chair. It may be partly attributed to insufficient public diplomacy, but 53 per cent of respondents to the nationwide opinion poll thought that Poland 'did not achieve much' (CBOS, 2012), while 77 per cent stated that the Presidency did not matter as it was the biggest Member States who had most influence on the policies. In spite of this, 63 per cent believed the international image of Poland improved.

This internal perception that its period at the helm contributed positively to Poland's international – or at least European – reputation may be more than just wishful thinking. As a country, which after more than 40 years of communism chose radically for reintegration into the west, Poland took its Presidency very seriously. It invested in the preparations and the otherwise rather assertive Poles showed a remarkable openness to learn from more experienced predecessors. One of these lessons was that it was imperative to set a small number of clear and limited objectives and that, rather than pushing for its own interests, it was important to listen to others and to operate as a bridge builder.

References

CBOS (Public Opinion Research Centre) (2012) *Evaluation of Polish Presidency of the Council of the European Union* (Warsaw: CBOS). Available at: «http://www.cbos.pl/EN/publications/reports/2012/011_12.pdf».

Copsey, N. and Pomorska, K (2010) 'Poland's Power and Influence in the European Union'. *Comparative European Politics*, Vol. 8, No. 3, pp. 304–26.

[13] *EUobserver*, 14 December 2011.

Dehousse, R. and Menon, A. (2009) 'The French Presidency'. *JCMS*, Vol. 47, No. S1, pp. 99–111.

Dinan, D. (2010) 'Institutions and Governance: A New Treaty, a Newly Elected Parliament and a New Commission'. *JCMS*, Vol. 48, No. S1, pp. 95–118.

European Council (2011a) 'Joint Declaration of the Eastern Partnership Summit', Warsaw, 29–30 September. Available at: «http://www.consilium.europa.eu/uedocs/cms_Data/docs/pressdata/en/ec/124843.pdf».

European Council (2011b) 'Communication on Security of Energy Supply and International Cooperation: 'The EU Energy Policy: Engaging with Partners beyond Our Borders', Brussels, 25 November.

Karaczun, Z. (2012) *Reflections on the Polish Presidency of the Council of the European Union: Climate and Energy* (Berlin: Heinrch Boll Stiftung). Available at: «http://www.boell.eu/web/270-803.html».

Łada, A. and Kucharczyk, J. (2012) *Pole Position: The Polish Presidency of the Council* (Warsaw: ISP). Available at: «http://www.isp.org.pl/aktualnosci,1,927.html».

Ministry of Foreign Affairs (MFA) (2011a) *Programme of the Polish Presidency of the Council of the European Union* (Warsaw: MFA). Available at: «http://www.pl2011.eu».

Ministry of Foreign Affairs (MFA) (2011b) *Towards a European Consensus on Growth: Report of the Polish Presidency of the Council of the European Union* (Warsaw: MFA). Available at: «http://www.mg.gov.pl/files/upload/14718/5-Raport_wersja%20angielska.pdf».

Ministry of Foreign Affairs (MFA) (2011c) 'Major Results of the Work of the Polish Presidency of the European Union Council'. Press Release, 22 December. Available at: «http://pl2011.eu/sites/default/files/users/shared/spotkania_i_wydarzenia/osiagniecia_en.pdf».

Missiroli, A. (2010) 'The New EU "Foreign Policy" System after Lisbon: A Work in Progress'. *European Foreign Affairs Review*, Vol. 15, No. 4, pp. 427–52.

Nowak, B. (2012) 'Ostatnia prezydencja dużych oczekiwań – refleksje po Prezydencji Polski w Radzie UE'. In *Raporty i Analizy Centrum Stosunków Międzynarodowych* (Warsaw: CSM).

Schout, A. and Vanhoonacker, S. (2006) 'Evaluating Presidencies of the Council of the EU: Revisiting Nice'. *JCMS*, Vol. 44, No. 5, pp. 1051–77.

Sikorski, R. (2011) 'Poland and the Future of the European Union'. Speech delivered in Berlin, 28 November. Available at: «http://www.msz.gov.pl/files/docs/komunikaty/20111128BERLIN/radoslaw_sikorski_poland_and_the_future_of_the_eu.pdf».

Spencer, T. *et al.* (2011) 'Linking an EU Emission Reduction Target Beyond 20% to Energy Security in Central and Eastern Europe'. FIIA Working Paper 16, March (Helsinki: Finnish Institute of International Affairs).

Świeboda, P. (2010) 'Poland: Island of Stability in the European Sea of Trouble', *demosEuropa*. Available at: «http://www.demoseuropa.eu/index.php?option=com_content&view=article&id=482&Itemid=104».

Tokarski, P. and Toporowski, P. (2012) 'The EU Budgetary Chess Game, the Polish Presidency and the Shadows of the Debt Crisis'. PISM Policy Paper 26 (Warsaw: Polish Institute of International Affairs).

Tusk, D. (2011a) 'Prime Minister Donald Tusk's Address on the Polish Presidency in the EU in the European Parliament', Brussels, 6 July.

Tusk, D. (2011b) 'Prime Minister Donald Tusk's Address to the European Parliament to Conclude the Polish Presidency in the EU', Strasbourg, 14 December.

Vanhoonacker, S., Pomorska, K. and Maurer, H. (2010) *The Council Presidency and European Foreign Policy: Challenges for Poland in 2011* (Warsaw: CSM).

Vanhoonacker, S., Pomorska, K. and Petrov, P. (eds) (2012) 'The Emerging EU Diplomatic System'. Special issue of the *Hague Journal of Diplomacy*, Vol. 7, No. 1.

JCMS 2012 Volume 50 Annual Review pp. 85–98 DOI: 10.1111/j.1468-5965.2012.02268.x

Governance and Institutions: Impact of the Escalating Crisis

DESMOND DINAN
George Mason University

Introduction

Economic governance was the most important item on the agenda of European integration in 2011 – a tumultuous year dominated by the eurozone crisis. Yet the meaning of 'economic governance' is notoriously imprecise, ranging from fiscal federalism, at one extreme, to loose intergovernmental co-ordination of various socio-economic policies, at the other. Despite predictable appeals to the notion of crisis as opportunity, few politicians argued in 2011 that the European Union should embrace full-fledged federalism. Instead, a consensus emerged on the need to strengthen the 'E' (economic) in 'EMU' (economic and monetary union) so that 'economic and monetary union [could] finally stand on both legs', as Commission President José Manuel Barroso put it, preferably within the confines of the existing treaty framework, supplemented, where necessary or desirable, by intergovernmental agreements (Barroso, 2011a).

Nevertheless, the year started and ended with negotiations on proposed changes to the Lisbon Treaty in response to the crisis. At the start of the year, work began on a minor modification to allow the establishment of the European Stability Mechanism (ESM) – a permanent rescue fund to supplement the temporary European Financial Stability Facility (EFSF), which had been used to bail out Greece and Ireland. At the end of the year, opposition from the United Kingdom thwarted agreement in the European Council on revising the Lisbon Treaty in order to incorporate a 'fiscal pact', thereby obliging the other Member States to negotiate the pact outside the formal Treaty framework.

The proposed Treaty changes served as bookends in a busy year that saw several other initiatives taken as a result of the crisis, with important implications for governance and institutions. Chief among these were the launch of the European Semester; negotiation, enactment and implementation of the 'Six Pack' of legislative measures intended to strengthen the Stability and Growth Pact (SGP); and commencement of the 'Euro Plus Pact' aimed at improving the competitiveness of Member States primarily in the eurozone. As in the cases of the proposed Treaty changes, these initiatives cast a new light on the dynamics of EU decision-making and inter-institutional relations.

The significance of the crisis for EU governance went far beyond the purely economic and institutional, however. For the first time in EU history, developments at the European level – notably the escalating crisis – had a profound and widespread impact on the national level of governance. Greece was the most dramatic example. In several other Member States, governments collapsed or lost elections as a direct result of the crisis. Populist politicians thrived and Euroscepticism soared. National parliaments, long the institutional Cinderellas of European integration, became crucial centres of action. Fissures over the crisis emerged not only between the government and opposition in the German Bundestag, but also within the ruling coalition. By the end of the year, the socialist candidate and front-runner in the French presidential election had come out against the proposed fiscal pact – a development with potentially far-reaching implications for France's role in the EU and for Franco–German relations.

Reviewing EU governance and institutions in 2011 is therefore unusually daunting. The crisis touched on so many issues, at so many levels, that providing a satisfactory synopsis is more difficult than ever. Key themes include the nature and quality of democracy in the EU; the Europeanization of domestic (national-level) politics; persistent tension between supranationalism (the 'Community Method') and intergovernmentalism; the undisguised emergence of reluctant German hegemony; significant changes in Franco–German relations and Franco–German leadership in the EU; the increasing predominance of the European Council and, on EMU issues, of the Eurozone Council (leaders of the Member States that have adopted the euro); the prominence of the elected European Council President; the residual importance of the rotating Council Presidency; the further marginalization of the Commission President; sharp political partisanship in the European Parliament (EP); and the growing assertiveness of the EP institutionally.

Yet another important development concerns the political cohesion of the EU. For a long time, the EU has been a highly flexible entity, accommodating opt-ins and opt-outs, derogations, and lengthy transposition periods on the part of its Member States. Cracks have opened over the years between older and newer, bigger and smaller, northern and southern, eastern and western Member States. Inevitably, the crisis accentuated the distinction between eurozone members and non-members – a distinction corresponding approximately to that between older and newer and eastern and western Member States. By the end of the year, however, as governments grappled with the proposed fiscal pact, a deep-rooted division, long apparent, became paramount: that between the United Kingdom and the other Member States on a fundamental issue affecting the EU's future.

The proliferation of so many consequential questions concerning governance and institutions suggests that the year 2011 may well have been one of the most momentous in recent EU history.

I. A Surfeit of Summits

Members of the European Council met no fewer than seven times in 2011: five times in a regular ('formal') European Council setting; once in an 'extraordinary' session; and once in an 'informal' session. The distinction between 'extraordinary' and 'informal' seems unclear, given that both sessions were out of the ordinary and less formal than regular European Council meetings. In practice, the meeting of the European Council in March was extraordinary in that Herman Van Rompuy, the institution's President, convened it outside the normal sequence of European Council sessions in order to discuss the crisis, whereas the meeting of 26 October was informal in that it was a continuation of the formal European Council session of 23 October – the gap between both being due to the vagaries of German politics (see below). All of the European Council meetings in 2011 were dominated by the crisis, which also triggered the separate summits of eurozone leaders.

Having separate summits of the EU-27 and the Euro-17 highlights the political distinction between membership and non-membership in the eurozone – a distinction that became acute as the crisis intensified. Most eurozone non-members see themselves as 'pre-ins', as countries waiting to meet the criteria for eurozone membership, despite the fading lustre of adopting the single currency. Only Denmark and the United Kingdom have opt-outs from the third stage of EMU, but even Denmark would like to participate in eurozone deliberations. Poland, the largest of the central and eastern European Member States and a country that weathered the global financial crisis and ensuing economic recession relatively well, is especially eager to participate in eurozone deliberations before formally becoming a member of the group. Poland's exclusion from meetings of eurozone leaders was especially galling during the country's Council Presidency in the second half of 2011.[1]

This is how *Spiegel*, the German news magazine, described the transition from the EU-27 to the Euro-17 on the evening of 26 October:

> At 7:45 p.m., Van Rompuy could no longer avoid the embarrassing and unpleasant task of throwing out the leaders of the ten non-euro countries. Friendliness was called for, of course, and nice words. But so too was firmness: their presence was no longer required, and they were asked to leave the assembly hall of the Justus Lipsius building in Brussels. [. . .] [The non-eurozone members] complained that the 17 eurozone nations were embarking on their own path and not involving them sufficiently. There was no shortage of grievances. Indeed, the full, 27-member session had already taken much longer than planned when Van Rompuy braced himself and asked [United Kingdom Prime Minister] Cameron, [Polish Prime Minister] Tusk and the other eight leaders of non-euro-zone nations to leave. He thanked them for the 'positive' discussion – a choice of words which belied the heated atmosphere which characterized the session – and went about his extremely unpleasant task. There was a break, and then dinner was served. Now the 17 [leaders] of the eurozone could finally tackle the important part of the meeting. Over dinner, they discussed how to save the euro. This is the reality of two-speed Europe.[2]

The frequency of summits, whether of the 27 or the 17, attested to the seriousness of the crisis and the extent to which 'the European Council has emerged as the centre of political gravity' in the EU (Puetter, 2012, p. 161). According to Van Rompuy: 'Saving the eurozone's financial stability was [. . .] the overriding objective during most of this year's meetings'. As the crisis deepened, each set of meetings (EU-27 and Euro-17) assumed a make-or-break aspect, despite Van Rompuy's stricture that 'raising expectation of a solve-it-all summit is not helpful' (Council, 2012, p. 6). Nevertheless, summits proved decisive in managing the crisis at crucial stages. Key meetings included the Euro-17 summit of 21 July, where leaders approved a second assistance programme for Greece, including voluntary private-sector involvement; the series of EU-27 and Euro-17 meetings in October, where leaders agreed on measures to maximize the capacity of the EFSF, on bank recapitalization and funding, and on regularizing eurozone summits; and the European Council and Euro-17 meetings of 9 December, where leaders decided to conclude the fiscal pact outside the Treaty framework.

These meetings were lengthy and lively affairs, characterized by intense discussions and often testy exchanges. For instance, during the October European Council, French President Nicolas Sarkozy, notorious for his outbursts at summit meetings, reportedly shouted at United Kingdom Prime Minister David Cameron: 'You have lost a good

[1] On the Polish EU Presidency, see Pomorska and Vanhoonacker in this issue.
[2] *Spiegel Online International*, 31 October 2011.

opportunity to shut up. [. . .] We are sick of you criticizing us and telling us what to do. You say you hate the euro and now you want to interfere in our meetings'.[3] Under the circumstances, it was hardly surprising either that Britain split from the other Member States at the end of the year over the proposed fiscal pact, or that France (and possibly other Member States) was not too sad to see Britain go its separate way.

Although supposedly equal, in practice some national leaders are more equal than others. Leaders of the larger Member States are generally at the top of the informal hierarchy at EU or eurozone summits, with the French and German leaders reigning supreme. Nevertheless, Silvio Berlusconi, though leader of Italy, a large Member State, was held in low regard by his peers, partly because of his presumed responsibility for the deteriorating state of Italy's public finances, which greatly exacerbated the crisis in the summer of 2011. Most of the other EU leaders were delighted when pressure from Merkel and Sarkozy, linked to EU assistance for Italy, finally forced Berlusconi, already weakened by a wave of domestic scandals, from office in early November. Despite not having been elected, Mario Monti, Berlusconi's successor, enjoyed enormous prestige among EU leaders because of his reputation as a successful ex-Commissioner and someone of unquestioned integrity. Donald Tusk, prime minister of another large Member State (Poland), was duly influential at meetings of the European Council, but could not attend eurozone summits because his country had not (yet) adopted the euro.

As in years past, only more so, France and Germany dominated meetings of the EU-27 and Euro-17. Invariably, the French and German leaders held bilateral summits before meetings of the EU-27 and Euro-17 to thrash out their differences and agree on a proposal or set of proposals for presentation at the forthcoming summits of EU and eurozone leaders. Without prior Franco–German agreement, Sarkozy declared after the December European Council, 'a deal [on the fiscal pact] would not have been possible'.[4] He may have been right, but Van Rompuy put France–German leadership in a slightly different light when he explained, after the October European Council, that agreement between France and Germany was 'necessary, but not sufficient' to ensure agreement in the European Council (European Council, 2011).

Also as in years past, only more so, Franco–German supremacy engendered the resentment of other leaders – and not only in the European Council. Thus Guy Verhofstadt, leader of the Liberals in the EP, warned in early December 'against the temptation of a Franco–German *coup de chefs d'état*' (Spinelli Group, 2011). Martin Schulz, leader of the Socialists and Democrats (S&D) in the EP, complained in August that France and Germany were 'once again [. . .] trying to force' their ideas on other Member States and were 'looking down their noses at the rest of the eurozone'.[5]

Despite the appearance of equality between France and Germany at the top of the EU pyramid, the balance of influence between both countries changed appreciably during the year. Germany, for a long time the most powerful economic player in the EU, became unquestionably the most influential Member State politically in 2011. With Germany contributing most to the bail-out funds, German politicians, including Merkel, were not shy about advancing German interests. At decisive junctures throughout the year, Merkel

[3] *The Guardian*, 23 October 2011.
[4] *Le Monde*, 9 December 2011.
[5] *Agence Europe*, 25 August 2011.

pushed successfully for a German-inspired solution to the crisis. The most striking example is the way in which Germany pressed towards the end of the year for a Treaty change to include 'debt brakes' in Member States' constitutions or national legislation as a powerful means of imposing budget discipline. Other actors, whether in the Commission, the EP or national capitals, frequently complained about the forcefulness and disputed the wisdom of Germany's approach. Nevertheless, Merkel continue to wrap German preferences in the cloak of Franco–German leadership and seemed determined to maintain the fiction of Franco–German equality. There were institutional and personal dynamics at play. Institutionally, the Franco–German duopoly is hard-wired into Germany's political elites. So too is an aversion to assertiveness and unilateralism on the international stage. Historically, France is Germany's inevitable partner in the EU; given the economic and political configuration of today's EU, Germany does not have a feasible alternative to France as possible co-leader.

Personally, Merkel and Sarkozy could not be more different. The crisis may not have caused them to like each other more, but it did cause them to appreciate each other better. François Hollande, Sarkozy's main rival in the 2012 presidential election, tipped the scales for Merkel when he came out against her cherished fiscal pact. Thereafter, Merkel saw the fate of the fiscal pact resting, in large part, on the outcome of the French election. Not surprisingly, she embraced Sarkozy wholeheartedly, offering to campaign with him in the run-up to the election. The idea of a German chancellor campaigning for a French president offended many French people, despite Merkel's popularity across the Rhine, and was in any case utterly impractical. Yet in an entity such as the EU, electioneering by members of the same pan-European party (Merkel and Sarkozy belong to the European Peoples' Party [EPP]) is surely a sign of political maturity. Even though she was the dominant partner, Merkel did not always get her own way with Sarkozy. Merkel's paradoxical dependence on Sarkozy gave him a degree of leverage over her, however slight. Similarly, France and Germany did not always get their way with the other Member States, often having to make concessions on the margins of whatever the core issue happened to be. Overall, however, France and Germany put their stamp on the EU's response to the crisis throughout 2011.

The predominance of the Franco–German tandem made the work of Van Rompuy, the EU's first elected President of the European Council, even more challenging. Van Rompuy was Merkel's and Sarkozy's candidate, which ensured that he got the job in November 2009, much to the chagrin of Luxembourg Prime Minister Jean-Claude Juncker and former Belgian Prime Minister Verhofstadt, who were the other contenders for the position. Because of this fulsome Franco–German support, many other European Council members assume that Van Rompuy does the bidding of Berlin and Paris. Juncker and Verhofstadt apparently think so, which matters more than it otherwise would because Juncker is also head of the Eurogroup (the informal Council of eurozone finance ministers) and Verhofstadt is head of the influential Liberal Group in the EP. Both Juncker and Verhofstadt have strongly criticized Van Rompuy's deference to France and Germany, suggesting that it is detrimental to the functioning of the European Council and to the interests of the EU as a whole.

Based on an evaluation of his second full year in the job, the switch in the Lisbon Treaty from a rotating to standing European Council Presidency seems like a worthwhile innovation. Van Rompuy may be unduly deferential to France and Germany, but the leaders of most countries in the rotating Presidency would be equally deferential. Not that Van Rompuy slavishly follows the Franco–German lead. In December 2011, he took a position contrary to that of Merkel and Sarkozy, advocating tighter fiscal policy co-ordination among Member States without recourse to a new Treaty, which he feared would prove divisive and difficult to ratify.

Van Rompuy's institutional profile rose when EU leaders decided in October that Euro-17 summits would take place regularly, with Van Rompuy as President. Although Van Rompuy's Presidency of both bodies would be subject to renewal in mid-2012, when his first term as European Council President ends, the presumption at the end of 2011 was not only that Van Rompuy would be renewed in both positions but also that, even after his second, non-renewable term, the Presidency of both bodies would be held by the same person. If so, the already tiny universe of potential European Council and eurozone summit presidents would shrink and become limited in effect to current or former leaders of eurozone countries.

It is tempting, when trying to evaluate Van Rompuy's performance, to imagine how the European Council would have fared under the old rotating Presidency. The answer in 2011 is easy, though mixed. Hungarian Prime Minister Victor Orbán, widely unpopular among other national leaders because of his authoritarian tendencies, would likely have been a disaster as President of the European Council, though Hungary generally performed well in the rotating Council Presidency in the first half of the year.[6] By contrast, the popular Donald Tusk would have made an excellent European Council President, just as Poland generally did a first-rate job in the rotating Council Presidency in the second half of the year. Van Rompuy himself is confident that having a standing President benefits the European Council. 'Thanks to the new continuity of my function', he wrote in his 2011 report, '[the European Council] is better equipped to steer change, to give orientations or quite practically to follow-up earlier decisions' (Council, 2012, p. 16). Meetings of the European Council seemed well-prepared and well-run under Van Rompuy's watch. Much of his success depends on having a good *cabinet* (small private office) and on having good working relationships with national leaders and foreign ministers (Van Rompuy works closely with the General Affairs Council) – especially with the prime minister and foreign minister of the country in the rotating Presidency – and with the President of the EP, political group leaders in the EP, the High Representative for the Common Foreign and Security Policy, and the head of the Eurogroup (despite Juncker's ambivalence towards him).

Commission President Barroso is a particularly important interlocutor for Van Rompuy. The relationship between the two presidents is inherently prickly, given that the Commission President had more to lose institutionally from the establishment of a standing European Council President than the standing European Council President had from the existence of the Commission President. Barroso and Van Rompuy seem to work harmoniously together, having been tasked jointly by the European Council in 2011 with drafting reports and taking initiatives to help resolve the crisis. They frequently take part in joint press conferences and appear together at the EP to report on European summits.

Regardless of the existence of a standing European Council President, the political influence of the Commission President is waning. The reasons are mostly institutional, but

[6] On the Hungarian EU Presidency, see Ágh in this issue.

partly personal. The onset of the crisis has further elevated the European Council. Despite being an *ex officio* member of it, the European Council is not a congenial environment for a Commission President, who lacks the stature and political heft of a national leader, especially if that Commission President comes from a small Member State (Barroso is Portuguese). Former Commission President Jacques Delors excelled in the European Council in the late 1980s, but he came from a leading Member State (France), was close to German Chancellor Helmut Kohl and benefited politically from the highly successful single market programme, which involved supranational decision-making.

With the exception of the Six Pack of legislative measures to strengthen the SGP, most of the major responses to the eurozone crisis have been intergovernmental. Even the Six Pack saw the Commission marginalized once the Council and EP launched the co-decision procedure (the Council Presidency, rather than the Commission, becoming the chief mediator). Traditionally, France is wary of the Commission, and Germany, though more sympathetic to supranationalism, is not a big fan of the EU executive. Merkel and Sarkozy are true to type and neither sees Barroso as a political heavyweight.

Barroso's frustration with Van Rompuy's prominence and with the primacy of the Merkel–Sarkozy tandem was palpable in 2011. Barroso may have been equally aggrieved in 2010, but he needed to put on a brave face in order to be reappointed Commission President. Once in his second term, and with no prospect of a third, Barroso became more critical of Franco–German leadership and what he saw as rampant intergovernmentalism in the EU. In a series of well-publicized speeches – notably his State of the Union address in September – Barroso launched a full-throated defence of the Community Method, in which the Commission and EP are central decision-makers and the European Court of Justice (ECJ) has the right of judicial review (Barroso, 2011b).

Most members of the European Parliament (MEPs) like to hear such rhetoric (Eurosceptics – a small minority of parliamentarians – are the obvious exception). As long as he spoke to MEPs about inter-institutional relations and the overall trajectory of European integration, Barroso was on solid ground. Whenever he spoke about the eurozone crisis or socio-economic policies, however, the EP split along left–right lines, with the centre-right EPP generally supporting Barroso, a former centre-right prime minister of Portugal, and the centre-left S&D denouncing him.

Barroso's limited political influence does not mean that the Commission itself lacked influence or authority in 2011. The Commission played an important part in what passed for economic governance before the 2011 reforms, whether in budgetary surveillance or the Europe 2020 process. Nor is the Community Method a thing of the past. Apart from specific legislative responses to the crisis, such as the Six Pack and a further 'Two Pack' of proposals submitted by the Commission in November to reinforce surveillance of fiscal policy in the eurozone, the Commission remains front and centre of other EU business, such as efforts to strengthen the single market – a work perpetually in progress. The Commission's most potent weapon is its exclusive right to initiate legislation, though pressure from the Council and the EP increasingly limits the Commission's freedom of manoeuvre.

The eurozone crisis did not represent a setback politically for the Commission, which, for instance, plays a key role monitoring compliance with bail-out conditionality, though this does not enhance the popularity of Commission officials working in Athens. The Commissioner for Economic and Monetary Affairs, Olli Rehn, is highly regarded in the priesthood of central bankers and senior government officials working exclusively on the crisis. Finally, the December agreement to negotiate an intergovernmental fiscal pact did not imply that the EU's supranational institutions would be entirely sidelined. As Angela Merkel pointed out, the fiscal pact would 'give a greater role to the Commission and the European Court of Justice, and EP observers [would] be invited to sit in on the drafting of the treaty' (Merkel, 2011).

II. The European Parliament and National Parliaments

The EP is a diverse body. Most MEPs are only peripherally involved in policy deliberation and decision-making. A minority, in leadership positions, take the institution and its role in EU governance extremely seriously. At the top, the institution's President plays largely a ceremonial role. Jerzy Buzek, in his final year as President in 2011, was no exception. Perhaps because he was the first politician from one of the central and eastern European Member States to head an EU institution, Buzek seemed unusually deferential in the post. Nor had he acquainted himself adequately with the organization and functioning of the EP. Other MEPs in leadership positions were far more outspoken. Not surprisingly, this was true especially of the political group leaders. Collectively, in the Conference of Presidents, the political group leaders pushed the interests of the EP in relation to the Commission and, in particular, the Council. Individually, while also upholding the EP's institutional interests, they pushed primarily the interests of their respective groups, arguing the merits of legislative proposals or other issues on ideological or party political grounds.

Who are the government and the opposition groups in the EP? Such a distinction does not exist in the EU, which lacks a readily identifiable government. Yet the overwhelming centre-right complexion of the Commission and the Council casts the EPP group, the largest in the EP, in the role of a quasi-government group. The other large groups – notably the S&D, Liberals and Greens – tend to see themselves as opposition parties.

The interaction between upholding institutional and political group interests came to light in 2011 during completion of the co-decision procedure to enact the Six Pack of measures to strengthen the SGP. Given the importance and complexity of the proposals, the legislative procedure was bound to be fraught. Providing overall political direction, the European Council urged the Council and EP to reach agreement in the first reading stage, thereby putting additional pressure on the EP and, in the view of many MEPs, limiting the effectiveness of parliamentary deliberation. The Council reached its common position on the draft legislation reasonably early, at the end of March. The most contentious issue within the Council concerned the automaticity of sanctions against countries contravening the terms of the SGP. A majority of national governments did not want the Commission to have the right to impose sanctions automatically with regard to the preventive arm of the pact, but wanted the Council to be able to approve sanctions by means of a qualified majority vote. A minority of governments – notably those from the Benelux countries – argued unsuccessfully that giving the Council the last word on sanctions risked undermining the effectiveness of a supposedly stronger SGP.

The six EP committees dealing with the draft legislation pored over the Commission's proposals, the Council's common position and a host of parliamentary amendments. 'Trialogues', bringing together representatives of the Commission, Council and EP, met in the spring and early summer, hoping to reach a political agreement before the end of June.

The two legislative bodies – the Council and EP – made remarkable progress, thanks in part to the successful mediation of the Hungarian Presidency, but the same issue that had most divided national governments proved even more divisive between the Council and the EP. Despite there being what Rehn described as '99.9% agreement' on the texts, concurrence on the imposition of sanctions proved elusive, with the EP insisting not that sanctions be fully automatic, but that national governments be allowed to prevent their imposition only by means of a reverse qualified majority (European Parliament, 2011). Thus, instead of being able to prevent the imposition of sanctions by forming a blocking minority, as the Council proposed, a country wanting to reject the Commission's recommendation would instead face the much more daunting task of having to form a qualified majority.

This was not simply a Council versus EP confrontation. The Benelux countries, which had opposed what became the Council position, remained vocal in their opposition and wholeheartedly supported the contending EP position. On the EP side, the political groups split. The EPP, the 'governing' group, supported the Council's position. It may not have been coincidental that France took the hardest line within the Council on the question of sanctions and that Joseph Daul, leader of the EPP, belonged to the ruling French centre-right party. Certainly, Sarkozy took a keen interest in the issue and mentioned more than once the importance of getting the EP behind the Council's position.

On the other side of the aisle, the S&D, under the aggressive leadership of Martin Schulz, defended the reverse majority rule. As a member of the opposition party in Germany, Schulz took particular pleasure blocking a solution favored by Chancellor Merkel. Verhofstadt, leader of the Liberals, also adamantly defended the reverse majority rule. As a former Belgian prime minister, Verhofstadt was in close touch with the Benelux countries, which had lost the battle in the Council over the rules for imposing sanctions but hoped to win the war in the larger Council–EP theatre of operations. Given his political stature, Verhofstadt felt supremely confident going head-to-head with the Council.

Despite intense pressure from Sarkozy and other national leaders, the EP collectively stuck to the reverse majority rule. The issue having passed the self-imposed deadline of June 2011, and from the Hungarian to the Polish Presidency, France, the final hold-out on the Council side, eventually relented. This allowed the Polish Presidency and the Polish President of the EP to enact the legislation in December. It was a sweet victory for the Benelux countries, the S&D and the Liberals, and for the EP as a whole, despite the EPP's position. More important, the reverse majority rule undoubtedly improved the effectiveness of the legislation by making it more difficult for national governments to wiggle out of their SGP commitments. Given that the purpose of the legislative package was to strengthen the SGP, the EP's insistence on reverse qualified majority was advantageous.

By the time the Six Pack saw the legislative light of day, Merkel was pushing to amend the Lisbon Treaty by including in it a fiscal pact. As usual, Merkel had brought Sarkozy on board and had built up sufficient political momentum to win support for the idea at the December European Council, although Britain's opposition meant that the pact would have to be negotiated as an intergovernmental treaty among the other Member States. Having reluctantly agreed to approve the earlier Treaty change on establishing the ESM by means of the simplified amendment procedure, thereby obviating the need for a Convention, the EP was reluctant in late 2011 to allow another, more far-reaching Treaty change to take place by means of the simplified procedure. Many MEPs wanted the

European Council to convene a Convention, in which the EP would be well-represented and correspondingly influential. National governments were averse to calling a Convention because of the amount of time that it would take, especially as the proposed Treaty reform sought to address the fast-moving fiscal crisis. Moreover, governments feared opening a Pandora's box – who knew what other items would pop up on the Convention's agenda? – and running the risk of contentious ratification procedures. The EP acquiesced, but many MEPs felt that, having gone along with the simplified procedure to establish the ESM and having acted constructively in the Six Pack negotiations, they and their institution were being steamrolled by national governments on the politically more consequential question of negotiating the fiscal pact.

Whether implemented by means of a Convention or simplified procedure, Treaty reform enhances the role of national parliaments in EU governance, as in most cases national parliaments are responsible for ratifying agreed-upon Treaty changes in each Member State. Moreover, the EFSF, the temporary eurozone bail-out fund, was an intergovernmental instrument whose establishment and modification required parliamentary approval in all Member States. Opposition in Slovakia to participation in the EFSF, together with political opportunism, resulted in rejection by the Slovak parliament in October of the EU agreement to bolster the rescue fund, which the other Member States had already approved. The government won a second vote with the help of the main opposition party, whose support was conditional on the general election being brought forward to March 2012. The Slovak saga was a colourful example of the interplay of EU and national-level politics during the eurozone crisis.

Going beyond the ratification of Treaty changes or the approval of intergovernmental instruments, national governments, sensitive to citizen concerns about the EU's democratic legitimacy, have long grappled with the declining power of national parliaments in the EU system – an inevitable result of more and more legislation being enacted by the Council and the EP rather than by national governments and national parliaments. Accordingly, the Lisbon Treaty gave national parliaments a voice in EU-level legislative decision-making by means of enforcing the subsidiarity principle.

As seen in the Slovak case, one of the most striking institutional developments in 2011 was the increasing prominence of national parliaments in EU governance not because of subsidiarity enforcement, but because of the unfolding eurozone crisis. The impact of the crisis on national political and parliamentary life was wide-ranging. The composition of national parliaments, and therefore of national governments, changed in several Member States (Ireland, Finland, Portugal, Spain and Denmark) because of elections whose outcome depended to some extent or other on the crisis. Governments changed as well in Belgium, Greece and Italy not following elections, but because of the fallout from the crisis. As Van Rompuy quaintly remarked: 'These are all signs of how European and national politics are now woven together ever more tightly' (Council, 2012, p. 5).

Although resulting in neither an election nor a change in government, the crisis had a direct and momentous impact on politics in Germany, with repercussions for the Bundestag and for Germany's role in the EU.[7] Hitherto, the German government had a relatively free hand domestically in EU affairs, although the Constitutional Court had

[7] On a discussion of Germany's evolving role in the EU, see Paterson (2011).

already flagged the necessity of greater parliamentary involvement. As the crisis escalated and the size of the bail-outs ballooned, German public and parliamentary opinion grew increasingly agitated. Ruptures opened in Merkel's ruling coalition, with the small Free Democratic Party coming out against additional assistance to Greece and members of Merkel's own Christian Democratic Party and sister Christian Social Union also voicing concern. As a result, Merkel found herself navigating dangerous internal shoals before acting on the EU stage. A Constitutional Court ruling in September rejected a challenge to the bail-outs, but reinforced the role of the Bundestag in approving future payments.[8] As a result, the Bundestag insisted on endorsing the chancellor's position on additional assistance to Greece before allowing her to conclude the 23 October summit. Merkel had no choice but to ask Van Rompuy to suspend the summit while she held and won a vote in parliament, which gave her the necessary mandate to conclude the summit on 26 October. This may have been a good example of democracy in action, but it was not conducive to rapid decision-making during a fast-moving crisis. It also aroused resentment of Germany on the part of other countries with restive parliaments but without the clout to keep the European Council in suspended animation for several days.

III. The Risk of Referendums

Democracy is a touchy issue in the EU (see, for instance, Follesdal and Hix, 2006; Habermas, 2012; Hobolt, 2012; Majone, 1998; Moravcsik, 2002). Many Eurosceptics are certain that the EU is not and never can be fully democratic and therefore legitimate. Perhaps the rise of Euroscepticism has made the EU political establishment too sensitive on the subject of the democratic deficit. The nature of the EU means that its democratic character cannot replicate that of a Member State, but the attributes of democracy, such as free and fair elections, wider citizen participation, political accountability and transparency, exist at the EU level. These features may be imperfect, and EU-level politics may lack the drama and range of national-level politics, but the EU is nonetheless a democratic polity.

One instrument of direct democracy, however, has become a lightning-rod for Eurosceptics and a scourge for EU politicians and officials: the national referendum. Eurosceptics see referendums as a means not of strengthening democracy in the EU (after all, many of them think that the EU cannot be fully democratic), but of weakening the EU politically. Knowing that EU-related referendums can easily be manipulated by Eurosceptics and are notoriously difficult to win, national governments usually do everything possible to avoid holding them. This, in turn, strengthens the Eurosceptic argument that the EU establishment is afraid of democracy and that the EU is inherently undemocratic.

The relevance of referendums to the tortuous debate about EU-level democracy emerged spectacularly in 2011 in three countries: Greece, Ireland and the United Kingdom. In Greece, Prime Minister Georges Papandreou, under massive pressure in late October from fellow national leaders to accept another bail-out and from domestic public opinion to resist onerous conditions for the loan, decided to hold a referendum on the issue. Other EU leaders, especially Merkel and Sarkozy, were outraged. While paying lip service to Greece's sovereign right to hold a referendum, they insisted that the question

[8] *Spiegel Online International*, 7 September 2011.

should be whether Greece wanted to stay in the eurozone – a question more likely to elicit a positive response than whether Greece should accept the conditions attached to the loan – and that the referendum take place as soon as possible. Opponents of the referendum justified their position on the grounds that Papandreou's initiative flew in the face of EU solidarity and risked destabilizing the eurozone. Papandreou soon agreed to drop the referendum, much to the relief of his eurozone partners. Nevertheless, the episode raised awkward questions about the nature of democracy in the EU, which Eurosceptics eagerly exploited.

The Greek case was unusual in that the government announced its intention of holding a referendum without having been obliged by constitutional or other constraints to do so. The situation in the United Kingdom was entirely different. There, parliament voted in October on a motion calling for a referendum on whether Britain should stay in the EU, leave or renegotiate its membership – a motion prompted by a citizens' initiative (a petition signed by more than 100,000 members of the public). Though Eurosceptical, Cameron did not want to have his hands tied in this way. He opposed the motion and instructed members of his Conservative Party to do so as well. Although the measure was overwhelmingly defeated, over 80 Conservatives defied the party leadership. Such a large-scale rebellion emboldened Conservative Eurosceptics and may have pushed Cameron to take a particularly tough stand at the December European Council on the question of the fiscal pact.

The possibility of an EU-related referendum anywhere, but especially in Ireland, filled the EU establishment with dread (memories of Ireland's rejection of the Lisbon Treaty were still vivid). As talk of Treaty change intensified toward the end of the year, Merkel and other national leaders made clear their intention to do everything possible to avoid triggering a ratification-related referendum. That partly explains their determination to keep Treaty change to a minimum and not convene a Convention. Following the December European Council, where leaders agreed to negotiate the fiscal pact, the Irish government was confident that a referendum would not be necessary to ratify the outcome. In the event, because it would not be a reform of the Lisbon Treaty, the new treaty would not require ratification in all Member States in order to come into effect. Moreover, because only those countries that had ratified the treaty would be eligible for an EU bail-out, national leaders were confident that, with or without a referendum, Ireland would ratify the fiscal pact.

Conclusions

The year 2011 was tumultuous for the EU. The escalating crisis resembled an ocean storm crashing towards shore. EU leaders responded by building an ever-higher seawall as ever-larger waves, in the form of rapidly deteriorating public finances in Greece, Portugal, Spain and Italy, risked inundating the eurozone. The seawall itself, consisting of the Six Pack, Euro Plus Pact, EFSF, ESM and finally the promised fiscal pact, appeared sufficiently sturdy by the end of the year, though the prospect of a rogue wave, capable of breaching the eurozone's defences, remained acute.

Some observers saw poor leadership and political weakness as the root causes of the crisis. On the monetary policy side, the ECB President, whether Jean-Claude Trichet or his successor Mario Draghi, faced fewer political constraints and were able to provide more decisive leadership. They did not hesitate to tell political leaders what they should be doing, while protecting the independence of their own institution. On the economic policy side, leadership rested on the shoulders of numerous national and EU-level actors. Merkel, the most important of them, was frequently criticized for not grasping the seriousness of the crisis, for responding too slowly and for advocating austerity *über alles*. By the end of the year, however, her increasingly alarmist statements about the implications of the crisis for the future of the EU suggested that she grasped the gravity, if not yet the complexity, of the situation.

Merkel and Sarkozy, as well as Trichet, and Draghi, were the key players combating the crisis in 2011; ad hoc meetings between them, as well as meetings of the EU-27 and Euro-17, were the main decision-making venues. As Van Rompuy observed with respect to the crisis, 'markets have the luxury of moving with the speed of the click of a mouse; political processes [. . .] cannot deliver so quickly'.[9] Having a plethora of people in leadership positions sharing responsibility for managing the eurozone inevitably makes matters worse. 'There are 17 governments sitting at the table in the Eurogroup, representing a total of more than 40 political parties', Juncker pointed out at the beginning of the year, 'it's no wonder that there are occasional difficulties with coordinating things'.[10] At the highest political level, the European Council and the Euro-17 face a similar constraint. Given the eurozone's political character and institutional architecture, EU leaders were simply unable to respond rapidly to a crisis, no matter how urgent the situation became.

Aware of the inadequacy of the EU's ability to cope with the crisis, Merkel and others repeatedly called for 'More Europe'. Federalists take that to mean more supranationalism in the conduct of EU affairs and greater EU competence for policy areas still subject to intergovernmental modes of governance. Few mainstream politicians saw the crisis as providing either the opportunity or necessity for deeper European integration along classic supranational lines (see Featherstone, 2011; Salines *et al.*, 2012). Yet there was definitely more Europe at the end of the year than at the beginning as the crisis penetrated deeper into national politics and political processes. Though still nominally the preserve of national parliaments and governments, fiscal policy – the final frontier of European integration – came under much greater scrutiny and became subject to much closer co-ordination among national authorities operating in a tighter EU context. By the end of 2011, economic governance at the EU level did not mean that fiscal policy was subject to supranational decision-making. Rather, economic governance had developed into a set of binding rules, expectations, institutions and obligations guiding fiscal policy and structural reform primarily among eurozone members.

Alongside its implications for economic governance, the crisis raised questions about how united the EU really is. The crisis accentuated the obvious distinction between eurozone members and non-members and opened other fissures. S&D leader Schulz saw a threefold distinction among EU Member States: the Franco–German decision-makers; other eurozone countries; and the rest.[11] Regardless of where exactly the dividing lines lay, just as the crisis had exposed the extent of economic divergence among Member States, the response to it would have to promote real convergence, thereby eradicating other

[9] *Agence Europe*, 28 October 2011.
[10] *Spiegel Online International*, 24 January 2011.
[11] *Agence Europe*, 26 October 2011.

distinctions and bringing about a more unitary EU. Being in or out of the eurozone would still matter politically as well as economically, but less than it had in 2011. Yet that would leave one distinction above all within the EU – a distinction that emerged forcefully by the end of the year: the difference between the United Kingdom and the rest.

References

Barroso, J.M.D. (2011a) 'Statement by President Barroso at the Press Conference following the European Council, Brussels, 25 March. Available at: «http://europa.eu/rapid/pressReleasesAction.do?reference=SPEECH/11/216».

Barroso, J.M.D. (2011b) 'European Renewal: State of the Union Address 2011'. Speech to the European Parliament, Strasbourg, 28 September. Available at: «http://ec.europa.eu/commission_2010-2014/president/pdf/speech_original.pdf».

Council (2012) *The European Council in 2011, General Secretariat of the Council*. Luxembourg: Publications Office of the European Union.

European Council (2011) Press Conference, 23 October. Available at: «http://tvnewsroom.consilium.europa.eu/event/european-council-october-2011/european-council-october-2011-press-conference/».

European Parliament (2011) Debates, Brussels, 22 June. Available at: «http://www.europarl.europa.eu/sides/getDoc.do?pubRef=-//EP//TEXT+CRE+20110622+ITEM-016+DOC+XML+V0//EN».

Featherstone, K. (2011) 'The JCMS Annual Lecture: The Greek Sovereign Debt Crisis and EMU: A Failing State in a Skewed Regime'. *JCMS*, Vol. 49, No. 2, pp. 193–217.

Follesdal, A. and Hix, S. (2006) 'Why There is a Democratic Deficit in the EU: A Response to Majone and Moravcsik'. *JCMS*, Vol. 44, No. 3, pp. 533–62.

Habermas, J. (2012) *The Crisis of the European Union: A Response* (London: Polity Press).

Hobolt, S. (2012) 'Citizen Satisfaction with Democracy in the European Union'. *JCMS*, Vol. 50, No. 1, pp. 88–105.

Majone, G. (1998) 'Europe's "Democratic Deficit": The Question of Standards'. *European Law Journal*, Vol. 4, No. 1, pp. 5–28.

Merkel, A. (2011) 'Europe will Emerge Stronger from the Crisis'. *Bundeskanzlerin News*, 14 December. Available at: «http://www.bundeskanzlerin.de/Content/EN/Artikel/_2011/12/2011-12-14-er-bk-regierungserklaerung_en.html;jsessionid=8A6CFF4C896DC7C18A8CC67AD274788C.s3t1?nn=77364».

Moravcsik, A. (2002) 'In Defence of the "Democratic Deficit": Reassessing the Legitimacy of the European Union'. *JCMS*, Vol. 40, No. 4, pp. 603–34.

Paterson, W. (2011) 'The Reluctant Hegemon? Germany Moves Centre Stage in the European Union'. *JCMS*, Vol. 49, No. S1, pp. 57–75.

Puetter, U. (2012) 'Europe's Deliberative Intergovernmentalism: The Role of the Council and European Council in EU Economic Governance'. *Journal of European Public Policy*, Vol. 19, No. 2, pp. 161–78.

Salines, M., Glöckler, G. and Truchlewski, Z. (2012) 'Existential Crisis, Incremental Response: The Eurozone's Dual Institutional Evolution, 2007–2011'. *Journal of European Public Policy*, Vol. 19, No. 5, pp. 665–81.

Spinelli Group (2011) 'Against the Temptation of a Franco–German "coup de chefs d'Etat"'. Available at: «http://www.spinelligroup.eu/2011/12/08/against-the-temptation-of-a-franco-german-coup-de-chefs-d%E2%80%99etat/».

JCMS 2012 Volume 50 Annual Review pp. 99–115 DOI: 10.1111/j.1468-5965.2012.02281.x

Internal Market: The Ongoing Struggle to 'Protect' Europe from Its Money Men*

JAMES BUCKLEY, DAVID HOWARTH[1] and LUCIA QUAGLIA[2]
[1] University of Luxembourg. [2] University of York

Introduction

Financial regulation dominated the European Union's internal market legislative agenda in 2011, as it had over the two previous years (Buckley and Howarth, 2010, 2011). The ongoing sovereign debt crisis in the eurozone and the funding difficulties facing many EU-based banks ensured that the international financial crisis continued to loom large in the minds of policy-makers, and financial sector stability remained a central preoccupation for most, if not all, EU Member State governments.

After a brief overview of the financial sector legislation adopted or developed during 2011, the focus of this contribution will be on two of the most hotly contested financial legislative packages over the year. Both are also noteworthy because they are useful case studies of the lobbying efforts by affected financial services and powerful Member States. Further, both are cases of national policies failing to correspond in significant ways to widely assumed and typical national positioning on national and EU-level financial regulation, with the British government pushing for legislation that would significantly restrict the operation of specific financial services and the French and German governments opting for 'lighter touch' regulation.[1] The structures of national financial – and more specifically, banking – systems and the perceived impact of EU legislation explain in large part differing policies.

The first piece of legislation examined is the European Market Infrastructure Regulation (EMIR) proposed by the European Commission in September 2010 (Commission, 2010). The Commission and supportive Member States sought to ensure the transparency of over-the-counter derivatives (OTC) transactions,[2] and to reduce the risks associated with these products by shifting where possible OTC derivatives trading to central counterparties. Under strong financial sector lobbying of MEPs, the Regulation was amended significantly. While expressing concerns about specific elements of the Commission's draft, the British government was largely supportive, while the German government was more cautious.

* Lucia Quaglia wishes to thank the European Research Council (Grant 204398 FINGOVEU) for financial support for this research. This article was written while she was a visiting fellow at the European University Institute (EUI) in Florence. We are grateful to Till Kaesbach for comments on an earlier draft.

[1] On the ideational dimension of the more typical positions, see Quaglia (2011).

[2] 'OTC derivatives' are contracts that are traded directly between two parties, without going through an exchange or other intermediary. 'Derivatives' are contracts used largely to extend credit that specify conditions under which payments are to be made between parties (notably, notional amounts, dates and resulting values of the underlying variables). Their complexity, lack of transparency and strong protections afforded to counterparties can cause capital markets to underprice credit risk, which made derivatives a major contributory factor to the outbreak of the international financial crisis in 2008.

The second draft legislative package examined is the Capital Requirements Directive (CRD)IV/and the Capital Requirements Regulation (CRR) adopted by the Commission in July 2011, which is likely to be the most substantial of all the post-financial crisis regulatory measures entertained to date at the EU level. CRDIV-CRR was adopted to implement the international agreement on capital requirements (the Basel III Accord) agreed in December 2010 by regulators from the world's leading economies meeting in the Basel Committee of Banking Supervisors (BCBS) of the Bank for International Settlements (BIS). However, the Commission's draft modified Basel III in various controversial ways, given the demands of Member State governments and national and EU-level bank lobbies. The application of Basel III guidelines to all 8,300 EU-based banks, fundamental differences in national banking systems and widespread fears over the exposure of national economies to bank recapitalization and de-leveraging meant that the adoption of Basel III into EU legislation would be likely to involve exemptions. The British government pushed actively for the full implementation of Basel III into EU law. Following this analysis, the role of the newly created European Banking Authority (EBA), in increasing the pressure on governments and banks to accept the need for recapitalization, is considered.[3]

I. Progress on a Range of Financial Legislation

Significant progress was made on several pieces of financial legislation during 2011. On 20 October, the Commission published a proposal to review the Markets in Financial Instruments Directive (MiFID). This legislation came into force in 2007, covering rules for all the investment services in financial products in the EU, including the trading of shares, and provides for consumer protection through information requirements. MiFID led to a deregulation of stock markets, putting stock exchanges into competition with new alternative trading venues. The latter benefited from softer rules – in particular on transparency which the Commission sought to tighten.[4] In addition to amendments to MiFID, which took the name 'MiFID II', the Commission also proposed the introduction of a new Markets in Financial Instruments Regulation (MiFIR) to make the requirements more binding and harmonized across Member States by eliminating the discretion in transposition allowed in the Directive. In addition to Multilateral Trading Facilities and regulated markets already covered by MiFID, the revision brought a new type of trading venue into its regulatory framework: the Organized Trading Facility (OTF). These were organized platforms that were not regulated but had come to play an increasingly important role – for example, for trading derivatives contracts (Commission, 2011c). The negotiations between the institutions on MiFID II and MiFIR were to proceed in 2012, with implementation in 2013 and 2014.

The European Commission brought forward legislation to restrict naked short-selling (that is, the sale of securities that are neither owned nor have been borrowed) to curb perceived excessive speculation. In September 2010, the Commission proposed a Regulation on short-selling and certain aspects of credit default swaps,[5] which was adopted in

[3] On the negotiations over the creation of the EBA, see Buckley and Howarth (2011).

[4] *Financial Times*, 21 October 2011.

[5] *COM*(2010) 482 final; 'Proposal for a Regulation of the European Parliament and of the Council on short-selling and certain aspects of credit default swaps', 2010/0251 (COD), SEC(2010) 1055, SEC(2010) 1056.

February 2012, following a decision by the European Parliament on 15 November 2011.[6] The Regulation proposes to increase the transparency of sovereign debt markets and to allow, during periods of crisis, the restriction or banning of the use of sovereign credit default swaps (CDS) – the financial products that had originally been created to hedge against the risk of sovereign default but had since become a mechanism to speculate on default. The Parliament voted on an amendment to strengthen the Commission's draft by limiting the use of credit default swaps to hedging; therefore, banning speculative transactions based on CDS. The new rules were to enter into force on 1 November 2012. This was a particularly controversial piece of legislation because it was driven by the problematic belief, widespread in the European Parliament and certain Member States, that the eurozone sovereign debt crisis was caused or at least exacerbated by 'Anglo-Saxon speculation', especially naked short-selling. It is not part of any G20 agreement. The Regulation was strongly supported by Germany, which had already adopted its own temporary unilateral ban on the naked short-selling of bank shares in May 2010 – and by France and certain Member States with real or potential solvency issues, notably Greece and Spain. It was strongly resisted by the British government as unnecessary on the grounds that short-selling was neither connected to the financial crisis nor a significant cause of the sovereign debt crisis. Italy also opposed some aspects of the proposals over concerns that they would reduce the liquidity of government bond markets, with potential consequences for the issuance of Italian debt.

In October, the Commission adopted proposals for a Regulation on insider dealing and market manipulation (market abuse) (Commission, 2011d), and for a Directive on criminal sanctions for insider dealing and market manipulation (Commission, 2011e). In November, the Commission put forward a proposal for a Regulation on the quality of audits of public-interest entities (Commission, 2011f), and a proposal for a Directive to enhance the single market for statutory audits (Commission, 2011g). Finally, the lack of developments in specific areas should be considered as significant. After prolonged consultations, the Commission was due to come forward with a proposal on crisis management – a key piece of legislation still missing from the EU's response to the financial crisis. However, due to major disagreement amongst the Member States and the Commission and concerns around the market impact of the proposal given ongoing bank funding proposals, this proposal was delayed.

II. Tightening the Rules on OTC Derivatives

In September 2010, the Commission proposed the European Market Infrastructure Regulation (EMIR). The proposed legislation aimed to ensure the transparency of OTC derivatives transactions and to reduce the risks associated with these products by shifting where possible OTC derivatives trading to central counterparties (CCPs). These CCPs would reduce counterparty risks because they act as intermediaries between sellers and buyers of derivative products. They would ensure the solvency of their participants by requesting deposits and margin calls. The proposed Regulation also would involve the creation of harmonized rules for CCPs and EU supervision of trade repositories. The reporting of all

[6] See the European Parliament's legislative observatory for an overview of the legislative process on the short-selling Regulation at: «http://www.europarl.europa.eu/oeil/popups/ficheprocedure.do?id=587269».

transactions would be mandatory and would provide supervisory authorities with the full picture of these markets.

EMIR was considered a critical piece of legislation by the Commission and Member States in order to meet G20 commitments at the September 2009 Pittsburgh summit. It was initially conceived by the Commission as a Directive, but it quickly changed to become a Regulation. This distinction is important, as Regulations are enacted into law with immediate effect in EU Member States, with no discretion over their interpretation. EMIR was driven by the Commission with general support from the German and French government,[7] although the Germans presented determined opposition to a core element of the Commission's draft Regulation. The British government was broadly in favour, but also opposed specific institutional elements of the Commission's draft (see below). The European Parliament and the Council agreed on their negotiating positions in July 2011 and October 2011, respectively. Subsequently, a series of trialogues between the Council, the Parliament and the Commission took place. The final (Level 1) text of the Regulation was finally agreed in March 2012. In early 2012, the European Securities Markets Authority (ESMA) was in the process of drafting Level 2 (specific) rules that support the Level 1 (framework) Regulation.

Despite the broad consensus about the two main pillars of the Regulation, the need for central clearing and reporting, there were a handful of controversial issues in the negotiation of EMIR, largely linked to national sensitivities, rooted in different configurations of the national financial system and competitiveness concerns. First, there were disagreements as to the scope of the Regulation and whether it should refer only to OTC derivatives (that is, derivatives not traded on a regulated market), as mandated by the G20 and as maintained by Germany, or to all derivatives, including those traded on stock exchanges, as argued by the United Kingdom.[8] The question of scope was linked to the issues of access and interoperability. All these issues had implications for competition between exchanges and clearing firms across the EU, as well as outside it.

According to the open access provisions, exchanges would have to allow clients to access any CCP, while clearing houses would be obliged to accept any trade executed at another venue. This presupposed 'interoperability' in terms of compatible technical requirements as well as compatible processes, business practices and fees. Germany's Deutsche Börse, which was a major player in trading and clearing derivatives, operated a 'vertical silos' structure, as in the Polish stock exchange and unlike other exchanges in Europe, including notably the London Stock Exchange (LSE). In a vertical structure, the stock exchange incorporates trading and post-trading services of clearing and settlement. The Deutsche Börse, therefore, had most to lose from open access provisions because these changes would split its vertical model.

Not surprisingly, German and Polish policy-makers opposed open access, arguing that the extension of the scope was not in line with G20 commitments. They also saw it as an attack on the successful business model of their national stock exchanges.[9] British policy-makers, supported by the Dutch and Scandinavians, were in favour of open access, arguing that it would allow independent CCPs to compete with those that were tied to an

[7] *European Voice*, 10 June 2010.
[8] *Financial Times*, 13 May 2011 and 4 October 2011.
[9] *Financial Times*, 4 October 2011; *Risk Magazine*, 29 September 2011.

exchange. The LSE could gain market share from any break-up in the vertical silos models, even though the British authorities claimed that they advocated open access with a view to closing potential loopholes in the legislation and ensuring end user choice.[10]

The initial Commission proposal only covered the OTC market, but in a hearing before the Parliament, Patrick Pearson, head of the Financial Markets Infrastructure Unit at the Commission, argued for the scope to be extended to all derivatives. The Council of Ministers considered the possibility of expanding the scope of new market infrastructure legislation to include exchange-traded derivatives, but Germany and German members in the European Parliament resisted this. The Commission backed down, agreeing to address the issue in later legislation and the proposal eventually approved limits on EMIR's scope of clearing to OTC derivatives. It covers all segments of the OTC derivatives market (interest rates, credit, equity, foreign exchange and commodities) and there are some exemptions from clearing and reporting requirements for non-financial firms. An article on the access of CCPs to venues of executions was included in the final draft, giving access rights of CCPs to transactions traded on a venue of execution. However, this provision does not imply the implementation of interoperability arrangements between those CCPs.[11]

The second controversial issue in EMIR concerned the location of CCPs and their access to central bank liquidity. Some regulators – notably the French – believed that CCPs clearing over-the-counter derivatives should have access to central bank liquidity in the same currency as the product being cleared. They linked the liquidity issue to the question of where CCPs should be physically located. In other words, a CCP would have to be located in the eurozone and clear euro-denominated products in order to access European Central Bank (ECB) liquidity. The British authorities opposed this view because it would be to the detriment of clearing houses located outside the eurozone – first and foremost those currently operating in the London OTC markets: LCH.Clearnet and Ice Clear Europe. These clearing houses argued that they did not need access to central bank liquidity to ensure their resilience. Central banks were reluctant to provide such support.[12] The final text established that CCPs' access to liquidity could result from access to central bank or to creditworthy and reliable commercial bank liquidity, or a combination of both. Regardless of the final provisions in EMIR, the position of London as the home of the eurozone's largest clearing house was already under threat. In the summer of 2011, the ECB issued a policy paper, requiring clearing houses to be based in the eurozone if they handle more than 5 per cent of the market in a euro-denominated financial product. The British government brought a legal case against the ECB on this, arguing that the ECB's policy restricted the free movement of capital and infringed on the right to establish cross-border businesses in the EU.[13]

The third issue concerned the powers of ESMA. MEPs wanted to give this newly created authority significant powers. By contrast, some Member States, including the United Kingdom and Germany, were reluctant to do so and had a blocking minority in the Council. The role of ESMA in authorizing CCPs for the OTC derivatives markets was particularly controversial. Neither the United Kingdom nor Germany wanted to allow a

[10] *Risk Magazine*, 12 March 2011.
[11] *Europa*, 29 March 2012. Available at: «http://europa.eu/rapid/pressReleasesAction.do?reference=MEMO/12/232&format=HTML&aged=0&language=EN&guiLanguage=en».
[12] *Risk Magazine*, 10 January 2011.
[13] *Financial Times*, 14 September 2011.

European entity to have the final word on CCP authorization to clear OTC products. The United Kingdom opposed ESMA binding mediation and sought to weaken the power of colleges for fear of being discriminated against as a clearing venue located outside the eurozone. Other policy-makers, such as the Czech central bank, opposed an expanded supervisory role for ESMA.[14] The final compromise largely preserved the powers of ESMA outlined in the Commission's original draft Regulation.

EMIR delegates responsibility to ESMA to draft and implement regulatory technical standards. As part of that responsibility, it would have to decide which classes of derivatives should be subject to mandatory clearing, and whether or not, for example, the EU should follow the lead of the United States Treasury in exempting foreign exchange swaps and forwards.[15] ESMA was to be responsible for the supervision of trade repositories and was to be a member of the colleges supporting national authorities supervising CCPs operating in several Member States.

According to the proposed legislation, authorities would be granted access to the data of trade repositories (owned by private companies) – in particular details of derivatives transactions. Issues such as the number and location of trade repositories, their regulation and data access were subject to a prolonged debate. For example, the American authorities argued in favour of one trade repository per asset class. The Depository Trust and Clearing Corporation (DTCC, an American post-trade group) was to launch an interest rate swap data repository in London in November 2012 and had another planned for commodities and foreign exchange.[16]

The Dodd-Frank Act – the most significant American regulatory response to the international financial crisis – mandated that American-based swap data repositories obtain indemnification from foreign regulators before sharing information. Foreign regulators, including EU regulators, were unlikely to accept such conditions and repositories based in the United States might be prevented from sharing information with EU regulators. The EU could thus have an incentive to create its own repositories. There were also fears that the EU could decide to include similar provisions in EMIR, which would have been unacceptable to American regulators.[17]

The debate on the third-country regime under EMIR was especially complex. These provisions needed to guarantee legal certainty while avoiding over- or 'under'-laps with similar legislation in other areas of the world and to ensure an international level playing field for EU CCPs while abiding by World Trade Organization (WTO) obligations. Some parties involved, including French policy-makers, called for reciprocal provisions – for example, concerning access to data held in repositories outside of a regulator's geographic jurisdiction, as mentioned above. Others, including the British, objected to the concept of reciprocity on the grounds of ensuring open markets. They also argued that it could jeopardize EU commitments under the WTO.[18] The final text established that recognition of a third-country CCP by ESMA would first require an equivalence decision by the Commission, after ascertaining that the legal and supervisory framework of that third country was equivalent to that of the EU. ESMA should also have established co-operation

[14] *Risk Magazine*, 12 February 2012.
[15] *Central Banking*, 12 March 2012.
[16] *Financial Times*, 25 August 2011.
[17] *Financial Times*, 10 October 2011.
[18] Interviews with senior Commission and Member State representation policy-makers, Brussels, March 2011–March 2012.

arrangements with the third-country competent authorities.[19] Recognition of a third-country trade repository would also be subject to equivalence decisions by the Commission. In addition, there was to be an international agreement in place between the Commission and that third country with regard to mutual access to data and exchange of information on OTC derivatives contracts held in trade repositories.

III. The Tussle over New EU Capital Legislation

At the international level, the G20 adopted a range of guidelines on financial matters in the aftermath of the international financial crisis, including higher capital requirements for banks and other financial institutions. At the BIS, the BCBS moved to adopt an agreement on tighter rules on bank capital requirements, which the EU and its Member States were expected to implement into Union and national legislation. In December 2010, the Basel III Accord was signed by the BCBS (BCBS, 2010). Intergovernmental and inter-institutional debates on the implementation of Basel III guidelines into EU law were intense throughout the year. In the past, the implementation of Basel Accord guidelines into EU law, as the Capital Requirements Directive (CRD) and amendments, proceeded with limited debate. This reflects in large part the less restrictive nature of previous versions of the accord. The implementation of the Basel III rules in the EU as the CRDIV-CRR met with considerably more disagreement among the Member States.

The new Basel III rules provide a more restrictive definition of what counts as capital, increase the proportion of capital that must be of proven loss absorbing capacity – that is, core Tier 1 (narrowly defined, equity) capital, over Basel II requirements. They increase the risk weight of several asset classes and introduce capital buffers; set up a recommended and potentially obligatory leverage ratio; and outline international rules on liquidity management. The rules are meant to be phased in gradually from January 2013 until 2019, allowing undercapitalized/heavily leveraged banks time to readjust.

In July 2011, after extensive consultation conducted in parallel with the work of the BCBS, the EU Commission adopted the CRDIV-CRR legislative package designed to replace the CRDII with a Directive that governs the access to deposit-taking activities (Commission, 2011a) and a Regulation that establishes prudential requirements for credit institutions (Commission, 2011b). After its approval, the proposed Directive would have to be transposed by the Member States in a manner suitable to their own national institutional framework environment. It covers the conditions for the freedom of establishment and the freedom to provide banking services, the supervisory review process and the definition of competent authorities.

The Directive incorporates an important element of the Basel III Accord – namely the introduction of two capital buffers on top of the minimum capital requirements. First, all EU-based banks would be expected to adopt a capital conservation buffer of 2.5 per cent core equity Tier 1 capital (CET1), which added to regulatory capital means that by 2019 banks would have to hold 7 per cent CET1. Second, the proposed Directive provides for a counter-cyclical capital buffer of up to 2.5 per cent to be determined at national level which, again, could only be met by CET1. The CRR implements Basel III's definitions of 'capital'

[19] *Europa*, 29 March 2012. Available at: «http://europa.eu/rapid/pressReleasesAction.do?reference=MEMO/12/232&format=HTML&aged=0&language=EN&guiLanguage=en».

(CET1, Tier 1 and Tier 2) and rules on increased own funds and the quality of these funds. The proposed Regulation introduces the Liquidity Coverage Ratio (LCR), which is to dictate the amount of liquid capital banks must hold to fund themselves for a limited period in the event of a crisis and the failure of wholesale markets. The LCR's exact composition and calibration would be determined after an observation and review period in 2015.

The Regulation also introduces the requirement to consider a leverage ratio, subject to supervisory review. The use of a Regulation, which once approved is directly applicable without the need for national transposition, was designed to ensure the creation of a single rule book in the EU. The Regulation eliminates a key source of national divergence. In the CRD II, more than a hundred national discretions (differences in national legislation transposing the EU Directive) remained. Further, the Commission proposed a *maximum* Tier 1 ratio in the context of the CRR, which differs from the Basel III guidelines that set a minimum level to be attained – that individual countries can choose to exceed. Many observers saw this as a plug to alleviate the concerns of banks and governments that feared that the stronger capital position of some banks could be used to gain competitive advantage.[20]

The Commission's CRDIV-CRR draft was the most substantial of all the post-financial crisis regulatory measures entertained to date at the EU level but the draft also involved watering down or modifying the Basel III guidelines in important ways to meet EU Member State demands and, as a result, was widely criticized by regulators and the IMF.[21] Several EU Member States (notably France and Germany), the European Parliament and the Commission itself called for the taking into account of 'European specificities' in incorporating the Basel III rules into the CRD IV, reopening some of the issues that had caused friction within the BCBS. Basel III applied to internationally active banks, whereas EU legislation was to apply to all banks, making some Basel III provisions (notably the calculation of CET1) impossible to apply without a significant shift in the structure of the liabilities of a large range of banks. The European Parliament also emphasized competition concerns and the need to ensure an 'international level playing field'. Of particular concern was the fact that in the United States, the Basel III Accord would be applied only to financial institutions with over US$50 billion in assets (EP, 2010, 2011).

The Commission 'softened' its definition of Core Equity Tier 1 capital relative to the Basel III recommendations in some areas, effectively allowing 'silent participations' – that is, state loans that make up a significant part of bank capital in a range of countries, notably German banks and specifically the public Landesbanken. The Commission's draft limits the role of the leverage ratio designed to limit risk-taking at banks and allows the double counting of banks' insurance subsidiaries' capital allowed under the 2002 Financial Conglomerates Directive (FiCOD). The almost unique reliance on the risk-weighted Core Equity Tier 1 ratio in the Commission's draft, which was in line with what was agreed in Basel IIII, was also criticized by the IMF, the Organisation for Economic Co-operation and Development (OECD) and several EU Member State governments for inadequately representing the health of the European banking sector.[22] These international bodies and Member State governments have argued in favour of the adoption of EU

[20] See IMF (2011a); *Financial Times*, 2 April 2012.
[21] See IMF (2011a); *Financial Times*, 30 January 2012.
[22] *Financial Times*, 30 January 2012.

standards that exceeded the Basel minimum because of prevailing balance sheet uncertainties in the EU, the lack of EU-wide resolution arrangements and a fully unified fiscal backstop. The Commission ignored these IMF and OECD recommendations.

On liquidity, the Commission adopted the less prescriptive definition of liquid assets for the LCR to include not only 'transferable assets that are of extremely high liquidity and credit quality' but also 'transferable assets that are of high liquidity and credit quality'. The Commission's draft lacks a firm commitment to implement the Net Stable Funding Ratio (NSFR) by 2018 called for in Basel III. The proposed Regulation also sets higher capital requirements for OTC derivatives that are not cleared though CCPs.

Most of the modifications to Basel III in CRDIV-CRR are due largely to French and German demands reflecting concerns over the capital position of their national banks, the likely impact of recapitalization on their competitiveness and/or the impact of de-leveraging on bank lending. The studies and impact assessments of the BCBS were conducted at the aggregate level. Nonetheless, even the BCBS warned about differentiated effects across countries, without identifying which banking systems were most affected. A perusal of the core and other Tier 1 capital for systemically important British, French and German banks shows why the German government in particular had good reason to oppose the rigid tightening of capital requirements (see Tables 1 and 2). Data on Tier 1 capital suggest that most of the main British, French and German banks would have

Table 1: Tier 1 Capital (as a Percentage of Total Assets) Main British, German and French Systematically Important Banks (Non-weighted Average)*

Recall: Basel III target of 6%, or 8.5% with the 'capital conservation buffer' by 2019	*2012 baseline scenario*	*2012 adverse conditions*	*2011 baseline scenario*	*2011 adverse conditions*
United Kingdom	10.4	7.45	9.75	7.95
France	9.0	7.4	8.5	7.7
Germany	8.8	6.4	7.85	6.75

Source: European Banking Authority.
Notes: * Results of the stress test based on the full static balance sheet assumption without any mitigating actions, mandatory restructuring or capital raisings post-31 December 2010/11 (all government support measures fully paid in before 31 December 2010/11 are included). Figures cover the largest four banks in United Kingdom and France and largest two in Germany.

Table 2: Bank Equity (Core Tier 1) as Percentage of Total Assets

Recall: Core Tier 1 ratio of 4.5%, or 7% with the 'capital conservation buffer' by 2019	*United Kingdom*	*France*	*Germany*
2008	3.7	3.8	2.93
2009	4.87	4.91	3.76
2010	5.37	5.07	3.88

Source: ECB statistical data warehouse: «http://sdw.ecb.europa.eu/».
Note: Domestic banking group and stand-alone banks only.

limited difficulties to meet the Basel III standards. However, many struggle to meet the target when the capital conservation buffer is added. The estimates for the adverse situation in 2012 include exposure to eurozone sovereign debt, to which German and French banks were particularly exposed. With the massive write-downs already agreed in the context of the March 2012 Greek debt swap, the baseline scenario presented an exaggerated picture of the health of French and German banks.

The data on Tier 1 capital holdings in Table 1 is misleading because of the double counting of insurance subsidiaries' capital which inflates figures in several EU Member States significantly, especially those for French banks. The Basel III ban on the double counting of capital in banks' insurance subsidiaries would hit French banks particularly hard because of the long-standing feature of *bancassurance*, in which insurance companies (often subsidiaries of banks) make use of banks to market their products. The IMF estimated a ban on double counting would result in French banks losing a total of 28.9 per cent of their Tier 1 capital, preventing several from meeting the 6 per cent threshold and all from meeting the 8.5 per cent threshold (with the capital conservation buffer to be in place from 2019) (IMF, 2011b). *Bancassurance* predominated in certain other EU Member States, including Spain and Austria. Heavy lobbying by banks ensured that the Commission's CRDIV draft removed the ban on double counting.

The implications of Basel III were potentially greatest for the many non-listed public sector and mutual banks on the continent which did not use equity, relying instead on other capital to meet requirements, including 'hybrid' capital.[23] Proportionately, the ban on hybrids would hit the German banking system hardest and in particular the Landesbanken which, lacking in equity, used 'silent participations' in their calculation of Tier 1 capital. However, as the efforts of Commerzbank in early 2012 to replace its hybrid capital with equity demonstrate, the German commercial banks are also exposed to Basel III rules on Tier 1 capital. The EBA stress tests in the autumn of 2011 found that NordLB, one of the most exposed Landesbanken, held 4.8 per cent Tier 1 capital on its baseline scenario and 3.7 per cent on the adverse scenario. Many of the Landesbanken fell far short of the 6 per cent threshold and all were far off the 8.5 per cent threshold that includes the 'capital conservation buffer'.

German opposition to the use of a leverage ratio owed to the much higher leverage ratios of most of its large commercial and public banks (compared to both France and the United Kingdom) and in particular the difficulty of the German Landesbanken in meeting the Basel III target. In 2010, no German Landesbanken came anywhere near the recommended threshold of 33.3 (or 3 per cent equity) and HSH Nordbank had a leverage ratio of 83.16. While the leverage ratios of British banks increased dramatically in the two years prior to the outbreak of the financial crisis, they had been historically amongst the lowest in the EU. The figures for French banks appear similarly low. However, the Basel III ban on double counting the capital of insurance subsidiaries – if adopted into EU legislation – would hit leverage ratios for several French banks. Previous Basel guidelines and current EU rules on bank capital allow banks to amass assets with high credit ratings without setting capital aside to cover potential losses. This has allowed many banks in Europe to become highly leveraged despite meeting international rules on capital cushions.

[23] 'Hybrids' are instruments that have some features of both debt and equity.

Table 3: Bank Customer Funding Gap (Loans – Deposits, in € billions) and as Percentage of Loans

	United Kingdom	*France*	*Germany*
2007	24	29.2	24.5
2011	8	20.4	17.4

Sources: Central bank data; Bank of England (2011, p. 17, chart 2.6).
Note: Non-MFI lending and deposits.

National positions on CRDIV-CRR reflect national banking systems and the likely impact of tighter capital rules on bank lending and the wider economy. British and French commercial banks were better capitalized because, on average, they relied more on equity finance in relative terms than banks in several other continental European countries including Germany (see Table 2). As noted above, many banks on the continent such as the publicly owned German Landesbanken, Co-operative and Savings Banks and most French Mutuals did not have equity finance. Indeed, this aspect proved problematic in the incorporation of the Basel III Accord into EU legislation, which contains specific provisions for the co-operative and mutual banks. Basel III was written having in mind banks funded by equity finance (hence the emphasis on common equities in core Tier 1 capital), whereas many banks in the EU are based on other sources of funding.

The capital position of British banks improved in part because of government intervention in the banking system which to the end of 2009 involved share purchases amounting to over 6 per cent of the United Kingdom's 2009 GDP. No other Member State share purchase programme came close to reaching British levels in real terms, and only Ireland exceeded the United Kingdom in terms relative to GDP.[24] Two of the systemically important British banks (RBS and Lloyds TSB) thus had a massive leg-up in meeting Basel III rules and two others, HSBC and Barclays, succeeded in raising capital in large equity issues in the early stages of the international financial crisis.

Basel III includes a prolonged phase-in period for the LCR (to 2015) and the NSFR (2018), while the Commission's CRDIV-CRR draft waters down the LCR and fails to impose the NSFR. This gradualism and flexibility can be explained by concerns about the potential impact of these liquidity measures on lending. Different national positions on CRDIV-CRR liquidity rules owed to differing reliance on short-term wholesale markets and the different rate at which exposure has been reduced since the height of the financial crisis in 2008. British banks had gone the furthest to reduce their reliance – down from over 60 per cent of GDP in 2007 to just over 30 per cent at the end of 2010 (Bank of England, 2011) – and increase the resilience of their funding positions. British banks and British authorities were broadly comfortable with Basel III's liquidity rules and ambitious phase-in dates.

Another metric to demonstrate bank exposure to 'non-traditional' forms of funding is the customer funding gap – the gap between non-financial companies (NFC) loans and deposits (Table 3). The substantial decline in the British bank funding gap largely stemmed from a massive decline in lending. (Further, major British banks' holdings of highly liquid assets almost tripled from 2008 to the end of 2011, accounting for 14 per cent of their total assets

[24] Source: National Central Bank figures.

in November 2011 [Bank of England, 2011].) The funding gap for French banks had also declined, but remained far higher than British figures in both real and relative terms. While German banks relied little on short-term funding, they were heavily dependent on covered bonds, the use of which Basel III liquidity rules would have discouraged with higher risk weighting. Funding gap figures for German banks help to explain the caution of the German government and regulators on liquidity rules and the less prescriptive definition of liquidity in CRDIV-CRR as opposed to Basel III.

The BCBS accepted the negative implications of pushing too hard and too fast with capital rules – especially in the aftermath of a deep post-crisis recession in many European countries (BCBS, 2010). These concerns were particularly acute in some national capitals, while the British government appeared less preoccupied. Since the outbreak of the financial crisis, the largest British banks had raised equity and cut lending dramatically (with 2011 national lending figures 22 per cent off the 2007 peak). In contrast, bank lending in France and Germany remained comparatively strong since the outbreak of the financial crisis – consistently and significantly above 2007 levels – limited principally by growth in the broader economy rather than the de-leveraging efforts of banks.[25] Forcing French and, more significantly, German banks to deleverage during a recessionary period could result in a credit crunch if banks reduced their lending instead of boosting their capital. Banks would struggle to lift the equity numerator and thus cut the risk-weighted assets denominator instead, which the French and German governments argued would hit lending to the real economy.

One IMF study from 2011 on the differential impact of Basel III rules on national banking systems echoes the findings in a range of other studies: to demonstrate a particularly significant impact upon bank lending in Germany and comparatively small drop in the United Kingdom, with France somewhere in between (Cosimano and Hakura, 2011). In April 2012, the IMF estimated that deleveraging would result in EU banks reducing their balance sheets by over €2.6 trillion (IMF, 2012). Particularly hard hit would be banks and economies in the eurozone periphery and in much of central and eastern Europe, which relied heavily on lending by western Europe-based banks (IMF, 2012).

It is important to note that the Commission draft did not just respond to the concerns of continental EU Member States: it also took on board the concerns of British banks and the British government. Notably, the Commission's CRDIV draft allows exposures to real estate to continue to benefit from a much more favourable risk weighting as compared to company loans. The bias towards real estate investments is maintained, with a risk weighting of half (or even less) of real exposure, even for commercial property.

Other national sensitivities remained to be negotiated. Basel III/CRDIV-CRR liquidity rules discourage the holding of a range of assets including covered bonds and encourage the holding of more liquid and historically reliable assets, including (some would argue ironically) government bonds. New rules forcing a reduction in covered bond holding would hit harder the banks and economies of specific European economies where banks were engaged in more covered bond issues, including Germany, whose Pfandbrief covered bond market was the biggest in the world. However, Denmark would likely be hit

[25] In 2007, French banks lent a total of €764.7 billion to NFCs in the eurozone with lending figures rising annually to €877.5 billion in 2011. In Germany, lending figures have fluctuated more, but remained consistently above 2007 levels (€859.4 billion) at €906.8 billion in 2011 (ECB statistical data warehouse: «http://sdw.ecb.europa.eu/»).

the hardest because Danish bank-covered bond issues were largely concentrated in home loans.[26] The two largest mortgage banks in the country, Nykredit and Realkredit, funded their mortgage lending entirely through covered bonds secured on the underlying mortgages. In 2009, Danish banks held only €11 billion of liquidity in government bonds but €140 billion in covered bonds. Liquidity rules discouraging the use of covered bonds would dramatically limit household access to credit. Ironically, covered bonds had previously been considered a very safe form of securitization, actively encouraged by the ECB, which purchased many billions of euros worth to encourage banks to lend in the aftermath of the financial crisis. Opponents of the new rules on covered bonds argued that they survived the financial crisis intact and in their long history had never defaulted and thus should not be treated by regulators with the same distrust as riskier securities such as collateralized debt obligations (CDOs) based on American sub-prime mortgages.

Not Going Far Enough?

There have been a range of criticisms of both Basel III and the CRDIV-CRR package by governments (notably the British and the Swedish), the IMF, the OECD and a range of independent think tanks (see, for example, Finance Watch, 2012). On 19 May, in anticipation of the adoption of a maximum ratio, the lack of a binding timetable and other deviations from key provisions in Basel III, the finance ministers of seven Member States (the United Kingdom, Sweden, Spain, Bulgaria, Estonia, Lithuania and Slovakia) sent an open letter to Michel Barnier and Olli Rehn, the Commissioners for Internal Market and Services and Economic and Monetary Affairs, respectively (Djankov *et al.*, 2011).[27] These finance ministers argued that proposed EU rules 'would be damaging to European financial stability and the EU's international credibility on these issues' (Djankov *et al.*, 2011, p. 3). More specifically, the seven finance ministers attacked maximum capital requirements to be imposed by the CRR. The Commission argued that a maximum rule was necessary to protect the integrity of the internal market and that Member States should not be allowed to set higher capital rules than others because activity would shift to those with the lowest standards, creating dangerous concentrations of risk.[28] The opposing finance ministers argued that the Basel III rules set minimum requirements which they wished to exceed to ensure that banks could cope better with a future crisis. They pointed out that there were several sound arguments against curtailing the ability of national authorities to set higher standards, including the different size of banking sectors to GDP across the EU and thus differences in the perceived appropriate level of loss absorbing capacity in the banking system. Further, they argued that 'applying macro-prudential policies required national authorities to retain the ability to increase levels of capital and liquidity requirements, or vary risk weights to address emerging financial risks' (Djankov *et al.*, 2011, p. 4). The move was also queried by the BIS as contrary to standard practice in the implementation of previous Basel guidelines on capital (Wellink, 2011). The seven finance ministers opposed any prohibitions on Member States seeking to implement new requirements earlier. The finance ministers opposed the Commission's intention to allow Member States to continue to use the Financial Conglomerates Directive approach in

[26] *Financial Times*, 6 July 2010.
[27] *Financial Times*, 25 May 2011.
[28] *Financial Times*, 2 August 2011.

relation to the deduction of material holdings in insurance entities – that is, to continue to allow the double counting of capital held by the insurance subsidiaries of banks.

IV. The European Banking Authority and European Systemic Risk Board in Action

The European System of Financial Supervisors and its three new European Supervisory Authorities (ESAs) to oversee supervision in the banking, securities and insurance markets came into existence at the start of 2011. The ESAs have the power to draw up harmonized technical standards for national supervisors to apply and they can mediate in the event of disputes between national regulators. The EBA, based in London, is assigned a significant role on stress-testing EU banks and resolution issues for cross-border systemically important financial institutions (SIFIs). In 2011, the EBA engaged in the second and third rounds of EU-wide stress tests. The results of the second, published in mid-July, found eight banks to have failed, including five Spanish banks, with the German Landesbank Helaba withdrawing from the tests. Yet, as with the first EU-wide tests, the second was widely criticized for not having rigorously tested banks.[29] The third, in December, was noteworthy for its improved rigour. The EBA enjoyed a degree of autonomy to set the standard for its tests, although it relied upon the ECB which designed them. In October, following widespread criticism of the first two EU-wide tests in 2010 and mid-2011, the EBA engaged in talks with European officials and governments over mechanisms that could be used to forcibly recapitalize banks, enabling them to cope with sovereign defaults. An important political signal to progress on bank recapitalization came from Angela Merkel, the German chancellor, who in October publicly accepted the need to recapitalize her country's banks, if necessary, and sought to discuss EU-wide bank support efforts at the October EU summit.[30] The EBA increased both the Tier 1 capital threshold demanded to 9 per cent (above the level required under Basel III) and tightened the modelling of the 'adverse scenario' to include write-downs on all eurozone periphery sovereign debt. A total of 37 banks failed the EBA's December test. The EBA gave them until the end of June 2012 to make up the €114.7 billion shortfall of core Tier 1 capital that was uncovered. The EBA also demanded that EU banks raise a €39.4 billion sovereign buffer to insulate themselves against losses in the government bond market. However, under pressure from governments and banks, the EBA subsequently acknowledged that this recapitalization might have to be relaxed given the difficulty that several banks faced in raising capital (Attwood, 2012).

The ESAs were not, however, to supervise financial institutions directly;[31] this was left to national authorities aided by cross-border 'colleges' created for all cross-border EEA banks and insurance companies with a strong international presence. There had been a significant clash between the European Parliament and the Council and disagreements among Member States on the powers of the new authorities over national supervisors, with notably the United Kingdom opposed to any transfer of powers (Buckley and

[29] *Financial Times*, 15 July 2011.
[30] *Financial Times*, 5 October 2011.
[31] One exception is credit rating agencies which were to be directly supervised by the ESMA. The ESMA was also likely to be given direct supervisory powers over trade repositories as a result of the EMIR Regulation, but this met resistance from the British government.

Howarth, 2010). While the creation of the Single Rulebook on technical standards for national supervisors might be considered as potentially significant, the actual contribution of the authorities to financial stability remained to be seen. Nonetheless, the aggressive positioning of the EBA on stress tests and recapitalization met with British government approval.[32]

The ESRB completed its first year of operation in 2011. Chaired by the president of the ECB and including representatives of national central banks and the heads of the ESAs on a revolving annual basis, the ESRB's core task was to monitor the build-up of risk at the level of the financial system. The Board focused on systemic issues resulting from dollar funding and lending in foreign currencies. It also weighed in on the negotiations around CRDIV-CRR, supporting calls by the United Kingdom, Sweden and others that Member States should be granted more powers to address macro-issues at a national level and to go beyond the requirements of Basel III if they believed it necessary for national stability. This prompted inter-institutional disagreement between the ESRB and Commission, which was likely to continue given their divergent mandates of, respectively, financial stability and internal market integrity.

Conclusions

This overview of two of the main pieces of EU financial legislation developed in 2011 demonstrates the extent to which they were designed and subsequently shaped to respond to the preoccupations of powerful EU Member States linked to domestic institutional frameworks and national financial systems. On OTC derivatives, EMIR was modified to accommodate German concerns about the incompatibility of the national stock exchange, a major European player in trading and clearing derivatives, with the legislation as initially drafted by the Commission. The CRDIV-CRR was drafted by the Commission to take into consideration European specificities in the implementation of international guidelines on capital requirements and, in particular, French and German concerns on, respectively, the double counting of insurance subsidiary capital and the use of hybrid capital to meet minimum capital thresholds and the definition of liquidity ratios. The Commission's draft and subsequent positioning directly challenged British and other Member State government's preference to push for higher requirements in order to reinforce the stability of nationally based banks and avoid a repeat of 2007–09 when huge amounts of public money were spent to avoid bank collapse.

Financial regulation continued to dominate the EU legislative agenda in the early months of 2012. The intergovernmental and inter-institutional debates over MiFID and CRDIV-CRR provisions, and specifically the maximum harmonization rule, intensified. Attention also turned to major disagreements on financial regulation between the Commission and the new ESAs and the ESRB. The Commission pushed to defend the integrity of the single market and continued to be sensitive to Member State concerns about the impact of financial regulation (and bank recapitalization) on national economies. The ESAs and the ESRB prioritized the reinforcement of financial system stability. The ESRB's public contradiction of the Commission for setting a maximum harmonization in the CRR was met with the Commission retort that the ESRB should not go public on

[32] *Financial Times*, 8 December 2011.

matters where the Commission has right of legislative initiative (PWC, 2011). Similarly, the ESMA and Commission expressed strongly diverging views on the implementation of the Alternative Investment Fund Managers Directive (adopted in 2010) affecting a range of issues including the treatment of third-country funds, depositories, delegation, leverage, own funds, professional indemnity insurance, appointment of prime brokers and calculation of assets under management (Agnew, 2012).

There were also new pieces of legislation and policy statements sparking debate, including proposed rules on auditors. In the summer of 2012, the Commission was to publish its report on the structure of EU banking, which was to be, in effect, its response to the Vickers Report on British banks.[33] In May 2012, the BCBS published its consultation for a fundamental review of the trading book, which would eventually feed into new EU legislation. Gaping holes in the EU's financial regulatory framework remained – notably its lack of cross-border resolution and crisis management regimes. Financial regulation, which dominated internal market legislation since 2008, looked set to continue this dominance for the foreseeable future.

References

Agnew, H. (2012) 'Hedge Fund Body Slams AIFMD Split'. *Financial News*, 17 April. Available at: «http://www.efinancialnews.com/story/2012-04-17/aima-report-aifmd-european-commission-divergence-esma».

Attwood, M. (2012) 'Thou Shalt Maintain 9% Core Tier 1 Capital'. *Financial News*, 20 February. Available at: «http://www.efinancialnews.com/story/2012-02-20/thou-shalt-maintain-9-percent-core-tier-1-capital».

Bank of England (2011) *Financial Stability Report* (London: Bank of England).

Basel Committee on Banking Supervision (BCBS) (2010) 'Assessing the Macroeconomic Impact of the Transition to Stronger Capital and Liquidity Requirements: Final Report', 17 December. Available at: «http://www.bis.org/publ/othp12.htm».

Buckley, J. and Howarth, D. (2010) 'Gesture Politics? Explaining Financial Regulatory Reform in the European Union'. *JCMS*, Vol. 48, No. S1, pp. 119–41.

Buckley, J. and Howarth, D. (2011) 'Regulating the So-Called "Vultures of Capitalism" '. *JCMS*, Vol. 49, No. S1, pp. 123–43.

Commission of the European Communities (2010) 'Proposal for a Regulation of the European Parliament and of the Council on OTC derivatives, central counterparties and trade repositories'. *COM*(2010)484, SEC(2010)1059.

Commission of the European Communities (2011a) 'Proposal for a Directive on the access to the activity of credit institutions and the prudential supervision of credit institutions and investment firms'. 2011/453/EC, 20 July.

Commission of the European Communities (2011b) 'Proposal for a Regulation on prudential requirements for credit institutions and investment firms'. 2011/452/EC, 20 July.

Commission of the European Communities (2011c). 'New rules for more efficient, resilient and transparent financial markets in Europe'. Press Release, 20 October. Available at: «http://europa.eu/rapid/pressReleasesAction.do?reference=IP/11/1219&format=HTML&aged=0&language=EN&guiLanguage=en».

Commission of the European Communities (2011d) 'Proposal for a Regulation of the European Parliament and of the Council on insider dealing and market manipulation (market abuse)'. *COM*(2011) 651 final, 2011/0295 (COD), Brussels, 20 October.

[33] Available at: «http://bankingcommission.independent.gov.uk/».

Commission of the European Communities (2011e) 'Proposal for a Directive of the European Parliament and of the Council on criminal sanctions for insider dealing and market manipulation'. *COM*(2011) 654 final, 2011/0297 (COD), Brussels, 20 October.

Commission of the European Communities (2011f) 'Proposal for a Regulation of the European Parliament and of the Council on specific requirements regarding statutory audit of public-interest entities'. *COM*(2011) 779/3, 2011/0359 (COD), Brussels.

Commission of the European Communities (2011g) 'Proposal for a Directive of the European Parliament and of the Council amending Directive 2006/43/EC on statutory audits of annual accounts and consolidated accounts'. *COM*(2011) 778, Brussels.

Cosimano, T.F. and Hakura, D.S. (2011) 'Bank Behavior in Response to Basel III: A Cross-country Analysis'. IMF Working Paper WP/11/119 (Washington, DC: International Monetary Fund).

Djankov, S. *et al.* (2011) 'Letter to Commissioners Michel Barnier and Olli Rehn', May. Available at: «http://www.secure-finance.com/analyses/1110.pdf».

European Parliament (EP) (2010) 'Resolution on Basel II and revision of the Capital Requirements Directives (CRD 4)'. Committee of Economic and Monetary Affairs, Brussels, 21 September.

European Parliament (EP) (2011) 'Draft Report on the proposal for a Regulation of the European Parliament and of the Council on prudential requirements for credit institutions and investment firms'. Committee on Economic and Monetary Affairs, Rapporteur: Othmar Karas.

Finance Watch (2012) 'To End All Crises? Implementing Basel III in the European Union: A Position Paper on CRDIV/CRR'. Available at: «http://www.finance-watch.org/2012/02/1-february-2012-download-finance-watchs-position-paper-on-crd-iv-crr-to-end-all-crises/».

International Monetary Fund (IMF) (2011a) *United Kingdom: 2011 Article IV Consultation – Staff Report*. IMF Country Report 11/220, July (Washington, DC: IMF).

International Monetary Fund (IMF) (2011b) *France: Selected Issues Paper*. IMF Country Report 11/212, July (Washington, DC: IMF).

International Monetary Fund (IMF) (2012) 'World Economic Outlook: Growth Resuming, Dangers Remain', April. Available at: «http://www.imf.org/external/pubs/ft/weo/2012/01/pdf/text.pdf».

PricewaterhouseCoopers (PWC) (2011) 'Special Edition on the Capital Requirements Directive IV'. Available at: «http://www.pwc.com/gx/en/financial-services/european-financial-regulation-updates/april-16-2012.jhtml#1».

Quaglia, L. (2011) 'The "Old" and "New" Political Economy of Hedge Funds Regulation in the European Union'. *West European Politics*, Vol. 34, No. 4, pp. 665–82.

Wellink, N. (2011) Speech at the ING Basel III Financing Conference, Amsterdam, 14 April. Available at: «http://www.bis.org/review/r110420a.pdf».

JCMS 2012 Volume 50 Annual Review pp. 116–131 DOI: 10.1111/j.1468-5965.2012.02271.x

Justice and Home Affairs

JÖRG MONAR
College of Europe/University of Sussex

Introduction

Developments in the justice and home affairs (JHA) domain in 2011 were much marked by the – mostly temporary – refugee and migrational movements resulting from the 'Arab Spring'. They led to serious tensions within the Schengen group, exposing the vulnerability of the Schengen open internal border system to asymmetric pressures in the absence of effective solidarity mechanisms. The reinforced role of the external border management agency Frontex could address this solidarity deficit only partially. The migratory pressures on the EU's southern borders, the EU's signing of a major Convention of the Hague Conference on Private International Law and new priorities defined for common action in the fight against organized crime highlighted the growing importance of the external dimension of EU policy-making in the JHA domain. The total annual output of the JHA Council increased slightly from 121 adopted texts the year before to 136 texts,[1] which included several substantive pieces of legislation, especially in the field of criminal justice co-operation, but also on asylum and immigration matters, where several other instruments remained under (difficult) negotiations.

I. Developments in Individual Policy Areas

Asylum Policy

Right at the start of the year the landmark ruling of the European Court of Human Rights (ECtHR) in case *M.S.S.* v *Belgium and Greece* rendered on 21 January (Monar, 2011) highlighted the persisting failure of the EU to ensure equal access of refugees to minimum protection standards in all Member States. The ruling increased the political pressure on the Greek government at the next JHA Council meeting on 24–25 February, although it had already been trying to address the critical humanitarian situation by a presidential decree to clear a backlog of over 50,000 asylum cases and the establishment of a new asylum service. The Greek efforts were not helped by the rapidly deteriorating Greek sovereign debt crisis, so that EU support became all the more important. This support took the form not only of €9.8 million made available by the Commission through the European Refugee Fund, the External Borders Fund and the Return Fund, but also the deployment of Asylum Support Teams (ASTs) consisting of an as yet undisclosed number of experts from a large number of Member States on the basis of an 'Operational Plan' signed with the Greek authorities on 1 April. This deployment of ASTs was the first operational test for the newly established European Asylum Support Office in Greece which had to

[1] Lists of texts provided by the General Secretariat of the Council and own calculations.

mobilize for the first time its 'Asylum Intervention Pool' eventually to consist of up to 300 deployable national experts in fields like registration and screening, quality and backlog management, development of reception systems and emergency accommodation (EASO, 2011). Assessing the situation in Greece at the beginning of January 2012 the Executive Director of the EASO, Robert Visser, reported 'significant progress' with the build-up of Greek asylum and reception services and a decrease of the asylum applications backlog by 30 per cent (EASO, 2012).

While the Greek asylum issues were still preoccupying the Commission and the Council, the 'Arab Spring' added to the challenges. In February and March, the number of Tunisians applying for asylum rose sharply from 50 per month in the year before to 1,100 and 1,200, respectively (Eurostat, 2011a). The increase in refugee numbers from Tunisia and the beginnings of the civil war in Libya were sufficient for Italian Interior Minister Roberto Maroni to warn his counterparts in the Council in February about an impending 'invasion' of up to 1.5 million refugees from Libya alone and to request a €100 million fund to help Mediterranean countries cope with this challenge.[2] This was rejected by the Council, and by June only a total of around 24,000 Tunisians and 20,000 persons of various nationalities had sought refuge in Italy and Malta from the unrest in Egypt and the civil war in Libya (UNHCR, 2011a) – most of whom were seeking temporary shelter and work rather than formal asylum status. Yet the 'invasion which never came' contributed to a serious temporary destabilization of the Schengen open internal border system (see below) and brought again to the fore the absence of an effective EU solidarity mechanism between Member States in case of major refugee movements. The EU did also not appear in the best possible light with regard to the large numbers of refugees fleeing from the violence in Libya – in August, an estimated 1,500 died in the Mediterranean while trying to reach the EU (UNHCR, 2011b). According to EU Commissioner Cecilia Malmström, Member States managed to agree only on accepting 400 of the 8,000 Libyan refugees in border camps between Libya and Tunisia which the UNHCR had – amongst the tens of thousands more – identified as being in particular need of help, which led the Home Affairs Commissioner to conclude that 2011 was the year in which Europe 'failed' the refugees.[3]

The problems in Greece and the wider Mediterranean increased the pressure on EU policy-makers to progress with the negotiations on the 'second-phase' legal instruments of the Common European Asylum System (CEAS) which had been proposed by the Commission from 2007 to 2009. On 1 June, the Commission tried to break the deadlock in the Council (the European Parliament was supporting most of the initial proposals) by recasting its original proposals on the Asylum Procedures and the Reception Conditions Directives. Regarding the Procedures Directive, the Commission proposed changes allowing for wider margins of flexibility for Member States in applying the procedures. This greater flexibility would apply, for instance, to decisions on the right to enter the territory and on the examination of applications at the border, as well as to new rules on addressing potential abuse of the right to asylum, including enhanced possibilities for national authorities to accelerate procedures and examine at the border claims where the applicant has made clearly false or obviously improbable representations which contradict

[2] *Deutsche Welle*, 24 February 2011.
[3] *The Times of Malta*, 19 January 2012.

sufficiently verified country-of-origin information (Commission, 2011a). With respect to the Reception Conditions Directive, the Commission tried to address the Member States concerns about high administrative constraints and costs by widening the latitude of implementation, particularly regarding guarantees for detained asylum seekers, reception conditions in detention facilities, deadlines for access to the labour market, the level of health care and access to material support. Although maintaining the general principle that detention of asylum seekers may only occur after an individual examination of each case under prescribed grounds and only if it is in line with the principles of proportionality and necessity, the Commission introduced more flexibility for national authorities on a number of particularly controversial issues in the Council such as access to free legal assistance and detention conditions in difficult geographical areas such as at border posts and in transit zones. While these proposals amounted overall to a certain lowering of the higher standards initially aimed at, the Commission – sure of strong backing from the European Parliament (EP) on this point – proposed strengthening the reception standards for vulnerable persons, especially minors (Commission, 2011b). The UNHCR broadly welcomed the proposals, but expressed concerns about the softening of the conditions under which national authorities can resort to 'accelerated' asylum procedures with reduced guarantees (UNHCR, 2011a). The proposals allowed for some new progress being made on these two instruments at Council working party level, but at the end of the year a political agreement was not yet in sight (European Council, 2011a).

Negotiations on two other key instruments remained inconclusive as well. In those on the recast Dublin Regulation, a large majority of the Member States rejected the emergency system proposed by the Commission which would allow for the temporary suspension of transfers of asylum seekers to Member States where the level of protection is considered to have fallen below EU standards (Greece having been the most obvious recent example). As this could result in a shift of the burden from Member States of first entry to those offering more attractive conditions further inside and in the north of the EU, it was perhaps not surprising that most of the Council members preferred to focus on how to better deal with asylum crises in the 'front-line' Member States (European Council, 2011a). The Commission tried to capitalize on this development in the Council through proposals under the heading of 'solidarity' and presented on 2 December on strengthening the operational support provision by the EASO, a more flexible, integrated and targeted use of the EU Return, Asylum and Migration Funds, and the introduction of early warning mechanisms and monitoring of national implementation capabilities in addition to the usual legislative monitoring (Commission, 2011c). Yet there was little movement in the negotiations on the recast EURODAC Regulation on the electronic comparison of fingerprints of asylum seekers in which an overwhelming majority of Council delegations continued to insist – against the declared position of the EP – on enabling law enforcement authorities access to the EURODAC central database (European Council, 2011a).

The year would have ended with an overall rather dismal record regarding the CEAS package were it not for the compromise on and adoption by the EP and the Council in December of the recast Asylum Qualification Directive (2011/95/EU). The Directive, which covers both refugees in the sense of the 1951 Geneva Convention and beneficiaries of subsidiary protection, clarifies the legal concepts of 'actors of protection' (outside of the EU, Article 7), 'internal protection' (in the countries of origin, Article 8) and 'membership of a particular social group' as a ground for persecution (including sexual orientation and gender identity, Article 10(d)). These changes adapt EU legislation to recent case law of the European Court of Justice (ECJ) and the ECtHR and provide greater legal certainty for decisions on granting or refusing protection status. The Directive provides for an enlarged family definition covering not only the spouse or unmarried partner and unmarried children, but also any other adult legally responsible for an unmarried minor who is applying (Article 2(j)). It also provides for improved access of refugees to employment-related education opportunities and vocational training as well as to accommodation and integration facilities. While the Commission did not achieve its initial aim to secure for beneficiaries of subsidiary protection rights equal to those of refugees in the sense of the 1951 Geneva Convention, the Directive improves the protection status of the former with regard to family unity, access to employment and health care, and the renewal of residence permits (European Parliament/European Council, 2011a). While the adoption of the first of the 'recast' CEAS instruments constituted clearly a step forward, the many open questions regarding the other four instruments made it as doubtful as ever at the end of the year whether the original deadline for completing the CEAS in 2012 could be met.

Migration Policy

In its Annual Report on Immigration and Asylum presented in May, the Commission emphasized again the demographic challenge of the EU with a projected fall in the ratio of persons of working age (20–64) for every person 65 and over from 3.5 in 2010 to 1.7 in 2060, reiterating its firmly held position that 'managed inward migration of suitably skilled third-country nationals' should be central to efforts addressing EU labour market needs (Commission, 2011d). Yet at a time of growing unemployment in most of the Member States as a result of the economic and financial crisis, the Commission's arguments for facilitating legal immigration from third countries did not find much positive resonance in the Council where its proposals from 2010 on seasonal workers and intra-corporate transferees (Monar, 2011) met a host of objections and requests for changes. As regards the proposed Seasonal Workers Directive, these focused on the definition of seasonal work, the admission criteria, permits or visas for seasonal workers and seasonal workers' rights; and in that of the intra-corporate transferees Directive on admission criteria, the rights to be granted to permit holders and to their family members, and, in particular, mobility between Member States for permit holders (European Council, 2011b). The prospects for a rapid decision were not improved by the EP's draft report on the Seasonal Workers Directive providing for a widening of the rights of seasonal workers proposed by the Commission which several delegations in the Council rather wanted to narrow down (European Parliament, 2011b).

Given the unfavourable political context, the adoption on 13 December of Directive 2011/98/EU on a single application procedure for a single work and residence permit for third-country nationals – although not opening up any new channels for legal immigration – appeared as at least one encouraging sign for the progressive framing of the EU's still rather fragmentary migration policy (European Parliament/European Council, 2011b). The Directive provides for a procedure leading to a combined title for third-country nationals which encompasses both residence and work permits in a single administrative act, thereby simplifying and partially harmonizing the rules currently applicable in the Member States. With several Member States already applying such a single procedure and permit system, the Directive can be regarded as a case of 'best practice' transfer across the EU. It applies to third-country nationals who either apply to reside in a Member State for the purpose of work or have already been admitted for that purpose, but not to long-term residents, refugees and posted workers – who are already covered by other EU legislation – and seasonal workers or intra-corporate transferees – who will be covered by the above instruments still under negotiation (Article 3). The single procedure is expected to make the process of application more effective for both migrants and employers, and at the same time reduce costs for national administrations and improve their controlling possibilities of the legality of residence and employment.

Yet the new Directive is not only about procedures, but also about the rights of the eventual single permit holders – and several of the latter had required difficult negotiations both within the Council and between Council and Parliament, with the latter in many cases advocating more generous definitions. As far as procedural guarantees are concerned, the applicant can appeal against a negative decision in accordance with national law, but Member States can declare an application inadmissible on the simple ground of wanting to limit overall volumes of admission of labour immigration (Article 8). The single permit entitles the holder to reside and work in the entire territory of the issuing Member State, but the right to work is limited to 'the specific employment activity' mentioned in the permit (Article 11). The third-country nationals are also generally entitled to equal treatment with nationals of the Member State where they reside with regard to working conditions (including pay and dismissal), freedom of association and affiliation (for example, trade unions), education and vocational training, recognition of diplomas, certificates and other professional qualifications, social security rights, tax benefits and access to public goods and services (including public housing). Yet as a result of the concerns of a large number of Member States, the Directive allows them on an individual basis to impose certain restriction of these equal treatment rights as regards education and vocational training (for example, as regards access to study grants), social security rights (for example, the possibility to exclude family benefits in cases of employment of under six months) and access to housing (Article 12). The EP successively insisted, however, on the right of permit holders to receive their pensions when moving back to their home countries under the same conditions and at the same rates as the nationals of the Member State concerned and on the principle of access to employment and vocational training for any permit holder who is registered as unemployed.

In July, Eurostat reported that in 2010 there were 20.2 million third-country nationals living within the territories of the Member States. While this made up 4 per cent of the total EU population, the full extent of immigration into the EU was highlighted by a reported total of 31.4 million (6.3 per cent) residents born outside the EU (Eurostat, 2011b). The effective integration of these significant and increasing numbers of third countries is crucial for preventing the risks of social exclusion and tension in the receiving societies which can fuel racism and xenophobia as well as maximizing the contribution legal immigration can make to the productivity of the EU economy.

With new Article 79(4) TFEU – introduced by the Treaty of Lisbon – providing for the first time a legal basis for EU support for the promotion of integration of third-country nationals, the Commission had an added justification for presenting on 20 July a

'European Agenda for the Integration of Third-country Nationals' (Commission, 2011e) which went beyond an earlier and more limited 'Common Agenda' in this field that had been endorsed by the Council back in 2005. In its Communication the Commission highlighted as current key problems of integration of non-EU immigrants their prevailing low employment levels, especially for immigrant women, rising unemployment and high levels of 'over-qualification', increasing risks of social exclusion, gaps in educational achievement and public concerns about the lack of integration of migrants. In order to address those problems the Commission proposed action focused on enhancing integration through participation (through, for instance, more support for language learning, facilitated access to the labour market as well as to adapted education facilities as well as removing obstacles to migrants' political participation), more action at the local level (by addressing especially disadvantaged urban areas, improving co-operation between the primarily responsible local authorities and higher governance levels and more EU support to local and regional action) and an increased involvement of countries of origin (including co-operation with third countries regarding the adequate information of migrants before their departure to the EU and 'mobility partnerships' with third countries providing temporary and circular migrants with a rights-based framework ensuring a clear legal status and facilitating mobility).

The Commission was obviously all too well aware of the high political sensitivity of the subject of integration of immigrants in most Member States – a fact which is reflected in the limitation of the aforementioned Article 79(4) TFEU to measures providing 'incentives and support for the action of Member States' and specifically excluding any harmonization of national laws and regulations. In its Communication the Commission therefore explicitly recognized that 'it is not the prerogative of the EU to determine integration strategies', but emphasized at the same time that the Union could provide a framework for monitoring, benchmarking and exchange of good practice and create incentives through EU financial instruments (Commission, 2011e, p. 3). Yet the Commission's proposals arguably went somewhat beyond the latter, and in their Conclusions on the proposed 'European Agenda' the Member States in the Council felt it necessary to assert the right in the first paragraph that 'developing and implementing integration policies falls within the competence and responsibility of the Member States', stressing also – in line with the toughening policies in several Member States – that migrants need to show responsibility for their own integration process through special efforts including acquiring the language and respecting the laws and values of the receiving society (European Council, 2011d, p. 4). The Council accepted certain principles of the Commission's proposed Agenda – such as a greater involvement of the local and regional level, a better targeted, needs-based use of EU funding instruments and exploring enhanced co-operation possibilities with third countries – but it did not take up any of the specific proposals of the Commission for enhancing participation possibilities of migrants and came out firmly in favour of a purely 'non-binding co-ordination mechanism' as regards knowledge exchange and best practice identification and transfer. In the light of both the very limited support in the Council for the Commission's integration policy and the slow progress made with the above-mentioned legal immigration instruments, the EU's migration policy appeared again to be dominated by a restrictive policy rationale on the side of the Member States. This all the more so as EU external border management during the year was as concentrated as ever on migration control challenges.

Border and Visa Policy

In its latest Frontex Risk Analysis Network (FRAN) Report (from January 2012 for the third quarter of 2011), the EU's external border management agency Frontex reported a 'consistently high level' of illegal external border crossings throughout the year, with an increase of 11 per cent compared to the same period the year before. The Mediterranean was once again shown to be the primary front line of the EU's irregular migration challenges, with the eastern, central and western Mediterranean accounting for 50, 33 and 10 per cent, respectively, of the EU total of illegal external border crossings. Much of the overall increase was due to the effects of the 'Arab Spring', which led in March to the arrival of 14,400 Tunisian migrants on the Italian Island of Lampedusa alone, followed later by significant numbers of sub-Saharan migrants – many of whom had been expelled from Libya – and, to a lesser extent, migrants from Egypt (Frontex, 2012a, pp. 5, 14).

While the immigration pressure from Northern Africa was not the only challenge during the year (Frontex reported in the third quarter similar to 2010 over 19,000 illegal crossings mainly by Afghans and Pakistani in the eastern Mediterranean concentrated at the Greek land border with Turkey), it was the surge of illegal crossings related to the 'Arab Spring' that sparked a political crisis which temporarily threatened the functioning of the entire Schengen border system. In Italy, Interior Minister Roberto Maroni not only warned about an impending 'invasion' of refugees (see above), but also asked for EU solidarity in the form of substantial financial means and an activation of Directive 2001/55/EC on temporary protection in the event of a mass influx of displaced persons. The Directive provides for a mechanism of burden-sharing through the transfers of displaced persons based on voluntary offers from a state and on the consent of the transferees. Having met little support in the Council (most other Member States considered the Italian threat perception and demands exaggerated, and only Greece and Spain supported the Italian position), the Italian government first concluded a bilateral return agreement with the new Tunisian government and then adopted on 5 April a Decree providing for a six-month visa for North African citizens present on Italian soil who could either not be returned back to their country of origin or had come before the date of the new agreement with Tunisia granting its holders the right 'to free movement in the European Union in accordance with the Schengen Implementing Convention of 14 June 1995 and Community Law' (Government of Italy, 2011, Article 3; my own translation).

As most of the likely beneficiaries were Tunisian, the French government immediately saw a risk of large numbers of the refugees/migrants moving across the 'open' internal Schengen borders to join the large French Tunisian immigrant community – and the Ministry of Interior issued on 6 April an instruction clearly aimed at the beneficiaries of the Italian measure under which Schengen visa holders not able to justify sufficient means of subsistence would be returned to the Schengen country from which they were coming (Ministère de l'intérieur, de l'outre-mer, des collectivités locales et de l'immigration, 2011). This led to tensions with Italy which further escalated when France temporarily suspended rail traffic at the Franco–Italian border at Ventimiglia on 17 April, justifying this by an unauthorized demonstration of Italian activists in favour of the Tunisian immigrants. Italian Foreign Minister Franco Frattini declared this to be a violation of the Schengen rules and openly questioned the continuing sustainability of the Schengen free movement regime.[4] In the meantime the Franco–Italian issue, which – given the limited numbers of migrants involved – owed much to domestic politics considerations of both governments, was spreading to other Member States, with the Bavarian Interior Minister Joachim Herrmann threatening the introduction of controls at the border towards Austria if the Italian visa issuing practice were to continue,[5] and the Danish government finding in this resurgence of national border protection measures an additional justification for announcing in May – under pressure from the right-wing populist Danish People's Party – increased border checks in response to crime and illegal immigration risks.[6]

The Schengen crisis was subsequently gradually brought under control. Italy benefited eventually not only from Frontex support in the context of the 'Hermes' joint operation, but also from emergency funding under the European Border Fund (EBF). France opened the Ventimiglia crossing again, and Italian Prime Minister Silvio Berlusconi and French President Nicolas Sarkozy defused the bilateral tensions by agreeing at a Franco–Italian summit on 26 April on a joint letter to the Presidents of the European Council and the Commission which called for more co-operation with third countries on illegal immigration challenges, more solidarity between Member States in migration management and changes to the Schengen rules making it easier to temporarily reintroduce border controls in case of 'exceptional difficulties' (Présidence de la République, 2011). The Commission responded on 4 May to the Franco–Italian initiative in the context of a Communication addressing the wider context of migration challenges in conjunction with the 'Arab Spring' by announcing proposals on a further strengthening of external border management as well as on a Schengen governance reform providing for a mechanism allowing for the temporary reintroduction of internal borders controls in critical situations (Commission, 2011f, pp. 7–8). A further destabilization of the Schengen system was also reined in by the Danish enhanced border checks – while being criticized by both the Commission and the incoming Polish Presidency – stopping short of any systematic reintroduction of border controls and by the EP adopting on 7 July a Resolution which forcefully stressed the fundamental importance of the Schengen free movement rules and condemned 'the attempt by several Member States to reintroduce border controls, which clearly jeopardizes the very spirit of the Schengen *acquis*' (European Parliament, 2011a).

With its political back strengthened by an EP clearly in favour of protecting the Schengen system against the potentially corrosive effects of national border emergency measures, the Commission presented on 16 September proposals for a 'reinforced EU-based approach' for the exceptional reintroduction of border controls. The main rule under the new approach would be that that any decision on the reintroduction of controls, which could be justified by the adverse consequences of either a Member State's persistent failure to adequately protect a part of the EU's external border or of a sudden and unexpected inflow of third-country nationals, would be taken by the Commission as an implementing act, determining the scope and duration of the controls for renewable periods of up to 30 days, with a maximum duration of six months (Commission, 2011g). The Commission combined this initiative with corresponding legislative proposals to amend the Schengen borders code (Commission, 2011h) and to further strengthen the

[4] *La Repubblica*, 18 April 2011.
[5] *Die Presse*, 11 April 2011.
[6] *BBC News Europe*, 11 May 2011.

Schengen evaluation mechanism (Commission, 2011i). The reinforcement of the latter was already under negotiation, but the Commission now added the possibility for it to ask Member States where serious deficiencies in carrying out of external border controls or return procedures have been identified to initiate the deployment of European border guard teams by Frontex or even close a specific border point temporarily until the weaknesses are remedied.

The Commission's September 'Schengen package' was met by a barrage of opposition from the Member States, with nearly all delegations in the Council – led by France, Germany and Spain and accompanied by subsidiarity objections from several national parliaments – being opposed to conferring the power to decide on the temporary reintroduction of controls at the internal borders on the Commission and also not wanting to leave it to the latter to decide on the need for deploying border guard teams at external borders or even closing specific border points (European Council, 2011d). By the end of the year it looked as if the Commission was going to suffer one of its biggest defeats ever in the JHA domain on the September 'Schengen package', highlighting both the risks of trying to use a temporary crisis for strengthening the Commission's 'supranational' management functions border and the Member States' determination to keep their borders firmly under national control.

The controversies about the Commission's potential border control emergency powers also pushed one of the key reasons for the year's Schengen crisis (the absence of an effective solidarity mechanism for 'front-line' Member States experiencing increased illegal immigration pressures) to the background, with the Commission itself not having gone beyond tackling the solidarity issue in an 'Annex' of its September package consisting essentially of a list of existing solidarity instruments such as Frontex assistance and the European Border Fund (Commission, 2011g, Annex 1). Yet because of its key role in initiating and supporting joint operations at external borders Frontex (which attained in 2011 a total budget of €118 million and 313 staff members) appeared indeed more than ever as the EU's primary solidarity instrument. The 68 per cent of its annual operations budget dedicated to sea borders also gave a clear indication where external border management needs were the most urgent during the year (Frontex, 2012b, pp. 6, 118). The future role of Frontex was strengthened by the adoption on 25 October of a Regulation amending the original 2004 Frontex Regulation which enables the agency to deploy European border guard teams drawn from a pool of national border guards (participation in which Member States can only refuse in an 'exceptional situation') and to acquire or lease its own equipment, such as mobile radars or vehicles, either by itself or in co-ownership with a Member State. The EP had successfully insisted on a reinforcement of the agency's fundamental rights protection framework through the establishment of a Fundamental Rights Officer and Consultative Forum and new provisions on the respect of the principle of non-refoulement of refugees (European Parliament/European Council, 2011c).

At the end of the year the EU's border management agenda was partially steered back into less rough waters by the Commission's legislative proposal for the establishment of the European Border Surveillance System (EUROSUR). This system, enjoying strong backing from most Member States, is to improve the situational awareness and reaction capability of Member States and Frontex when preventing irregular migration and cross-border crime at the external land and maritime borders. The system is planned to consist of national co-ordination centres for border surveillance in charge of putting together national border 'situational pictures', a special communication network, 'European situational pictures', which Frontex will establish on the basis of the national pictures as well as common (external) pre-frontier intelligence pictures also managed by Frontex and the common application of technical surveillance tools, such as satellite and ship reporting systems (Commission, 2011j). While the pooling of border surveillance capabilities and common situation assessments may help with a better, and potentially earlier, assessment of border management risks, it will do little to even out the differences in burden Member States are facing in this respect and which can only be addressed by a – still missing – comprehensive solidarity system.

Compared to the political controversies regarding border management issues, developments in the visa policy appeared primarily technical. After a successful final test, the Commission could take, on 21 September, the Decision to start the operations of the new Visa Information System (VIS) on 11 October, although the collection and transmission of visa application data were, as previously planned, initially limited to applications from Algeria, Egypt, Libya, Mauritania, Morocco and Tunisia (Commission, 2011k). The successful start of operation of the VIS stood in sharp contrast to the continuing delays affecting the second-generation Schengen Information System (SIS II), for which, at the beginning of the year, new risks regarding the availability of the required advanced test environment and the readiness of Member States to participate in the scheduled 'extended compliance test' were identified, although the EU's financial investment in the development of the system since 2002 had by then reached over €135 million (Commission, 2011l).

A contribution to both the fight against visa fraud and legal uncertainty was made by a Decision of Parliament and Council on the list of third-country travel documents which may be endorsed with a visa, providing a mechanism for establishing and regular updating of that list (European Parliament/European Council, 2011d). While not harmonizing Member States' differing practices with regard to the recognition of third-country travel documents for visa purposes (this remains a national competence), the mechanism should reduce the uncertainties of third-country nationals applying for, or travelling with, a Schengen visa in the Schengen zone. The external dimension of the common visa policy continued to grow with the conclusion of agreements with Georgia (visa facilitation) and Brazil (short-stay visa waiver) and the opening of negotiations on a first visa facilitation agreement with Belarus and more advanced visa facilitation agreements with Russia, Ukraine and Moldova.

Judicial Co-operation

The EU's growing international role in the field of civil justice co-operation was underlined by the signing by the EU on 6 April of the 2007 Hague Convention on the International Recovery of Child Support and Other Forms of Family Maintenance (European Council, 2011e). The Convention, whose signatories currently include the United States, Norway, Ukraine, Bosnia-Herzegovina and Burkina Faso, is to ensure the effective international recovery of child support and other forms of family maintenance, in particular by enhancing co-operation between the authorities of the Contracting States, making available applications for the establishment of maintenance decisions, providing for the recognition and enforcement of maintenance decisions and requiring effective measures for the prompt enforcement of maintenance decisions. In line with the case law of the Court of Justice on EU external competence, the Union was in a position to sign the Convention alone and with exclusive competence for all matters governed by the Convention as a result of it already having exercised its competence with regard to these matters internally by Council Regulation (EC) No 4/2009, which showed again the extent of the dependency of EU external action capacity on internal legislative progress.

The corpus of common EU criminal law was expanded with regard to two of the most repellent forms of cross-border crime: trafficking in human beings and sexual abuse of children. In each case, the adoption of a Directive showed the real potential for progress offered by the replacement of existing ex-'third-pillar' Framework Decisions. On 5 April the Council and Parliament adopted Directive 2011/36/EU on preventing and combating trafficking in human beings which replaced a Council Framework Decision from 2002 on the same issue (European Parliament/European Council, 2011e). The Directive introduces in Article 2 a broader definition of offences involving trafficking in human beings which now includes 'forced begging', 'exploitation of criminal activities' (meant to cover the exploitation of a person to commit, *inter alia*, pick-pocketing, shoplifting or drug trafficking) as well trafficking in human beings for the purpose of the removal of organs, and is wide enough to cover also acts of trafficking relating to illegal adoption or forced marriage. Article 4 provides for increased criminal penalties for trafficking offences, based on a maximum term of imprisonment of not less than five years and, in case of aggravating circumstances (if the victim's life has been endangered or if they are children, for instance), ten years. By virtue of Article 10, Member States now also have to take extraterritorial jurisdiction as regards any nationals who traffic people anywhere in the world for the purpose of exploitation. Articles 11–17 comprise extended and detailed provisions on assistance and support for victims – and especially child victims – of human trafficking, several of which go beyond the standards of the 2005 Council of Europe Convention on the subject. The Directive reflects the major concerns in the EU about the growth of various forms of human trafficking, which have also become an important source of revenue for organized crime.

The adoption of Directive 2011/92/EU on combating the sexual abuse and sexual exploitation of children and child pornography on 13 December, which also replaced an earlier Framework Decision from 2004, was motivated by similar objectives of adapting crime definitions, penalty levels and protection provisions to the growth and increasing variety of this form of crime which keeps spreading, in particular, through the use of modern technologies and the Internet (European Parliament/European Council, 2011f). The new Directive provides for new levels of maximum penalties for the sexual abuse of children ranging from at least one year's imprisonment for causing a child to witness sexual activities to at least ten years for coercing a child into sexual actions; for the sexual exploitation of children it ranges from at least two years' imprisonment for attending pornographic performances involving children to a minimum of ten years for forcing a child into prostitution. It also covers child pornography, foreseeing for its possession at least one year's imprisonment, for its production at least three years' imprisonment, and for the solicitation of children for sexual purposes at least one year's imprisonment (Articles 3–6). It also provides for mandatory disqualifications of convicted offenders from professional activities involving direct and regular contacts with children, and the information of other Member States about such disqualifications (Article 10) introduces compulsory jurisdiction over nationals who commit crimes abroad (Article 17) – a measure aimed at 'sex tourism' – and obliges Member States to ensure the prompt removal of child pornography websites hosted in their territory and to endeavour to obtain their removal if hosted outside of their territory (Article 25). These repressive provisions are complemented by an extension of the already existing measures on the assistance, support and protection measures of child victims, especially during investigations and legal proceedings (Articles 18–20).

The progress in terms of harmonization of substantive criminal law marked by the two new Directives was accompanied by a smaller step forward on the mutual recognition side through the adoption, on 13 December, of Directive 2011/99/EU on the 'European Protection Order' (EPO) (European Parliament/European Council, 2011g). The new EPO is aimed at protecting a person anywhere in the EU against a criminal act of another person which may, in any way, endanger that person's life or physical, psychological and sexual integrity – by preventing, for instance, any form of harassment – as well as that person's dignity or personal liberty – by preventing, for instance, abductions, stalking and other forms of indirect coercion. The EPO is essentially an extension, by way of mutual recognition, of a national protection measure providing for a prohibition from entering certain localities, places or defined areas where the protected person resides or visits, a prohibition or regulation of contact, in any form, with the protected person, and/or a prohibition or regulation on approaching the protected person closer than a prescribed distance. It can be issued at the request of a protected person when they decide to reside or already reside in another Member State (Article 6), but only if a protection measure is already in place in the issuing Member State (Article 5). Apart from being a new cross-border criminal justice instrument the EPO can also be regarded as an instrument facilitating the exercise of the free movement rights of actual or potential crime victims. The adoption of the instrument, although backed by both Council and EP, had been delayed by objections of the Commission against the original 2010 initiative by 12 Member States on grounds of it covering also protection orders issued on a civil law basis for the latter of which the Commission has – unlike in the criminal law domain – an exclusive right of initiative under the Treaty. This legal dispute will make the adoption of a parallel civil law instrument based on a Commission initiative necessary, highlighting both the Commission's combative defensiveness with regard to its prerogatives and an unhelpful leftover of the former 'first/third pillar' divide.

Internal Security Co-operation

The year 2011 marked the start of the 2011–13 EU policy cycle for organized and serious international crime. As foreseen by this new programming mechanism, the Standing Committee on operational co-operation on internal security (COSI) – introduced by the Lisbon Treaty – and the Commission established a Policy Advisory Document (PAD) on the basis of the 2011 EU Organized Crime Threat Assessment (OCTA 2011) presented by Europol (European Council, 2011f). A draft PAD was produced by the Presidency with input from the Commission building upon the executive summary of the OCTA 2011 with the aim of assisting COSI in submitting to the Council draft conclusions setting the EU's new priorities for the fight against organized crime for 2011–13. At its meeting of 1 June

2011, COSI reached agreement on both the PAD for the years 2011–13 (European Council, 2011g), which highlighted the increasing diversification of organized crime activities and the need for more flexible responses and more preventive measures, and on the draft Council conclusions on setting the EU's priorities for the fight against organized crime between 2011 and 2013. These conclusions, which were approved by the JHA Council in its meeting on 9–10 June, are marked by a strong emphasis on the links between external and internal organized crime threats. Priorities include the weakening of the capacity of organized crime groups active or based in West Africa to traffic cocaine and heroin to and within the EU, the mitigation of the role of the Western Balkans as a key transit and storage zone for illicit commodities destined for the EU and logistical centre for organized crime groups (including Albanian-speaking organized crime groups), the reduction of the capacity of organized crime groups to facilitate illegal immigration to the EU (particularly via southern, southeastern and eastern Europe and notably at the Greek–Turkish border and in crisis areas of the Mediterranean close to North Africa) and, within the EU, measures against the production and distribution in the EU of synthetic drugs, including new psychoactive substances and action against all forms of trafficking in human beings and human smuggling by targeting the organized crime groups conducting such criminal activities in particular at the southern, southwestern and southeastern criminal hubs in the EU (European Council, 2011h).

While the progressive strengthening of internal law enforcement co-operation remains of primary importance in the fight against organized crime and terrorism,[7] the strong focus on external organized crime threats in the Council priorities for 2011–13 indicated the growing importance of the external dimension of EU internal security objectives. This was also reflected in the adoption of a number of new guidelines for enhancing the links between internal and external aspects of counter-terrorism (European Council, 2011j), adopted in June, and in the new 'JHA External Relations Trio Programme' of the Polish, Danish and Cyprus Presidencies (European Council, 2011k), presented on 4 July. Both texts identified a number of persisting coherence deficits between internal and external action which were partially due to the complexity of the institutional framework, especially as regards the interaction between the JHA and CFSP domains. As external action needs in relation with internal security objectives are likely to keep growing, shortcomings on the institutional co-ordination side will clearly need to be addressed.

Conclusions

The second year of implementation of the 2010–14 Stockholm Programme was clearly not marked by any spectacular progress, and some of the deadline linked objectives of the Programme, such as the completion of the CEAS by the end of 2012 are now clearly at risk. Yet this should not be taken as a sign of the Union's 'area of freedom, security and justice', which, it should be recalled, ranks high on the list of fundamental treaty objectives in Article 3(2) TEU, losing political momentum. It is rather a case of decision-making, especially in the legislative field, becoming more complex and difficult as the EU tries to move beyond the relatively 'easier' range of initial least common denominator

[7] The Council admonished Member States in June to accelerate their so far partially insufficient efforts for a full implementation of the 2009 Prüm Decisions on the automated cross-border access to and searching and comparison of DNA profiles, dactyloscopic data and vehicle registration data (European Council, 2011i).

instruments. The passage from the first-phase asylum policy legislation to the second (CEAS) is a case in point, and it is also evident that the harmonizing rules on the admission of seasonal workers certainly raises more sensitive issues at the domestic level than those on admission of students already approved in 2004. On the other hand, there is also evidence for developments in justice and home affairs benefiting from the growing experience with certain mechanisms. An example is the ASTs of the EASO which were for the first time deployed in 2011 and are clearly modelled upon the Rapid Border Intervention Teams (RABITs) already deployed by Frontex for several years. All of this points towards an increasingly 'mature' policy domain in which developments are slower and more differentiated as there are no new and relatively uncontroversial fields for common action left, but where real progress nevertheless continues to be made.

Key Readings

Carrera, S., Guild, E., Merlino, M. and Parkin, J. (2011) *A Race against Solidarity: The Schengen-Regime and the Franco–Italian Affair* (Brussels: Centre for European Policy Studies).

Cremona, M., Monar, J. and Poli, S. (eds) (2011) *The External Dimension of the European Union's Area of Freedom, Security and Justice* (Brussels: P.I.E. Peter Lang).

Eckes, C. and Konstadinides, T. (eds) (2011) *Crime within the Area of Freedom, Security and Justice: A European Public Order* (Cambridge: Cambridge University Press).

References

Commission of the European Communities (2011a) 'Amended proposal for a Directive [. . .] on common procedures for granting and withdrawing international protection status'. *COM*(2011)319, 1 June.

Commission of the European Communities (2011b) 'Amended proposal for a Directive [. . .] laying down standards for the reception of asylum seekers'. *COM*(2011)320, 1 June.

Commission of the European Communities (2011c) 'Communication [. . .] on enhanced intra-EU solidarity in the field of asylum: An EU agenda for better responsibility-sharing and more mutual trust'. *COM*(2011)835, 2 December.

Commission of the European Communities (2011d) 'Annual Report on Immigration and Asylum (2010)'. *COM*(2011)291, 24 May.

Commission of the European Communities (2011e) 'Communication [. . .] European Agenda for the Integration of Third-country Nationals'. *COM*(2011)455, 20 July.

Commission of the European Communities (2011f) 'Communication on migration'. *COM*(2011)248, 4 May.

Commission of the European Communities (2011g) 'Communication [. . .] Schengen governance: Strengthening the area without internal border control'. *COM*(2011)561, 16 September.

Commission of the European Communities (2011h) 'Proposal for a Regulation of the European Parliament and of the Council amending Regulation (EC) No 562/2006 in order to provide for common rules on the temporary reintroduction of border control at internal borders in exceptional circumstances'. *COM*(2011)560, 16 September.

Commission of the European Communities (2011i) 'Amended proposal for a Regulation of the European Parliament and of the Council on the establishment of an evaluation and monitoring mechanism to verify the application of the Schengen acquis'. *COM*(2011)559, 16 September.

Commission of the European Communities (2011j) 'Proposal for a Regulation of the European Parliament and of the Council establishing the European Border Surveillance System (EUROSUR)'. *COM*(2011)837, 12 December.

Commission of the European Communities (2011k) 'Commission implementing Decision of 21 September 2011 determining the date from which the Visa Information System (VIS) is to start operations in a first region'. OJ L 249, 27 September.

Commission of the European Communities (2011l) 'Report from the Commission to the European Parliament and the Council Progress report on the development of the second-generation Schengen Information System (SIS II), January 2011–June 2011'. *COM*(2011)907, 20 December.

European Asylum Support Office (EASO) (2011) 'Decision No. 3 of the Management Board [. . .] on the profiles and overall number of experts to be made available for the asylum support teams. EASO/MB/2011/03, Valletta Harbour, February.

European Asylum Support Office (EASO) (2012) 'European Asylum Support Office delegation visits Greece to discuss progress made since the deployment of Asylum Support Teams'. Press Release, Valletta Harbour, 19 January.

European Council (2011a) 'Common European Asylum System: State of play', 18170/11, 7 December.

European Council (2011b) '3096th Council meeting: Justice and Home Affairs'. Press Release, 11008/11, 10 June.

European Council (2011c) 'Draft Conclusions of the Council and the Representatives of the Governments of the Member States on the European Agenda for the Integration of Third-Country Nationals'. 18296/1/11 REV 1, 12 December.

European Council (2011d) 'Amended proposal for a regulation of the European Parliament and of the Council on the establishment of an evaluation and monitoring mechanism to verify the application of the Schengen acquis [. . .]: State of play'. 18196/1/11 REV 1, 9 December.

European Council (2011e) 'Council Decision of 31 March 2011 on the signing, on behalf of the European Union, of the Hague Convention of 23 November 2007 on the International Recovery of Child Support and Other Forms of Family Maintenance'. OJ L 93, 7 April.

European Council (2011f) 'EU Organized Crime Threat Assessment 2011 (OCTA)'. [Europol], 8709/11, 6 April.

European Council (2011g) 'Policy advisory document for 2011 to 2013'. [COSI], 9225/4/11 REV 4, 8 June.

European Council (2011h) 'Council conclusions on setting the EU's priorities for the fight against organized crime between 2011 and 2013'. 11050/11, 6 June.

European Council (2011i) 'Council Conclusions on the implementation of the "Prüm Decisions" '. 10653/11, 26 May.

European Council (2011j) 'Council Conclusions on enhancing the links between internal and external aspects of counter-terrorism'. 11075/11, 6 June.

European Council (2011k) 'JHA External Relations: Trio Programme'. [Polish, Danish and Cyprus Presidencies], 12004/11, 4 July.

European Parliament (2011a) 'European Parliament resolution of 7 July 2011 on changes to Schengen'. P7_TA(2011)0336, 7 July.

European Parliament (2011b) 'Draft report on the proposal for a directive of the European Parliament and of the Council on the conditions of entry and residence of third-country nationals for the purposes of seasonal employment (Rapporteur: Claude Moraes)'. PE 464.960v02-00, 8 June.

European Parliament/European Council (2011a) 'Directive 2011/95/EU [. . .] of 13 December 2011 on standards for the qualification of third-country nationals or stateless persons as beneficiaries of international protection, for a uniform status for refugees or for persons eligible for subsidiary protection, and for the content of the protection granted'. OJ L 337, 20 December.

European Parliament/European Council (2011b) 'Directive 2011/98/EU [. . .] of 13 December 2011 on a single application procedure for a single permit for third-country nationals to reside and work in the territory of a Member State and on a common set of rights for third-country workers legally residing in a Member State'. OJ L 343, 23 December.

European Parliament/European Council (2011c) 'Regulation 1168/2011 [. . .] of 25 October 2011 amending Council Regulation (EC) No 2007/2004 establishing a European Agency for the Management of Operational Co-operation at the External Borders of the Member States of the European Union'. OJ 304, 11 November.

European Parliament/European Council (2011d) 'Decision No. 1105/2011/EU [. . .] of 25 October 2011 on the list of travel documents which entitle the holder to cross the external borders and which may be endorsed with a visa and on setting up a mechanism for establishing this list'. OJ L 287, 4 November.

European Parliament/European Council (2011e) 'Directive 2011/36/EU [. . .] of 5 April 2011 on preventing and combating trafficking in human beings and protecting its victims, and replacing Council Framework Decision 2002/629/JHA'. OJ L 101, 15 April.

European Parliament/European Council (2011f) 'Directive 2011/92/EU [. . .] of 13 December 2011 on combating the sexual abuse and sexual exploitation of children and child pornography, and replacing Council Framework Decision 2004/68/JHA'. OJ L 335, 17 December.

European Parliament/European Council (2011g) 'Directive 2011/99/EU [. . .] of 13 December 2011 on the European protection order'. OJ L 338, 21 December.

Eurostat (2011a) 'Number of asylum applicants on rise during the first quarter of 2011'. *Statistics in Focus* 48/2011.

Eurostat (2011b) '6.5% of the EU population are foreigners and 9.4% are born abroad'. *Statistics in Focus* 34/2011.

Frontex (2012a) *FRAN Quarterly*, No. 3, July–September 2011, January 2012.

Frontex (2012b) *Programme of Work 2012* (Warsaw: Frontex).

Government of Italy (2011) 'Decreto del Presidente del Consiglio dei Ministri, 5 Aprile 2011: Misure di protezione temporanea per i cittadini stranieri affluiti dai Paesi nordafricani'. No. 11A04818, *Gazzetta Ufficiale*, No. 81, 8 April.

Ministère de l'intérieur, de l'outre-mer, des collectivités locales et de l'immigration (2011) 'Autorisations de séjour délivrées à des ressortissants de pays tiers par les Etats membres de Schengen'. [Circular letter by the Chef de Cabinet Stéphane Bouillon], Paris, 6 April.

Monar, J. (2011), 'Justice and Home Affairs'. *JCMS*, Vol. 49, No. S1, pp. 145–64.

Présidence de la République (2011) 'Lettre de MM. Sarkozy et Berlusconi adressée à MM. Van Rompuy et Barroso'. Rome, 26 April.

United Nations High Commission for Refugees (UNHCR) (2011a) 'UNHCR's Recommendations to Poland for its EU Presidency', Brussels, June.

United Nations High Commission for Refugees (UNHCR) (2011b) 'Hundreds of new arrivals in Italy from Libya and Tunisia'. Briefing Notes, Brussels, 16 August.

JCMS 2012 Volume 50 Annual Review pp. 132–146 DOI: 10.1111/j.1468-5965.2012.02279.x

Legal Developments

FABIAN AMTENBRINK
Erasmus University Rotterdam

Introduction

Last year's review of legal developments largely focused on the European Union's regulatory response to the global financial and economic crisis in the sphere of financial market regulation and supervision (Amtenbrink, 2011). Yet, this crisis has also revealed the shortcomings in the system of economic governance in European economic and monetary union (EMU). Indeed, in parallel and to some extent triggered by the financial market crisis, there was a dramatic deterioration of the budgetary position of several Member States resulting in – at least in one instance – the quasi-insolvency of a eurozone country.[1] While 2010 was arguably mainly geared towards ad hoc emergency measures, in 2011 the EU could be seen taking steps towards more structural reform of the system of economic governance. This culminated in the signing, in February 2012, of the much talked about Fiscal Compact. Correspondingly, the first part of this review is dedicated to these important legal developments that not only change the character of EMU to some extent, but also put pressure on the Community Method. The second part of this contribution will turn to the jurisprudence of the Court of Justice of the European Union (ECJ). Given the vastness of developments relating to the reform of EU economic governance that require recording, and considering the limited space available, it is by no means possible to offer a comprehensive or even wider overview of the judgments of the ECJ in 2011. Thus, following last year's approach, the focus is on a number of important judgments of the ECJ that have the potential to substantially (re)shape the scope of EU citizenship and the free movement of persons.

I. Dealing with the Eurozone Debt Crisis: The Reform of Economic Governance

The global financial and economic crisis has not only revealed the weakness, if not absence, of the European financial market regulatory and supervisory system, but also the costs of a failing system of economic governance in EMU in the shape of the economic policy co-ordination foreseen in Title VIII of the Treaty on the Functioning of the European Union (TFEU) and related secondary Union law acts. Arguably, the bilateral loans by the Member States to Greece and, thereafter, the granting of financial assistance to Ireland and Portugal as part of the hastily established European Financial Stability Mechanism (EFSM) and of the European Financial Stability Facility (EFSF),[2] not only stemmed from the financial market crisis and the need for a large-scale bail-out of financial institutions and fiscal stimuli in Member States, but also from the absence, for a

[1] On the crisis in the eurozone, see the contributions written by Hodson, Gros and Buiter and Rahbari in this issue.
[2] See Amtenbrink (2011, p. 173).

long time, of a regulatory framework capable of enforcing the budgetary rules that have been agreed upon in the Maastricht Treaty. The shortcomings of this system have been well documented[3] and have resulted in several attempts to reinforce the regulatory framework – most notably by means of the 1997 Stability and Growth Pact[4] that introduced detailed rules for the two main components of European economic policy co-ordination: the multilateral surveillance procedure and the excessive deficit procedure.[5]

Yet these efforts have not substantially altered the governance mode applicable in EMU, characterized by self-commitment and peer review. Indeed, even long before the global financial and economic crisis could be felt, excessive deficit procedures had become a regular occurrence, whereby the events in late 2003 surrounding the (failed) application of the excessive deficit procedure to Germany and France that ended in a dispute between the European Commission and the Council before the ECJ, highlight the legal limitations and political substance of the so-called 'corrective arm' of economic policy co-ordination in EMU.[6]

Strengthening the corrective as well as the preventive arm of economic policy co-ordination in EMU – that is, the multilateral surveillance procedure – was the main aim of several European Commission proposals that led to the 2011 reform of economic governance. Indeed, 'experience gained and mistakes made during the first decade of the economic and monetary union show a need for improved economic governance in the Union, which should be built on a stronger national ownership of commonly agreed rules and policies and on a more robust framework at the level of the Union for the surveillance of national economic policies'.[7] The legal framework meant to establish this 'robust framework' was the so-called 'Six Pack'.[8]

Highlighting the speed of developments – not least triggered by the rather lukewarm reception of the financial markets to the reform package barely weeks after their introduction in November 2011 – the heads of state or government of the Member States of the eurozone in December announced 'a new deal between euro area Member States to be enshrined in common, ambitious rules that translate their strong political commitment into a new legal framework' in order to move 'towards a stronger economic union' (European Council, 2011, pp. 2–3).

The Six Pack

The Six Pack consists of six Union measures, five Regulations and one Directive.[9] In essence, these measures are geared towards enhancing the working of the multilateral

[3] See, for example, Hahn (1998); Amtenbrink *et al.* (1997).

[4] Resolution of the European Council on the Stability and Growth Pact, OJ 1997 C 236.

[5] Council Regulation 1466/97 on the strengthening of the surveillance of budgetary positions and the surveillance and co-ordination of economic policies, OJ 1997 L 209/1; Council Regulation 1467/97 on speeding up and clarifying the implementation of the excessive deficit procedure, OJ 1997 L 209/6.

[6] Case C-27/04, *European Commission* v *Council* [2004] ECR I-6649. See Maher (2004).

[7] See preamble 8, Regulation 1175/2011 amending Council Regulation (EC) No. 1466/97 on the strengthening of the surveillance of budgetary positions and the surveillance and co-ordination of economic policies, OJ 2011 L 306/12.

[8] This contribution does not cover the Treaty establishing the European Stability Mechanism that was originally signed on 11 July 2011, but thereafter modified and signed again by the eurozone Member States on 2 February 2012. For a brief overview, see ECB (2011).

[9] Regulation 1173/2011 on the effective enforcement of budgetary surveillance in the euro area, OJ 2011 L 306/1; Regulation 1174/2011 on enforcement measures to correct excessive macroeconomic imbalances in the euro area, OJ 2011 L 306/8; Regulation 1175/2011 amending Council Regulation (EC) No. 1466/97 on the strengthening of the surveillance of budgetary positions and the surveillance and co-ordination of economic policies, OJ 2011 L 306/12; Regulation 1176/2011

surveillance procedure and excessive deficit procedure, laid down in Articles 121 and 126 TFEU, which form the core of economic policy co-ordination in EMU and namely in the eurozone.[10] At the same time, the scope of economic policy co-ordination is extended, as a new procedure is introduced to monitor macroeconomic developments in Member States and address (emerging) imbalances.

Turning first to the multilateral surveillance and excessive deficit procedure, a clear attempt has been made to commit Member States – more so than in the past – to implementing a sound economic policy in line with the basic fiscal rules laid down in primary Union law and especially the obligation to avoid excessive government deficits.[11] Previously, the surveillance of the national economic policy measures was largely centred on annual updated Convergence and Stability Programmes that the Member States had to forward to the European Commission and to the Council. From 2011, following an amendment of the Code of Conduct for the implementation of the Stability and Growth Pact in September 2010, a new six-month cycle for economic policy co-ordination has been introduced. As part of this so-called 'European Semester', the European Commission as well as the European Council get involved in the early stages of the preparation of the national budgets. The cycle commences in January with the European Commission's annual growth survey that establishes economic priorities for the EU as a whole and for individual Member States. Thereafter, based on strategic advice provided by the European Council, Member States determine their budgetary strategies and prepare any required reform programmes.[12] The national plans are then assessed by the European Commission, which advices the Council on the guidance the latter should issue to individual Member States.[13] While the Member States and, more precisely, national governments and parliaments remain, in principle, in charge of adopting the national budget, the European Semester is clearly geared towards getting a better grip on national budgets, whereby the European Commission is bound to take on the role of a strong defender of Union (budgetary) interests.

This early engagement with the economic developments in the Member States can also be highlighted for the actual surveillance system laid down in Article 121 TFEU and in the revised Regulation 1466/97. First, the reform of the multilateral surveillance procedure aims at better achieving the medium-term balanced budget or budget surplus objective (MTO) stated in Regulation 1466/97. What is more, in the future more attention will be paid to prudent fiscal policies in the Member States. In the Commission's analysis, 'the structural balance has in practice proved an insufficient measure of a country's underlying fiscal position' (Commission, 2010d, section 3). This may in the past have resulted in a distorted picture of a Member State's budgetary situation. For the Member States this new

of the European Parliament and of the Council of 16 November 2011 on the prevention and correction of macroeconomic imbalances, OJ 2011 L 306/25; Council Regulation 1177/2011 amending Regulation (EC) No. 1467/97 on speeding up and clarifying the implementation of the excessive deficit procedure, OJ 2011 L 306/33; Council Directive 2011/85/EU on requirements for budgetary frameworks of the Member States, OJ 2011 L 306/41.

[10] It should be noted, however, that Articles 121 and 126 TFEU, with the exception of the sanction regime described in Article 126(11) TFEU, also applies to Member States outside the eurozone (so-called 'Member States with a derogation', including the United Kingdom and Denmark).

[11] As stated in Article 126(1) TFEU and the Protocol on the excessive deficit procedure attached to the Treaty on European Union (TEU) and the TFEU.

[12] These programmes must take into account Europe 2020 objectives.

[13] For more details, see Commission (2010b, section III.3; 2010c, section 5).

focus means that their annual expenditure growth should not exceed 'a prudent medium-term rate of growth of GDP, unless the MTO has been significantly overachieved or unless the excess of expenditure growth over the prudent medium-term rate is matched by discretionary measures on the revenue side' (Commission, 2010a). Essentially, Member States are not to spend revenue windfalls, but rather allocate them to debt reduction first (Commission, 2010a).

Two more important amendments to the old multilateral surveillance regime concern the introduction of reversed voting and the possibility of imposing non-interest-bearing deposits on Member States that do not comply with Council recommendations. Where a Member State to which the Council has addressed recommendations in accordance with Article 121(4) TFEU fails to take the appropriate corrective measures, the Commission must immediately recommend that the Council adopt, by qualified majority, a decision establishing that no effective action has been taken. The Council is then in principle expected to take a decision to that effect. If this is not the case, the Commission, after one month from its earlier recommendation, will make a new recommendation to the Council that it adopt the decision establishing that no effective action has been taken. Different to the first recommendation, the implementation of which rests on the Council, this latter recommended decision is 'deemed to be adopted by the Council unless it decides, by simple majority, to reject the recommendation within 10 days of its adoption by the Commission'.[14] The Commission can also recommend adopting a revised recommendation on necessary policy measures. The reversed voting procedure is supposed to prevent the Council remaining inactive despite clear indications of a failure on the part of a Member State to comply with the previously issued recommendations. Indeed, in the past the Council has not in all instances been very effective in strictly following the multilateral surveillance procedure.[15]

Introducing more stringency into the multilateral surveillance procedure is also the aim of the new possibility to demand an interest-bearing deposit. This is provided in Regulation 1173/2011 on the effective enforcement of budgetary surveillance in the eurozone. Under the new framework the continuation or even deterioration of the divergence of the budgetary situation of Member States from the path of a prudent fiscal policy not only results in new Council recommendations, but the decision that a Member State has not followed up the initial Council recommendations also results in the obligation of the Member State in question to pay an interest-bearing deposit. For this, the Commission will 'recommend that the Council, by a further decision, require the Member State in question to lodge with the Commission an interest-bearing deposit amounting to 0.2 % of its GDP in the preceding year'.[16] Similar to the decision on the lack of effective action by a Member State, a reversed voting procedure applies, whereby the Council has a period of ten days to reject the Commission's recommendation.[17]

Next to the multilateral surveillance procedure a new focus in economic policy co-ordination comes to rest on macroeconomic imbalances in Member States. The preamble to Regulation 1176/2011 states in this regard that 'surveillance of the economic

[14] Article 6(2), Regulation 1466/97 (as amended).
[15] See, for example, the conclusions of the Council with regard to Germany in 2002: 2407th Council meeting – Ecofin – Brussels, 12 February 2002.
[16] Article 4(1), Regulation 1173/2011.
[17] Article 4(2), Regulation 1173/2011.

policies of the Member States should be broadened beyond budgetary surveillance to include a more detailed and formal framework to prevent excessive macroeconomic imbalances and to help the Member States affected to establish corrective plans before divergences become entrenched'. To this end, the Commission monitors the macroeconomic developments in the Member States based on a 'scoreboard' comprising indicative thresholds in order to detect any 'severe imbalances, including imbalances that jeopardise or risk jeopardising the proper functioning of the economic and monetary union' and that require corrective action by the Member States.[18] The list of indicators foreseen to detect such imbalances at an early stage, in parts, reads like a listing of the macroeconomic deficiencies currently found in several eurozone Member States, including public and private indebtedness, financial and asset market developments in areas such as housing, as well as developments in private sector credit flow and unemployment.[19]

Where the Commission detects excessive imbalances in a Member State, the Council, on a recommendation from the Commission, can adopt a recommendation establishing the existence of an excessive imbalance and recommend that the Member State concerned takes corrective action.[20] The Member State is also set a deadline to draw up a corrective action plan, which it has to submit to the Council and the Commission for approval. The implementation of the plan is then monitored. Subject to Regulation 1174/2011 on enforcement measures to correct excessive macroeconomic imbalances in the eurozone, Member States that do not take the necessary corrective action face an interest-bearing deposit.[21] This deposit can turn into a fine if the Member State continuously fails to comply. Moreover, an annual fine can be imposed by the Council if a Member State continuously fails to submit a sufficient corrective action plan. For these decisions, the above-mentioned reversed voting procedure applies.[22]

The excessive deficit procedure is also strengthened. Two amendments are most notable: the reinforced focus on government debt levels and the application of non-interest-bearing deposits early on in the excessive deficit procedure. With regard to the former, it should be observed that certainly up to 2005 the focus in economic co-ordination in EMU was very much on government deficits.[23] Little attention was paid to government debts when assessing the economic situation in a Member State. Under the new system, the Commission must explicitly take into account:

> the developments in the medium-term government debt position, its dynamics and sustainability, including, in particular, risk factors including the maturity structure and currency denomination of the debt, stock-flow adjustment and its composition, accumulated reserves and other financial assets, guarantees, in particular those linked to the financial sector, and any implicit liabilities related to ageing and private debt, to the extent that it may represent a contingent implicit liability for the government.[24]

[18] Article 2, Regulation 1176/2011.
[19] Article 4(3), Regulation 1176/2011. For more details, see Commission (2012).
[20] Article 7, Regulation 1176/2011.
[21] Article 3(1), Regulation 1174/2011.
[22] Articles 3(2)–(3), Regulation 1174/2011.
[23] This neglecting of the government debt criterion was already acknowledged in the 2005 reform of the Stability and Growth Pact – that is, Regulation 1466/97 and Regulation 1467/97.
[24] Article 2(3)(c), Regulation 1467/97 (as amended).

In the context of the excessive deficit procedure Member States are now obliged to define targets for 'government expenditure and revenue and for the discretionary measures on both the expenditure and the revenue side consistent with the Council's recommendation'.[25]

The second major change in the excessive deficit procedure concerns the application of sanctions. Until recently this was only possible at a late stage in the procedure and in practice had never occurred.[26] Based on the new Regulation 1173/2011 on the effective enforcement of budgetary surveillance in the eurozone, the decision on the application of a non-interest-bearing deposit is taken at the time of the decision on the existence of an excessive deficit in a Member State and thus in the opening phase of the excessive deficit procedure. Where an interest-bearing deposit has been imposed upon a Member State in the multilateral surveillance procedure, it is turned into a non-interest-bearing deposit. Moreover, such a deposit may be imposed if the Commission detects the existence of serious non-compliance of a Member State with its budgetary policy obligations.[27] In such a case, the Commission can recommend that 'the Council, by a further decision, requires the Member State concerned to lodge with the Commission a non-interest-bearing deposit amounting to 0.2% of its GDP in the preceding year'.[28] Once more, reversed voting applies.[29]

Finally, experience in the past with unreliable economic data forwarded by Member States in the context of the multilateral surveillance and excessive deficit procedure has resulted in the adoption of Council Directive 2011/85/EU which seeks to establish 'detailed rules concerning the characteristics of the budgetary frameworks of the Member States'.[30] Fiscal planning by Member States must be 'based on realistic macroeconomic and budgetary forecasts using the most up-to-date information' and 'fiscal data for all sub-sectors of general government' must be made public.[31] Indeed, as stated in the preamble to the Directive: 'Complete and reliable public accounting practices for all sub-sectors of general government are a precondition for the production of high-quality statistics that are comparable across Member States'.[32] What is more, under the reformed regime, the manipulation, whether intentionally or by serious negligence, of deficit and debt data can trigger a fine imposed by the Council, acting on a recommendation by the Commission.[33]

The Fiscal Compact

The signing of the Treaty on Stability, Co-ordination and Governance in the economic and monetary union (known as the 'Fiscal Compact') highlights first and foremost that major reforms of the existing system of economic governance requiring an amendment of the existing primary Union law face major, if not at times insurmountable, obstacles. Indeed,

[25] Articles 3(4a) and 5(1a), Regulation 1467/97.
[26] See Article 126(11) TFEU.
[27] Article 5(1), Regulation 1173/2011.
[28] Article 5(1), Regulation 1173/2011.
[29] Article 5(2), Regulation 1173/2011.
[30] Article 1, Council Directive 2011/85.
[31] Articles 4(1) and 3(2), Council Directive 2011/85.
[32] Preamble 3, Council Directive 2011/85.
[33] Article 8, Regulation 1173/2011.

the often applied characterization of Treaty amendment as the opening of a Pandora's box appears to have been borne out in the recent negotiations on an amendment of the TFEU in order to strengthen economic governance in EMU. What was true in the European Communities of the six is even truer in the European Union of the 27: any one Member State can hold all others and the Union hostage when it comes to negotiating treaty amendments for which the ordinary revision procedure applies.[34]

The way out has been – and not for the first time – the creation of a legal framework outside the existing EU treaties by means of the signing of an international treaty.[35] Leaving aside the legal policy issue of what the general effects of the application of such intergovernmental instruments are on the constitutional framework of the EU,[36] it is clear that the relationship of the Fiscal Compact with existing Union law is a delicate one. Indeed, several references in the Fiscal Compact to the existing Treaties suggest that the drafters were very much aware of this issue. Article 2 of the Fiscal Compact, for example, states that: 'This Treaty shall be applied and interpreted by the Contracting Parties in conformity with the Treaties on which the European Union is founded'. Moreover, it 'shall apply insofar as it is compatible with the Treaties on which the European Union is founded and with European Union law' and 'shall not encroach upon the competence of the Union to act in the area of the economic union'. Yet whether the budgetary constraints on Member States introduced by the Fiscal Compact can be easily reconciled with the rather restricted scope of Articles 121 and 126 TFEU is questionable, to say the least.

Among the main elements of the Fiscal Compact is the obligation for Member States to have budgetary positions that are balanced or in surplus. The structural deficit must not exceed 0.5 per cent of nominal gross domestic product (GDP). Only in the case where the debt ratio is 'significantly below' the 60 per cent of GDP margin laid down in Article 126(1) TFEU and the Protocol on the excessive deficit procedure, and only if the long-term sustainability of public finances is secured, does a Member State have the right to operate a structural deficit of up to 1 per cent of GDP.[37] Member States must also provide for an automatic correction mechanism that forces them to take action to correct significant deviations from the medium-term objective or the adjustment path deficits within a specified period of time.[38] What is more, Member States are required to incorporate rules of a 'binding and permanent character' to this effect into their own legal systems. The Fiscal Compact gives preference to a constitutional safeguard in this regard. In the case of non-compliance with this requirement, Member States can find themselves before the ECJ and, thereafter, in case of non-compliance with the latter's judgment may even face a lump sum or a penalty payment that can amount to up to 0.1 per cent of its GDP.[39] Interestingly,

[34] Article 48(2) TEU: by common accord.

[35] Another prominent example is the Convention on the stepping up of cross-border co-operation, particularly in combating terrorism, cross-border crime and illegal migration (known as the 'Prüm Convention') that was concluded outside the Treaties framework by Belgium, Germany, Spain, France, Luxembourg, the Netherlands and Austria. By Council Decision 2008/615/JHA of 23 June 2008 on the stepping up of cross-border co-operation, particularly in combating terrorism and cross-border crime, this convention was included in the EU legal framework.

[36] See in this regard, for example, the comments by Paul Craig as reported in House of Lords, European Union Committee, 'The euro area crisis', 25th Report of Session 2010–12, p. 28.

[37] Article 3(1), Fiscal Compact.

[38] Based on common principles decided upon by the European Commission. See Article 3(2), Fiscal Compact.

[39] Article 8, Fiscal Compact. The jurisdiction of the ECJ outside the EU Treaty framework is established through Article 273 TFEU. For this purpose the Fiscal Compact is considered a special agreement.

the Fiscal Compact does not foresee judicial enforcement when a Member State does not reduce its excessive deficits.[40]

Under the Fiscal Compact, Member States are supposed to discuss all 'major economic reforms they plan to undertake' *ex ante*.[41] Moreover, they are obliged to 'report ex ante on their public debt issuing plans to the Council [. . .] and to the European Commission'.[42] Interestingly, the provision in question explains this with the need to 'better co-ordinate the planning of their national debt issuance'. One may wonder whether this clear attempt to get a grip on sovereign debt issuance by eurozone Member States and thus (irresponsible) lending on the capital markets is a first, cautious step towards a centralization of sovereign debt issuance in the eurozone.[43]

In case of debt rates above 60 per cent of GDP, Member States must reduce their debt at an average rate of 0.05 per cent per year.[44] What is more, a Member State that is subject to an excessive deficit procedure becomes obliged to establish a so-called 'budgetary and economic partnership programme' that has to include details on structural reforms that are implemented 'to ensure an effective and durable correction of its excessive deficit'.[45] The programme has to be endorsed by the Council and the Commission.

The Fiscal Compact also attempts to address one of the main weaknesses of the excessive deficit procedure as defined by Article 126 TFEU and Regulation 1467/97 – that is, the dependency of the procedure on the political will in the Council to take action. The example of the unsatisfactory application of the procedure to Germany and France in 2003 has highlighted the constraining effect of this quasi-intergovernmental method of economic policy co-ordination (Collignon, 2004). Article 7 of the Fiscal Compact somewhat convolutedly hints at the general application of reversed voting in the excessive deficit procedure beyond the application of a non-interest-bearing deposit introduced as part of the Six Pack when stating that the Member States 'commit to supporting the proposals or recommendations submitted by the European Commission where it considers that a Member State of the European Union whose currency is the euro is in breach of the deficit criterion in the framework of an excessive deficit procedure'. At the same time Article 7 states that this is not the case if a qualified majority of the eurozone Member States, without taking into account the Member State concerned, is opposed to the decision proposed or recommended. This wording seems to suggest that in the case of inaction on parts of the Council during the different stages of the excessive deficit procedure, Member States are expected to accept the Commission's recommendations. In this context, the reference in Article 7 to the observance of 'the procedural requirements of the Treaties on which the European Union is founded' is somewhat puzzling as Article 126 TFEU does not foresee such a procedure, but rather explicitly makes any procedural steps subject to a qualified majority decision in the Council.

Despite these clear attempts to commit Member States to sound budgetary policies, the Fiscal Compact also introduces some loopholes that may jeopardize its aims in the

[40] Article 126(10) TFEU continues to exclude an application of the infringement procedure foreseen in Articles 258 and 259 TFEU.

[41] Article 11, Fiscal Compact.

[42] See Article 6, Fiscal Compact.

[43] Reference can be made in this context to the discussion on Eurobonds. See, for example, Commission (2011).

[44] Article 4, Fiscal Compact.

[45] Article 5, Fiscal Compact.

future. In exceptional circumstances Member States are allowed to temporarily deviate from their MTO or the adjustment path towards it.[46] What is more, the rather critical statements by the new president of the French Republic during his election campaign, as well as the election results on – at the time of writing of this contribution – ongoing government formation talks in Greece, highlight that the new consensus on economic governance in the EU may already be eroding and is in any event fragile.

II. Development of the *Acquis Union* in the Jurisprudence of the ECJ

The reminder of this contribution will focus on several developments in the jurisprudence of the ECJ that shape the *acquis Union* pertaining to EU citizenship and the free movement of persons. Here, the ECJ continues to be confronted with individuals that test the outer limits of the rights provided by primary and secondary Union law in national courts. In dealing with such cases, the ECJ in 2011 seems to have taken a novel approach to the scope of EU citizenship that some observers consider to be the beginning of real European citizenship (for example, Kochenov, 2011) and the identification of citizens with the EU (Hailbronner and Iglesias Sánchez, 2011; also Hailbronner and Thym, 2011).

In *Gerardo Ruiz Zambrano* v *Office national de l'emploi (ONEm)*,[47] the Court had to deal with the question of whether Union law gave a third-country national a right of residence and a right to a work permit in the Member State of residence and nationality of the third-country national's minor dependent children. In its decision from March 2011, the ECJ briefly discussed the application of Article 3(1) of Directive 2004/38 on the right of citizens of the Union and their family members to move and reside freely within the territory of the Member State only to come to the conclusion that this provision does not cover the situation in question as the minors were residing in the Member State of which they were nationals and had never left the territory of that Member State.[48] The ECJ then moved on to assess the implications of the fact that the dependent minor children of the third-country national were in possession of an EU nationality and as such were covered by Article 20 TFEU establishing the Union citizenship.

Emphasizing its established case law that 'citizenship of the Union is intended to be the fundamental status of nationals of the Member States', the Court stated that: 'Article 20 TFEU precludes national measures which have the effect of depriving citizens of the Union of the genuine enjoyment of the substance of the rights conferred by virtue of their status as citizens of the Union'. In the opinion of the ECJ, in the given circumstances the refusal to grant a residency and work permit to the third-country father would have effectively amounted to depriving the dependent minors of 'the genuine enjoyment of the substance of the rights attaching to the status of European Union citizen' as they would have to leave the EU as well 'in order to accompany their parents'.[49] Remarkably, the question of whether the case in the main proceedings would have to be considered a purely internal situation, as the minors had not made use of their right to freedom of movement, was not as such discussed by the ECJ in this context.

[46] Articles 3(1)(c) and (3)(b), Fiscal Compact.
[47] C-34/09 [2011] ECR I-nyr. See the brief mention in last year's Annual Review (Amtenbrink, 2011, p. 180).
[48] C-34/09 [2011] ECR I-nyr, paragraphs 37–39.
[49] C-34/09 [2011] ECR I-nyr, paragraphs 40–45.

This decision by the ECJ has been acknowledged not only for recognizing a fundamental legal status of EU citizenship, but for defining 'a new jurisdiction test' (Kochenov, 2011, p. 108) and even for (potentially) being 'at the centre of the emergence of a constitutional patriotism' (Hailbronner and Iglesias Sánchez, 2011, p. 498). At the same time, the uncertainties surrounding this new approach by the ECJ have been pointed out (Hailbronner and Iglesias Sánchez, 2011). Against this background it could be argued that the expectations for the subsequent case law of the ECJ were high on all sides.

In the case *Shirley MacCarthy* v *Secretary of State for the Home Department*,[50] which was decided in May 2011, the ECJ once more had to interpret the scope of Directive 2004/38 and of EU citizenship in a case involving a British citizen who also had Irish nationality but had always lived in the United Kingdom. In essence the first issue was, whether such a person could be considered a 'beneficiary' within the meaning of Article 3(1), Directive 2004/38, according to which this provision applies to 'all Union citizens who move to or reside in a Member State other than that of which they are a national, and to their family members as defined in point 2 of Article 2 who accompany or join them'. In the case before the national court, the British citizen with dual nationality had married a Jamaican national who had no right of residence in the United Kingdom under the national immigration rules. The couple therefore applied for a residence permit and residence document as, respectively, a Union citizen and the third-country spouse of a Union citizen. Before doing so, the British national for the first time applied for an Irish passport and obtained it. The application for a residence permit was refused by the British authorities on the grounds that despite her dual nationality the British citizen could not be considered a worker, self-employed person or self-sufficient person in accordance with Articles 2 and 3, Regulation 2004/38.

For the ECJ, '[a] literal, teleological and contextual interpretation of that provision leads to a negative reply' to the question whether Regulation 2004/38 applies.[51] It becomes not only apparent from the wording of Article 3(1) that refers to moving to, or residing in, a Member State *other than that* of which the Union citizen is a national, but in the view of the ECJ also from 'Directive 2004/38, taken as a whole, that the residence to which it refers is linked to the exercise of the freedom of movement for persons'.[52] Consequently, the Jamaican national was not considered to have a right of residence as a third-country spouse under EU law.[53] As such, the ECJ verified in this case what mainstream textbooks on EU law will usually state – that is, the right to rely on Directive 2004/38 is intrinsically linked to the exercising of the right of free movement. This is not the case if an EU citizen has always resided in the Member State of which he or she is a national, regardless of whether the citizen is also a national of another Member State. Dual EU nationality does not amount to a use of the freedom of movement.[54]

Turning to EU citizenship, the ECJ pointed out once more that 'citizenship of the Union is intended to be the fundamental status of nationals of the Member States' and that 'Article 20 TFEU precludes national measures which have the effect of depriving Union citizens of the genuine enjoyment of the substance of the rights conferred by

[50] Case C-434/09 [2011] ECR I-nyr.
[51] Case C-434/09 [2011] ECR I-nyr, paragraph 31.
[52] Case C-434/09 [2011] ECR I-nyr, paragraph 35.
[53] Case C-434/09 [2011] ECR I-nyr, paragraphs 14–17.
[54] Case C-434/09 [2011] ECR I-nyr, paragraphs 39–41.

virtue of that status'.[55] From this fundamental status the ECJ concluded that the fact that a EU citizen has not made use of the right to freedom of movement 'cannot, for that reason alone, be assimilated to a purely internal situation' to which Union law does not apply.[56] Thus the absence of a cross-border movement as a factor linking a situation to the free movement provisions is not per se sufficient to deny the protection of EU law with regard to EU citizenship. In the given case, the ECJ considered, however, that the British citizen could not rely on Article 21 TFEU as she was not deprived of her rights associated with her status as a Union citizen and that the exercise of her right of free movement and residence within the territory of the Member States was not impeded as a result of the refusal of the United Kingdom authorities to grand her a residence permit as an EU citizen.[57]

In an effort to explain the difference with its *Zambrano* judgment earlier that year, the ECJ pointed out that different to the situation in that case, the effect of the British measure would not be that of 'obliging' the British national to leave the territory of the EU.[58] Yet whether this argument is convincing is questionable, since in *Zambrano* it was not established either that the EU national minor children of the third-country national would have been *de jure* obliged to leave the EU. Rather in that case it was stated as a matter of fact that given the situation that would arise if the third-country national was forced to leave the EU, the children would have to accompany their parents. So while Mrs MacCarthy would surely not be obliged to leave the United Kingdom as a result of the refusal to grant her a EU residence permit, the consequence of this denial by the British authorities, being that her husband would have to leave the territory of the EU, could certainly lead to a situation whereby she would at least feel forced to leave the country if she intends to live with her husband.

The question that one could have is if the Court would have decided differently, if it had been established that Mrs MacCarthy was a dependent spouse of the third-country national? The answer was arguably indirectly provided by the ECJ shortly after this decision in its judgment in the case *Dereci and others* v *Bundesministerium für Inneres*.[59] This case involved several instances of third-country nationals that had unsuccessfully applied for residence permits in Austria on grounds of being family members of Austrian citizens residing in Austria. Apparently none of the Austrian citizens had ever exercised their right to free movement. Moreover, none of the Austrian family members was dependent on any of the third-country nationals. In its November 2011 judgment, the ECJ once more referred to the scope of Directive 2004/38 which did not cover the situation in the given case either. Turning thereafter to the protective scope of EU citizenship, the ECJ once more adopted the *Zambrano* formula to test the existence of a denial of 'genuine enjoyment of the substance of the rights' conferred by the status of being an EU citizen.[60] In doing so, the Court seemed eager to emphasize the exceptional circumstances existing in *Zambrano* that resulted in the establishment, in that case, of a right of a residence and work permit for a third-country national relying on the EU citizenship rights of its

[55] Case C-434/09 [2011] ECR I-nyr, paragraph 47.
[56] Case C-434/09 [2011] ECR I-nyr.
[57] Case C-434/09 [2011] ECR I-nyr, paragraph 56.
[58] Case C-434/09 [2011] ECR I-nyr, paragraph 50.
[59] C-256/11 [2011] ECR I-nyr.
[60] C-256/11 [2011] ECR I-nyr, paragraph 64.

dependent minor children.[61] In the opinion of the ECJ in *Dereci* it derives from the facts of its earlier judgment that:

> [T]he mere fact that it might appear desirable to a national of a Member State, for economic reasons or in order to keep his family together in the territory of the Union, for the members of his family who do not have the nationality of a Member State to be able to reside with him in the territory of the Union, is not sufficient in itself to support the view that the Union citizen will be forced to leave Union territory if such a right is not granted.[62]

Rather, in the view of the Court circumstances must exist:

> in which, although subordinate legislation on the right of residence of third-country nationals is not applicable, a right of residence may not, exceptionally, be refused to a third-country national, who is a family member of a Member State national, as the effectiveness of Union citizenship enjoyed by that national would otherwise be undermined.[63]

Exactly in what situations this would be the case, if at all, apart from the specific situation of *Zambrano* (EU national minor that is economically dependent on third-country national) remains unclear. What seems to become clear though from *Dereci* is that the dependence on a third-country national requires that the EU citizen is actually maintained by the former. This can be derived from the fact that in describing the actions in the main proceedings the ECJ in its judgment made a point of stating that this was not the case for any of the applicants.[64]

The reception of the ECJ's approach to EU citizenship in and since *Zambrano* has been rather mixed. Exemplary for this are the observations by Niamh Nic Shuibhne who, on the one hand, recognizes the judgments *McCarthy* and *Dereci* for seeking to 'refine a core new premise of EU citizenship law: the deprivation/genuine enjoyment test' and for establishing 'the primacy of EU citizenship law over national measures that either threaten the loss of the status of citizenship per se or deprive citizens of the genuine enjoyment of the substance of associated rights', while on the other hand rightly pointing the problematic side of the inconsistencies that can be observed in the approach taken by the Court in its judgments since *Zambrano* (Nic Shuibhne, 2012, pp. 363, 365).[65] Moreover, this author points towards the broader case law on the right to respect for family law protected by Article 7 of the Charter of Fundamental Rights of the European Union and Article 8 of the European Convention for the Protection of Human Rights and Fundamental Freedoms.[66] Indeed, it can certainly be debated whether the ECJ's decisions in the cases *McCarthy* and *Dereci* add to the protection of family life in EU law or rather signify attempts by the ECJ to kerb the potentially far-reaching implications of its reasoning in *Zambrano*.

[61] C-256/11[2011] ECR I-nyr, paragraph 67.
[62] C-256/11[2011] ECR I-nyr, paragraph 68. On the implications of the decision on family reunification, see Thym (2012, pp. 103ff.).
[63] C-256/11[2011] ECR I-nyr, paragraph 67.
[64] C-256/11[2011] ECR I-nyr, paragraph 22.
[65] See also Kochenov (2011), who offers a somewhat more positive assessment.
[66] With regard to the implications of this case law for the national judiciary, see, for example, Van Eijken (2012), who also raises questions with regard to the compatibility with Article 8 ECHR.

Concluding Reflections

Similar to what has already been observed in the 2010 *Annual Review* the most salient legal developments in 2011 were in the regulatory sphere. This can be explained by the vast number of highly significant measures that have been taken in a very short space of time that not only (re)shape the landscape of economic policy co-ordination in EMU, but in the view of some decide over the faith of the European integration as we know it. Somewhat less dramatically it may be observed that these developments have the potential to shape EU governance beyond EMU.

The Fiscal Compact is a case in point. On the one hand, it can be argued that the substantive provisions of the Treaty are really not substantially new as a considerable number of the arrangements included therein can be traced back to the two Regulations of the Stability and Growth Pact – namely Regulations 1466/97 and 1467/97. This is certainly the case for the obligation of Member States to aim for a balanced or surplus budget and to aim for an annual deficit reduction. On the other hand, the elevation of these duties to the status of an international treaty, paired with the requirement to enshrine them in national (constitutional) law, arguably gives them a somewhat different quality. The possibility to refer to the ECJ in order to enforce the requirement to introduce budgetary restraints into national law, as well as the implied reversed voting for all Council decisions in the excessive deficit procedure have to be considered real novelties. What is more, the significance of the Fiscal Compact may only be recognized when considering that any financial assistance to Member States under the new European Stability Mechanism will be subject to the ratification of the Fiscal Compact.[67] Finally, the fact that a reform of economic governance within the EU Treaty framework proved to be impossible to realize once more raises questions about the ability of the EU to advance under its present constitutional structure.

The new mode of economic governance certainly results in a vertical and horizontal shift in the balance of power. First, the obligation on parts of the Member States of a (constitutional) *Schuldenbremse* (debt brake), as well as the new requirements as part of the European Semester and of the macroeconomic imbalances procedure result, to some extent, in a further technocratization of economic policy at the national level, arguably at the expense of national parliaments. The influence of the Council and Commission, and thus the influence of the supranational level, has been increased at the expense of the Member State's constitutional systems. Next to this vertical shift in power, there is also a remarkable change in the inter-institutional balance at the EU level. As has become clear from the description of the new regulatory structure, the power of the Commission is substantially increased compared to the previous arrangements. Thanks to the application of reversed voting, but also through the increased involvement in all parts of the process of economic surveillance, the Commission is moving towards becoming the main source of economic policy in the EU. It is questionable whether this vertical and horizontal shift in power is sufficiently backed by (democratic) accountability structures. Be that as it may, the recent victory of the socialist candidate for the French presidency who has already announced that the Fiscal Compact would have to be renegotiated, underlines the continuing vulnerability of developments in the EU to political developments in the Member States.

[67] Treaty establishing the European Stability Mechanism, Preamble 5.

Turning to the developments in the jurisprudence of the ECJ in the area of EU citizenship and the free movement of persons, it can be observed that the ECJ further builds its case law on the citizenship of the Union as a fundamental status of nationals of the Member States as observed in the 2010 *Annual Review*.[68] Whether the new formula applied in the context of Articles 20 and 21 TFEU, established first in *Zambrano*, can actually be considered strengthening this fundamental status of nationals of the Member States as EU citizens is open to debate. While the subsequent judgments in *McCarthy* and *Dereci* can be viewed as useful clarification, they may also be criticized for being somewhat inconsistent and possibly even a retreat from the initial position taken in *Zambrano*.

References

Amtenbrink, F. (2011) 'Legal Developments'. *JCMS*, Vol. 49, No. S1, pp. 165–86.

Amtenbrink, F., De Haan, J. and Sleijpen, O.C.H.M. (1997) 'Stability and Growth Pact: Placebo or Panacea?' *European Business Law Review*, Vol. 8, No. 9, pp. 202–10, 223–38.

Collignon, S. (2004) 'The End of the Stability and Growth Pact?' *International Economics and Economic Policy*, Vol. 1, No. 1, pp. 15–19.

Commission of the European Communities (2010a) 'Proposal for a Regulation of the European Parliament and of the Council amending Regulation (EC) No 1466/97 on the strengthening of the surveillance of budgetary positions and the surveillance and co-ordination of economic policies'. *COM*(2010) 526 final.

Commission of the European Communities (2010b) 'Communication from the Commission to the European Parliament, the European Council, the Council, the European Central Bank, the Economic and Social Committee and the Committee of the Regions: Reinforcing economic policy co-ordination'. *COM*(2010) 250 final.

Commission of the European Communities (2010c) 'Communication from the Commission to the European Parliament, the European Council, the Council, the European Central Bank, the Economic and Social Committee and the Committee of the Regions: Enhancing economic policy co-ordination for stability, growth and jobs: tools for stronger EU economic governance'. *COM*(2010) 367 final.

Commission of the European Communities (2010d) 'Proposal for a Regulation of the European Parliament and of the Council on the effective enforcement of budgetary surveillance in the euro area'. *COM*(2010) 524 final.

Commission of the European Communities (2011) 'Green Paper on the feasibility of introducing Stability Bonds'. *COM*(2011) 818 final.

Commission of the European Communities (2012) 'Scoreboard for the surveillance of macroeconomic imbalances'. European Economy Occasional Paper 92, February.

European Central Bank (ECB) (2011) 'The European Stability Mechanism'. *Monthly Bulletin*, July.

European Council (2011) 'Statement by the euro area heads of state or government', Brussels, 9 December.

Hahn, H.J. (1998) 'The Stability Pact for European Monetary Union: Compliance with Deficit Limit as a Constant Legal Duty'. *Common Market Law Review*, Vol. 35, No. 1, pp. 77–100.

Hailbronner, K. and Iglesias Sánchez, S. (2011) 'The European Court of Justice and Citizenship of the European Union: New Developments towards a Truly Fundamental Status'. *Vienna Journal on International Constitutional Law*, Vol. 5, No. 4, pp. 498–537.

[68] Amtenbrink (2011, pp. 179ff.), with further references.

Hailbronner, K. and Thym, D. (2011) 'Case C-34/09, *Gerardo Ruiz Zambrano* v *Office national de l'emploi (ONEm)*, Judgment of the Court of Justice (Grand Chamber) of 8 March 2011'. *Common Market Law Review*, Vol. 48, No. 4, pp. 1253–70.

Kochenov, D. (2011) 'A Real European Citizenship; A New Jurisdiction Test; A Novel Chapter in the Development of the Union in Europe'. *Columbia Journal of European Law*, Vol. 18, No. 1, pp. 56–109.

Maher, I. (2004) 'Economic Policy Co-ordination and the European Court: Excessive Deficits and Ecofin Discretion'. *European Law Review*, Vol. 29, No. 6, pp. 831–41.

Nic Shuibhne, N. (2012) '(Some of) the Kids are All Right'. *Common Market Law Review*, Vol. 49, No. 1, pp. 349–80.

Thym, D. (2012), 'Aufenthaltsrechtliche Wirkungen der Unionsbürgerschaft – Dereci u. a.'. *Neue Zeitschrift für Verwaltungsrecht*, pp. 97–104.

Van Eijken, H. (2012) 'Ruiz Zambrano the Aftermath: de impact van artikel 20 VWEU op de Nederlandse rechtspraak'. *Nederlands Tijdschrift voor Europees*, No. 2, pp. 41–8.

JCMS 2012 Volume 50 Annual Review pp. 147–161 DOI: 10.1111/j.1468-5965.2012.02278.x

The Arab Spring, the Eurozone Crisis and the Neighbourhood: A Region in Flux

RICHARD G. WHITMAN[1] and ANA E. JUNCOS[2]
[1] University of Kent. [2] University of Bristol

Introduction

The year 2011 was momentous in the European Union's neighbourhood. Struggling to deal with the effects of the eurozone crisis and with the European External Action Service (EEAS) in the process of being established, the Union was confronted with one of its greatest foreign policy challenges yet: the popular uprisings in its southern neighbourhood. The EU's efforts concentrated on providing a new response to these events through a revised European Neighbourhood Policy (ENP) and supporting the international efforts in Tunisia, Egypt and elsewhere. However, the EU was criticized once again for its failure to act forcefully and coherently during the Libyan crisis. Meanwhile, developments in the east and particularly in Belarus and Ukraine also provided evidence of the limited effectiveness of the ENP, with democratic reforms stalling in most of the region. The EU's enlargement policy made some progress with the closure of accession negotiations with Croatia, but the usual problems (bilateral disputes, ethno-nationalism and corruption) remained.

To be sure, Croatian accession was one of the few success stories in 2011. It was even more remarkable considering that 2011 marked 20 years since the declaration of independence of Croatia and the start of the war in the country. However, the signing of the Accession Treaty was largely forgotten during the European Council in December because of the eurozone crisis and the United Kingdom's position on the Fiscal Compact. Notwithstanding this success, the EU was unable to have a distinct impact in its neighbourhood because of a combination of factors: the sovereign debt crisis, institutional problems linked to the implementation of the EEAS and a lack of consensus among its Member States.

This article first provides an overview of the impact of the eurozone crisis on the EU's neighbourhood policies and the enlargement process. The crisis raises important challenges not just for the EU itself, but also for the candidate countries and EU neighbours. It also risks undermining one of the cornerstones of EU foreign policy: conditionality. Second, the article examines the role of the newly established EEAS in dealing with the political and security challenges coming from the neighbourhood. As will be shown below, the picture here is mixed. The EEAS was able to achieve some successes in the Balkans, where the EU can hold out the prospect of membership; however, it failed to deliver in the ENP region during its first year of operation. The article then moves on to discuss developments in the EU's neighbourhood – in particular, in relation to the Arab Spring, eastern Europe and the enlargement process. Just as the EU had to respond to unprecedented popular uprisings in the Middle East and North Africa, the tendency in the eastern neighbourhood was towards more authoritarianism. Although there might be a temptation to become inward-looking given the internal problems affecting the EU, the neighbourhood still remains a key challenge for European policy-makers.

I. The Impact of the Eurozone Crisis on the Neighbourhood

The eurozone crisis threatens not only the internal dimension of the integration process, but also the EU's role in the world and its international image. In the neighbourhood, the sovereign debt crisis has had a fourfold impact. First, although the EU remains officially committed to its enlargement policy and the ENP, the eurozone crisis risks increasing the 'enlargement fatigue' among political leaders and draining support from public opinion within the Member States. Second, in times of economic crisis, Member States might become more reluctant to share the financial burden of further enlargement (and other neighbourhood policies). Third, the economic crisis has worsened the economic problems that some of the candidate and neighbouring countries face. And last but not least, the euro crisis is set to decrease the EU's attraction power among candidate countries and neighbours, especially where the EU does not hold out the prospect of membership. Let us examine each of these in turn.

After years of institutional reform, the entry into force of the Lisbon Treaty was meant to mark a new phase in the EU's foreign policy with the appointment of the new High Representative and the establishment of the EEAS (Dinan, 2010; Whitman and Juncos, 2009b). However, the sovereign debt crisis has put a new brake on those ambitions. A more inward-looking Europe, concentrated on how to solve the crisis through the negotiation of a new fiscal treaty, means that European leaders have less time for the neighbourhood, enlargement and European foreign policy more generally – and indeed many other policy areas. Among the public support for enlargement is also at a low at 42 per cent, while opposition to further enlargement is up to 47 per cent (Eurobarometer, 2011, p. 58). And although public support for a common foreign and security policy remains high (at 64 per cent), polls consistently show that the economic situation continues to be the main concern among EU citizens (Eurobarometer, 2011, pp. 23–6).

While financial considerations have always played a part in discussions about EU enlargement,[1] the sovereign debt crisis is set to complicate matters even more. Financially, the neighbourhood policy does not constitute a significant burden for the EU. At around €24.3 billion, the financial commitment to the candidate countries and neighbours through the Instrument Pre-Accession (IPA) and the European Neighbourhood and Partnership Instrument (ENPI) represents a very small percentage of the EU's budget (less than 3 per cent). For instance, in the new Multiannual Financial Framework (2014–20) presented by the Commission in June 2011, the proposed budget for IPA stands at €14.1 billion, which according to the Commission represents a stable budget, at the same level as the current funding programme running from 2007 to 2013 (European Union, 2011). Despite these modest figures, the eurozone crisis has drawn attention to the lack of convergence between European economies, in particular between the north and the south, and the risks associated with it. This will weigh in any decision to enlarge the EU as it will require more

[1] For example, the French and Italians raised concerns with the 1981/86 enlargement fearing transfers would be diverted to Greece and the Iberian Peninsula and Spain raised similar questions about the enlargement to the central and eastern European states (CEEs).

transfers to the poorer economies of the candidate countries; with the exception of Iceland, GDP per capita in the candidate countries is well under the EU-27.

The economic crisis has also been felt in the EU's neighbourhood, with some of the candidate countries (Serbia, Bosnia and Iceland) amongst the most affected (see Whitman and Juncos, 2011). For instance, in 2009, the EU had to create an IPA crisis package of €200 million to support the economies of the Western Balkans. Iceland's decision to apply for EU membership was also directly linked to the consequences of the collapse of its bank sector. The eurozone crisis raises new doubts regarding Iceland's membership bid, though. The weakness of the euro and the fact that the new fiscal pact will require a stronger budgetary discipline has reduced the economic and political incentives of joining the EU. Hence, more recently, Icelandic politicians even floated the idea of adopting the Canadian dollar instead of the single currency.[2]

More worryingly, the euro crisis risks decreasing the power of conditionality which is at the heart of the EU's most successful foreign policy – that of enlargement. A case in point is that of Turkey. As its economy continues to grow as well as its confidence as a regional power, the attractiveness of EU membership recedes, particularly since membership talks have been at a standstill for the last five years. In the words of Turkey's former ambassador to the EU, Volkan Bozkir: 'The EU dream has come to an end for the world. There is a paradigm shift. The EU is no longer the same Union that provided comfort, prosperity and wealth to its citizens as in the past'.[3] The soft power that the EU has traditionally been able to exercise in its neighbourhood is now being eroded. The success of the EU's model has been put into question as the financial and economic crisis bites into the economies of the Member States and leads to economic stagnation (see the contributions by Hodson and Connolly in this issue). With Europe in decline, Russia will also exert more attraction on the countries of eastern Europe. For many of the eastern European countries, Russia currently offers more incentives than the EU in the form of potentially cheaper gas – as the deal between Ukraine and Russia about the Russian Black Sea naval base in Sebastopol illustrates. By comparison, the ENPI offers more modest financial rewards at higher costs of adaptation. And although the EU has committed more money to the Middle East and North Africa as a response to the Arab Spring (see below), the economic crisis has also limited the financial response to the crisis. Despite having agreed on a policy that promised more access to funding, EU markets and mobility,

> [M]ember [S]tates have so far failed to deliver much: Budget constraints limited the money they were prepared to offer to 5.8 billion euros in direct funding; populist fears about immigration restricted offers of greater mobility for students and workers; and protectionist sentiment, fuelled by economic difficulties, precluded any real opening of markets, especially to North African agricultural products. (Vaïsse, 2012)

In sum, in the short and medium terms, the financial and economic crisis has limited the time and attention to these policies, but also the range of tools that the EU can deploy in its neighbourhood to support the transitions of countries in the Mediterranean, eastern Europe and the Balkans. In the long term, it could have an even more damaging and

[2] *EUobserver.com*, 15 March 2012.
[3] *EUobserver.com*, 18 November 2011.

lasting impact on the EU's ability to promote its values and norms as the incentives of joining the single market and the single currency continue to wane.

II. The EEAS and the Neighbourhood

The establishment of the EEAS at the end of 2010 was seen as an opportunity to re-energize the EU's foreign policy more generally and its neighbourhood policy in particular (Allen and Smith, 2011). However, even before it was fully operational, the EEAS was presented with a vast challenge in the form of the Arab uprisings. As stated in its first year report:

> The political and economic context for the launch of the EEAS has been particularly challenging. The global economic crisis and tensions within the euro zone, together with the Arab Spring, have dominated the international agenda. At the same time, public administrations across Europe are under acute budget pressure, with consequences for the diplomatic services of Member States. This is hardly the ideal backdrop for the launch of a new service for the external relations of the Union. (EEAS, 2011, p. 1)

Despite these challenges, the EEAS achieved some relative successes, especially in the Western Balkans. Under the leadership of Catherine Ashton, it was instrumental in promoting talks between Serbia and Kosovo. Launched in March 2011, the talks have not been ground-breaking (Serbia still does not recognize Kosovo's independence) and were severely disrupted by violence in North Kosovo, but have led to some (yet limited) progress in the normalization of relations between the two. For instance, Kosovo and Serbia have agreed to recognize their university diplomas, and to carry out joint custom checkpoints in North Kosovo. There has also been progress on issues of civil registry, car insurance and licence plates. Moreover, since December, Serbia allows Kosovo citizens to come to the country and move freely with documents issued at the border.[4] The EEAS also played a crucial role in promoting stability in Bosnia and Herzegovina, helping avert a crisis when the president of Republika Srpska, Milorad Dodik, decided to drop his proposal of organizing a referendum after his meeting with Catherine Ashton on 13 May 2011.[5] The referendum on the State Court and the prosecution was seen as a direct assault on the role of the international community in Bosnia, the High Representative and the Dayton Agreement.[6]

Beyond the Balkans, the role of the EEAS has been more modest and somehow disappointing (Brattberg, 2011; Menon, 2011). This can be explained by the fact that the EU has less tools at its disposal in the ENP region (notably, it lacks the membership prospect). In addition, the lack of consensus among the Member States has undermined the role of the EEAS. On Libya, the High Representative issued several declarations on behalf of the EU (see, for example, European Council, 2011d). The High Representative was also active in the preparation of EUFOR Libya (European Council, 2011b) – a military operation to support humanitarian assistance operations in Libya if requested by

[4] *EUobserver.com*, 23 December 2011.

[5] *BalkanInsight*, 13 May 2011.

[6] The referendum would have asked Republika Srpska citizens: 'Do you support laws imposed by High Representative in Bosnia, in particular the laws on Bosnia's state court and prosecution?'

the United Nations Office for the Co-ordination of Humanitarian Affairs (OCHA). However, the operation was never deployed. On 22 May, Ashton opened a liaison office in Benghazi and later an EU delegation was opened in Tripoli.

As discussed below, there was some evidence of improved co-ordination between the EEAS and the Commission in the form of joint crisis platforms and joint initiatives such as the March communication *Partnership for Democracy and Shared Prosperity in the Southern Mediterranean* (Commission, 2011f) and the revised Neighbourhood Strategy. However, the response of the EU to the Arab uprisings still suffered from a lack of coherence, in particular, between Member State and EU policies – a perennial problem in many policy areas. The biggest failure was the fact that the EU could not agree on a united response to the Libya crisis and that a decision on military action was taken outside the EU's framework. The vote on Palestinian membership in Unesco was also another example of the inability of the EEAS to provide for a more coherent action where the Member States remain divided.

III. The Arab Spring and the EU's Neighbourhood Policies

The high degree of stability and stasis in the EU's south and eastern neighbourhood changed dramatically in early 2011. The events in North Africa that were subsequently to be dubbed the 'Arab Spring' ushered in changes within the EU's southern neighbourhood that were akin to those in eastern Europe in 1989. The pace and interconnectedness of the uprisings matched the changes in CEE two decades earlier, but a 'return to Europe' was not the central leitmotif of the Arab Spring – rather a set of uprisings against long-entrenched forms of authoritarianism.

The EU, alongside other external actors such as the United States, was unprepared for the events of the Arab Spring and struggled to formulate an appropriate policy response. In addressing the events in its southern neighbourhood the EU grappled with two issues. First, as mentioned in the previous section, the new foreign policy innovations introduced by the Lisbon Treaty were not yet fully operational and the new EEAS was still being constructed. This created a capacity deficit in the EU's mechanisms to respond to a foreign policy challenge. Furthermore, it severely constrained the capacity of the High Representative to fully exploit the main innovation of the Lisbon Treaty – that is, the drawing together of the EU's common foreign and security policy (CFSP) and its external relations.

The second issue was that the ENP was not designed as a policy for crisis management, but rather as a policy for the EU's medium- and long-term engagement with its neighbours. Consequently, the architecture of the ENP remained largely unchanged by the events across North Africa and the eastern Mediterranean in 2011 and 2012. Moreover, the EU's objectives for the region have not changed substantially with the Arab Spring. This is primarily because the EU has not posited an alternative policy offering with, for example, enlargement to the south and eastern Mediterranean not a policy option.

In many ways, 2011 presented a major juncture for the ENP: never before did the EU produce as many strategy documents on the ENP in one year as it did in 2011 (European Council, 2011c; Commission, 2011a, c, e, f), nor was the increase in the ENP budget ever as significant in relative and absolute terms, not to mention the fact that it comes at a time of profound economic crisis within the EU.[7] This was partly in response to the momentous developments in its southern neighbourhood, partly the result of a longer review process triggered by the implementation of the Lisbon Treaty, but also due to a flawed policy design and the mismatch between ambitions and resources (despite the increases to the latter).

The ground for the reinvigoration that the ENP has seen over the past 12 months was partially prepared in recent years as we have noted in the preceding three reviews of the neighbourhood (see Whitman and Juncos, 2009a, 2010, 2011). In recent years the Eastern Partnership has been the primary centre of developing activity within the wider ENP and with the Union for the Mediterranean (UfM) a much less successful initiative (see Whitman and Juncos, 2009a, 2010, 2011). In 2011, despite another Eastern Partnership summit in September, the focus of the ENP shifted decidedly to the southern neighbourhood as the Arab Spring began to engulf the region from early 2011 onwards in developments at least partly reminiscent of the events in CEE after 1989. The relatively routine policy process of the ENP was thus suddenly presented with significant challenges and opportunities at a time when its place and role in the post-Lisbon environment was still being defined.

On 25 May 2011, the High Representative of the Union for Foreign Affairs and Security Policy and Commission Vice-President, Baroness Catherine Ashton, and the European Commissioner for Enlargement and Neighbourhood Policy, Štefan Füle, presented a new communication from the Commission to the European Parliament, the Council, the European Economic and Social Committee and the Committee of the Regions, underlining the new possibilities for close co-operation between the emerging EEAS and the enlargement and ENP portfolio (in the Commission). Boldly entitled *A New Response to a Changing Neighbourhood* (Commission, 2011e), the document was the outcome of a review of the ENP that began in summer 2010 in response to the changes of the Union's new foreign affairs set-up under the Lisbon Treaty. The *New Response* communication proclaims the need for a new approach 'to build and consolidate healthy democracies, pursue sustainable economic growth and manage cross-border links' and specifically mentions 'stronger political cooperation on [. . .] security [and] conflict resolution matters' (Commission, 2011e, pp. 1, 3). Crucially, and thus reaffirming a persistent theme across a decade of EU strategy papers on the ENP, the communication insists that 'the new approach must be based on mutual accountability and a shared commitment to the universal values of human rights, democracy and the rule of law' and puts significant emphasis on both positive and negative conditionality (Commission, 2011e, pp. 2, 4).

The new ENP mission statement recognizes that addressing threats to stability is an interest that the EU shares with the countries of the southern neighbourhood and, at least implicitly, makes a connection between the two categories in seeing problems in the neighbourhood among the causes of security threats beyond its geographical boundaries, including for the EU. More to the point, organized crime, international terrorism, and so on are, to some extent, symptoms of underlying problems, such as the lack of civil and political liberties and economic opportunities, in the countries of the southern and eastern

[7] The Commission proposed a total budget for the ENP for the period 2014–20 of €18.2 billion, reflecting a 40 per cent increase on the current budget (Commission, 2011d).

Mediterranean, which may be addressed by the breadth of policies that comprise the ENP, including institution building, economic co-operation, and co-operation on a range of security issues that fall into the areas of common security and defence policy (CSDP) and justice and home affairs (JHA).

Looking back over close to a decade of ENP, the track record of these policies to achieve their strategic goals of strengthening the prosperity, stability and security of the EU and its neighbours is less than stellar. Among all the countries of the southern neighbourhood, only two – Morocco and Jordan – have fully implemented, and moved beyond, their original action plans. In recognition of this, the EU granted them 'advanced status' in 2008 and 2010, respectively. Yet, one might question, for example, how much Morocco really has advanced since the inauguration of the ENP in 2003: the conflict in the western Sahara (after all, one of the security challenges in the southern Neighbourhood constantly referred to in EU documents) is nowhere nearer a resolution than it was eight years ago.

Is this likely to change now? The *New Response* document signifies a certain degree of continuity in its commitment to democracy, economic development, sub-regional co-operation and regional differentiation that has characterized the ENP since 2003. What is, if not new, so far at least more explicit, is a greater emphasis on conditionality and political and security co-operation. The revised ENP strategy proposes a 'more-for-more' approach to guide the EU's relations with its neighbours: more trade and mobility in return for more political and economic reforms. Thus, the EU seeks to 'enhance [its] involvement in solving protracted conflicts' (Commission, 2011e, p. 5). However, rather than outlining concrete steps that go beyond the implementation of ENP (and CFSP/CSDP) to date, the emphasis is on continuing what already happens (and has arguably not been very effective): membership in the Middle East Quartet,[8] opposition to violent border changes, using operational presence through existing missions to back reform efforts, and employing instruments that promote economic integration and sectoral reform to support confidence-building measures and conflict resolution objectives (Commission, 2011e). The only partially innovative new initiative is that the 'EU intends to enhance its support for confidence-building and outreach to breakaway territories, for international efforts and structures related to the conflicts, and, once that stage is reached, for the implementation of settlements' (Commission, 2011e, p. 5).

Here is where the EU may be able to find (yet again) a niche for an effective contribution to stability in its neighbourhood through the instruments that the ENP offers. Consider, briefly, the case of Libya. While the UN-authorized military intervention was a Nato operation almost solely conducted and led by Europeans – first and foremost the United Kingdom and France – the EU has not so far played any significant role. Clearly constrained by its economic and financial crisis, the real blow to concerted and unified EU action was dealt by the German abstention during the vote on UN Security Council Resolution 1973.[9] Until then, the EU had been fully supportive of UN actions and contributed to enforcing sanctions against the Gaddafi regime. A joint statement by the President of the European Council, Herman Van Rompuy, and the EU High Representative, Catherine Ashton, on the day the crucial UN resolution was passed already indicated

[8] The members of the Quartet are the United Nations, the United States, the European Union and Russia.
[9] For a record of the 6498th Meeting of the UN Security Council, see UN Security Council (2011).

more lukewarm support of the EU, noting its readiness 'to implement this Resolution *within its mandate and competences*' (Rompuy and Ashton, 2011; emphasis added) and the subsequent Council Conclusions three days later unsurprisingly offered no more than 'CSDP *support to humanitarian assistance* in response to a request from OCHA and under the coordinating role of the UN' (European Council, 2011a; emphasis added). At that time, the Nato military operation, carried out predominantly by military forces of EU members Britain and France, was already in full swing. A starker contrast could hardly be imagined.

The EU did follow up with a Council Decision on an EU military operation in support of humanitarian assistance operations in Libya, setting up operational headquarters in Rome and preparing various scenarios (European Council, 2011b). Embarrassingly, a request for the activation of EU military assistance was never made. EU Military Staff and assets were, however, involved in the evacuation of EU citizens from Libya and third-country refugees via Tunisia.

While it is easy (and not wrong) to belittle the inability of the EU to offer any substantial military support during the Libyan crisis (even though it did, through its Member States, clearly have the necessary capabilities), the EU has been an important player in a different way: by providing significant humanitarian assistance, worth over €150 million by October 2011. An additional €25 million is available for short-term stabilization needs, as well as a further €60 million for assistance in the transition process. These will include measures decided together with the transitional government to build up state institutions; to support civil society, human rights and democratization; to provide health services; and to assist with border management and security sector reform (Commission, 2011b).

The statement by the High Representative following the fall of Sirte and the death of Gaddafi clearly indicates the Union's willingness to become a strong partner of the new Libya (Ashton, 2011). The case of Libya demonstrates in an exemplary way that the countries of the Arab Spring in the southern neighbourhood, which are going through a challenging, and at times violent, transition process now, and the EU need each other economically and politically (as did and do the CEE countries that joined the EU in 2004 and 2007 or are now covered by the Eastern Partnership). These countries' successful transition to democracy is crucial to stability in the EU's southern neighbourhood, and thus to the EU's security, and it is here where the ENP will have to prove its mettle.

IV. Eastern Europe

In a year that saw the democratic revolutions in the EU's southern neighbourhood, the trend in the east was the opposite: towards political stagnation and a deterioration of the political climate. For instance, Freedom House ratings for many of the countries in the eastern periphery have worsened since 2006 (for example, Armenia, Georgia, Ukraine and Kyrgyzstan); the only country that experienced an improvement during this period was Moldova.[10] These trends are particularly worrying given the fact that it was in this part of the world that the EU had actively sought to exercise its normative power through the ENP – by contrast, the Union had mostly supported the status quo in its southern flank.

[10] See rankings at: «http://www.freedomhouse.org».

Moreover, the shift of focus in EU policies from the east to the south is taking place as Russia seeks to increase its influence in its former sphere of influence. For instance, in October, Vladimir Putin outlined his plans to establish a 'Euroasian Union' with other former Soviet countries, based on the EU model.[11]

The response by the EU to these developments was timid, reactive and inconsistent at times, concentrated as it was on trying to deal with the consequences of the eurozone crisis and the Arab Spring. Its strategy towards the region continued to be framed within the ENP and the Eastern Partnership. However, it is clear that the main targets of the renewed ENP policy discussed in the previous section and its emphasis on 'more-for-more' were not its eastern neighbours – which had already enjoyed such an approach in the context of the Eastern Partnership – but the southern Mediterranean countries. While this focus is understandable bearing in mind the historic nature of the revolutions taking place in the south, it might be short-sighted if one considers the worrying trends in the east. It is still unclear, however, how eastern countries might benefit from the increase in funding promised by Brussels and new initiatives aimed at promoting 'deep democracy' such as the Civil Society Facility and the Polish-sponsored idea of establishing an American-style European Endowment for Democracy.

As far as the Eastern Partnership is concerned, the Polish Presidency organized the biannual summit in Warsaw in September (which had originally been planned to take place during the Hungarian Presidency) (see Ágh on the Hungarian Presidency and Pomorska and Vanhoonacker on the Polish Presidency in this issue). Belarus and visa liberalization were high on the summit's agenda. The Eastern Partnership summit did not produce any concrete outcomes beyond a joint declaration of the parties expressing their commitment to the guiding principles of the Eastern Partnership already agreed at the 2009 Prague summit (European Council, 2011c). However, it presented another opportunity for the EU to remind its eastern neighbours that increasing political association and economic integration with the EU remains directly linked to progress in the areas of democracy and the rule of law.

In 2011, the Rose and Orange Revolutions seemed a thing of the past, with many of the regimes in the region turning towards authoritarianism. A case in point was that of Ukraine, which was downgraded by Freedom House to 'partly free' in 2011. The detention and then sentencing to seven years of prison of former Prime Minister Yulia Tymoshenko was for many a clear example of the increasing politicization of the rule of law in the country. Mrs Tymoshenko was charged with procedural irregularities over a gas deal with Russia.[12] The Ukrainian security forces were also accused of other human rights violations and clamping down on civil liberties (Amnesty International, 2011). As a result of these developments, Yanukovych's visit to Brussels in mid-October was postponed. Yet, the EU's response was rather hesitant, alternating between those that threatened with suspending the negotiations on the Association Agreement and the Deep and Comprehensive Free Trade Agreement;[13] and those that called for a more tepid response and the mobilization of more financial and non-financial incentives (such as visa liberalization) to trigger pro-democracy changes in the country (see European Parliament, 2011). Despite these

[11] *EUobserver.com*, 4 October 2011.

[12] For his part, President Yanukovych made his own gas deal, trading a reduction in the price of gas for an extension of the lease of the port of Sebastapol to the Russian Black Sea fleet.

[13] *European Voice*, 19 December 2011.

concerns, the final text of the Association Agreement was agreed in December with a view to initialling the Agreement in 2012. Once again, Ukrainian negotiators failed to get a promise to join the EU explicitly recognized in the text of the Treaty, which only refers to 'Ukraine's European choice and aspirations and confirms its European identity'.

The situation in Belarus also deteriorated further in 2011. The crackdown that followed the presidential elections of 19 December led to the arrest of hundreds of protesters and of opposition leaders (see Whitman and Juncos, 2011). Notwithstanding initial disagreements on the appropriateness of sanctions to deal with the Belarusian regime, on 31 January the Council decided to (re)impose sanctions including travel restrictions and an asset freeze on those individuals involved in the events. These measures were subsequently extended to include other officials and an arms embargo. Some Member States also continued to lobby for more 'people-to-people' contacts and other policies aimed at facilitating the development of Belarusian civil society and democratic opposition. Lithuania's President Dalia Grybauskaitė also wrote a letter to the Commission to look into ways to promote visa facilitation for Belarusian citizens. These measures, however, did not seem to have any impact on Lukashenko's regime, with more evidence of a clamp down on independent media emerging during the second half of the year.

Moldova constituted the exception in terms of democratic development, although a two-year stalemate over the election of the president by the parliament raised some concerns among EU policy-makers about the ability of Moldova's political parties to reach an agreement.[14] Despite these problems, Moldova continued to make progress in the negotiation of an Association Agreement and visa dialogue and was also preparing to launch negotiations on a Deep and Comprehensive Free Trade Area (DCFTA).

Relations with countries in the South Caucasus remained hostage to political instability and the unresolved frozen conflicts of South Ossetia and Nagorno-Karabakh. Developments in Azerbaijan were particularly worrying regarding violations of freedom of expression and assembly, with non-governmental organizations (NGOs) reporting increasing levels of harassment of political opponents, activists and journalists in the country. Despite some statements by High Representative Catherine Ashton, the position of the EU was always going to be a difficult one, given Member States' economic interests in the country's energy resources. Relations with Georgia made more progress with the conclusion of two agreements on visa facilitation and readmission at the beginning of the year.

V. Enlargement

As mentioned earlier, the economic crisis has put more (financial and political) strains on the enlargement project. Although this trend was already visible after the big bang enlargement of 2004–07, enlargement has receded even further in the list of priorities of the Union, with EU policy-makers' attention concentrated on the euro crisis. This, no doubt, has caused disillusionment among candidate countries, reflected in declining popular support for EU membership in candidate and potential candidate countries. For instance, when asked whether EU membership was a 'good thing', only 41 per cent of Turkish respondents, 30 per cent of Croatian respondents and 26 per cent of Icelandic respondents agreed with this statement (Eurobarometer, 2011, p. 35). Yet, despite these

[14] *EUobserver.com*, 16 November 2011.

difficulties, the enlargement process continued to move forward in Croatia, Iceland, Montenegro and Serbia in 2011, although not much progress was reported in the cases of Turkey, Macedonia, Albania and Kosovo.

In its 2011 annual report, the Commission announced a new 'enlargement approach'. With a view to avoiding the kind of problems faced during the 2007 enlargement to Romania and Bulgaria, the Commission is set to focus even more on the rule of law. From now on, the first chapters to be opened during accession negotiations will be those dealing with the judiciary, justice and home affairs and fundamental rights; they will also be among the last to be closed (Commission, 2011g).[15] Apart from its emphasis on the rule of law, the 2011 enlargement strategy identified the following priorities: strengthening public administration reform, ensuring freedom of expression in the media, boosting regional co-operation and reconciliation in the Western Balkans, promoting sustainable economic recovery and growth, and extending transport and energy networks.

The year 2011 was momentous for Croatia as it concluded accession negotiations with the EU. Although some progress was still needed in areas such as public administration reform, reform of the judiciary and in the fight against corruption, the last four chapters were closed in June 2011 paving the way for Croatia to join the EU on 1 July 2013. This date was confirmed by the European Council in its December's Conclusions, which also agreed that Croatia will from now on participate as an active observer in all Council meetings (European Council, 2011f). The Commission annual report noted that there was 'a high-degree of alignment with EU rules in most sectors' (Commission, 2011g, p. 34), but that Croatia still needed to strengthen the administrative capacity necessary for the implementation of the *acquis*. Croatia and Slovenia met on several occasions to discuss the implementation of the Border Arbitration Agreement signed in 2009 to resolve the border dispute between the two countries. Given the negative impact that bilateral disputes are having on the enlargement process, it was remarkable to see the adoption by the Croatian parliament of a declaration on promoting European values in southeast Europe stating that bilateral issues, such as border issues, must not obstruct the accession of candidate countries to the EU. The referendum on accession was held by Croatia in January 2012, with 66 per cent of the voters supporting EU membership (33 per cent voted against). However, as it was the case with prior referendums held in CEE countries, the turnout was very low (at 44 per cent).

The other two candidate countries to have made some progress were Iceland and Montenegro. The former continued to advance in its process of accession to the EU with the opening of six chapters in 2011, of which four were provisionally closed. Although Iceland shows a high level of alignment with EU rules, in particular in the chapters covered by the European Economic Area and the Schengen Agreement, there are still significant challenges, for instance, in the area of fisheries. A solution to the Icesave dispute with the Netherlands and the United Kingdom was still out of reach after a second referendum rejected a proposed package to compensate British and Dutch depositors. Waning public support for EU membership is still a concern. In a recent poll, only 26.3 per cent of the respondents supported accession to the EU, while 56.2 opposed membership.[16]

[15] It is worth noting, however, that chapters are only 'provisionally closed' (that is, they can be reopened if a candidate country does not fulfil its commitments). It is only when all negotiations with the candidate country are concluded that chapters are definitively closed.
[16] Bloomberg, 29 February 2012.

Montenegro continued to make headway in its process of accession to the EU, fulfilling the recommendations made by the Commission in its opinion the previous year. This led to the European Commission recommending the opening of accession negotiations in its October Progress Report. Following the Commission's recommendation, the European Council gave a green light to the launch of the process on 9 December 2011 with a view to opening accession negotiations in June 2012. In line with the new enlargement approach, the Council tasked the Commission to examine compliance in the area of rule of law – especially regarding corruption and the fight against organized crime – in a report to be presented in the first half of 2012.

By contrast, progress in the case of the other two candidate countries, Macedonia and Turkey, remained stalled because of bilateral issues. The opening of accession negotiations with Macedonia continued to be blocked by Greece because of the name dispute. In the case of Turkey, the Cyprus issue meant that no new chapters were opened or closed during 2011. Although rhetorically both the EU and Turkey remain committed to the process, in practice there were many signs of a deterioration in EU–Turkey relations. Tensions between Turkey and Cyprus also rose over offshore gas exploitations. Turkey complained after the Greek Cypriot government announced drilling for oil and gas in the eastern Mediterranean sea. Turkey retaliated a week later by sending its own exploration ship to the north of the island. In relation to these rising tensions in the area, the Council affirmed the need to avoid 'any kind of threat or action directed against a Member State, or source of friction or actions, which could damage good neighbourly relations and the peaceful settlement of disputes' and also stressed 'the sovereign rights of EU Member States [. . .] to explore and exploit their natural resources' (European Council, 2011e, p. 5). The declaration by the French Assembly about the Armenian genocide issue did not help European–Turkish co-operation either. Observers pointed to the worsening of the freedom of the press and minority rights as an indication of a weakening of the EU's influence. Turkey has also grown more confident in its foreign policy and remained actively involved in the Arab revolutions and the Middle East.

Serbia made significant headway towards membership during 2011. With the arrest by Serb authorities of the two remaining war criminals wanted by the International Criminal Tribunal for the former Yugoslavia (ICTY), Ratko Mladić and Goran Hadžić, one of the main obstacles in its path to the EU was removed. This also showed that EU conditionality might still have some leverage in the Western Balkans. Serbia also demonstrated goodwill with its participation in the EU-mediated talks with Kosovo (see above). For these reasons, the Commission recommended granting candidate status to Serbia in October, ahead of the next parliamentary elections in the country in May 2012. Notwithstanding this progress, tensions in the north of Kosovo increased during 2011. Violence broke out in July after Kosovo police were deployed to two custom gates in the border with Serbia. A border checkpoint was burned down and a policeman shot dead by Kosovo Serb protesters in the Jarinje crossing. New violent events took place later in the year when Kosovo Serbs erected barricades in the area to impede the access to the border points by Kosovo officials, which led to clashes with the Nato-led mission, KFOR. Serb President Tadić called on the protesters to remove the blockade, but some Member States did not feel Serbia was doing enough to put an end to the violence in Kosovo. The December European Council seemed to take this view as it postponed a decision on the status of candidate country until the next European Council meeting in

March. The European Council also noted the following conditions relating to the issue of Kosovo: the need 'to show credible commitment [and] further progress in moving forward with the implementation in good faith of agreements reached in the dialogue, including on IBM [Integrated Border Management] [. . .] an agreement on inclusive regional cooperation [in order to] enable EULEX and KFOR to execute their mandates' (European Council, 2011e, p. 5). However, some Member States are becoming more open to the idea of finding an alternative solution to the situation in the north of Kosovo which could entail some form of autonomy.[17]

Bosnia and Albania, together with Kosovo, remained the laggards in the region. Political instability in these cases prevented further progress towards accession. In Bosnia, the country remained without a government for most of 2011 as political parties failed to agree on the terms of a new one following the general elections of October 2010. It was not until December that the main political parties agreed to the formation of a coalition government, which was a requirement for the disbursement of much needed funds from the International Monetary Fund (IMF) and the EU.[18] Although a potential crisis was averted by the High Representative in the spring (see above), ethnic tensions remained high and stalled the reform agenda. The only notable development was the appointment of Peter Sørensen as Head of the Union Delegation and EU Special Representative (EUSR) in July – a first step in the process of disbanding the Office of the High Representative and increasing the EU's presence in the country.[19]

In Albania, the continuing political stalemate that followed the 2009 elections (see Bechev, 2011) affected the adoption of reforms and, for another year, the Commission's report noted that not enough progress had been made to recommend candidate status. The year began with opposition-led protests against the government which turned violent, resulting in four deaths. The local elections that took place in May were also marred by irregularities, mainly in the capital Tirana. By the end of the year, however, there were some signs that the main political parties were willing to find a solution to the crisis.

Conclusions

The year finished with the EU's relations with its neighbourhood in a greater condition of uncertainly than has existed since the early 1990s. The combination of the eurozone crisis and the events of the Arab Spring have created a high degree of uncertainty as to how the EU's role might develop in the coming year.

The eurozone crisis has already had a spillover effect on the EU's neighbourhood policies and the enlargement process and is impinging on the candidate countries and EU neighbours. The prolongation of the crisis risks undermining one of the cornerstones of EU foreign policy within the neighbourhood which is the EU's conditionality requirements for a deepening of relationships and the EU's capacity to offer rewards in response. The bright spot was Croatian accession being secured. For other candidate states the record was highly variable with limited progress for Montenegro, Iceland and Serbia. All

[17] *EUobserver*, 28 November 2011.
[18] *European Voice*, 29 December 2011.
[19] Prior to this, the international High Representative was also double-hatted as the EUSR.

other candidate states made little headway in tackling the underlying problems that they need to confront if membership is to be a realistic prospect.

The EEAS has had a very mixed record over the past 12 months in dealing with the political and security challenges within the neighbourhood. The EEAS was able to achieve some minor policy successes in the Balkans, where the EU can hold out the prospect of membership. But it largely failed to deliver in the ENP region during its first year of operation and struggled to provide a cogent response to the Arab Spring and events in eastern Europe. The EEAS' scope for the development of a greater capacity to define and implement appropriate policy responses to challenging events on the ground within the EU's neighbourhood is still unproven. Furthermore, a greater capacity for an active and leading role in crisis management in the neighbourhood remains elusive.

References

Allen, D. and Smith, M. (2011) 'Relations with the Rest of the World'. *JCMS*, Vol. 49, No. S1, pp. 209–30.

Amnesty International (2011) 'Ukraine Must Act to Deal with Endemic Police Criminality'. Available at: «http://www.amnestyusa.org/research/reports/ukraine-must-act-to-deal-with-endemic-police-criminality».

Ashton, C. (2011) 'Statement by High Representative Catherine Ashton on the fall of Sirte and reports of the death of Colonel Gaddafi' (Brussels: European Union).

Bechev, D. (2011) 'The Protracted Death of Democratic Albania'. *EUobserver.com*, 8 September.

Brattberg, E. (2011) 'Opportunities Lost, Opportunities Seized: The Libya Crisis as Europe's Perfect Storm'. Policy Brief (Brussels: European Policy Centre).

Commission of the European Communities (2011a) *Dialogue for Migration, Mobility and Security with the Southern Mediterranean Countries* (Brussels: Commission of the European Communities).

Commission of the European Communities (2011b) *EU Support to Libya* (Brussels: Commission of the European Communities).

Commission of the European Communities (2011c) *A Medium Term Programme for a Renewed European Neighbourhood Policy (2011–2014)* (Brussels: Commission of the European Communities).

Commission of the European Communities (2011d) *The Multiannual Financial Framework: The Proposals on External Action Instruments* (Brussels: Commission of the European Communities).

Commission of the European Communities (2011e) *A New Response to a Changing Neighbourhood* (Brussels: Commission of the European Communities).

Commission of the European Communities (2011f) *Partnership for Democracy and Shared Prosperity in the Southern Mediterranean* (Brussels: Commission of the European Communities).

Commission of the European Communities (2011g) 'Communication from the Commission to the European Parliament and the Council "Enlargement Strategy and Main Challenges 2011–2012" '. *COM*(2011)666 final, Brussels, 12 October.

Dinan, D. (2010) 'Institutions and Governance: A New Treaty, a Newly Elected Parliament and a New Commission'. *JCMS*, Vol. 48, No. S1, pp. 95–118.

Eurobarometer (2011) 'Public Opinion in the European Union'. Eurobarometer 75. Available at: «http://ec.europa.eu/public_opinion/archives/eb_arch_en.htm».

European Council (2011a) *Council Conclusions on Libya (3076th Foreign Affairs Council Meeting)* (Brussels: European Council).

European Council (2011b) *Council Decides on EU Military Operation in Support of Humanitarian Assistance Operations in Libya* (Brussels: European Council).

European Council (2011c) *Joint Declaration of the Eastern Partnership Summit, Warsaw, 29–30 September* (Brussels: European Council).

European Council (2011d) 'Declaration by the High Representative, Catherine Ashton, on behalf of the European Union on events in Libya'. 6795/1/11 Presse 33, Brussels, 20 February.

European Council (2011e) 'Council Conclusions on Enlargement and Stabilization and Association Process'. 3132nd General Affairs Council Meeting, Brussels, 5 December.

European Council (2011f) 'European Council Conclusion'. Brussels, 9 December. Available at: «http://www.consilium.europa.eu/uedocs/cms_data/docs/pressdata/en/ec/126714.pdf».

European External Action Service (EEAS) (2011) 'Report by the High Representative to the European Parliament, the Council and the Commission'. Brussels, 22 December.

European Parliament (2011) 'Motion for a European Parliament Resolution containing the European Parliament's recommendation to the Council, the Commission and the EEAS on the negotiations of the EU–Ukraine Association Agreement'. Brussels, 22 November.

European Union (2011) 'The Multiannual Financial Framework: The proposals on External Action Instruments'. MEMO/11/878, Brussels, 7 December. Available at: «http://europa.eu/rapid/pressReleasesAction.do?reference=MEMO/11/878&format=HTML&aged=0&language=EN&guiLanguage=fr».

Menon, A. (2011) 'European Defence Policy from Lisbon to Libya'. *Survival: Global Politics and Strategy*, Vol. 53, No. 3, pp. 75–90.

Rompuy, H. van and Ashton, C. (2011) *Joint Statement on UN Security Council Resolution on Libya* (Brussels: European Union).

United Nations (UN) Security Council (2011) *Security Council Approves 'No-Fly Zone' over Libya, Authorizing 'All Necessary Measures' to Protect Civilians by Vote of 10 in Favour with 5 Abstentions* (New York: UN Department of Public Information).

Vaïsse, J. (2012) 'The Sick Man of Europe is Europe'. *Foreign Policy*, 16 February. Available at: «http://www.foreignpolicy.com/articles/2012/02/16/the_sick_man_of_europe_is_europe?page=full».

Whitman, R. and Juncos, A.E. (2009a) 'Relations with the Wider Europe'. *JCMS*, Vol. 47, No. S1, pp. 193–211.

Whitman, R. and Juncos, A.E. (2009b) 'The Lisbon Treaty and the Foreign, Security and Defence Policy: Reforms, Implementation and the Consequences of (Non-)ratification'. *European Foreign Affairs Review*, Vol. 14, No. 1, pp. 25–46.

Whitman, R. and Juncos, A.E. (2010) 'Relations with the Wider Europe'. *JCMS*, Vol. 48, No. S1, pp. 183–204.

Whitman, R. and Juncos, A.E. (2011) 'Relations with the Wider Europe'. *JCMS*, Vol. 49, No. S1, pp. 187–208.

JCMS 2012 Volume 50 Annual Review pp. 162–177 DOI: 10.1111/j.1468-5965.2012.02277.x

Relations with the Rest of the World

DAVID ALLEN and MICHAEL SMITH
Loughborough University

Introduction

In our review of 2010 we focused on the need for, and the relative absence of, a 'grand strategy' in European Union policies towards the rest of the world, and concluded that there were several reasons for the apparent failure of the Union to develop a focused, well-resourced and effective set of external policies (Allen and Smith, 2011). Our review of 2011 has a rather different focus, although it builds upon these continuing areas of concern. To put it crudely, 2011 saw the impact across the EU's external policies of major internal crises as well as external turbulence, to such an extent that the EU became a perceived 'problem' for many of its key international partners and the credibility and legitimacy of some of its major external policy initiatives came into question.

Whilst it has been possible in the past to see external policy as focusing on the projection of European 'solutions' to problems of global governance, development or conflict management (and this has been a key feature of self-perceptions by EU policy-makers), in 2011 this was not possible. Indeed, the impact of the crisis within the eurozone and its corrosive effect on a broader range of EU external policy activities has arguably become one of the key limiting factors on the EU's international role and status – for example, in the context of the G20 and its attempts to develop a consensus on global economic management (Jokela, 2011; see also Woolcock, 2012; Youngs, 2010). Not surprisingly, this characteristic has also impressed itself on the EU's major international partners, with effects that are so far difficult to discern but that unquestionably have created a new dynamic in several of the Union's key external relationships. This set of forces will act as a central constraint on EU international activities for years to come, but our concern here is to identify its impact on the international arena thus far.

I. General Themes

Foreign, Security and Defence Policy

The year 2011 was an important year for the European External Action Service (EEAS), which after an uncertain and prolonged birth finally got down to work in January. As the High Representative (HR/VP) Catherine Ashton made clear in her rather defensive report to the European Council, Parliament and Commission (EEAS, 2011) at the end of the year, she considered that the twin pressures that came from the immediate need to respond to the events surrounding the Arab Spring[1] and from the immense distraction that was the ongoing crisis in the eurozone made life even more difficult for the new service than it

[1] On the EU and the Arab Spring, see Whitman and Juncos in this issue.

might otherwise have been. Whilst the eurozone crisis certainly prevented the President of the European Council from giving EU external relations as much attention as he might have liked, it could be argued that the Arab Spring provided as many opportunities as it did challenges to Baroness Ashton and her team, particularly as the need to produce a co-ordinated and coherent response to events, which was part of the rationale for creating the EEAS, was all the more necessary given the partial failure of previous EU policies towards the region.[2] In many cases, the EU had found itself with an unenviable record of having financially aided the very regimes that were being overturned.

Many officials appointed to the new EEAS from both the Commission and the Council went home for Christmas at the end of 2010 knowing that they would return to make up the new service but uncertain as to their role within it. As David O'Sullivan (2012), the EEAS Chief Operating Officer, reported, the first priority was to 'ensure business continuity' both in Brussels with the creation of a new integrated structure and around the world where 140 plus Commission delegations had been transformed into EU Delegations, each headed by an officer of the EEAS. Despite one or two technical glitches, by and large this was achieved procedurally, but at the expense of any significant substantive policy initiatives. Thus Baroness Ashton was able to report that progress had been made in recruiting staff to the EEAS although the major problems remain both financial with the Member States in no mood to find further resources for much needed posts[3] and with recruiting the agreed number of national diplomats to join those already transferred from the Commission and the Council Secretariat. At the end of the year there were 3,611 officials in the EEAS, 1,551 at the Brussels headquarters and 2,060 in the EU Delegations. It was indicative of the relatively low morale in the EEAS that by early 2012 there were probably more EU officials interested in voluntarily transferring back out of the EEAS than into it.

Last year, we reported that the EU had encountered problems after the coming into force of the Lisbon Treaty maintaining its (limited) rights to speak in the UN (Allen and Smith, 2011). That problem at least was resolved in 2011 when in May, in the face of criticism from the European Parliament (EP),[4] the EU was able to secure the passage of a UN General Assembly Resolution giving the EU upgraded status and speaking rights and the possibility of presenting common positions in the General Assembly at least. The problems arising from France and the United Kingdom's separate and permanent membership of the United Nations Security Council, of course, remain. As noted above, a feature of 2011 was the renewed activism on external relations of the EP as it sought to build on the additional powers of scrutiny that it obtained in the Lisbon Treaty. It seems likely that the Parliament will be much more of a player particularly on issues that result in any contractual relations with third countries. The example of the relationship between the United States Congress and American foreign policy may well prove to be instructive in the future for those conducting the EU's external relations.

The EU came in for general criticism for its lack of clear leadership in 2011. The area of foreign policy was no exception. Whilst the President of the European Council received a generally good press and sympathetic understanding for the amount of his time that he was forced to devote to the complex internal negotiations about the euro rather than to

[2] *Financial Times*, 25 May 2011.
[3] *The Guardian* and *Financial Times*, 24 May 2011.
[4] *European Voice*, 5 May 2011.

representing the EU externally (see Dinan's contribution to this issue), the HR/VP was criticized throughout the year and especially as the time for her annual report drew near. In a 'non-paper' and a letter (Foreign Ministers, 2011), the foreign ministers of 12 of the Member States complained, amongst other things, that the HR/VP had not done enough to replace the agenda-setting and meeting preparation role of the now defunct Foreign Affairs Council Presidency. She chaired the Foreign Affairs Council and her staff chaired the Political and Security Committee and a host of Council/Commission Working Groups, but it was not clear what use was being made of this 'directing' role. The foreign ministers were also critical of Catherine Ashton's failure to use her role as a Vice-President of the Commission to improve working relations between the EEAS and the Commission, and in particular, for her failure to use her powers to take full co-ordinating control of all the external aspects of the Commission's ongoing competences. In particular, there was a feeling that those responsible in the Commission for Trade – and to a certain extent for Development – were not properly aware of all the foreign policy consequences of their actions.

The EEAS was designed to bring coherence to the EU's many external activities and the feeling was that this aspect still needed considerable work despite the best efforts of those working within the EEAS when faced with blatant obstructionism from the Commission in particular. It is interesting to note that whilst the EEAS was requested to provide 243 briefings for the HR/VP, 67 for the President of the European Council, 125 for the President of the European Commission and 235 for the Commissioner for Enlargement (EEAS, 2011), it received no such requests from other Commissioners such as those responsible for Trade, Humanitarian Assistance, Research, Agriculture or Competition – all policy areas with significant external dimensions. Thus Baroness Ashton continued to receive a generally bad press[5] for her handling of what was, nevertheless, also generally conceded to be an impossible job as the High Representative, Vice-President of the Commission, Chair of the Foreign Affairs Council and, of course, Head of the EEAS.

Baroness Ashton did, however, receive praise, particularly from the United States for her leadership work with Special Adviser Robert Cooper (who was also notably involved in the delicate negotiations with Serbia and Kosovo), on the Middle East Peace Process,[6] as well as the latest round of negotiations with the Iranian government[7] in relation to their potential nuclear weapons capability. Despite the efforts in 2011 to bargain with Iran, the EU nevertheless ended up in December[8] extending its sanctions by targeting 180 new Iranian officials, but still resisted a potentially more effective ban on crude oil imports from Iran because of the vulnerability of Greece. When the British embassy in Tehran came under attack, also in December, Germany, France and the Netherlands recalled their ambassadors in a gesture of EU solidarity.

The first major substantive challenge for the EU's new foreign policy procedures came with the development of events within Libya and here the lessons are rather mixed. Amid growing concern in the first few months of the year about the reactions of the Libyan government to the turmoil in its country, the governments of the United Kingdom and

[5] *Financial Times*, 24 May 2011; *European Voice*, 5 January 2011, 20 July 2011 and in particular 2 February 2012; *The Guardian*, 24 May 2011; *The Economist*, 2 February 2012.
[6] *Financial Times*, 16 September 2011.
[7] *European Voice*, 20 January 2011.
[8] *The Guardian*, 2 December 2011.

France took the lead in pushing for international action against General Gaddafi, who used his military forces to attack his own people. Whilst the EU collectively was prepared to make critical statements and provide humanitarian assistance, the Member States were quite bitterly divided about the desirability of using military force and there was never any real prospect of EU military intervention.

Although in the early stages of the Libyan episode plans were mooted for a EUFOR Libya, they would have proved difficult to implement as, of the two EU battlegroups on standby at the time, one was led by the Dutch and included 700 Germans and the other was led by Sweden and included troops drawn from Finland.[9] All four of these EU Member States were opposed to the use of military force in Libya, The outcome, with the United States in the new and very significant position of 'leading from behind',[10] was that both the United Kingdom and France participated, at first with and shortly afterwards without, active American participation, in a Nato-branded air operation that played a significant role in the eventual downfall of the Libyan government. However, the use of force did not command the support of all EU states, with Germany – the most prominent dissenter[11] – even abstaining, along with China and Russia, from support for a UN Security Council Resolution underpinning the Nato action.

Although the United Kingdom and France did not necessarily share the same precise motives for pursuing military action in Libya, their ability to work together underlined the fact that 'European' military activity was more likely to emerge from their enhanced bilateral relationship[12] (a mini-coalition of the willing!) than from the further development of the EU's European security and defence policy (ESDP). The pressure on EU Members from the United States to do more collectively in the defence area increased in 2011 with American Defense Secretary Robert Gates warning that Europe's lack of political will to either undertake military action or fund defence projects could lead to a new generation of American leaders unprepared to maintain the Nato alliance.[13]

For the British, EU defence activity provides a means by which the United States can be reassured, whilst for France EU defence activity provides a potential alternative to Nato, which is why France was so keen in 2011 to once again raise the issue of the perceived need for a separate EU military headquarters capable of overseeing EU operations without the use of Nato command resources.[14] The chances of the further development of ESDP after the Libyan intervention were negligible, however, because, as Garton Ash put it: 'Libya has exposed Europe's fault lines'.[15] Following their successful intervention in Libya, both the United Kingdom and France have been in the vanguard of urging both UN and EU action against Syria.[16] Although, in the end, no EU Member State attempted to veto the Nato Libyan mission, less than half of them participated in any way and only a third took part in the air strike missions. It was certainly the case that the EU's pretensions to act as an independent global power were once again cruelly exposed[17] by

[9] *European Voice*, 5 May 2011.
[10] *Financial Times*, 24 March 2011.
[11] *The Guardian*, 12 March 2011.
[12] *Financial Times*, 2 May 2011.
[13] *The Guardian*, 11 June 2011.
[14] *The Guardian*, 26 March 2011; *European Voice*, 30 June 2011 and 15 September 2011.
[15] *The Guardian*, 24 March 2011.
[16] *The Guardian*, 9 June 2011; *Financial Times*, 24 November 2011.
[17] *The Guardian*, 16 March 2011.

this aspect of the Arab Spring. Although there were still 20 ongoing ESDP missions at the end of 2011 (three military and 17 civilian), it was significant that no new missions were proposed and that, with most Member States making significant cuts in their national defence budgets, it seemed most unlikely that there would be much enthusiasm in the short to medium term for enhancing this particular aspect of EU foreign and security policy.

The Common Commercial Policy

As noted above, it is impossible to consider the development of EU external commercial policy during 2011 without reference to the internal crisis focused on the eurozone. For the purposes of the argument here, the key repercussion of the general crisis was the growth – or threat of growth – of protectionism. The Union remained strongly in favour of multilateral solutions to international problems (for example, a lot of 2011 was taken up with the eventually successful effort to finalize Russia's entry into the World Trade Organization (WTO),[18] and the Union remained committed in principle to the conclusion of the Doha Development Round of WTO negotiations), but this commitment could not always be maintained in the face of inexorable internal and international forces.

The new package of EU commercial policy provisions introduced in November 2010 (Commission, 2010) was premised on the need for an 'open' EU in an 'open' world trading system, but also contained the germs of something less multilateral in its focus on reciprocity and 'trade defence', and on the enforcement of trade rules.[19] As the year unfolded, these tensions became more apparent, with Karel de Gucht, the Trade Commissioner, emphasizing the need for market opening and reciprocity and underlining the search for competitiveness in a way that had not been seen since the late 1990s.[20] By the end of the year, there were apparently contradictory indications: the EU had contributed to a major revision within the WTO of the Government Procurement Agreement, which could be seen as a victory for multilateralism, but this was actually a 'plurilateral' agreement which aroused the suspicions of a number of developing countries.[21] At the same time, the pursuit of ever more extensive free trade agreements with individual partners or small groups (see below) created further potential for discrimination, even though such agreements had to be WTO-compliant. The Doha Round itself remained stuck, despite efforts by the EU and others to move it ahead with new concessions or bargaining offers.[22]

One area in which paralysis seemed to have been avoided was that of free trade agreements. The trail-blazing agreement with South Korea was finalized during the year, and came into force in July 2011, and agreements were signed with a number of Latin American countries (see below), whilst negotiations with Singapore and Ukraine moved into their final phases. The agreement with Ukraine was signed late in the year, but its implementation was delayed by the EU because of political issues in Ukraine itself. Negotiations with Canada and India continued, but for reasons to be explored later in this

[18] *Financial Times*, 11 November 2011.
[19] *European Voice*, 13 January 2011.
[20] *European Voice*, 17 March 2011.
[21] *Financial Times*, 16 December 2011.
[22] *Financial Times*, 13 December 2011.

chapter, the hopes that they might be signed during the year were disappointed. By the end of 2011, there was also progress in laying the basis for negotiations with two of the EU's most 'strategic' partners – the United States and Japan (see below) – and plans were laid for new negotiations with countries such as Egypt in the context of political change following the 'Arab Spring'.

During the year, the EU also continued its review of the Generalized System of Preferences (GSP) (see Allen and Smith, 2011). This is a classic example of a measure that might be thought to be liberalizing and a major contribution to the multilateral system, but which embodies large helpings of unilateral EU action and has a potentially damaging impact on a number of developing countries. During recent years there has been a move to greater discrimination in the preferences accorded with the GSP – for example, through the so-called 'GSP+' scheme which rewards good governance and similar achievements on the part of EU partners. The review proposed to incorporate still greater selectivity by radically reducing the number of countries admitted to the GSP. The proposals published in early May envisaged a reduction from 176 to 80 in the number of beneficiaries.[23] Amongst those to be relegated were Argentina, Brazil, Qatar, Russia and Saudi Arabia.

The Union also spent a good deal of 2011 expressing its concern about the availability of raw materials, and especially of the so-called 'rare earths', of which China produces the vast majority at present. Early in the year, the Commission published a paper setting out proposals for maintaining the Union's access to strategic raw materials, and despite the confusion caused by the inclusion of agriculture and commodities more generally in the discussion, this came to be the centrepiece of discussion within the European institutions.[24] As the year wore on, the focus on 'rare earths' intensified, with action in the WTO by both the EU and the United States aimed at reducing China's restrictions on exports. The Chinese resisted stoutly, defending their restrictions on environmental grounds, until late in the year they relaxed them to a degree. The opening up of new sources of production also promised to change the situation in future years, but the Chinese would be likely to still hold a preponderance of the reserves.

Whilst many of these commercial policy issues might seem to be 'external' and the focus of technocratic negotiations, it is important in conclusion to this section to point out that many trade and related issues have become increasingly politicized in recent years – not least because of the growing influence of the EP. The Parliament played a substantial role in the end-game of the South Korea Free Trade Agreement (FTA) negotiations and in the consideration of FTAs more generally. It also made its voice heard in the consideration of a range of more specialized trade issues, such as the Anti-Counterfeiting Trade Agreement signed by the Commission on behalf of the EU, and late in the year its rejection of a fisheries agreement with Morocco.

Development Co-operation Policy and Humanitarian Aid

In 2011 the EU, under pressure from the Member States for tangible results, adopted yet another development policy framework (Commission, 2011). Concern had been expressed about the amount of Commission aid that was being sent directly to the treasuries of recipient countries rather than being allocated by the EU to specific development

[23] *European Voice*, 12 May 2011.
[24] *European Voice*, 20 January 2011.

projects.[25] In particular, the realization that in a number of cases the EU had been supporting undesirable governments, which had come under pressure in the Arab Spring, forced a reconsideration of how EU aid could be best dispersed so as to reach its intended targets rather than be used to support governments that did not meet EU standards of acceptable governance.

In October in its *Agenda for Change* the Commission introduced the notion of 'differentiated partnerships' whereby the Commission would decide on the mix of assistance directly to recipient governments or to specific projects depending on factors such as administrative capacity and willingness to reform governmental practices.[26] The Commission also introduced the notion of 'inclusive growth', by which it meant focusing on development aid that reached the very poorest sections of recipient states, although some felt that this objective would be in conflict with the aim of reducing the number of states in receipt of development aid as opposed to loans, technical co-operation and so on. A country like India, for example, which could be seen as a middle-income country undeserving of development aid would qualify because of its significant numbers of very poor people. Demands from the Member States that EU development aid be more specifically concentrated on those recipients most in need rather than spread thinly over a wide range of targets meant that decisions were taken to privilege sub-Saharan Africa, but with a recognized cost to less assistance being made available to the Asian and Latin American programmes.

Within the Commission there was recognition that there needed to be better co-ordination between those administering development aid and those responsible for emergency aid – the former being the responsibility of the Development Commissioner and the latter of the Commissioner for Crisis Response, Kristalina Georgieva. Following a spate of natural disasters, the links between long-term development aid and emergency relief aid have become more sensitive. Whilst in 2006 Mozambique failed to obtain just €2 million in development aid to prepare for floods, the subsequent flooding of the country caused damage worth €70 million and triggered EU emergency aid worth considerably more than €2 million. In the post-Lisbon EU, foreign policy, development policy and humanitarian aid policy are still all handled by different parts of the Commission and EEAS, with each competing for their own share of an increasingly tight EU budget. Thus Mrs Georgieva was also active in her determination to make Member State pledges of emergency equipment for humanitarian relief legally binding and, where such promised equipment was not forthcoming, she also sought authority to use EU finance to purchase it for the Commission.[27]

II. Regional Themes

Russia

During the year little real progress was made between the EU and Russia towards their declared objective of creating a 'partnership for modernization' (European Council, 2010c). This was partly a result of the uncertainty that developed as Russia's presidential

[25] *European Voice*, 16 June 2011.
[26] *European Voice*, 13 October 2011.
[27] *European Voice*, 21 December 2011.

election approached. Once it became clear that Prime Minister Putin and President Medvedev had agreed to once again 'swap' roles, the result of the March 2012 election could be anticipated, giving the EU some cause for concern. It was felt within the EU that the return of Mr Putin to the presidency would significantly reduce the chances of further modernization in Russia as well as marking a consolidation of Putin's notion of Russia as a centralized and 'sovereign democracy'[28] as opposed to a more competitive and decentralized polity that seemed to be one of the objectives of Mr Medvedev.[29] It was probably concern about the likely return of Mr Putin to the presidency in 2012 that encouraged the EU to do as much as it did (which included putting pressure on Georgia) to ensure Russia's final entry into the WTO, which came at the end of the year. Mr Putin is well known for his nostalgia for the Soviet Union and for his enthusiasm less for Russian acceptance of the commitments required of WTO membership and more for creating new institutional arrangements to attract Russia's former partners such as the customs union with Belarus and Kazakhstan as well as his more recent proposal for the creation of a Eurasian Union[30] to include states such as Tajikistan and Kyrgyzstan.

There were, as scheduled, two EU–Russia summits in 2011 which enabled the President of the European Council to deepen his relationship with the Russian leadership under the Lisbon Treaty arrangements, but which produced little else of substance other than a resolution, at the meeting in Nizhny Novograd in June, of the 'vegetable dispute' that had flared up after Russia responded to an outbreak of the E. coli bacteria inside the EU by banning the sale of all EU-sourced vegetables in Russia. At both summits, and despite reaching agreement on some important preliminaries, the EU was able to resist strong Russian demands for immediate negotiations to create a visa-free regime for ordinary travellers between the EU and Russia.[31] On the international scene, during 2011 Russia continued to frustrate EU ambitions to obtain United Nations Security Council (UNSC) agreement on enhanced sanctions against Iran and Syria,[32] although Russia under Medvedev did eventually abstain rather than veto the UNSC resolution on action against the Libyan government. The feeling inside the EU was that obtaining even this degree of Russian co-operation would probably prove to be more difficult under Mr Putin and that the prospects for further enhancement of the strategic partnership in the immediate future were slim. What was needed was not so much a 'reset' as a 'rethink' of relations with Putin's as opposed to Medvedev's Russia.[33]

Africa

Events in sub-Saharan Africa took second place to those associated with the Arab Spring that swept through North Africa in 2011 (see Whitman and Juncos in this issue). The EU continued with its four African ESDP missions, with EUNAVFOR continuing to provide protection against piracy off the coast of Somalia especially for vessels transporting food aid to Somalia as well as to ships supporting the African Union Mission in that country. In addition, the EU had a small number of troops engaged in a military training mission

[28] *Washington Post*, 15 July 2006.
[29] *Financial Times*, 20 June 2011.
[30] *The Guardian*, 5 October 2011.
[31] *European Voice*, 8 December 2011.
[32] *The Guardian*, 10 November 2011.
[33] *European Voice*, 29 September 2011.

for Somalia forces. In the Democratic Republic of the Congo, the EU has two ongoing missions engaged in security-sector reform and reforming the Congolese National Police.

In Sudan, the EU was involved in 2011 in an exercise to oversee and assist the division of the country following a referendum (scrutinized by 100 EU observers) which approved the secession of Southern Sudan. In Cote d'Ivoire the EU used 'soft power' (visa and travel bans, freezing of assets, etc.) and the threat at least of a French-led military intervention to eventually force the former President Laurent Gbagbo to accept his electoral defeat and to stand down in favour of the winner Alassane Ouattara. Events in Cote d'Ivoire provided the EEAS with an opportunity to test its new EU Situation Centre in Brussels for the first time as well as to oversee the temporary evacuation of non-essential EU staff from the Delegation in Abidjan. Once Ouattara was in place, the European Commission, presumably in consultation with the EEAS, was able to announce the opening of an ECHO office in Cote d'Ivoire as well as extensive emergency assistance to neighbouring Liberia where many refugees from the conflict within Cote d'Ivoire had sought shelter.[34] Finally, a terrorist attack on the UN headquarters in Nigeria led many in Brussels to argue that the EU's efforts to enhance security in the Sahel area of West Africa, which to date have been concentrated on Mali, Mauritania and Niger, would also now need to take greater account of Nigeria, with whom a strategic partnership had been proposed but not as yet implemented.[35]

Asia

Economic diplomacy has always been a key element – if not the dominant element – of the EU's relationship with many Asian countries, and most notably China, but in recent years it has been supplemented with a strong dose of political concern for regional order in such areas as South Asia. We highlighted in last year's *Review* the ways in which this entered into EU policies towards Sri Lanka, Pakistan, Afghanistan and Burma (Myanmar), and at that point it appeared that the Union might be carving out for itself a significant role in the South Asian regional order, to its political as well as its commercial benefit (Allen and Smith, 2011).

At least in terms of public diplomacy and impact, this role was curiously muted in 2011. This might have been because a number of the key issues (as in Sri Lanka) have been at least temporarily resolved, and some others (for example, the relaxation of political constraints in dealings with Burma) only made themselves fully felt towards the end of the year. Concern with the future of Pakistan persisted, and was part of a strategic reappraisal of the EU's relationship with Islamabad (Commission, 2012, p. 149), but in a broader sense, political Asia retreated in 2011 and became a function of the EU's overwhelming concern with its own internal economic order. Even where there was an attempt to respond to South Asian political demands – for example, in the handling of trade relations with Pakistan, and specifically the proposal for a waiver of import duties on Pakistan's exports to the EU – this was constrained by internal opposition from a number of Member States and by external pressure from Pakistan's key regional competitors.

The more ambitious and wide-ranging negotiations with India over a potential free trade agreement proceeded slowly during the year, and hopes that the agreement might be

[34] *European Voice*, 10 April 2011.
[35] *European Voice*, 8 September 2011.

signed during early 2011 were rapidly replaced by similar aspirations for early 2012. The interaction of these negotiations with the stagnation, if not paralysis, of the Doha Round negotiations (see above) is significant, but whereas in some cases the Doha problem has been seen as a stimulus to the conclusion of a more limited agreement, in the case of India the problem seems to be different. India does not see the need for an agreement that would give away cherished areas of control over market access in return for what might be relatively small benefits of access to the EU.[36]

As in 2011, much of the EU's policy towards Asia could be summarized in one word: China. During this year, there was a new tone to the relationship, and one that drew unmistakably on the broader financial and economic crises affecting the Union. To put it crudely, China's growing economic power encompasses not only trade power but also financial power (itself the reflection of the years in which China has traded very profitably with both the EU and the United States). The financial weakness of the EU creates opportunities for the exercise of financial power by the Chinese, and in 2011 the reality and the anticipation of this were both apparent. Early in the year there were fears expressed that China was accumulating disproportionately high amounts of EU members' sovereign debt – a position that might of course translate into political influence.[37] As the year went on, it became apparent that some EU Member States were rather eager to explore the potential for Chinese involvement, and Spain and Italy were to be seen negotiating for contributions from Beijing. These negotiations did not come to full fruition, but in the later months of the year there was a sustained effort to get China to contribute to the European Financial Stability Facility (EFSF) which was at the core of attempts to stabilize the eurozone economies.[38]

At the same time, relations with China also followed a somewhat familiar course during 2011. The two key dialogues between the EU and China – the high-level strategic dialogue, led by Catherine Ashton and Herman Van Rompuy, and the high-level economic and trade dialogue, led by Trade Commissioner Karel de Gucht and Commission president José Manuel Barroso – were both consolidated during 2011, and there were preparations for the launching of negotiations on a bilateral investment agreement (Commission, 2012, p. 119). On the other hand, and significantly, the scheduled EU–China summit due to be held in November was postponed – on this occasion because of the clash with an emergency European Council meeting focused on the eurozone crisis. Despite this very public indication of the EU's troubles, the infrastructure of EU–China economic relations, with its wide array of dialogues and working groups, is well established and contributes significantly to the management of relations even in times of considerable turbulence.

This is not to say that relations were uniformly harmonious during 2011. There was, for example, a continuing dispute over the Chinese policy of export controls over 'rare earths', which the EU, the United States and Japan made the subject of a WTO complaint (see above). Early in the year, the EU for the first time used its powers to impose retaliatory duties in an anti-subsidy case involving exports of coated paper from China, and an important element in the finding that lay behind these duties was the fact that China

[36] *European Voice*, 17 March 2011.
[37] *European Voice*, 20 January 2011.
[38] *Financial Times*, 28 October 2011.

is not yet recognized as a market economy by the Union. Perhaps significantly, it has been suggested that one *quid pro quo* for Chinese financial support in the eurozone crisis might be a change of position on this issue by Brussels. The Union also imposed a series of checks on imports of Chinese rice in order to guard against their contamination with genetically modified elements. And finally, the Chinese found themselves united with the United States and almost everyone else against the extension of the EU's Emissions Trading Scheme (ETS) to include air transport (see below).

Latin America

During 2011, developments in EU–Latin America relations were largely devoted to following through on the initiatives taken the year before (Allen and Smith, 2011), but as in other areas of EU external activity, the impact of financial and economic crisis could not be ignored. Perhaps the most obvious expression of this was to be seen early in the year, when Brazilian leaders raised the possibility of 'currency wars' arising out of the misalignment and subsequent manipulation of currencies as a form of protectionism.[39] This indicated at one and the same time a new assertiveness by Brazil and an awareness of its relative vulnerability in the face of a rapidly appreciating *real*. The Brazilians are, of course, a key component of the BRIC grouping, in which they are joined by Russia, India and China – and increasingly by South Africa – as a group of concerned emerging economies with potentially significant leverage on international financial dealings. This trend was borne out in late 2011 by the news that finance ministers and central bank governors from the five BRICS were to meet in Washington, DC, with one of their topics for discussion being aid to the eurozone.[40]

This development aside, the EU's relationship with Brazil, its key Latin American 'strategic partner', was further solidified during 2011. The fifth EU–Brazil summit was held in October in Brussels and adopted a revised joint action plan for the relationship as well as initialling an EU–Brazil aviation agreement. Interestingly, the new Brazilian president, Dilma Roussef, confined her visits to other European countries to Bulgaria (where she has family links) and Turkey, another rising regional power which has collaborated with Brazil, for example, over the question of Iran's nuclear programme.

There were renewed efforts during 2011 to make progress with negotiations for an EU–Mercosur (common southern market) free trade agreement. These negotiations have been going on for many years, and have always encountered great difficulties when they turn to the subject of agricultural trade. A number of EU Member States – and now increasingly the EP – have strong views on this topic, and predictably they reacted strongly to the proposed new rounds of negotiations. By the end of the year, two rounds of talks had been held, but it was clear that there would be no further negotiations until after the French elections in spring 2012.[41] At the same time, the EU felt moved to complain against elements of protectionism in Argentinian and Brazilian trade policies – reinforcing a theme that has been central to this chapter.

Despite the problems with Mercosur, Latin America also saw progress for the EU in its search for free trade agreements. In March, a comprehensive association agreement was

[39] *Financial Times*, 10 January 2011.
[40] *Financial Times*, 14 September 2011.
[41] *European Voice*, 3 November 2011.

initialled with six Central American countries – Costa Rica, El Salvador, Guatemala, Honduras, Nicaragua and Panama – and agreements were also made with Peru and Colombia later in the year. The latter were the fruits of negotiations with the Andean Community, but two of its member states – Bolivia and Ecuador – refused to proceed with similar agreements. More broadly, the development framework agreed in Madrid in 2010 at the EU–Latin America and Caribbean Summit was pursued, with €454 million to be made available for the Latin American and Caribbean countries, strongly focused on the fostering of social cohesion, the rule of law and good governance, and the Latin American Investment Facility was consolidated.

The United States, Japan and Other Industrialized Countries

When it comes to relations between the EU and its key partners in the advanced industrial world, it becomes clear that there was a high degree of shared pain in 2011. Indeed, the relationship particularly between the EU and the United States was characterized by intense interdependence of economic challenges and by linkages between the two partners of a type rarely seen before.

One element in this interdependence between the EU and the United States was clearly perceptions of government inadequacy, in the broadest sense. On the EU side, there was the intractability of problems surrounding sovereign debt, austerity and the impact on both of these for the prospects of growth. On the American side, there was faltering recovery, accompanied by severe conflicts between the White House and Congress over such issues as the government debt ceiling and potential economic stimulus, and the approach of what was likely to be a bitterly contested presidential election campaign. As the year developed, it became painfully clear that the fate of the euro preoccupied the administration in Washington. Treasury Secretary Tim Geithner, for example, spent considerable time in Europe and at meetings such as those of EU finance ministers calling for a more assertive policy stance.[42] At the G20 summit in Cannes during November 2011, President Obama actually sat in on EU discussions of the eurozone crisis that came to dominate the broader agenda, and the EU–US summit held later in November saw further focus on the debt crisis and the need for a strengthening of the so-called 'firewall' set up to combat potential further debt crises.[43] To put it bluntly, it appeared that in its weakness and prevarication the EU was receiving far greater attention in American policy and politics than at almost any other time in recent memory.

Alongside this fixation with the financial crisis, a series of other issues were prominent on the EU–US economic agenda. Some were very familiar indeed, such as the latest round of the dispute between Boeing and Airbus in which WTO findings on the subsidization of Boeing's Dreamliner passenger aircraft enabled the Europeans to claim that they had been right all along (whilst the Americans retorted that Airbus was much more of an offender than they ever had been).[44] There was also continuing evidence of the growing competition from China and Brazil, especially in the 100–200-seat aircraft range. By the end of the year, another aviation issue was much more prominent – that of the EU's Emissions Trading Scheme (ETS), which established permits and a trading system related to

[42] *Financial Times*, 17 September 2011.
[43] *European Voice*, 10 and 24 November 2011.
[44] *Financial Times*, 19 May 2011.

emissions by industry and is designed thereby to exert market pressures as a means of limiting the release of 'greenhouse gases' in the EU, and its extension to civil aviation. American airline companies were the leaders of the opposition to this measure, due to be introduced on 1 January 2012, although they were joined by others such as the Chinese and the Japanese. Significantly, they pursued their opposition through the European Court of Justice (ECJ), which found against them in terms of the legality of the measures towards the end of the year, but they were also supported by the State Department in the form of a letter from Secretary of State Hillary Clinton.[45]

Despite these areas of turbulence, there were others in which EU–US co-operation was extended. Early in the year there was an agreement on civil aviation and air traffic control, and later there were agreements on customs clearance and on public procurement (the latter also including Japan, which was significant and was linked with progress on the WTO Government Procurement Agreement as noted earlier), whilst the EU and the United States also collaborated in the challenge to China's export controls over 'rare earths' (see above). The EU–US summit in November discussed the potential for a comprehensive bilateral trade agreement, and set up studies led by de Gucht and the United States Trade Representative Ron Kirk to explore this (European Council, 2010a). As noted earlier in this chapter, this is a key element in the extension of the EU's search for such agreements to include its major advanced industrial partners.[46]

In an important sense, the economic and regulatory issues noted above were also the key political issues of the year for EU–US relations. The Obama administration's pragmatic foreign policies, combined with the effects of economic crisis, can be given the credit for this situation, but that does not mean that everything has been plain sailing. During 2011, the long-standing dispute over the use of air passenger data (PNR) rumbled on. The Commission came to a new agreement with Washington on this issue, but it did not resolve the doubts of the EP, especially in relation to the retention and use of passenger data. The EP threatened to take the issue to the ECJ for a judgment on whether the agreement exceeded the legal boundaries set in the EU treaties. In a related area, there were continuing tensions between Brussels and Washington over issues of data protection.

On many other areas there were signs of important collaborative (or at least convergent) ventures, especially on the diplomacy of a number of major international conflicts. Thus, the EU and the United States were anxious to concert their positions on the issue of Palestinian statehood when it was raised at the UN General Assembly in the autumn (although there were significant differences of view within the EU itself). Whilst the position was held on this occasion, there might be others when it is less easy to ensure policy convergence on this issue. The EU and the United States continued to co-operate in developing policy towards Iran and its nuclear programme (an issue where Catherine Ashton holds the key role of co-ordinator of the 'E3 + 3' diplomatic effort), although there was increasing talk in Washington and elsewhere of a potential military strike against Iran's facilities.[47] A major strengthening of sanctions, including against oil exports, was mooted for introduction early in 2012. At the same time, sanctions undertaken against regimes such as that in Libya and later in Syria during 2011 were also the subject of

[45] *Financial Times*, 20 December 2011.
[46] *European Voice*, 1 December 2011.
[47] *Financial Times*, 9 November 2011.

intense discussion between the EU and the United States. In all of this talk about sanctions, one thing became clear: the EU was actually in a position to exert more significant pressure than the United States, partly because of their dependence on exports from the Middle East and North Africa, but also partly because of the leverage given by their willingness to suffer the political and other losses in imposing the measures, which could be contrasted with American prevarication in some of the areas concerned.

Relations between the EU and two of its other major industrial-world partners – Canada and Japan – remained positive during the year, but in at least one case there were signs of problems to come. The EU has set out to negotiate a Comprehensive Economic and Trade Agreement (CETA) with Canada, which also involves negotiating with all of the ten Canadian provinces. Although this seemed to have gone smoothly during the year, the negotiations were complicated by the impact of another issue – that of oil derived from so-called 'tar sands'. The EU's environmental arm sees these as more polluting and more damaging to the atmosphere than other forms of hydrocarbons, and proposed to regulate them accordingly. The Canadians, not surprisingly, objected, and the issue began to rise strongly up the political scale in autumn 2011, revealing internal divisions within the EU about how far it should push its proposals.[48]

The EU–Japan relationship was furthered during 2011 with broad proposals for a free trade agreement, discussed at the EU–Japan summit in May (Council, 2010b). These proposals led to the setting up of a 'scoping exercise' to be completed during 2012. This progress, for some at least, reflected the impact of the EU–South Korea free trade area and the leverage it added to the EU search for further such agreements.[49] In the case of Japan, the link is quite significant given its geographical proximity and intense competition with Korea in a number of key sectors.[50] The tsunami and earthquake that hit Japan in spring 2011 also led to significant areas of co-operation, and to the donation of emergency aid by the EU.

Conclusions

It is clear that the EU spent most of 2011 on the back foot as far as its external relations were concerned. Failure to get to grips fully with the crisis in the eurozone and the challenging impact of the Arab Spring resulted in critical scrutiny of the EU from its international partners to whom it was also forced to turn for financial assistance in 2011. The United States, in particular, expressed both frustration and concern with the EU's weak response to the fiscal crisis and to its inability to meet a number of military and diplomatic challenges, even though, at the personal level, Baroness Ashton clearly has been able to develop a positive relationship with the United States secretary of state, Hillary Clinton.

In its first year of operation the EEAS found itself fully occupied with just keeping the EU's diplomatic show on the road and with coming to terms with the new institutional arrangements which have given rise both to a new set of 'turf wars' and to an enhanced and more significant role for the EP in EU external relations. For this, and other reasons discussed above, the EU was limited almost exclusively to reacting to events and was not

[48] *The Guardian*, 5 October 2011.
[49] *European Voice*, 26 May 2011.
[50] *European Voice*, 26 May and 1 June 2011.

able to produce any significant external policy initiatives. Indeed, it is hard to disagree with the ECFR's conclusions that the EU's *acquis diplomatique* has 'started to slowly erode' (ECFR, 2012, p. 9). The EU generally suffered from a crisis of leadership in 2011, reflected in Baroness Ashton's failure to get an overall grip on all aspects of EU external relations, and from a re-nationalization of European foreign policy despite (or perhaps because of) the cuts that most EU Member States were forced to make in their foreign and security policy budgets. This crisis of leadership was reflected in the EU's overall performance in its relations with the outside world and in the call for the EEAS to provide what was described as 'global vision'.[51]

Key Readings

As in previous years, Commission (2012) provides a good general (if sometimes selective) overview. Reports on their activities by the President of the European Council (General Secretariat of the Council, 2012) and by the High Representative (EEAS, 2011) are also useful. The European Council on Foreign Relations ((ECRF, 2012) published a *European Foreign Policy Scorecard* for 2011 and *European Voice* continues to provide comprehensive coverage of all aspects of EU external relations. Much of the *European Voice* coverage is provided by Toby Vogel, and his highly critical article (Vogel, 2012) on Baroness Ashton attracted a great deal of attention (see *The Economist*, 2012).

References

Allen, D. and Smith, M. (2011) 'Relations with the Rest of the World', *JCMS*, Vol. 49, No. S1, pp. 209–30.

Commission of the European Communities (2010) 'Trade, growth and world affairs: trade policy as a core component of the EU's 2020 Strategy'. *COM*(2010)612, November.

Commission of the European Communities (2011) 'Increasing the impact of EU development policy: an agenda for change'. *COM*(2011) 637.

Commission of the European Communities (2012) *General Report on the Activities of the European Union 2011* (Brussels: European Commission).

The Economist (2012) 'The Berlusconi Option for Lady Ashton', Charlemagne's Notebook. *The Economist*, 2 February. Available at: «http://www.economist.com/blogs/charlemagne/2012/02/european-foreign-policy».

European Council (2010a) 'EU–US Summit Lisbon, 20 November 2010: Joint Statement'. Available at: «http://www.consilium.europa.eu/press».

European Council (2010b) 'Joint Statement Following the EU–Japan Summit'. Available at: «http://www.consilium.europa.eu/press».

European Council (2010c) *EU–Russia: Partnership for Modernisation*. Available at: «http://www.consilium.europa.eu/homepage/highlights/eu-russia-partnership-for-modernisation?lang=en».

European Council on Foreign Relations (ECRF) (2012) *European Foreign Policy Scorecard, 2012*. Available at: «http://www.ecfr.eu/scorecard/2012/extras/introduction».

European External Action Service (EEAS) (2011) 'Report by the High Representative to the European Parliament, the Council and the Commission', 22 December. Available at: «http://www.eeas.europa.eu/images/top_stories/2011_eeas_report_cor.pdf».

[51] *European Voice*, 24 November 2011.

Foreign Ministers (2011) 'Joint Letter from the Foreign Ministers of Belgium, Estonia, Finland, France, Germany, Italy, Latvia, Lithuania, Luxembourg, the Netherlands, Poland and Sweden to the HR/VP Catherine Ashton'. Available at: «http://www.eurotradeunion.eu/documents/20111208Lettredes12.pdf».

General Secretariat of the Council (2012) *The European Council in 2011* (Luxembourg: Publications Office of the European Union).

Jokela, J. (2011) 'The G-20: A Pathway to Effective Multilateralism?' Chaillot Paper 125 (Paris: EU Institute for Security Studies).

O'Sullivan, D. (2012) 'The European External Action Service One Year On: Note of Comments Made at European Policy Centre Breakfast Meeting', 25 January. Available at: «http://eeas.europa.eu/images/top_stories/2012_dos_speech.pdf».

Vogel, T. (2012) 'A Year On and Still Failing'. *European Voice*, 5 January.

Woolcock, S. (2012) *European Union Economic Diplomacy: The Role of the EU in External Economic Relations* (Aldershot: Ashgate).

Youngs, R. (2010) *The EU's Role in World Politics: A Retreat from Liberal Internationalism* (London: Routledge).

JCMS 2012 Volume 50 Annual Review pp. 178–194 DOI: 10.1111/j.1468-5965.2012.02270.x

The Eurozone in 2011

DERMOT HODSON
Birkbeck College, University of London

Introduction

The year 2011 saw the eurozone sovereign debt crisis go from bad to considerably worse. Although budget deficits fell in almost all Member States, continued concerns over debt sustainability and the fragility of eurozone banks contributed to a sharp slowdown in economic growth, which, in turn, cast doubt on the credibility of further fiscal consolidation. These tensions came to a head in Portugal in March 2011 after the government failed to win approval for its deficit reduction plans against the backdrop of a double dip recession. Rising interest rates on government debt and downgrades by the three major ratings agencies saw Portugal become the third eurozone member, after Greece and Ireland, to seek financial support from the European Union (EU) and the International Monetary Fund (IMF) – a package of loans worth €78 billion being agreed in May 2011.

Greece's precarious public finances remained a real and present danger for the eurozone in 2011. Facing widespread social unrest over the scale of budget cuts and a deepening recession, the authorities in Athens struggled to stick to the terms of the EU–IMF financial support package agreed in May 2010. A round of further expenditure cuts and emergency revenue-raising measures in 2011 ensured that this support continued to flow, but it was by now clear that more needed to be done to avoid a disorderly default by Greece with potentially disastrous consequences for the rest of the eurozone. The tentative offer of a second round of EU–IMF loans, combined with a preliminary deal on private sector involvement in debt restructuring, failed to convince financial markets, with only George Papandreou's resignation as prime minister in November 2011 and the appointment of a caretaker government led by former European Central Bank (ECB) Vice-President Lucas Papademos bringing some semblance of calm.

Running reforms to eurozone governance were another feature of 2011. In January, the new European Systemic Risk Board (ESRB) held its inaugural meeting, thus beginning a bold new experiment in pan-European financial supervision. In February, the heads of state or government signed a treaty establishing the European Stability Mechanism (ESM) – a permanent successor to the ad hoc Financial Stability Facility (ESFS) created in May 2010. This was followed in March 2011 by a final agreement by the European Council on changes to Article 136 of the Treaty on the Functioning of the European Union (TFEU) to ensure the legality of the ESM. November 2011, meanwhile, saw the entry into force of the so-called 'Six Pack' – a set of six legislative reforms designed to reinforce the Stability and Growth Pact and other aspects of eurozone governance. Within a month, all EU Member States (except the United Kingdom and the Czech Republic) had agreed on an additional, intergovernmental treaty – the Fiscal Compact – designed to reinforce Member States' commitment to fiscal discipline and foster closer economic policy co-ordination.

This flurry of reforms did little to reassure financial markets in the short term that eurozone members were both willing and able to bring about a resolution to the eurozone sovereign debt crisis. A series of inconclusive discussions between eurozone leaders failed to increase the financial firepower of either the EFSF or the embryonic ESM to the point where support for a large eurozone member was feasible. This left the eurozone without a credible course of action when interest rates on Italy's burgeoning debt soared, leaving all eyes on the G20 leaders' summit in Cannes in November 2011.

This summit came and went without a concrete solution, with only the subsequent resignation of Silvio Berlusconi as prime minister and his replacement with a caretaker government led by former European Commissioner Mario Monti bringing respite to, and from, financial markets. The European Council's agreement on the Fiscal Compact in December 2011 failed to diffuse this situation, with Standard and Poor's downgrade of Austria, Cyprus, France, Italy, Malta, Portugal, Slovakia, Slovenia and Spain offering proof, if it were needed, that the sovereign debt crisis was no longer confined to the periphery of the eurozone (Standard and Poor's, 2012).

The year 2011, finally, saw a changing of the guard at the ECB. In November 2011, Jean-Claude Trichet's tumultuous eight-year term of office came to an end. His successor, Mario Draghi, was a surprise choice, with the former governor of the Banca d'Italia winning the backing of France and Germany after the front-runner, Axel Weber, resigned as Bundesbank president and ruled himself out of the race for the ECB. Hopes that Draghi might be more open to large-scale bond purchases were ruled out in the short run, but the new ECB President did win plaudits for announcing a new long-term financing operation in December 2011 that provided banks with cheap three-year loans.

This article takes stock of these and other key developments in its review of the eurozone for 2011. Section I summarizes the economic outlook for the eurozone in 2011. Section II explores key developments in eurozone monetary policy. Section III examines the ESRB's first full year. Section III discusses compliance with the Stability and Growth Pact in 2011 and the launch of the new European Semester. Section IV takes stock of the key reforms to eurozone governance in 2011. Section V examines the eurozone's international role in 2011, focusing on its interaction with the IMF and the Group of Twenty (G20).

I. The Economic Situation in 2011

Having rebounded from recession in 2010, real gross domestic product (GDP) in the eurozone fell from 1.9 to 1.5 per cent in 2011 (see Table 1).[1] The worsening outlook for the world economy was partly to blame here, with the eurozone's top three trading partners – the United Kingdom, the United States and China – all experiencing slowdowns of varying degrees of severity in 2011 as the effects of earlier fiscal stimulus packages faded and various other factors took their toll; the eurozone's sovereign debt crisis was itself among these factors, with investors fearing another international banking crisis in the event of a disorderly default by Greece and/or the break-up of the eurozone. Similar fears weighed on domestic demand in the eurozone in 2011, with consumer and business confidence declining and credit conditions for individuals and industry tightening as the year progressed.

[1] The data for this article are taken from Commission (2011a) unless otherwise stated.

Table 1: Real GDP Growth (% Annual Change) – Eurozone Area (2007–12)

	2007	*2008*	*2009*	*2010*	*2011[e]*	*2012[f]*
Belgium	2.9	1.0	−2.8	2.3	2.3	0.9
Germany	3.3	1.1	−5.1	3.7	2.9	0.8
Estonia	7.5	−3.7	−14.3	2.3	8.0	3.2
Ireland	5.2	−3.0	−7.0	−0.4	1.1	1.1
Greece	3.0	−0.2	−3.2	−3.5	−5.5	−2.8
Spain	3.5	0.9	−3.7	−0.1	0.7	0.7
France	2.3	−0.1	−2.7	1.5	1.6	0.6
Italy	1.7	−1.2	−5.1	1.5	0.5	0.1
Cyprus	5.1	3.6	−1.9	1.1	0.3	0.0
Luxembourg	6.6	0.8	−5.3	2.7	1.6	1.0
Malta	4.3	4.4	−2.7	2.7	2.1	1.3
Netherlands	3.9	1.8	−3.5	1.7	1.8	0.5
Austria	3.7	1.4	−3.8	2.3	2.9	0.9
Portugal	2.4	0.0	−2.5	1.4	−1.9	−3.0
Slovenia	6.9	3.6	−8.0	1.4	1.1	1.0
Slovakia	10.5	5.9	−4.9	4.2	2.9	1.1
Finland	5.3	1.0	−8.2	3.6	3.1	1.4
Eurozone	3.0	0.4	−4.2	1.9	1.5	0.5

Source: Commission (2011a, p. 206, table 1).
Note: Estimates are denoted by *e* and forecasts by *f*.

A few eurozone economies managed to buck this trend,[2] but the outlook for most members was bleak. Particularly worrying in this regard was the case of Germany, which saw its impressive economic recovery in 2010 derailed by falling demand for its exports; for the year as a whole, net exports contributed just 0.4 percentage points to real GDP growth in Germany, compared to 2.2 and 0.3 percentage points for domestic demand and inventories, respectively. The slowdown was of a different order of magnitude in the geographic periphery of the eurozone, with Portugal seeing real GDP contract by 1.9 per cent in 2011 after a relatively strong showing in 2010. Greece, meanwhile, saw real GDP contract by 5.5 per cent in 2011, with public and private consumption falling by 8.5 and 6.2 per cent, respectively, as the effects of austerity took their toll.

The eurozone's unemployment rate fell fractionally to 10.0 per cent in 2011 and is expected to remain close to this level for the foreseeable future (see Table 2). Germany is a unique case here among the eurozone's largest members, with just 6.5 per cent of its civilian labour force registered as unemployed in 2011 – lower than at any other time since 1991. Burda and Hunt (2011) attribute this 'labour market miracle' not only to wage moderation, the traditional mainstay of German competitiveness, or to adjustment in the number of hours worked during the recession of 2009, but also to the fact that firms were unusually cautious about hiring new workers during the economic upturn of 2005–07, thus resulting in fewer layoffs than usual when economic conditions slowed.

Inflationary pressures in the eurozone picked up in 2011, with the harmonized index of consumer prices rising by 2.6 per cent, as compared with 1.6 per cent 12 months earlier (Table 3). Whether the ECB's historically low interest rates were a factor here is difficult

[2] Estonia, which became the 17th country to join the eurozone in January 2011, saw GDP rise by 8.0 per cent thanks to a surge in demand for its exports.

Table 2: Unemployment (% of the Civilian Labour Force) – Eurozone (2007–12)

	2007	*2008*	*2009*	*2010*	*2011[e]*	*2012[f]*
Belgium	7.5	7.0	7.9	8.3	7.6	7.7
Germany	8.7	7.5	7.8	7.1	6.1	5.9
Estonia	4.7	5.5	13.8	16.9	12.5	11.2
Ireland	4.6	6.3	11.9	13.7	14.4	14.3
Greece	8.3	7.7	9.5	12.6	16.6	18.4
Spain	8.3	11.3	18.0	20.1	20.9	20.9
France	8.4	7.8	9.5	9.8	9.8	10.0
Italy	6.1	6.7	7.8	8.4	8.1	8.2
Cyprus	3.9	3.7	5.3	6.2	7.2	7.5
Luxembourg	4.2	4.9	5.1	4.6	4.5	4.8
Malta	6.5	6.0	6.9	6.9	6.7	6.8
Netherlands	3.6	3.1	3.7	4.5	4.5	4.7
Austria	4.4	3.8	4.8	4.4	4.2	4.5
Portugal	8.9	8.5	10.6	12.0	12.6	13.6
Slovenia	4.9	4.4	5.9	7.3	8.2	8.4
Slovakia	11.1	9.5	12.0	14.4	13.2	13.2
Finland	6.9	6.4	8.2	8.4	7.8	7.7
Eurozone	7.6	7.6	9.6	10.1	10.0	10.1

Source: Commission (2011a, p. 217, table 23).
Note: Estimates are denoted by *e* and forecasts by *f*.

Table 3: Inflation Rates (% Change on Preceding Year) – Eurozone (2007–12)

	2007	*2008*	*2009*	*2010*	*2011[e]*	*2012[f]*
Belgium	1.8	4.5	0.0	2.3	3.5	2.0
Germany	2.3	2.8	0.2	1.2	2.4	1.7
Estonia	6.7	10.6	0.2	2.7	5.2	3.3
Ireland	2.9	3.1	–1.7	–1.5	1.1	0.7
Greece	3.0	4.2	1.3	4.7	3.0	0.8
Spain	2.8	4.1	–0.2	2.0	3.0	1.1
France	1.6	3.2	0.1	1.7	2.2	1.5
Italy	2.0	3.5	0.8	1.6	2.7	2.0
Cyprus	2.2	4.4	0.2	2.6	3.4	2.8
Luxembourg	2.7	4.1	0.0	2.8	3.6	2.1
Malta	0.7	4.7	1.8	2.0	2.6	2.2
Netherlands	1.6	2.2	1.0	0.9	2.5	1.9
Austria	2.2	3.2	0.4	1.7	3.4	2.2
Portugal	2.4	2.7	–0.9	1.4	3.5	3.0
Slovenia	3.8	5.5	0.9	2.1	1.9	1.3
Slovakia	1.9	3.9	0.9	0.7	4.0	1.7
Finland	1.6	3.9	1.6	1.7	3.2	2.6
Eurozone	2.1	3.3	0.3	1.6	2.6	1.7

Source: Commission (2011a, p. 213, table 16).
Note: Estimates are denoted by *e* and forecasts by *f*.

Table 4: Net Lending (+) or Net Borrowing (–) General Government Balance (% of GDP) – Eurozone (2007–12)

	2007	*2008*	*2009*	*2010*	*2011*[e]	*2012*[f]
Belgium	–0.3	–1.3	–5.8	–4.1	–3.6	–4.6
Germany	0.2	0.1	–3.2	–4.3	–1.3	–1.0
Estonia	2.4	–2.9	–2.0	–0.2	–0.8	–1.8
Ireland	0.1	–7.3	–14.2	–31.3	–10.3	–8.6
Greece	–6.5	–9.8	–15.8	–10.6	–8.9	–7.0
Spain	1.9	–4.5	–11.2	–9.3	–6.6	–5.9
France	–2.7	–3.3	–7.5	–7.1	–5.8	–5.3
Italy	–1.6	–2.7	–5.4	–4.6	–4.0	–2.3
Cyprus	3.5	0.9	–6.1	–5.3	–6.7	–4.9
Luxembourg	3.7	3.0	–0.9	–1.1	–0.6	–1.1
Malta	–2.4	–4.6	–3.7	–3.6	–3.0	–3.5
Netherlands	0.2	0.5	–5.6	–5.1	–4.3	–3.1
Austria	–0.9	–0.9	–4.1	–4.4	–3.4	–3.1
Portugal	–3.1	–3.6	–10.1	–9.8	–5.8	–4.5
Slovenia	0.0	–1.9	–6.1	–5.8	–5.7	–5.3
Slovakia	–1.8	–2.1	–8.0	–7.7	–5.8	–4.9
Finland	5.3	4.3	–2.5	–2.5	–1.0	–0.7
Eurozone	–0.6	–2.1	–6.4	–6.2	–4.1	–3.4

Source: Commission (2011b, p. 223, table 35).
Note: Estimates are denoted by *e* and forecasts by *f*.

to discern since the traditional transmission mechanisms for eurozone monetary policy have been impaired by the financial crisis. Other factors that may have had an impact here are high commodity prices, with concerns over supply disruptions due to the Arab Spring causing oil prices to surge at the beginning of the year, and the effects of value added tax (VAT) increases in Portugal, Greece, Italy and Slovakia on consumer prices (see Table 4).

The eurozone budget deficit fell from 6.2 per cent in 2010 to 4.1 per cent in 2011. With the exception of Cyprus, all eurozone members that posted budget deficits in 2010 saw government borrowing fall in 2011.[3] The pace of fiscal consolidation was, however, greater in some countries than in others. Leaving to one side the case of Ireland, which saw its budget deficit in 2010 balloon because of one-off capital injections into certain financial institutions, the pace of fiscal consolidation was greatest in Portugal, which cut four percentage points off its budget deficit, first, in an effort to reassure financial markets and, later, to meet its commitments to the EU–IMF financial support package. Germany, too, saw its budget deficit fall by three percentage points, reflecting its strong economic performance in 2010.

II. Monetary Policy in 2011

Last year's review of the eurozone took note of increasing tensions within the ECB Governing Council over the Bank's response to the unfolding crisis (Hodson, 2011a). Particularly controversial in this regard was the ECB's Securities Markets Programme

[3] Exposure to Greece's economic crisis was a key contributory factor behind Cyprus's fiscal difficulties in 2011, as was the explosion at the Evangelos Florakis naval base that incapacitated the country's largest power station.

(SMP) – an initiative launched in May 2010 to allow the Bank to buy government bonds. Such purchases are limited to the secondary rather than the primary bond market, meaning that the ECB cannot buy bonds directly from national governments. Bundesbank President Axel Weber was the most vocal critic of the SMP, criticizing ECB bond purchases for being ineffective and for blurring the line between monetary and fiscal policies. Tensions over the SMP came to a head in 2011, with Weber announcing his resignation as Bundesbank president in February. This was followed in September 2011 by the resignation of Jürgen Stark – an ECB Executive Board Member with his own misgivings about the SMP (Reuters, 2011a).

For Germany, the resignation of two of the country's most senior central bankers prompted a reshuffle that Chancellor Angela Merkel could arguably ill-afford, with her economic adviser, Jens Weidmann, becoming the new Bundesbank president and her deputy finance minister, Jörg Asmussen, joining the ECB Executive Board. At the European level, Weber's resignation robbed the race to succeed Jean-Claude Trichet as ECB President of its front-runner. With Germany failing to field an alternative candidate, the European Council finally agreed that Mario Draghi, the president of the Banca d'Italia, would become the third President of the ECB after Trichet's eight-year, non-renewable term of office came to an end in November 2011 (European Council, 2011a).

When Draghi assumed office, the ECB Executive Board found itself in the unusual position of having two Italians and no French person on this six-strong body. Traditionally, the four largest eurozone members – France, Italy, Spain and Germany – have 'reserved' a seat on the ECB Executive Board, with the remaining two seats rotated between central bankers from smaller eurozone members. In keeping with this tradition, French President Nicolas Sarkozy reportedly put Draghi's compatriot, Lorenzo Bini Smaghi, under considerable pressure to resign his seat, even though his term of office did not expire until May 2013 (Atkins, 2011). That Bini Smaghi eventually agreed to make way for Benoît Cœuré, a well-respected French economist, was not unexpected, but it surely went against the spirit of the Treaty, which imposes no nationality requirements on ECB Executive Board Members. This move, coupled with Trichet's departure and the appointment of Belgian central banker, Peter Praet, to the ECB Executive Board in June 2011, also left the Bank with comparatively inexperienced leadership at a time of unprecedented turmoil for the eurozone.

Turning from institutional developments to monetary policy decisions, the ECB, it should be recalled, initiated a series of interest rate cuts in October 2008 at the height of the financial crisis, bringing the rate on its main refinancing operation to a historic low of 1.0 per cent in June 2009. In so doing, the Bank was behind the curve compared to other monetary authorities; the United States Federal Reserve, for example, started cutting its overnight federal funds rate in October 2007 until it reached a band of between 0.00–0.25 per cent in December 2008. Far from seeking to change course in 2011, the Fed took the unusual step of announcing that the federal funds rate would likely remain unchanged until at least mid-2013. The ECB Governing Council, in contrast, raised interest rates on its main refinancing operation by 25 basis points in April 2011 and again in July.

As ever, the ECB sought to justify its actions with reference to its overarching commitment to price stability. At a press conference following the first interest rate cut, ECB President Jean-Claude Trichet warned of the second-round effects of higher energy and food prices on price and wage setting in the eurozone (Trichet, 2011). The fact that commodity price rises subsequently peaked in mid-2011 raises questions about whether the ECB acted too soon in raising interest rates, as does the fact that the growth outlook for the eurozone deteriorated so sharply in the second half of the year. These decisions were, in any case, quickly reversed, with the ECB Governing Council voting to cut interest rates by 0.25 basis points in both November and December 2011, as the sovereign debt crisis escalated.

The interest rate increases of April and June 2011 were not the only questionable judgement call by the Bank since the beginning of the financial crisis. In July 2008, the ECB raised interest rates, citing familiar concerns over high energy and food prices, only to start cutting interest rates three months later once the scale of the economic slowdown facing the eurozone became apparent. Also inopportune was the ECB President's reference in November 2009 to the phasing out of unconventional monetary policies – a remark that served only to inflame financial market concerns over Greece (Trichet, 2009). As a prediction it also proved wide of the mark, with the ECB introducing the SMP in May 2010 and spending around €211 billion on bond purchases as of December 2011 (ECB, 2011).

A recurring criticism of the ECB in 2011 was that the SMP went nowhere near far enough; by way of comparison, the Fed spent $600 billion on United States government bonds between November 2010 and June 2011. As the year progressed, many commentators came to the view that only large-scale purchases of government bonds of this sort could bring an end to the eurozone sovereign debt crisis (see Friedman, 2011). Hopes that Mario Draghi might engineer a U-turn on this issue were dashed nonetheless in December 2011, with the new ECB President seen as ruling out any drastic change in policy direction from the ECB. Actually, Draghi left himself with some wiggle room, implying that the purchase of government bonds on primary markets was against the Treaty but implicitly leaving open the possibility of increased intervention on secondary markets (Draghi, 2011a). Such subtleties notwithstanding, Draghi gave no indication that the Bank would significantly step up government bond purchases anytime soon, thus further frustrating financial markets over the lack of viable solutions to the eurozone's sovereign debt crisis.

Financial markets took some consolation, however, from the ECB's decision to launch a new long-term refinancing operation (LTRO) in December 2011. Under this initiative, the ECB agreed to offer low-cost three-year loans to European banks, with more than €500 billion allocated between December 2011 and March 2012 (see ECB, 2012). These loans helped to stabilize European banks in the short term, which appeared to be on the brink of another systemic crisis in late 2011 as fears over the eurozone sovereign debt crisis mounted. Some commentators also credit the LTRO with helping to reduce interest rates on the government debt of countries such as Italy and Spain by encouraging commercial banks to buy government bonds issued by these countries. De Grauwe (2012), for one, is critical of the LTRO, arguing that it would have been both cheaper and less risky for the ECB to purchase government bonds rather than delegating this role to risk-averse commercial banks that might choose to offload these purchases at any point.

III. Financial Supervision in 2011

Last year's review of the eurozone recorded the launch of the ESRB in December 2010 – one of several new EU watchdogs created in the light of the financial crisis (Hodson, 2011a). Questions were raised over the ESRB's nebulous mandate, its cumbrous governance structure, its lack of ready-made policy instruments and its democratic accountability. The year 2011 provided the first chance to see if such concerns were warranted, with the ESRB holding its first meeting in January and convening on three occasions thereafter.

The initial meetings of the ESRB were low-key affairs, preoccupied with procedural rules and offering only tentative thoughts on the outlook for financial stability in the eurozone. Thereafter, the new watchdog showed a willingness to sound the alarm, with Jean-Claude Trichet, the inaugural chair of the ESRB, using post-meeting press releases to issue increasingly terse warnings about threats posed by rising sovereign risks and concerns over another systemic banking crisis (see, for example, ESRB, 2011a). Trichet and other senior members of the ESRB also used their periodic appearances before the European Parliament's Economic and Monetary Affairs Committee (Econ) to reinforce this message, thus mimicking the approach used by the ECB in its regular Monetary Dialogue with Members of the European Parliament (MEPs). These appearances also shed some light on the inner workings of the ESRB, thus helping to enhance the new body's transparency, if not necessarily its democratic accountability.

Alongside this general watchdog function, the ESRB acted on a number of specific supervisory concerns in 2011. One such concern was the systemic risks associated with foreign currency loans, with the Board's newly assembled Advisory Technical Committee finding that such loans accounted for over 20 per cent of lending to households in seven EU Member States and over half of lending to non-financial corporations in five Member States. Having flagged up this issue at its meeting in September 2011, the ESRB followed up a month later with its first formal recommendation on lending in foreign currencies (ESRB, 2011b).

Addressed to national financial supervisors, this detailed recommendation called for measures to encourage, *inter alia*, financial institutions to inform borrowers against the risks associated with foreign currency loans and the use of hedging instruments to protect against this risk. The recommendation also urged national supervisors to monitor levels of foreign currency lending closely and to adopt more stringent standards in cases where a systemic threat exists. Compliance with these provisions will be a crucial test case of the ESRB's so-called 'ask and explain' mechanism.[4] This mechanism is an interesting exercise in soft co-ordination, with Member States under no legal obligation to follow ESRB recommendations but non-compliant countries required to justify their inaction. In cases where the ESRB is not convinced by this justification, it has the authority to refer this matter to the Council and, where relevant, the European Supervisory Authorities, although the ESRB statutes remain vague on precisely what happens next.

IV. The Stability and Growth Pact in 2011

While the sovereign debt crisis continued to rage in 2011, the year was rather paradoxically a relatively quiet one for the Stability and Growth Pact. In July 2010, it should be recalled, the Economic and Financial Affairs Council (Ecofin) decided that Austria, Belgium, Germany, Ireland, France, Italy, the Netherlands, Portugal, Slovenia, Slovakia and Spain had complied with earlier recommendations under Article 126 TFEU to take corrective action to get their budget deficits below 3 per cent and that, in consequence, no

[4] Article 20, Regulation EU No. 1092/2010.

additional steps were foreseen. With the exception of Ireland, this assessment remained unchanged in 2011, meaning that the Commission made surprisingly few public pronouncements on the pace of fiscal consolidation in these countries and initiated no further disciplinary measures. Such flexibility was arguably justified by the fact that Member States' plans for fiscal consolidation remained more or less on track in 2011. It provided yet further proof, however, of the discord between EU fiscal surveillance and market expectations, with Portugal's compliance with the Stability and Growth Pact doing little to reassure ratings agencies about the sustainability of the country's public finances.

Ireland, as noted in last year's review of the eurozone, was issued with a revised Article 126(7) recommendation in December 2010 taking account of unforeseen circumstances and extending the deadline for correcting the excessive deficit from 2014 to 2015 (Hodson, 2011a). A European Commission assessment in August 2011 concluded that Ireland was on course to meet this target and that consequently no further action under the excessive deficit procedure would be required (Commission, 2011b). This assessment was consistent with the quarterly reviews of the country's Economic Adjustment Programme, which concluded that Ireland had made significant progress in 2011 in getting its government borrowing under control (see, for example, Commission, 2011c).

If the excessive deficit procedure thus faded into the background for Ireland and Portugal in 2011, it remained in the foreground for Greece, which faced revised recommendations under Article 126(9) in March, July and November 2011 to coincide with the quarterly reviews of its Economic Adjustment Programme.[5] The stakes surrounding these recommendations could not have been higher, since compliance with the Economic Adjustment Programme is a condition for receiving further tranches of the loans extended by eurozone members to Greece in May 2010. For their part, eurozone finance ministers proved willing to engage in a degree of brinksmanship with Greece, delaying, for example, a decision over a loan instalment in September 2011 until Athens offered further fiscal concessions (see Ewing and Kitsantonis, 2011).

Of the three other eurozone members that posted excessive budget deficits in 2011, Ecofin agreed in February that Finland, Cyprus and Malta were on track to get government borrowing below 3 per cent of GDP within the time frame agreed and that, consequently, no further disciplinary measures were envisaged under Article 126 TFEU (Council, 2011a). Finland saw its excessive deficit procedure formally closed by Ecofin in July 2011, becoming the first country to get government borrowing below 3 per cent of GDP in the wake of the financial crisis (Council, 2011b). This fact is of relevance for understanding this country's reticence about financial transfers to other eurozone members, with the government refusing to sign off on a second support package for Greece until the Greek government agreed to put up collateral for the Finnish portion of these loans.

Finally, on the issue of fiscal surveillance, 2011 was the first full year of the so-called 'European Semester'. This change to the calendar for monitoring Member States' economic policies, signed off in September 2010 by EU leaders, began in December 2010 with the Commission's presentation of a new Annual Growth Survey (Commission, 2011d). This document identified a set of overarching economic priorities for the year ahead, covering fiscal policy issues, labour market reforms and 'growth enhancing measures'. These priorities were then endorsed by EU leaders at the Spring European Council

[5] Available at: «http://ec.europa.eu/economy_finance/economic_governance/sgp/deficit/countries/Greece_en.htm».

in March 2011, with Member States invited, in particular, to present medium-term plans for bringing government debt back to sustainable levels and getting budget deficits below 3 per cent of GDP (European Council, 2011a).

Prior to the European Semester, Member States set out their medium-term plans for fiscal policy in stability programmes submitted at the end of the budget year. Thus, for example, Belgium's stability programme for the period 2009–12 was submitted in January 2010 before being assessed by the Commission in March and subject to a Council opinion in April. Under the European Semester, Member States now set out their medium-term fiscal plans at the beginning of the budget year, with Belgium, for example, presenting its stability programme for the period 2011–14 in April 2011 before facing a Commission recommendation in June and a Council recommendation in July. The rationale for this change is to allow the Commission and Council to offer a view on Member States' fiscal policies before budgetary negotiations back home are at an advanced stage. In the case of Belgium, the Council's July 2011 recommendations were delivered some six months before the government presented the 2012 budget to parliament.

The idea that the Commission and Council should offer a view on Member States' draft budgets before national parliaments have had a chance to do so has understandably reignited concerns about a democratic deficit at the heart of economic and monetary union (EMU).[6] Such criticisms assume that recommendations issued under the European Semester will be 'more or less binding' (Tsoukalis, 2011, p. 29), but this surely exaggerates the significance of the new arrangements, with Member States subject to the same non-binding recommendations from the Commission and the Council as before. A key question for the evolution of the European Semester is how willing the EU executive and EU finance ministers will be to apply peer pressure through this process and how Member States might respond to such naming and shaming. That the Commission might have been emboldened by the crisis is suggested by Olli Rehn's leaked letter to Belgian Finance Minister Steven Vanackere, which identified changes to the draft 2012 budget needed to avoid disciplinary action under the excessive deficit procedure (see Robinson, 2012). That the Belgian government took steps to address these concerns may suggest a new spirit of co-operation from Member States, although reports that several Member States fought back against the Commission's June 2011 recommendations under the European Semester suggest otherwise.

V. The Future of Eurozone Governance

As discussed in last year's review, the Commission presented a set of six legislative proposals for strengthening the Stability and Growth Pact and other aspects of eurozone governance in September 2010 (Hodson, 2011a). The year 2011 saw several long months of negotiation between the Council and EP on the so-called 'Six Pack', with agreement finally reached in September and the new legislation entering into force in November. That the EP played such an active role in these negotiations rested on a rather expansive reading of the Lisbon Treaty, which extends for the first time the ordinary legislative procedure to regulations governing the conduct of multilateral surveillance.[7] A narrow reading of this

[6] See, for example, European Parliament Resolution 2011/2071[INI]).
[7] Article 121(6) TFEU.

provision would have, perhaps, restricted the EU legislature's powers of co-decision to those aspects of the Six Pack that are explicitly referred to in Article 121 TFEU (for example, the proposal on the excessive imbalance procedure) but the Parliament insisted from the outset that it would treat the Commission's proposals as a single legislative package.

Further investigation is required to understand precisely what role the EP played in these negotiations, with initial indications suggesting that MEPs fought a successful rearguard action against France and others' attempt to limit the use of reverse voting under the excessive deficit procedure – a principle whereby a Commission proposal for corrective action will be carried unless it is opposed by a qualified majority of Member States (see Brand, 2012). In principle, this should make it more difficult for EU finance ministers to override EMU's fiscal rules, as occurred in November 2003 after Ecofin failed to reach agreement on the Commission's recommendations to step up disciplinary measures against France and Germany. The EP is also credited with the decision to create a new Economic Dialogue, which will invite representatives of the Commission, Council and the EP for regular discussions with MEPs on matters relating to fiscal surveillance and economic policy co-ordination more generally.

Alongside these legislative reforms, 2011 saw not one, but several, attempts to push through treaty reforms as part of eurozone members' ongoing efforts to combat the sovereign debt crisis. In March 2011, the European Council formally agreed on the revised wording to Article 136 TFEU, allowing eurozone members to establish 'a stability mechanism to be activated if indispensable to safeguard the stability of the euro area as a whole', thus paving the way for the creation of a permanent successor to the EFSF by January 2013 (European Council, 2011b). This was followed in July 2011 by the signing of a new ESM Treaty setting out the statutes of this new body.[8] Under this treaty, the ESM, which will be based in Luxembourg, will be authorized to lend up to €500 billion to eurozone members facing dire fiscal circumstances that pose a threat to the stability of the eurozone. Such assistance will come with significant strings attached, with Member States bound by a macroeconomic adjustment programme. Responsibility for negotiating the terms of this programme falls to the Commission, with input from the ECB. Significantly, the ESM Treaty allows for the possibility that the ESM can, in extreme circumstances, buy government bonds on primary markets.

The ink on the ESM treaty was barely dry before Member States began to have second thoughts. Perhaps the most immediate concern was that the ESM was nowhere near large enough to provide a credible crisis resolution mechanism for the eurozone, particularly if a large Member State such as Spain or Italy found itself in need of financial support. Buiter and Rahbari (2011) suggest that the sum required under such circumstances would be closer to €2,500 billion than the €500 billion envisaged by the ESM Treaty.[9] A second major concern was that the ESM's insistence on private sector involvement in debt restructuring could do more harm than good if extended beyond the case of Greece. By late 2011, a political consensus was beginning to emerge on revising the ESM Treaty even before it was ratified.

[8] Available at: «http://www.european-council.europa.eu/media/582311/05-tesm2.en12.pdf».
[9] For Willem Buiter's views on the ECB as a Lender of Last Resort, see his contribution with Ebrahim Rahbari in this issue.

Having embarked on one messy treaty change in 2011, eurozone leaders found time for another one before the year was out. In December 2011, all EU Member States with the exception of the United Kingdom and the Czech Republic (both non-members of the eurozone) agreed to take forward a new Treaty on Stability, Co-ordination and Governance in the EMU.[10] Under this treaty, better known as the 'Fiscal Compact', Member States are required to codify their commitment to the Stability and Growth Pact's country-specific medium-term budgetary objectives in fiscal rules embedded in national law. It falls to the Commission to monitor the implementation of these laws, with Member States entitled to refer any country that fails to enforce sufficiently robust national fiscal rules to the Court of Justice of the EU. The Court's judgment in such circumstances will be binding, with errant Member States facing fines of up to 0.1 per cent of GDP.

Under the Fiscal Compact, Member States have also agreed 'to strengthen the co-ordination of economic policies and to improve the governance of the euro area'. To this end, the Treaty states that the heads of state of eurozone members will meet at least twice per year. The Euro Area summit, it was further agreed, would be chaired by a President, who will be appointed for a $2^1/_2$-year term of office at the same time as the President of the European Council. The aim of these summits will be to discuss specific responsibilities relating to the single currency and matters relating to eurozone governance and to issue 'strategic orientations for the conduct of economic policies to increase convergence in the euro area'.

What France and Germany gained by signing the Fiscal Compact and what the United Kingdom gained by opting out is a key question for students of EU politics. The big win for France from the new treaty, it would appear, is the Euro Area summit, with Nicolas Sarkozy having pushed for greater involvement by the heads of state or government in eurozone issues since before this financial crisis began (see Hodson, 2011b, chapter 3). For Germany, the Fiscal Compact provides yet further proof of Member States' commitment to fiscal discipline, thus helping to counter suggestions that German taxpayers are being asked to provide financial support to 'profligate' Member States, such as Greece, Ireland and Portugal. Significant in this respect is the preamble to the Fiscal Compact, which states that only Member States that have ratified the Treaty will have access to financial support under the ESM.

Quite why British Prime Minister David Cameron opposed the Treaty is a matter of debate. At the time, he objected to the idea that two EU institutions – the European Commission and Court of Justice of the EU – should be involved in the modalities of closer economic policy co-operation under the new Treaty, but this objection was later quietly shelved. Concern was also expressed at the time about the Treaty's implications for EU financial market policy, although references to the pursuit of 'deeper integration in the internal market' in early drafts of the Treaty were removed. Some point to a failure of diplomacy at the December European Council, with the United Kingdom's 11th-hour request for safeguards on certain sensitive financial market issues standing little chance of success (see House of Lords, 2012).

Another explanation for the United Kingdom's self-imposed exclusion is the fact that David Cameron would have struggled to win the approval of his Conservative Party for a new EU treaty of any description. In October 2011, it should be recalled, 81 Conservative

[10] Available at: «http://www.european-council.europa.eu/media/639235/st00tscg26_en12.pdf».

MPs defied Cameron in voting for a referendum on the United Kingdom's continued membership of the EU. Although this motion was ultimately unsuccessful, it nonetheless constituted the biggest ever backbench rebellion in Conservative Party history over Europe. By refusing to sign up to the Fiscal Compact in December 2011, the British prime minister won few friends in the European Council but he avoided a further, potentially calamitous confrontation with rebels back home.

For political economists, the key issue is not why Member States signed up to the Fiscal Compact, but what the consequences of the new Treaty might be. In the short term, some viewed the Treaty as an enticement to the ECB to reconsider its opposition to large-scale government bond purchases, with Mario Draghi's comments to the EP in December 2011 about the importance of 'sequencing' in restoring credibility to EMU giving rise to speculation that a grand bargain of this sort might be on the cards (Draghi, 2011b). No such bargain emerged by the end of 2011, suggesting that the ECB may refuse to play its hand until the Treaty has been ratified or, conversely, that Mario Draghi's game plan has been entirely misconstrued.

VI. The Eurozone as a Global Actor

A recurring theme in the last two reviews of the eurozone is how the Member States that share the euro have shown a surprising degree of influence on the international stage in spite of EMU's fragmented system of external representation (Hodson, 2010, 2011a). Further evidence in support of this hypothesis in 2011 was the appointment of French Finance Minister Christine Lagarde as the new Managing Director of the IMF in July 2011. Following the previous Managing Director Dominique Strauss Kahn's sudden and spectacular fall from grace in May 2011, eurozone members moved within a matter of days to champion Lagarde's candidacy. Non-euro EU Member States put up little protest against this choice, with David Cameron's refusal to nominate his old rival, Gordon Brown, removing the only other serious EU contender from the ring. Once Lagarde had formally declared her candidacy for the position of IMF Managing Director she faced criticism from some developing countries but no credible competitor, allowing EU Member States to maintain their monopoly on the IMF's top job for the time being (Reuters, 2011b).

Ironically, the eurozone sovereign debt crisis strengthened rather than weakened the case for a European Managing Director of the IMF, with EU Member States insisting on a candidate who could work closely with eurozone policy-makers. Lagarde wasted little time in playing this mediating role, making regular appearances at meetings of the Eurogroup, European Council and eurozone heads of state or government meetings in 2011. She was also invited to join the so-called 'Frankfurt Group' – an ad hoc crisis cell created in November 2011 that also includes the president of France, the chancellor of Germany, the Presidents of the ECB and the European Commission, and the Commissioner for Economic and Monetary Affairs. It remains to be seen how much influence this body will yield, although early indications suggest that it could be considerable. According to Taylor (2011), the Frankfurt Group met no less than four times in the margins of the G20 Leaders' summit in Cannes in November 2011, dealing directly with United States President Barack Obama and exerting considerable behind-the-scenes pressure on both Italy and Greece to get their public finances in order.

A question that remained unanswered in 2011 is whether the IMF is prepared to play a more prominent role in the eurozone's escalating sovereign debt crisis. As of the end of the year, the Fund had around US$385 billion on standby, leaving it no better placed than the EU to provide financial support to large eurozone members. Among the more innovative ideas for tackling the eurozone sovereign debt crisis put forward in 2011 was that the ECB – or more accurately the eurozone national central banks – should lend to the IMF so that the Fund could lend in turn to eurozone members (see McDermott, 2011), but Mario Draghi appeared to rule out such an approach in December 2011 as being against the spirit of the Treaty. This left Lagarde, with little choice but to encourage eurozone members to boost the financial firepower of the EFSF and ESM, while at the same time encouraging the IMF's shareholders to increase the Fund's own financial resources.

Having been at the forefront of efforts to forge a co-ordinated international response to the financial crisis, the G20 showed little appetite for leadership in relation to the eurozone sovereign debt crisis in 2011. Billed by Britain's Chancellor George Osborne as the last chance to save the euro, the G20 Leaders' summit in Cannes produced few concessions from eurozone leaders and no concrete commitment to increase the amount of funding available to the IMF (G20, 2011). The reluctance of both the United States and China to commit further resources to resolving the eurozone sovereign debt crisis may explain this lack of progress. A lack of co-ordination between EU Member States in the run up to the Cannes summit may be partly to blame too. Although the Presidents of the Commission and European Council continued their practice of circulating a 'key issues' letter to Member States, this document was couched in generalities. The EU's largest Member States also found themselves divided on the question of further IMF financing, with David Cameron facing the prospect of yet another backlash from Eurosceptic MPs over financial contributions to the Fund that might be diverted to the eurozone.

Conclusions

Discussing the year gone by is a bit like looking at an Impressionist painting close up; it allows for an appreciation of individual details, but not always a sense of how these images will appear from a distance. With this proviso in mind, this article has explored those developments in 2011 that seem most relevant in near retrospect for students of EMU. In short, this was the year in which the eurozone's sovereign debt crisis escalated to an alarming degree, with Portugal becoming the third Member State to turn to the EU and IMF for financial support and markets becoming increasingly sceptical about the sustainability of public debt and the state of the banking sector in the eurozone as a whole. This uncertainty weighed heavily on the economic outlook, with the slowdown in the eurozone economy in late 2011 further complicating Member States' efforts to get government borrowing under control.

In the monetary sphere, 2011 was another fraught year for the ECB. Having increased interest rates in the first half of the year over concerns about high fuel and food prices, the Bank cut them again in the second half as the outlook for the eurozone economy deteriorated. The purchase of government bonds through the SMP, meanwhile, continued to cause controversy both inside and outside the Bank. Internally, a vocal minority within the ECB Governing Council viewed the SMP as an unacceptable threat to price stability, with Bundesbank President Axel Weber and Executive Board Member Jürgen Stark resigning in protest. Externally, a vocal majority of economists viewed the SMP as going nowhere near far enough to diffuse the eurozone's sovereign debt crisis. Mario Draghi's appointment as ECB President in November 2011 made little immediate impact in this respect, although the provision of cheap three-year loans through the LTRO helped to stabilize eurozone banks in the short term.

In the financial sphere, 2011 provided the first opportunity to see the ESRB in action. This new supervisory watchdog showed its willingness to bark, with Eurogroup President Jean-Claude Juncker becoming increasingly vocal as the year went on about rising risks to financial stability from the eurozone sovereign debt crisis. Whether the ESRB can also bite remains to be seen, with its recommendation on foreign currency lending an important test case of the new body's 'ask and explain' approach to enforcement.

In the fiscal sphere, 2011 was a surprisingly quite time for the Stability and Growth Pact given the heightened concerns over Member States' public finances. All eurozone members were eventually deemed to have taken adequate steps in response to recommendations under the excessive deficit procedure. Such compliance was of little consolation to financial markets, which lost confidence in Portugal's efforts at fiscal consolidation and grew increasingly sceptical about the sustainability of public debt in other eurozone members. Greece, meanwhile, remained a source of serious instability for the eurozone, with agreement, in principle, on a second bail-out and private sector involvement in debt structuring failing to convince.

In the sphere of external relations, the eurozone continued to show leadership in international financial institutions and forums in 2011, with the appointment of French Finance Minister Christine Lagarde as the new Managing Director of the IMF a coup for the eurozone. International financial institutions and forums were less keen about showing leadership on the eurozone sovereign debt crisis, with the G20 leaders' summit in Cannes in November 2011 failing to deliver a concrete commitment to increase the financial resources available to the IMF.

Eurozone leaders cannot be accused of standing still in the face of the sovereign debt crisis, with 2011 witnessing a raft of reforms to eurozone governance. The year saw no fewer than three proposed treaty changes, with Member States agreeing to revise Article 136 TFEU to allow for the establishment of a permanent crisis resolution mechanism for the eurozone, signing the ESM Treaty to give effect to this mechanism and agreeing on a new Fiscal Compact in an attempt to reinforce fiscal discipline and strengthen economic policy co-ordination. The entry into force of the Six Pack in November 2011, finally, means that fiscal and economic surveillance will take place in a radically different institutional context next year. Whether any of these reforms leave the eurozone better placed to tackle the sovereign debt crisis remains a moot point, with financial markets seemingly unconvinced in the short term.

References

Atkins, R. (2011) 'Bini Smaghi Quits ECB after French Pressure'. *Financial Times*, 11 November.

Brand, C. (2012) 'MEPs Claim Success in 'Six-Pack' Negotiations'. *European Voice*, 8 September.

Buiter, W. and Rahbari, E. (2011) 'Global Growth Generators; Moving beyond "Emerging Markets" and "BRIC" '. *Citi Global Economics*, 21 February.

Burda, M. and Hunt, J. (2011) 'What Explains the German Labor Market Miracle in the Great Recession?' Discussion Paper 8520 (London: Centre for Economic Policy Research).

Commission of the European Communities (2011a) 'European economic forecasts: Autumn 2011', European Economy 6 (Brussels: DG Economic and Financial Affairs).

Commission of the European Communities (2011b) 'Communication', Brussels, 24 August. *COM*(2011) 509 final.

Commission of the European Communities (2011c) 'The economic adjustment programme for Ireland: Spring 2011 review'. European Economy Occasional Papers 78 (Brussels: DG Economic and Financial Affairs).

Commission of the European Communities (2011d) 'Communication', Brussels, 12 January. *COM*(2011) 11 final.

Council (2011a) '3067th Council Meeting: Economic and Financial Affairs'. Press Release 6514/1125, 15 February.

Council (2011b) Council Decision of 12 July 2011 abrogating Decision 2010/408/EU on the existence of an excessive deficit in Finland (2011/417/EU).

De Grauwe, P. (2012) 'ECB Intervention is the Only Way to End the Crisis'. *Financial Times*, 12 March.

Draghi, M. (2011a) 'Introductory Statement to the Press Conference', 8 December (Frankfurt am Main: European Central Bank).

Draghi, M. (2011b) 'Introductory Statement at a Hearing before the Plenary of the European Parliament', 19 December (Frankfurt am Main: European Central Bank).

European Central Bank (2011) 'Consolidated Financial Statement of the Eurosystem as at 23 December 2011', 28 December (Frankfurt am Main: European Central Bank).

European Central Bank (2012) 'Impact of the Two Three-Year Longer-Term Refinancing Operations'. Monthly Bulletin, March (Frankfurt am Main: European Central Bank).

European Council (2011a) 'Conclusions', 23–24 June. EUCO 23/11.

European Council (2011b) 'Conclusions', 24–25 March. EUCO 10/1/11 REV 1.

European Systemic Risk Board (ESRB) (2011a) 'Press Release', 21 September (Frankfurt am Main: ESRB).

European Systemic Risk Board (ESRB) (2011b) Recommendation of the ESRB of 21 September 2011 on lending in foreign currencies (ESRB/2011/1), OJ C 342.

Ewing, J. and Kitsantonis, N. (2011) 'Greek Vote Approves a Despised Property Tax'. *New York Times*, 27 September.

Friedman, A. (2011) 'It's Time for You to Fire the Silver Bullet, Mr Draghi'. *Financial Times*, 9 November.

G20 (2011) 'Building Our Common Future: Renewed Collective Action for the Benefit of All', Cannes, 4 November. Available at: «http://www.g20.utoronto.ca/2011/2011-cannes-declaration-111104-en.html».

Hodson, D. (2010) 'The EU Economy: The Euro Area in 2009'. *JCMS*, Vol. 48, No. S1, pp. 225–42.

Hodson, D. (2011a) 'The EU Economy: The Eurozone in 2010'. *JCMS*, Vol. 49, No. S1, pp. 231–50.

Hodson, D. (2011b) *Governing the Euro Area in Good Times and Bad* (Oxford: Oxford University Press).

House of Lords (2012) *European Union Committee: The Euro Area Crisis* (London: The Stationery Office).

McDermott, J. (2011) 'The ECB–IMF–Italy Roundabout Switcheroo'. *Financial Times Alphaville Blog*, 17 November. Available at: «http://ftalphaville.ft.com/blog/2011/11/17/752101/the-ecb-imf-italy-roundabout-switcheroo/».

Reuters (2011a) 'Top German Quits ECB over Bond-Buying Row'. *Reuters*, 9 September.
Reuters (2011b) 'Lagarde Launches IMF Bid, BRICs Pile on Pressure'. *Reuters*, 25 May.
Robinson, F. (2012) 'Belgium Planning Budget Reserve of Around EUR1.3 Bln'. *Dow Jones*, 6 January.
Standard and Poor's (2012) 'Standard & Poor's Takes Various Rating Actions on 16 Eurozone Sovereign Governments'. *Standard and Poor's*, 13 January.
Taylor, P. (2011) 'Insight: Euro has New Politburo but No Solution Yet'. *Reuters*, 7 November.
Trichet, J.C. (2009) 'Introductory Statement to the Press Conference', 5 November (Frankfurt am Main: European Central Bank).
Trichet, J.C. (2011) 'Introductory Statement to the Press Conference', 7 April (Frankfurt am Main: European Central Bank).
Tsoukalis, L. (2011) 'The JCMS Annual Review Lecture: The Shattering of Illusions – and What Next?' *JCMS*, Vol. 49, No. S1, pp. 19–44.

JCMS 2012 Volume 50 Annual Review pp. 195–209 DOI: 10.1111/j.1468-5965.2012.02267.x

Developments in the Economies of Member States Outside the Eurozone

RICHARD CONNOLLY
University of Birmingham

Introduction

Throughout 2011 the repercussions from the deepest recession in the post-war period continued to be felt, with the eurozone at the epicentre of worries about the future trajectory of the global economy. In 2010, there were signs of a pick-up in domestic demand across the European economy (Connolly, 2011), offering the prospect of a self-sustaining recovery. However, the first half of 2011 saw domestic demand across Europe weaken, with only net exports driving growth across the continent, causing it to be dependent on demand from North America and, especially, the emerging markets of East Asia. In the spring, the Fukushima disaster in Japan caused a downturn in international trade that was quickly followed by a broader slowdown in economic output across the world. By the summer, the outlook worsened abruptly as concerns about the sovereign debt crisis in the eurozone (see Hodson in this issue), especially in the countries located at the so-called 'periphery', such as Greece, Ireland and Portugal, intensified.

The aggravation of the sovereign debt crisis and the deteriorating outlook for the global economy triggered global financial market turmoil. Across the globe, equities tumbled, although most sharply in Europe. While the bond yields of eurozone Member States with vulnerable fiscal positions increased, the yields in so-called 'safe havens' fell to record lows, including Germany and the United Kingdom. Uncertainty about the exposure of banks to eurozone sovereigns resulted in a freeze of inter-bank lending and a sharp deterioration of the banking sector's funding conditions. While the predicaments of individual banks differed, banks were, on aggregate, expected to accelerate efforts at strengthening their capital buffers, with adverse consequences for access to finance across the European economy. By the end of 2011, the weakening real economy, fragile public finances and the vulnerabilities present across the European financial sector appeared to be contriving to send the European economy back into recession or at least a period of extended stagnation.

This article assesses how the broader trends in the wider global and European economies outlined above affected the performance of the ten EU economies outside the eurozone in 2011. Section I gives an overview of key economic performance indicators. Section II summarizes key developments in each of the ten European economies outside the eurozone, focusing on whether domestic demand and/or external demand have driven output growth in these economies. Section III examines how far the United Kingdom – the largest economy covered here – fared in deleveraging (that is, reducing its debt burden) since the onset of the Great Recession in 2008. Given that financial vulnerabilities were at the heart of the Great Recession, it is worth considering what progress the United Kingdom made in reducing financial imbalances (Eichengreen, 2007; Wolf, 2009; Connolly, 2012).

I. Economic Performance Outside the Eurozone: Main Economic Indicators

Economic Growth

The data presented in Table 1 reveal the heterogeneity of the recovery across the countries outside the non-eurozone. Sweden and Poland again were among the fastest growing economies of the region, with both growing significantly faster than the EU and eurozone average. In addition, Latvia and Lithuania also enjoyed a period of sharp growth – something that was especially welcome given the extreme recessions both countries experienced over 2008–09. Rates of growth approximating the EU and eurozone average were observed in Bulgaria, Czech Republic, Denmark, Hungary and Romania. The worst performing economy of the non-eurozone was the United Kingdom, where economic activity contracted in the final quarter of the year. The fact that many of the countries with the lowest levels of per capita income in the EU (that is, the countries of central and eastern europe) were recovering at a sluggish rate continued to be a source of concern: conditional convergence suggests that poorer countries should grow faster than richer countries, but this was not the case across much of the non-eurozone in 2011, with perhaps the exceptions of Latvia and Lithuania.

Employment

The unemployment rate is an indicator that lags developments in overall output. As such, an economy may experience positive output growth, yet still see unemployment rise. As Table 2 illustrates, the sluggish rate of growth in many non-eurozone economies meant that unemployment continued to grow, albeit at a much slower rate than in previous years. A rise in unemployment was observed in Bulgaria, Romania and the United Kingdom. In

Table 1: Real GDP Growth (% Annual Change) – Non-eurozone (2007–11)

	2007	*2008*	*2009*	*2010*	*2011*[e]
Bulgaria	6.2	6.0	–5.5	0.2	2.2
Czech Republic	6.1	2.5	–4.7	2.7	1.8
Denmark	1.6	–1.2	–5.2	1.7	1.2
Latvia	10.0	–4.6	–17.7	–0.3	4.5
Lithuania	9.8	2.8	–14.8	1.4	6.1
Hungary	1.0	0.6	–6.8	1.3	1.4
Poland	6.8	5.0	1.6	3.9	4.0
Romania	6.3	6.2	–6.6	–1.9	1.7
Sweden	2.6	–0.2	–5.2	5.6	4.0
United Kingdom	2.6	–1.1	–4.4	1.8	0.7
Eurozone	2.8	0.6	–4.2	1.9	1.5
EU average	3.0	0.5	–4.2	2.0	1.6

Source: Commission (2011, p. 206, table 1).
Note: Estimates are denoted by *e*.

Table 2: Unemployment (% of the Civilian Labour Force) – Non-eurozone (2007–11)

	2007	*2008*	*2009*	*2010[e]*	*2011[e]*
Bulgaria	6.9	5.6	6.8	10.8	12.2
Czech Republic	5.3	4.4	6.7	7.3	6.8
Denmark	3.8	3.3	6.0	7.4	7.4
Latvia	6.0	7.5	17.1	18.7	16.1
Lithuania	4.3	5.8	13.7	17.8	15.1
Hungary	7.4	7.8	10.0	11.2	11.2
Poland	9.6	7.1	8.2	9.6	9.3
Romania	6.4	5.8	6.9	7.3	8.2
Sweden	6.1	6.2	8.3	8.4	7.4
United Kingdom	5.3	5.6	7.6	7.8	7.9
Eurozone	7.5	7.5	9.5	10.1	10.0
EU average	7.2	7.0	8.9	9.7	9.7

Source: Commission (2011, p. 217, table 23).
Note: Estimates are denoted by *e*.

Denmark and Hungary, unemployment levels stayed roughly the same as the previous year. Unemployment went down in the Czech Republic, Latvia, Lithuania and Sweden. Despite the different trajectories of unemployment growth, two groups within the non-eurozone can be identified. The first group, comprising Bulgaria, Hungary, Latvia and Lithuania, all exhibited unemployment rates significantly higher than the EU average. Indeed, in the two Baltic economies, Latvia and Lithuania, unemployment remained at levels not seen since the 'transition depression' of the 1990s, more than twice as high as that observed during the pre-crisis boom. The second group of countries, including all the other countries of the non-eurozone registered unemployment rates lower than both the eurozone average and the overall EU average.

Inflation

The sharp decline in inflation caused by the collapse in output over the course of 2008–09 continued to be reversed over 2011 (Table 3). Commodity prices rose throughout 2010, and the spike in commodity prices that followed political instability across the Middle East and North Africa (the 'Arab Spring', see Whitman and Juncos in this issue) added to these pressures. Consequently, despite severely subdued domestic demand across many economies of the non-eurozone, the general trajectory for prices was upwards, largely due to negative terms of trade developments. Only in Romania and Sweden did the rate of inflation grow at a slower rate than in 2010. The fact that Swedish inflation rates continued to be relatively low was due to the strength of the Swedish krona, which continued to appreciate throughout 2011. Changes in nominal exchange rates were not as important in determining prices in the economies outside the eurozone as they were in 2010. Bulgaria, Latvia, Lithuania, Hungary and Romania all experienced nominal effective exchange rate appreciation alongside rising domestic prices, suggesting that the growth of commodity prices was a much more important driver of inflationary pressures than exchange rate movements. Whether inflation would prove to be a persistent problem over the long term appeared unclear. On the one hand, monetary policy across the globe continued to be historically loose, fuelling growth in asset prices and commodities. On the other hand,

Table 3: Inflation Rate[a] (% Change on Preceding Year) – Non-eurozone (2007–11)

	2007	2008	2009	2010[e]	2011[e]
Bulgaria	7.6	12.0	2.5	3.0	3.6
Czech Republic	3.0	6.3	0.6	1.2	1.8
Denmark	1.7	3.6	1.1	2.2	2.6
Latvia	10.1	15.3	3.3	−1.2	4.2
Lithuania	5.8	11.1	4.2	1.2	4.0
Hungary	7.9	6.0	4.0	4.7	4.0
Poland	2.6	4.2	4.0	2.7	3.7
Romania	4.9	7.9	5.6	6.1	5.9
Sweden	1.7	3.3	1.9	1.9	1.5
United Kingdom	2.3	3.6	2.2	3.3	4.3
Eurozone	2.1	3.3	0.3	1.6	2.6
EU average	2.4	3.7	1.0	2.1	3.0

Source: Commission (2011, p. 213, table 16).
Notes: Estimates are denoted by *e*. [a] Harmonized index of consumer prices.

Figure 1: Change in Private Sector Financial Balance,[a] 2010–11 (% of GDP) – Non-eurozone

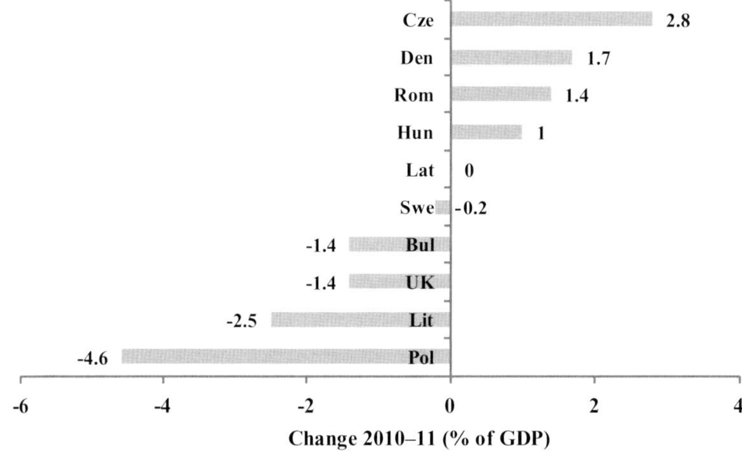

Source: Commission (2011); author's calculations.
Notes: Estimates are denoted by *e*. [a] The Private Sector Financial Balance is the difference between private income and private spending. It can be written as: Private Sector Financial Balance = Government Balance + Current Account Balance.

wage inflation showed little evidence of matching overall price inflation, thus dampening fears of a 'cost-push' inflationary spiral.

Private Sector Financial Balances

The private sector financial balance measures the extent to which the private sector – both household and corporate (financial and non-financial) – is either a net acquirer of financial assets (if it is in surplus), or a net borrower. In the pre-crisis period, many of the economies in the non-eurozone ran persistent and often large private sector financial deficits (Figure 1). This fuelled the boom that preceded the recession. However, as the Great Recession struck, private sector agents cut back spending, causing financial balances to shift towards surplus in most cases. As households and financial sector organizations repaid debt amid tightening credit conditions, firms also cut investment expenditure. In 2009, this contraction in private sector spending contributed towards the severe recessions that were observed across the region, and dampened consumption and investment growth afterwards (see Connolly, 2010, 2011). Private sector financial balances continued to shift towards surplus in several countries, including the Czech Republic, Denmark, Hungary and Romania, demonstrating a weakness in domestic demand. However, compared to the previous year, private sector financial surpluses fell, most notably in Poland and Lithuania, but also in the United Kingdom, Bulgaria and Sweden, suggesting that private sector demand was recovering, albeit at a restrained pace. The downside to a fall in private sector balances was that it threatened to slow the necessary process of deleveraging within the private sector.

Public Finances

The state of public finances, and the issue of sovereign debt, continued to be particularly important issues across the world in 2011. Although the focus was on the eurozone periphery countries, it was clear that a failure to demonstrate sufficient standards of sovereign fiscal rectitude might invite financial turbulence. Because, however, of the continued private sector retrenchment described above, the role of the public sector in supporting domestic demand remained important; without public spending, private sector weakness may have restrained the recovery even further. It was, therefore, perhaps unsurprising that governments tended to reduce fiscal deficits only slowly, particularly as the recession and subsequent anaemic private sector recovery limited the growth of the tax base. As Table 4 illustrates, fiscal balances across the non-eurozone varied quite dramatically. Sweden and Hungary were the only countries in which the government balance was in surplus. At the other end of the spectrum, the United Kingdom's level of net borrowing was among the largest in the world, and certainly within the group of rich Organisation for Economic Co-operation and Development countries (OECD, 2011). In all cases, though,

Table 4: Net Lending (+) or Net Borrowing (–), General Government Balance (% of GDP) – Non-eurozone (2007–11)

	2007	*2008*	*2009*	*2010*^{e}	*2011*^{e}
Bulgaria	0.1	1.8	–4.7	–3.1	–2.5
Czech Republic	–0.7	–2.1	–5.8	–4.8	–4.1
Denmark	4.5	3.4	–2.7	–2.6	–4.0
Latvia	–0.3	–4.1	–10.2	–8.3	–4.2
Lithuania	–1.0	–3.2	–9.2	–7.0	–5.0
Hungary	–5.0	–3.8	–4.4	–4.2	–3.6
Poland	–1.9	–3.6	–7.2	–7.8	–5.6
Romania	–2.5	–5.5	–8.6	–6.9	–4.9
Sweden	3.8	2.5	–0.9	0.2	0.9
United Kingdom	–2.7	–5.0	–11.4	–10.3	–9.4
Eurozone	–0.6	–2.0	–6.3	–6.2	–4.1
EU average	–0.9	–2.3	–6.8	–6.6	–4.7

Source: Commission (2011, p. 223, table 35).
Note: Estimates are denoted by *e*.

Table 5: Gross General Government Debt (% of GDP) – Non-eurozone (2007–11)

	2007	*2008*	*2009*	*2010*	*2011*
Bulgaria	18.2	14.1	14.7	16.3	17.5
Czech Republic	29.0	30.0	35.3	37.6	39.9
Denmark	26.8	33.5	41.5	43.7	44.1
Latvia	9.0	19.5	36.7	44.7	44.8
Lithuania	16.9	15.6	29.5	38.0	37.7
Hungary	65.9	72.9	78.4	81.3	75.9
Poland	45.0	47.2	50.9	54.9	56.7
Romania	12.6	13.6	23.9	31.0	34.0
Sweden	40.5	38.0	41.9	39.7	36.3
United Kingdom	44.2	52.0	68.2	79.9	84.0
Eurozone	66.0	61.5	79.1	85.6	88.0
EU average	58.8	61.8	74.0	80.3	82.5

Source: Commission (2010), p. 225, table 40.

the government net borrowing/lending balance tended to improve, with the exception of Denmark, where government borrowing increased.

Continued flows of government borrowing resulted in an expansion of the stock of government debt across nearly all countries of the non-eurozone throughout 2011, albeit at a considerably slower rate than in previous years (Table 5). Stocks of gross government debt declined in only three countries: Lithuania, Hungary and Sweden. Nevertheless, the total levels of government debt were lower than both the EU and eurozone average in all cases. Unfortunately, the fact that private debt levels tended to be much higher in the non-eurozone meant that sovereign default risk was not necessarily any less likely. This was because public balance sheets were exposed to the contingent liabilities of the private sector, leading to a worsening of the overall consolidated balance sheets of these economies (Roubini and Setser, 2004; see section III below).

Competitiveness

Competitiveness – that is, the potential to increase exports – remained an important consideration for policy-makers in 2011 (Table 6). Because onerous private and public sector debt burdens were dampening domestic demand, the potential for achieving robust rates of economic growth (that is, rates sufficient to reduce debt-to-GDP ratios) needed to be based on strong export performance. This was of particular importance in those countries that experienced large increases in the Real Effective Exchange Rate (REER) in the pre-crisis boom, especially Bulgaria, Latvia and Romania. In all three cases, the REER in 2011 appreciated, going some way towards reversing the progress made in regaining cost competitiveness over 2009–10. Indeed, the only countries to experience even a modest level of REER depreciation in 2011 were Denmark, Lithuania and Poland.

Overall, the economic performance of the Member States from outside the eurozone was broadly positive in 2011. Whether this performance would have been better or worse if countries had been part of the eurozone is, of course, impossible to know. Nevertheless, several basic observations can be made which suggest that non-adoption of the euro may have benefited the countries under examination here. First, much of the financial market

Table 6: Real Effective Exchange Rate (% Change on Preceding Year) – Non-eurozone (2007–11)

	2007	*2008*	*2009*	*2010[e]*	*2011[e]*
Bulgaria	11.0	12.5	7.8	–2.0	6.9
Czech Republic	3.4	13.5	–4.5	2.2	3.5
Denmark	3.8	5.2	3.0	–4.5	–1.3
Latvia	23.0	19.1	–7.0	–11.8	1.3
Lithuania	3.0	5.1	4.1	–8.6	–0.1
Hungary	9.0	1.2	–10.9	–3.1	1.5
Poland	3.8	12.8	–19.9	9.2	–0.9
Romania	19.4	8.0	–1.2	0.1	4.0
Sweden	3.2	–3.3	–7.8	6.1	6.0
United Kingdom	2.8	–14.0	–9.0	3.1	0.4
Eurozone	1.6	3.4	3.9	–7.5	1.6
EU average	6.0	1.6	–3.4	–8.0	4.1

Source: Commission (2011, p. 221, table 32).
Note: Estimates are denoted by *e*.

turmoil of 2011 was focused on eurozone countries. This was likely to have been at least partially the result of investors betting against growth returning to countries where rigidities imposed by the single currency (for example, the inability to experience nominal exchange rate depreciation that might restore competitiveness) looked to be constraining growth. In the Member States outside the eurozone, this was less of a problem (although the Baltic economies fixed their currencies to the euro). Second, growth in the economies outside the eurozone was, on the whole, export-led. This was likely to have been boosted by the significant exchange rate depreciation that nearly all economies of the sample experienced over the course of 2008–11. Membership of the eurozone, however, would have removed this safety valve. Nevertheless, some countries continued to exhibit vulnerabilities that could not be masked by flexible exchange rates. For example, Hungarian public debt levels remained dangerously high, whilst the size of overall stocks of debt in the United Kingdom was higher than the pre-crisis period (see below).

II. Economic Developments in the Non-eurozone

Bulgaria

Over the course of 2011, GDP was estimated to have grown by 2.2 per cent. This represented an end to a long and deep recession in Bulgaria, although given the depth of the recession the rebound from recession was still relatively muted. This slow rate of recovery was driven by continued depressed domestic demand, with gross fixed capital formation continuing to fall by 4.5 per cent, and private consumption rising slowly at only 1.0 per cent. Public expenditure, however, rose by 2.6 per cent – a relatively fast pace given the fiscal constraints imposed upon the government. Bulgaria had previously experienced a higher than average pre-crisis expansion in private credit – an expansion that was in the process of unwinding since 2008. As a result, private sector balance sheet adjustments were important factors in restraining domestic demand growth. Fortunately, exports grew faster (10.9 per cent) than imports (7.0 per cent), helping net exports make the largest contribution to GDP growth during the year. However, unemployment continued to rise, reaching 12.2 per cent, with many labour-intensive sectors, such as construction, particularly badly affected.

Czech Republic

The Czech Republic experienced growth that was based almost entirely on external demand, with net exports driving GDP growth of 1.8 per cent in 2011. As an open economy (trade openness of 142 per cent of GDP in 2007) that was tightly integrated into international production networks (IPNs) that were focused on machinery exports, the Czech Republic was boosted by robust growth in Germany and Slovakia. This strong export performance was achieved despite a 3.5 per cent appreciation in the REER, generated more by a rise in the nominal exchange rate than in unit labour costs, which stayed roughly stable. By contrast, domestic demand contracted in 2011. Private consumption fell by 0.3 per cent, although gross fixed capital formation grew by 1.7 per cent, bucking the trend across most of the other non-eurozone countries. Public consumption also contracted by 1 per cent. Subdued domestic demand helped real unit labour costs grow at a restrained rate (0.4 per cent), with unemployment falling from 7.3 per cent in 2010 to 6.8 per cent. Exports grew at an annual rate of 9.8 per cent, exceeding imports, which grew at 7.7 per cent, to ensure that the Czech Republic continued to grow despite the continued downturn in domestic demand.

Denmark

After a strong performance in 2010, the Danish recovery began to lose momentum in 2011. Private consumption was subdued, contracting by 0.5 per cent, and held back by low consumer confidence and comparatively high levels of household debt. Investment grew by just 0.4 per cent, primarily due to negative credit growth for non-financial corporations as the weak banking sector deleveraged. Public consumption, which helped boost growth in the previous year, grew by just 0.1 per cent in 2011. As a result, GDP grew by a mere 1.2 per cent in 2011. The fact that growth was positive was, as in the Czech Republic, due to export growth (6.5 per cent) exceeding import growth (4.4 per cent). Denmark, as a relatively small and open economy, benefited from rising demand from its two main trading partners, Germany and Sweden. This was likely aided by the fact that Denmark continued to experience REER depreciation (–1.3 per cent), going against the trend observed in most other non-eurozone countries. The dual track performance observed in Denmark – with a resilient export sector and a stagnant domestic sector – caused unemployment to remain stable at 7.4 per cent in 2011, although any reduction in this level looked to require a turnaround in private sector activity, which at the end of 2011 looked especially weak.

Hungary

The Hungarian economy experienced another year of subdued economic expansion, registering overall GDP growth of an estimated 1.4 per cent in 2011. Domestic consumption remained especially subdued, with private consumption declining by 0.9 per cent amidst continued fiscal austerity in the face of persistent concerns over the sustainability of Hungarian sovereign debt. This was exacerbated by a fall in fixed capital investment of 4.9 per cent. Indeed, only a strong performance in exports caused the Hungarian economy to expand at all in 2011, with exports growing at 9.1 per cent – faster than import growth of 7.1 per cent, which was itself a function of depressed domestic demand. Domestic sentiment was especially gloomy, largely due to the severe financial vulnerabilities built up during the pre-crisis period. The banking sector faced higher funding costs and tighter liquidity, squeezing access to finance for the wider economy. Moreover, instalment payments on foreign currency-denominated loans surged as the forint depreciated, depressing consumption: around 65 per cent of household loans from banks were denominated in foreign currencies, overwhelmingly in Swiss francs. Against a backdrop of weak domestic demand and faltering external demand as the eurozone sovereign debt crisis deepened, Hungarian unemployment stayed constant at 11.2 per cent despite avoiding recession.

Latvia

Latvia experienced one of the most severe recessions in the world over the course of 2008–10, although its economy began to grow in the last three quarters of 2010. This expansion continued into 2011, with GDP growing by 4.5 per cent – one of the fastest rates observed in the European economy. This recovery was, unlike most other countries, driven by domestic demand, with gross fixed capital formation growing by an extraordinary 21.5 per cent in 2011. This, however, came after investment had fallen by a cumulative rate of approximately 60 per cent between 2008 and 2010. The scope for an investment-based recovery, therefore, remained considerable. Private consumption rose by 3.5 per cent, while public consumption grew by a modest 1 per cent in the face of fiscal austerity. Nevertheless, the contribution of investment meant that domestic demand as a whole made a positive contribution of 7.2 per cent in 2011, with net exports exerting a drag on GDP growth, as imports grew faster (14.9 per cent) than exports (11.0 per cent). After several years of deflation, Latvia experienced REER growth of 1.3 per cent in 2011. This boosted domestic demand, but in the long run threatened to reduce Latvian competitiveness in export markets, despite the fact that real unit costs continued to fall (by 1.3 per cent). However, the fact that unemployment fell from 18.7 per cent in 2010 to 16.1 per cent in 2011 hinted that the worst might have been over for a country that had experienced one of the most severe recessions in the world.

Lithuania

As in Latvia, a recovery in domestic demand acted as the engine of growth in a country that had also experienced a deep and protracted recession. After recovering slightly in 2010 with GDP growth of 1.4 per cent, the Lithuanian economy experienced a brisk out-turn of 6.1 per cent in 2011. Like Latvia, this recovery was also based on a rapid expansion of investment, growing at 18.9 per cent, with nearly half of this accounted for by new equipment, suggesting that Lithuanian industry was upgrading its capital stock and boosting its long-run productivity potential. Private consumption also grew at a rapid rate (6.1 per cent) with public consumption making a more modest contribution, expanding at 1.2 per cent. Although imports grew (13.9 per cent), they only exceeded export growth by a small amount (exports grew 12.2 per cent), causing net exports to exert only a modest drag of 1.3 per cent on GDP growth. The fact that the REER continued to remain negative, albeit by just 0.1 per cent, gave added belief that Lithuania would not return quickly to the pre-crisis current account imbalances. Indeed, the fact that the current balance was in a modest deficit of −1.7 per cent – down from deficits of over 15 per cent in the pre-crisis period – suggested that Lithuania has experienced a rapid rebalancing of its economy, laying the foundations for more balanced and sustained growth in the future. Falling unemployment (from 17.8 to 15.1 per cent) meant that, like Latvia, the worst looked to be behind Lithuania.

Poland

The Polish economy, which was the only EU economy to avoid recession in 2008–09, continued to grow, with growth increasing in pace to 4.0 per cent in 2011, up slightly from the 3.9 per cent expansion registered in 2010. This was driven by positive developments in export growth (7.3 per cent) and domestic demand (3.4 per cent), as well as inflows of EU structural adjustment funds. Most importantly, gross fixed capital formation growth of 7 per cent acted as the engine of growth in 2011 as infrastructure projects linked to the 2012 European Championships were carried out. However, while exports grew at a healthy rate, imports also grew (7 per cent) on the back of nominal exchange rate appreciation and strong domestic demand. The contribution of net exports was, as a result, flat (that is, around 0 per cent of GDP growth). As the Polish economy experienced one of the fastest rates of growth in the European economy, unemployment fell from 9.6 to 9.3 per cent. The strong growth performance also helped the government reduce the fiscal deficit from –7.8 per cent of GDP in 2010 to –5.6 per cent in 2011, helping reduce pressure on the public finances.

Romania

The Romanian economy grew at a brisk pace in the first half of 2011, but weakened in the second half of the year. Progress in implementing the measures required under the multilateral financial assistance programmes of the EU, the International Monetary Fund and the World Bank reduced the imbalances built up during the pre-crisis period when Romania proved excessively reliant on external financing, manifested in the form of dangerously large current account deficits. Following the successful completion of the 2009–11 balance of payments assistance programme, Romania returned to the financial markets and in 2001 was able to finance itself both on the domestic and the external market. As a result, GDP expanded by 1.7 per cent in 2011, with public consumption continuing to shrink (by 1.5 per cent), but aided by an increase in private consumption (0.7 per cent), investment growth of 2.4 per cent and export growth of 7.3 per cent (compared to import growth of 4.7 per cent). As a result, domestic demand, inventory restocking and external demand made roughly equal contributions to GDP growth over the year. Nevertheless, unemployment continued to rise from 7.3 per cent of the labour force in 2010 to 8.2 per cent in 2011. Notwithstanding this deterioration of the overall unemployment rate, the labour market showed signs of improvement towards the end of the year. The second quarter of 2011 saw significant improvement, probably also driven by important reforms implemented in April 2011 in the areas of labour market legislation (Labour Code) and social dialogue (Social Dialogue Code).

Sweden

The Swedish economy continued to experience a robust recovery from the recession of 2008–09, with GDP growing by 4.0 per cent in 2011, down from 5.6 per cent in 2010, but still amongst the fastest growing economies of the EU. Most sectors of the economy contributed to this performance, with private consumption (growth of 2.6 per cent) and investment (8.5 per cent) showing particular strength. Although retail sales had a difficult year, household consumption held up well thanks to brisk sales of durable consumer goods in the first half of the year. In the second half of 2011, however, increased uncertainty regarding sovereign risk in the eurozone and its implications for economic growth sapped business and consumer confidence, which fell sharply to levels usually observed in connection with very slow or even negative output growth. Moreover, the stock market also fell by some 20 per cent over the summer. Unlike the previous year, the role of public consumption was less important, growing at just 1.1 per cent. In addition, net exports, which played such an important role in the recovery in 2010, made only a modest contribution of 0.5 per cent to GDP growth in 2011. Thus, Swedish growth became increasingly dependent on investment growth, and to a lesser extent, household consumption, throughout the year. The continued uncertainty in the eurozone suggested that this would be likely to continue. In the labour market, unemployment fell markedly from 8.4 to 7.4 per cent, further strengthening domestic demand. However, whilst the outlook was comparatively rosy, a number of potential weaknesses remained that were not addressed during the recession – not least the high level of household indebtedness (*c.*160 per cent of disposable income) that was inextricably linked to the Swedish housing market. While the debt dynamics appeared relatively benign in an environment of low interest rates and only mild levels of unemployment, the risk from any increase in interest rates was substantial, especially given the fact that Swedish banks active in the mortgage market were particularly dependent on short-term funding, rendering them vulnerable to any deterioration in liquidity conditions on financial markets.

United Kingdom

After registering only modest GDP growth in 2010 of 1.8 per cent, the British recovery began to lose momentum in 2011, growing at a rate of just 0.7 per cent – the worst performance in the non-eurozone. Despite the continuation of exceptionally loose monetary policy, economic activity was slow and volatile. Output in the second quarter of 2011 was just 0.6 per cent higher than in the same quarter of 2010. Indeed, quarterly output did not grow at all in the three quarters to the second quarter of 2011, remaining 4.4 per cent below its pre-crisis peak. Much of this weakness was related to weak household consumption, which, weighed down by a large debt burden, contracted for four successive quarters. Households spent 6.4 per cent less in the second quarter of 2011 than at the pre-crisis peak in the fourth quarter of 2007. Survey indicators suggested that this weakness would continue, with consumer confidence as measured by the Commission's Business and Consumer survey falling sharply throughout the year to a level below its average for 2008 and 2009. Overall, private consumption fell by 1.1 per cent in 2011. A renewed contraction in investment (down 1.6 per cent) completed the sorry picture of British private sector sentiment. With the private sector so weak in the United Kingdom, it was perhaps surprising that the government continued to implement a severe fiscal austerity package, unprecedented in depth and scope. Nevertheless, because only a small proportion of government spending cuts was implemented by the end of 2011, public consumption made a positive contribution to GDP growth. However, the other hope for the United Kingdom's economic recovery – a growth in net exports – showed signs of materializing throughout the year. Exports grew at a brisk rate of 5.1 per cent, while imports barely grew at all (0.2 per cent) in the face of weak domestic demand, causing net exports to make the largest contribution to growth. The weak and volatile nature of economic activity in the United Kingdom had a negative effect on the labour market, with unemployment rising for the third successive year, from 7.8 to 7.9 per cent.

III. Reducing Financial Vulnerabilities after the Crisis: The Case of the United Kingdom

This section briefly considers the progress made by the largest economy under review here – the United Kingdom – in deleveraging after a sustained period of credit expansion before the crisis caused it to develop a number of dangerous financial vulnerabilities. In order to assess the extent of a country's financial vulnerability it is useful to employ a balance sheet framework (see, for example, Roubini and Setser, 2004). It suggests that a useful way to analyze financial vulnerabilities is to conceptualize an economy as a system composed of the balance sheet of all its agents, including the government sector (including the central bank), the private financial sector (mainly banks) and the non-financial sector (corporations and households).

It is also necessary to examine both financial flows and stocks. First, financial *flows* that occur over a defined period of time are considered, such as the annual output, fiscal balance, current account balance or capital flows. However, balance sheet analysis also involves an examination of financial *stocks* – that is, of assets and liabilities, such as debt and foreign exchange reserves. These two approaches are, of course, closely connected as the difference in a stock variable at two points in time is related to the flow in the period between them. This synthetic framework enables us to consider the risk created by mismatches between a country's existing debt stock and its assets; two countries may display identical debt-to-GDP ratios, but the degree of vulnerability will be a function of whether one country's debt is short or long term, or denominated in foreign or local currency.

Each sector of the economy has claims on and liabilities to each other, as well as to external (non-resident) entities. When consolidating the sectoral balance sheets into the country's balance sheet, the assets and liabilities held between residents net out, leaving the country's external balance *vis-à-vis* the rest of the world (non-residents). Times of economic strain can see the rapid changes across sectoral balance sheets. For instance, default on, say, mortgage debt in the household sector can lead to the impairment of the balance sheets of the private financial (banking) sector. This in turn might lead to state-led bank bail-outs that can reduce the debt and/or increase the assets of banks while increasing the stock of debt held by the government sector.

A full balance sheet analysis is beyond the scope of this small section. It is, however, possible to make several observations about the nature and extent of delivering the United

Kingdom since 2008. The United Kingdom is the largest economy within the non-eurozone, one of the largest economies in the EU and home to one of the largest financial sectors in the world. As such, the financial health of the British economy is of crucial importance to the rest of Europe. Moreover, while this section focuses on the United Kingdom, the issue of deleveraging was of wider importance as many of the countries of central and eastern Europe exhibited similar financial vulnerabilities.

Since 2008, the size of private sector financial flows in the United Kingdom diminished significantly. For example, consumer credit, which grew at an annual rate of over 6 per cent before the crisis, slowed down to an annual rate of around 2 per cent (Bank of England, 2012). Business lending, which grew at a rate of nearly 20 per cent prior to the crisis, became negative, with businesses making net repayments to banks. Finally, mortgage lending, which was growing at an annualized rate of 11 per cent before the crisis was, in 2011, barely growing at all. In short, the non-financial private sector (households and corporations) either slowed down their borrowing or started to make net repayments. The financial sector, however, continued to issue debt, growing by over 20 per cent since the end of 2008. Finally, increased government borrowing (see Table 4) in the wake of the recession increased dramatically after 2007 and only started to diminish in 2010.

This mixed picture of non-financial sector retrenchment contrasting with increased government and financial sector borrowing has caused the consolidated balance sheet of the United Kingdom to expand, not contract, since 2008. By the middle of 2011, total United Kingdom debt stood at 507 per cent of GDP, up from 487 per cent at the end of 2008 and 310 per cent in 2000 (McKinsey Global Institute, 2012). Non-financial corporate debt, as a share of GDP, declined since 2008, although it remained 31 per cent above its 2000 level. The financial sector stock of debt reached 219 per cent of GDP in 2011, up from 209 per cent in 2008, accounting for the largest proportion of total United Kingdom debt. Nevertheless, British banks improved their capital ratios by reducing lending and raising capital, and they replaced short-term debt funding with longer-term debt. Non-bank financial institutions were responsible for the increase in financial-sector debt. Overall, the United Kingdom financial sector remained heavily exposed to the euro crisis, particularly loans to private borrowers in countries at the heart of the crisis, especially Ireland and Spain.

While households started to reduce their debt burdens, they succeeded in reducing the total stock of household debt by just 14 per cent of GDP, from over 122 per cent in 2008 to 109 per cent in 2011. Moreover, the ratio of household debt to disposable income declined from 156 per cent in 2008 to 146 per cent in mid-2011 – a level that was still significantly higher than that of American households in 2007, suggesting that British households had some way to go before their debt levels would reach safer and more sustainable levels. Residential mortgage lending continued to grow, albeit at a much slower rate than before the recession. While house prices had not collapsed (the national average price was over 20 per cent off the pre-crisis peak in real terms), the future of the housing market remained uncertain. The Bank of England estimated that up to 12 per cent of United Kingdom mortgages were in some stage of forbearance, with an additional 2 per cent in full default. In total, this was comparable to the 14 per cent of mortgages outstanding in the United States where house prices had fallen much lower.

Finally, the stock of government debt also increased (Table 5) due to falling tax revenue, expenditure on 'automatic stabilizers', and public support for the banking system

Figure 2: Distribution of Debt across Sectors in the United Kingdom and Selected Comparator Economies, 2011 (% of GDP)

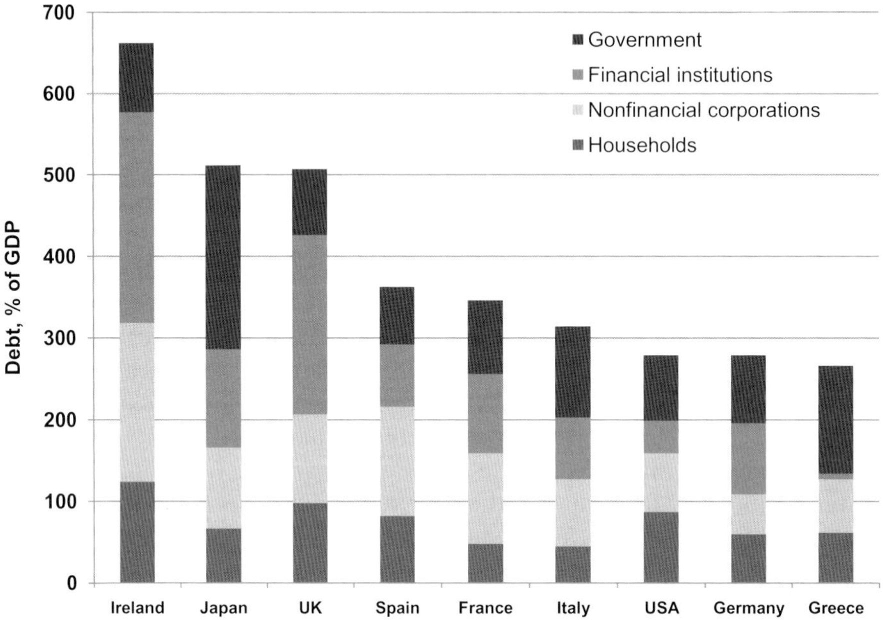

Source: Data derived from McKinsey (2012).

(the figure would be even greater were the Bank of England's bloated balance sheet included). Reducing the stock of government debt, therefore, required a return to relatively fast economic growth. However, as the private sector continued to save, and thereby fund the government's increased borrowing, the economy could only count on net exports as an engine of growth. Unfortunately, growth in this area was not sufficient to ignite a broader-based growth. As a result, growth remained anaemic at best and the process of deleveraging appeared to be just beginning even though the onset of the recession was over three years behind the United Kingdom. Such protracted patterns of deleveraging are entirely consistent with the aftermath of previous episodes of financial crisis throughout history (Reinhart and Rogoff, 2009).

The extent of the United Kingdom's debt vulnerabilities is illustrated in Figure 2. Compared to most of the world's largest developed economies (that is, the United States, Germany, France), the United Kingdom's overall debt profile appeared quite alarming. Of the large economies, only Japan had a larger consolidated debt profile, although this was a function of two decades of deficient domestic demand and persistent government deficits. As is clear, the huge stock of debt attributed to the financial sector accounted for much of the difference between the United Kingdom's consolidated debt profile and those of other countries. Of course, much of the financial sector's liabilities were likely to have been relatively safe assets. However, some of these liabilities also included exposure to sovereign debt across the eurozone, especially in Ireland and Spain, suggesting that any escalation of the sovereign debt crisis in the eurozone could have exerted a significant and negative impact on the financial sector in the United Kingdom. For the United Kingdom, and indeed for many of the countries of central and eastern Europe which had also built up large financial vulnerabilities during the pre-crisis period, the challenge for 2012 and beyond was to generate significant and sustained economic growth without exacerbating already fragile financial balance sheet vulnerabilities.

Conclusions

Over the course of 2011 the economies of the non-eurozone continued to make an uncertain and unsteady recovery from the severe recession of 2008–09. For the first year since the crisis, all of the countries under review here registered positive GDP growth. This was welcome. However, the pace of recovery remained, on the whole, much slower than is usual after a recession. Evidently, post-financial crisis recessions are characterized by lower growth as excessive debt burdens limit the propensity of affected agents and sectors to spend, thus restraining the growth of the wider economy. As the example of deleveraging in the United Kingdom illustrates, the reduction of financial vulnerabilities in an economy is a long and drawn out process that is, above all, contingent on robust economic growth. Unemployment was still either high or rising (in some cases both), meaning that the level of human suffering associated with economic turmoil remained at high levels. Most growth observed across the countries covered here came from external demand. The prospect of further strain in the eurozone sovereign debt markets, however, threatened to disable this remaining engine of growth for many countries of the non-eurozone. Looking to 2012, then, economic prospects for the countries of the non-eurozone appeared more uncertain than usual, with the threat of renewed, and possibly severe, recession never far away.

References

Bank of England (2012) *Trends in Lending* (London: Bank of England).

Commission of the European Communities (2011) *European Economic Forecast: Autumn 2011* (Brussels: Ecofin).

Connolly, R. (2010) 'The EU Economy: Member States Outside the Euro Area in 2009'. *JCMS*, Vol. 48, No. S1, pp. 243–66.

Connolly, R. (2011) 'Developments in the Economies of Member States Outside the Eurozone'. *JCMS*, Vol. 49, No. S1, pp. 251–73.

Connolly, R. (2012) 'The Determinants of the Economic Crisis in Post-Socialist Europe'. *Europe-Asia Studies*, Vol. 64, No. 1, pp. 35–67.

Eichengreen, B. (2007) *Global Imbalances and the Lessons of Bretton Woods* (Cambridge, MA: MIT Press).

McKinsey Global Institute (2012) *Debt and Deleveraging: Uneven Progress on the Path to Growth* (London: McKinsey Global Institute).

Organisation for Economic Co-operation and Development (OECD) (2011) *World Economic Outlook* (Paris: OECD Press).

Reinhart, C. and Rogoff, K. (2009) *This Time is Different: Eight Centuries of Financial Folly* (Princeton, NJ: Princeton University Press).

Roubini, N and Setser, B (2004) *Bail-outs or Bail-ins? Responding to Financial Crises in Emerging Economies* (Washington, DC: Institute for International Economics).

Wolf, M. (2009) *Fixing Global Finance: How to Curb Financial Crises in the 21st Century* (New Haven, CT: Yale University Press).

JCMS 2012 Volume 50 Annual Review pp. 210–216 DOI: 10.1111/j.1468-5965.2012.02274.x

Chronology: The European Union in 2011

FABIAN GUY NEUNER
University of Oxford

At a Glance

Presidencies of the EU Council: Hungary (1 January–30 June) and Poland (1 July–31 December).

January

1	Hungary takes over the EU Council Presidency.
1	Estonia becomes the 17th member of the eurozone.
1	The European Banking Authority (EBA), European Insurance and Occupational Pensions Authority (EIOPA) and the European Securities and Markets Authority (ESMA) start work supervising their respective areas of financial activity.
1	The European External Action Service (EEAS) enters a new phase as staff are officially transferred from the Commission and Council.
8	Official launch event for the 'European Year of Volunteering' takes place in Budapest.
11	Launch of 'EU–China Year of Youth'.
15	Commission gives favourable opinion on the limited Treaty change needed for the creation of the European Stability Mechanism (ESM).
17	Claude-France Arnould becomes Chief Executive of the European Defence Agency (EDA) after the post had been vacant since October 2010.
18	Beginning of the first 'European Semester': a cycle of budgetary and economic policy co-ordination between EU Member States.
23	Aníbal Cavaco Silva is re-elected president of Portugal.
26	Commission presents a set of measures aimed at reducing the number of young people who leave education with low-level qualifications.
26–29	World Economic Forum in Davos.

February

1	Commission launches High-level Expert Group on literacy.
1	Inaugural presentation of European Innovation Scoreboard results.
1	Foreign Ministerial Conference on the European Neighbourhood Policy (ENP).
4	European Council. The focus was on energy and innovation as well as ongoing discussions on economic governance. There was a separate declaration in support of the Egyptian and Tunisian peoples' democratic aspirations and any violent responses were condemned.

10–12 Launch of 'MEDIA Mundus' programme aimed at strengthening co-operation between the European film industry and those in third countries.
11 Axel Weber, president of the German Bundesbank, resigns.
15 Commission communication on the promotion and protection of the rights of children.
16 Adoption of the legislation on the implementation of the European Citizens' Initiative.
17 European Parliament (EP) adopts a resolution in support of Egypt's transition to democracy.
20 Frontex launches operation Hermes after requests from Italian authorities for help with managing the inflow of migrants from North Africa.
25 Fianna Fáil is defeated in the Irish general election and Fine Gael's Enda Kenny becomes prime minister after his party forms a government in coalition with Labour.
28 EU adopts sanctions against Libya. Measures include the freezing of assets of Libyan leader Muammar Gaddafi and his associates as well as an arms embargo.

March

3 The Agency for the Co-operation of Energy Regulators (ACER) – an EU agency tasked with working towards a single energy market – opens its headquarters in Ljubljana.
6 Estonian parliamentary election sees incumbent Prime Minister Andrus Ansip's Reform Party remain in power.
11 Extraordinary European Council on the situation in Libya produces a declaration calling on Colonel Gaddafi to stand down. The heads of state and government of the eurozone countries adopt a Pact for the Euro to strengthen economic policy co-ordination.
11 EU activates its Civil Protection mechanism to support Japan after the earthquake and the resulting tsunami disaster.
16 Commission proposes a Common Consolidated Corporate Tax Base (CCCTB) which would provide companies operating in the EU with a single set of rules to calculate taxable profits.
23 Portuguese Prime Minister José Sócrates resigns following parliament's rejection of austerity measures proposed by his government.
24–25 European Council. Discussions centred on the economic recovery and measures on financial stability and economic growth were adopted. There was further discussion of the situation in Libya and the broader Southern Neighbourhood. Condolences for the loss of life following the earthquake and tsunami in Japan were expressed.

April

1 Council approves EUFOR Libya military operation to provide possible humanitarian assistance.
4 Commission launches European Union Space Strategy aimed at improving citizens' safety and quality of life through space technologies.

6	Portugal becomes the third EU Member State to request EU–IMF support officially.
7	EP adopts a resolution condemning the use of violence against protesters in Syria, Yemen and Bahrain.
9	Icelanders vote in a referendum to reject proposals on providing loan guarantees to the United Kingdom and the Netherlands.
17	Finnish parliamentary election sees breakthrough of populist True Finns Party. The National Coalition Party's Jyrki Katainen becomes prime minister, heading a government comprising six parties.
19	EU–Turkey Association Council.
26	25th anniversary of Chernobyl nuclear power plant disaster.

May

2	Osama Bin Laden is killed in a targeted American military raid.
15–21	5th European Youth Week.
16	€78 billion EU–IMF bail-out deal for Portugal is agreed.
18	Brussels Economic Forum.
19	EU Culture Ministers agree to launch the 'European Heritage Label' with a view to naming the first sites in 2013.
22	Local and regional elections in Spain see a landslide victory for the opposition People's Party.
22	Cypriot parliamentary election sees Democratic Rally Party win the largest number of seats.
26	Arrest of war crimes fugitive Ratko Mladić. He is extradited to the International Criminal Tribunal for the former Yugoslavia (ICTY) on 31 May.
26–27	G8 Summit in Deauville. The key discussions centred on the Arab Spring, seeing financial support pledged to aid democratic reforms in Tunisia and Egypt, and on further measures to support the global economic recovery.
28	20th EU–Japan Summit in Brussels.

June

2	Andris Bērziņš is elected Latvian president in an indirect election.
5	Portuguese parliamentary election sees the Social Democratic Party win the largest number of seats, and Pedro Passos Coelho is designated as the new prime minister.
5	Slovenes reject three proposals including pension reform in a referendum.
6–7	10th Asia–Europe Meeting (ASEM) at the level of foreign ministers.
9–10	EU–Russia Summit in Nizhny Novgorod.
12	A general election in Turkey sees Recep Tayyip Erdoğan securing a third term as prime minister.
20	Screening stage of Icelandic EU membership bid concluded.
20	Western Balkans Forum.
23	The Commission and the EP launch a joint transparency register of EU lobbyists.

23–24 European Council. The first 'European Semester' was closed and Commission guidelines for budgetary consultation were approved. Further discussions centred on the development of the EU's migration policy, the situation in the Southern Neighbourhood and Croatia's accession.
27 Negotiations on accession chapters with Iceland commence. Four chapters are opened, of which two are provisionally closed immediately.
28 Christine Lagarde named as the new managing director of the International Monetary Fund (IMF) after former director Dominique Strauss-Kahn resigns following his arrest in New York on charges of sexual assault and attempted rape. The charges are dropped in August.
30 Commission publishes proposed multi-annual spending plan aimed at boosting growth.
30 Greek parliament agrees terms of a fourth set of austerity measures.
30 The final accession negotiation chapters with Croatia are closed.

July
1 Poland takes over the EU Council Presidency.
1 EU–Korea Free Trade Agreement enters into force.
6–7 'Eastern Dimension of Mobility' conference in Warsaw aimed at reinforcing mobility flows of certain societal groups between the EU and Eastern Partnership countries.
11 Eurozone countries sign agreement on the European Stability Mechanism (ESM) with the provision to lend up to €500 billion to European countries in financial crisis.
15 Italian parliament passes first austerity package including cuts worth €48 billion.
15 The European Banking Authority (EBA) presents the results of its stress tests of 90 European banks. Eight fail.
20 Serbian authorities arrest Goran Hadžić, the last remaining fugitive sought by the ICTY.
21 Meeting of heads of state and government of the Member States of the eurozone. Additional financial support for Greece is agreed and the scope of the EFSF and the ESM are increased.
23 Latvians vote in favour of a referendum to dissolve parliament early.

August
1 Council adopts restrictive measures against five Syrian individuals associated with the repression of the Syrian people.
24 Commission announces humanitarian support measures for Libya.
24 France announces deficit reduction measures worth €12 billion.
29 Toomas Hendrik Ilves is re-elected president of Estonia in an indirect election.

September
7 Germany's highest court rejects challenges questioning the lawfulness of the country's participation in EU bail-outs.
9 Jürgen Stark, a member of the ECB's executive board, resigns.

12 Council adopts directive to extend copyright protection of sound recordings from 50 to 70 years.

15 Danish parliamentary election sees the Venstre Party gain the largest number of seats, but the Social Democrats form a centre-left coalition government. Helle Thorning-Schmidt is designated the country's first female prime minister.

15 South Africa–EU Summit.

17 Latvian parliamentary election sees Harmony Centre Party win the most seats, but Unity Party leader and incumbent Valdis Dombrovskis is designated prime minister after he manages to form a coalition with Zatlers' Reform Party and the National Alliance Party.

28 Commission President José Manuel Barroso delivers State of the Union address in which he outlines his vision for a global financial transaction tax.

29–30 Eastern Partnership Summit in Warsaw.

October

3–4 EU–Brazil Summit.

9 Polish parliamentary election sees Prime Minister Donald Tusk's Civil Platform Party and his Peasant Party coalition partners returned to office.

12 Commission publishes annual overview of enlargement policy and country progress reports. Highlights include a favourable opinion on Croatian accession as well as a recommendation to grant official candidate status to Serbia.

13 Eurozone members agree upon EFSF enlargement.

14 The EP opens a new visitors' centre named 'Parlamentarium'.

20–21 European Culture Forum.

21 Launch of the first two Galileo satellites, representing a milestone for Europe's satellite navigation efforts.

23 European Council. Discussions centred on economic policy, preparations for the Cannes G20 Summit and the Durban conference on climate change as well as the developments in the Southern Neighbourhood.

23 Swiss legislative election sees Swiss People's Party retain the largest seat share despite electoral losses.

24 The United Kingdom government defeats a parliamentary bid calling for a referendum on the country's EU membership despite the largest party rebellion against a British Conservative prime minister over Europe.

26 Meeting of heads of state and government of the Member States of the eurozone. Agreement is reached on new measures aimed at tackling the sovereign debt crisis.

27 Michael D. Higgins is elected president of Ireland.

27 Launch of mobility partnership between Armenia and the EU.

30 Rosen Plevneliev is elected Bulgarian president in a second-round run-off election.

31 The UN declares that the world population has reached 7 billion.

November

1	Mario Draghi takes over as President of the European Central Bank (ECB).
3–4	G20 Summit in Cannes. Discussions centre on co-ordination of growth policies and measures to ensure financial stability.
8	Economic and Financial Affairs Council adopts a package of legislative proposals on economic governance aimed at performance surveillance and enhanced financial supervision.
8	Inauguration of Nord Stream gas pipeline between Europe and Russia.
11	Georg Papandreou resigns as Greek prime minister. He is succeeded by Lucas Papademos.
12	Italian Prime Minister Silvio Berlusconi resigns after the Italian parliament successfully passes austerity measures.
18–19	Agreement is reached on the 2012 European budget.
20	Spanish legislative election sees the People's Party win an absolute majority and Mariano Rajoy is designated as the new prime minister.
23	Commission proposes a package of measures to strengthen budgetary and economic co-ordination and scrutiny.
24	External dimension of EU energy policy is agreed upon.
28	EU–US Summit in Washington.
30	Commission presents 'Horizon 2020' – a framework programme proposing €80 billion investment in research and innovation.

December

4	A centre-left coalition wins an absolute majority in the Croatian parliamentary election with Zoran Milanović designated as the new prime minister.
4	Slovenian parliamentary election. Zoran Janković's new centre-left party, Positive Slovenia, wins the largest number of seats, but Janez Janša becomes prime minister leading a five-party centre-right coalition.
5	Rating agency Standard and Poor's places debt of 15 eurozone countries on credit watch.
6	Elio Di Rupo becomes Belgian prime minister, thereby ending a record-breaking 541-day period without a government.
8	The European Banking Authority publishes its recommendations on bank recapitalisation.
9	European Council. A 'Fiscal Compact' among members of the eurozone is agreed which includes fiscal rules and correction mechanisms. Other Member States are invited to join, but the United Kingdom declares it will not opt in, thus preventing the Compact from being part of the existing EU treaty structure. The accession treaty with Croatia is signed.
11	Conclusion of Durban Climate Change Conference.
12	Ministerial-level intergovernmental conference on Iceland's EU membership application. Four chapters are provisionally closed bringing the number of closed chapters to eight.
12	EU launches trade negotiations with Georgia and Moldova.
13	EU economic governance measures come into force.

15 EU–Russia Summit in Brussels.
15 Adoption of the declaration on the European Endowment for Democracy – a new tool to support political and civil society actors working towards transition to democracy.
16 The Italian lower house approves an emergency austerity budget aimed at reducing the deficit by around €20 billion.
19 Liechtenstein becomes the 26th member of the Schengen area.
19 15th EU–Ukraine Summit in Kyiv.
22 The European Court of Justice rules that asylum seekers should not be transferred to a Member State in which they are at risk of inhumane treatment.

JCMS 2012 Volume 50 Annual Review pp. 217–225 DOI: 10.1111/j.1468-5965.2012.02283.x

Index

Note: Italicized page references indicate information contained in tables.

accession candidates
  Albania 159
  Bosnia-Herzegovina 159
  Bulgaria 72
  Croatia 2, 3, 70, 80, 147, 157, 159
  Iceland 149, 157, 159
  Kosovo 159
  Macedonia 158
  Montenegro 157, 158, 159
  Romania 72
  Serbia 149, 158, 159
  Turkey 149, 158
Afghanistan 50, 170
Ahern, Bertie 59
Albania 54, 157, 159
Alert Mechanism Report (AMR) 34
Algeria 1, 125
Aliot-Marie, Michèle 1
Arab Spring 1, 72, 116, 117, 122, 123, 147, 149, 150, 151–4, 155, 162–3, 166, 167, 168, 169, 175, 197
Argentina 167, 172
Armenia 80, 154
Art 3(2) TEU 128
Art. 20 TFEU 140, 145
Art. 21 TFEU 142, 145
Art. 79(4) TFEU 120, 121
Art. 121 TFEU 134, 135, 138, 188
Art. 123 TFEU 6, 26, 30, 33
Art. 126 TFEU 134, 138, 139, 185, 186
Art. 136 TFEU 178, 188, 192
Ashton, Catherine 2, 77, 79, 150, 151, 152, 153, 156, 162–3, 164, 171, 174, 175, 176
Asmussen, Jörg 183
asylum policy 116–19
  Asylum Procedures Directive 117
  Asylum Qualification Directive 118
  Asylum Support Teams (ASTs) 116
  Common European Asylum System (CEAS) 117–19, 128–9
  Dublin Regulation 118
  European Asylum Support Office (EASO) 116–17, 118, 129
  European Refugee Fund 116, 118
  External Borders Fund 116, 118
  Reception Conditions Directive 117–18
  Return Fund 116, 118
Austria 70, 123
  economy 185
  financial regulation 108
  residence permits 142–3
  sovereign debt 22, 179
authoritarianism 90, 148
Azerbaijan 80, 81, 156

Bahrain 1
bail-outs 1, 95, 132
  Greece 36, 60–1, 85, 87, 95, 189, 192
  Ireland 36, 85, 189
  Portugal 36, 189, 191
Baker, James 51
Bank for International Settlements (BIS) 99, 105, 111
  Basel Committee of Banking Supervisors (BCBS) 99, 105–7, 110, 114
Barnier, Michel 111
Barroso, José Manuel 77, 85, 90, 91, 171
Basel III Accord 99, 105–7, *107*, 108, 109–10, 111, 112, 113
Belarus 80, 82, 125, 147, 155, 156, 169
Belgian Presidency 69
Belgium
  economy 185, 187
  national parliament 94
  sovereign debt 22
Berlusconi, Silvio 61, 62, 63, 88, 123, 179
border and visa policy 122–5, 138
  European Border Fund (EBF) 123, 124
  European Border Surveillance System (EUROSUR) 124
  Frontex 122–5, 129
  Schengen Information System (SIS II) 125
  Visa and Information System (VIS) 125
Bosnia-Herzegovina 54, 62, 125, 149, 150, 159
Bozkir, Volkan 149
Brazil 125, 167, 173
  relations with EU 172
Brown, Gordon 190

Bulgaria 72, 82, 111, 157, 172
economic developments 201–2
economic growth 196
government debt 200
inflation 197
private sector financial balances 199
unemployment 196, 197
Burkina Faso 125
Burma (Myanmar) 170
Bush, George W. Sr 51
Buzek, Jerzy 79, 82, 92

Cameron, David 2, 87, 96, 189–90, 191
Canada 7, 166
relations with EU 175
Charter of Fundamental Rights of the European Union 143
China 167, 173, 174
economy 179
foreign policy 50, 51, 165
relations with EU 170, 171–2
climate change 50, 68
Clinton, Hillary 174, 175
Cœuré, Benoît 183
cohesion policy 68, 70, 86
Committee of Permanent Representatives (Coreper II) 80
common agricultural policy 59
Common European Asylum System (CEAS) 117–19, 128–9
common foreign and security policy (CFSP) 77, 90, 148, 151
common security and defence policy (CSDP) 81, 153
communism 65
Community Method 86, 91, 132
Cooper, Robert 164
Cote d'Ivoire 170
Council of Economics and Finance Ministers (Ecofin Council) 59, 61, 77, 185, 186, 188
Council of Europe 59, 65
Council of Ministers 59, 103
credit rating agencies 112 n 31
Croatia
accession 2, 3, 70, 80, 147, 156, 157, 159
Cyprus 158
economy 182, 186
sovereign debt 21, 179
Czech Republic 104, 189
economic developments 202
economic growth 196
private sector financial balances 199
unemployment 196

Danube Strategy (DRS) 70, 72
Daul, Joseph 93
de Gaulle, Charles 59
de Gucht, Karel 166, 171, 174
Deep and Comprehensive Free Trade Area (DCFTA) 80
Delors, Jacques 91
democracy 95–6
Democratic Republic of the Congo 170
Denmark 87
economic developments 202
economic growth 196
financial regulation 110–11
government debt 200
immigration 123
national parliament 94
private sector financial balances 199
unemployment 196
Dereci and others v *Bundesministerium für Inneres* 142–3, 145
Dobrindt, Alexander 53
Dodik, Milorad 150
Doha Round negotiations 166, 171
Draghi, Mario 96–7, 179, 183, 184, 190, 191, 192

Eastern Partnership (EaP) 68, 70, 78, 80, 82, 152, 154, 155
Eastern Partnership Academy 80, 82
economic developments
austerity measures 1
competitiveness *201*
economic stagnation 1
eurozone 178–94
GDP growth *196*
government debt *200*
non-eurozone 195–209
private sector financial balances *198*
public finances *199*
rescue packages 1
economic and monetary union (EMU) 3, 7, 85, 86, 132, 133, 134, 138, 187, 188, 189, 190, 191
public debt 36–48
educational exchange programmes 62
Egypt 1, 117, 122, 125, 147, 167
elections
French presidential 86
Slovenian parliamentary 64

Emissions Trading Scheme (ETS) 172, 173
energy security 65, 72
enlargement 2, 3, 54, 60, 70, 147, 148, 149, 156–9
environment 62
Estonia 3, 111, 180 n 2
EU citizenship 132, 140–3, 145
EU external relations 162–77
 common commercial policy 166–7
 development co-operation policy and humanitarian aid 167–8
 EU–Africa relations 169–70
 EU–Asia relations 170–2
 EU–Canada relation 175
 EU–Japan relations 175
 EU–Latin America relations 172–3
 EU–Russia relations 168–9
 EU–United States relations 173–5
 foreign, security and defence policy 162–6
 Generalized System of Preferences (GSP) 167
EU Patent 79, 82
EU rotating Presidency 3
euro *see* single currency
Euro+ Pact 34, 85, 96
Eurogroup 77, 89, 90, 97, 190
Europe 2020 strategy 62, 68, 78, 91
European Asylum Support Office (EASO) 116–17, 118, 129
European Banking Authority (EBA) 28, 34, 99, 108, 112–13
European Border Fund (EBF) 123, 124
European Border Surveillance System (EUROSUR) 124
European Central Bank (ECB) 3, 36–8, 47, 60, 61, 62, 63, 96, 103, 112, 113, 178, 179, 183–4, 185, 188, 190, 191
 as lender of last resort 6–35
 longer-term refinancing operation (LTRO) 39–40, 179, 184, 192
 Securities Market Programme (SMP) 6, 25–6, 28–9, 33, 37, 182–3, 184, 191
European Commission 59, 60, 62, 63, 71, 78, 164
 Alternative Investment Fund Managers Directive 114
 asylum policy 117, 118
 border controls 123–4
 Capital Requirements Directive/Capital Requirements Regulation (CRDIV-CRR) 100, 105–7, 108, 109, 111, 113
 development aid 168
 economic policy 144
 enlargement 157–8
 European Market Infrastructure Regulation (EMIR) 100, 101–5, 113
 Financial Conglomerates Directive (FiCOD) 106, 111
 Fiscal Compact 2, 31, 34, 62, 85, 86, 89, 92, 94, 96, 132, 137–40, 144, 147, 178, 179, 189, 190, 192
 Markets in Financial Instruments Directive (MiFID) 100, 113
 Markets in Financial Instruments Regulation (MiFIR) 100
 Multiannual Financial Framework 148
 Six Pack reforms 2, 34, 69, 72, 77, 79, 82, 85, 91, 92, 93–4, 96, 133–7, 139, 178, 187–8, 192
 troika programmes 6
European Commission v *Council* 133 n 6
European Constitutional Treaty 60, 64
European Convention for the Protection of Human Rights and Fundamental Freedoms 143
European Council 38, 60, 70, 77, 85, 86, 93, 97, 102, 112
 Croatia accession treaty 2
 standing Presidency 69, 76, 89–90
 summits 86–92, 95, 96, 158–9
European Court of Human Rights (ECtHR) 116, 119
European Court of Justice (ECJ) 55, 91, 92, 119, 132, 133, 138 n 39, 140–3, 144, 145, 174, 189
European Defence Agency 81
European Economic Area 157
European Economic Community 59
European employment strategy 56, 62
European Endowment for Democracy 80, 82
European External Action Service (EEAS) 2, 77, 79, 147, 148, 150–1, 152, 160, 162–3, 164, 170, 175
European Financial Stability Facility (EFSF) 7, *22*, 23, 25, 34, 37, 85, 87, 94, 96, 132, 171, 178, 179, 188, 191
European Financial Stability Mechanism (EFSM) *22*, 34, 132
European identity 57
European Insurance and Occupational Pensions Authority (EIOPA) 34
European Monetary System (EMS) 43, 55, 56
European neighbourhood 147–61
 Arab Spring 147, 149, 150, 151–4, 155
 Dayton Agreement 150
 Deep and Comprehensive Free Trade Area (DCFTA) 156
 Eastern Europe 154–6
 enlargement 156–9
 European External Action Service (EEAS) 147, 148, 150–1, 152, 160

European Neighbourhood and Partnership Instrument (ENPI) 148, 149
European Neighbourhood Policy (ENP) 68, 147, 151–3, 155
eurozone crisis 148–50, 155
Instrument Pre-Accession (IPA) 148, 149
Multiannual Financial Framework 148
Neighbourhood Strategy 151
European Parliament 8, 63, 65, 77, 78, 79, 80, 83, 86, 90, 91
asylum policy 117
external relations 163
financial regulation 101, 102, 103, 106
free trade agreements 167
governance 187–8
and national parliaments 92–5
political groups 92
European Protection Order (EPO) 81, 82
European Rate Mechanism (ERM) 44 n 7
European Securities and Markets Authority (ESMA) 34, 102, 103–4, 114
European security and defence policy (ESDP) 165, 166, 169
European Semester 34, 85, 134, 144, 186–7
European Stability Mechanism (ESM) 6, 22, 23, 25, 29, 30, 31, 32, 33–4, 37, 85, 93–4, 96, 133 n 8, 144, 178, 179, 188, 189, 191, 192
European System of Financial Supervisors 112
European Supervisory Authorities (ESAs) 112, 113
European Systemic Risk Board (ESRB) 34, 113, 178, 184–5, 192
Europol 127
Euroscepticism 73, 85, 91, 95, 96, 191
eurozone 178–94
banking union 31–2
budget deficit 182
budgetary surveillance 135
economic outlook 179–82
financial supervision 184–5
GDP growth *180*
general government balance *182*
as global actor 190–1
governance 178, 187–90
inflation 180, *181*
membership issues 86–7
monetary policy 182–4
sovereign debt crisis 1, 2, 3, 6–35, *14–16*, *19–20*, *21*, *28*, 36, 39, 40–2, 46, 47, 53, 64, 69, 76, 77–8, 82, 85, 90–1, 94, 96, 97, 99, 108, 119, 132–40, 147, 148–50, 155, 156, 159, 162–3, 166, 171, 173, 175, 178–9, 184, 185, 188, 190, 191, 192, 195, 209
Stability and Growth Pact 185–7, 192
unemployment 180, *181*
excessive imbalance procedure (EIP) 34

financial crisis *see* eurozone crisis, global financial crisis
financial regulation 99–115, 132
Alternative Investment Fund Managers Directive 114
Capital Requirements Directive/Capital Requirements Regulation (CRDIV-CRR) 100, 105–7, 108, 109, 111, 113
European Market Infrastructure Regulation (EMIR) 100, 101–5, 113
Financial Conglomerates Directive (FiCOD) 106, 111
Markets in Financial Instruments Directive (MiFID) 100, 113
Markets in Financial Instruments Regulation (MiFIR) 100
Organized Trading Facility (OTF) 100
Finland 82, 165
economy 186
national parliament 94
Fiscal Compact 2, 31, 34, 62, 85, 86, 89, 92, 94, 96, 132, 137–40, 144, 147, 178, 189, 190, 192
Foreign Affairs Council 81
foreign policy 49–52, 54, 150, 162–6
France 49, 158, 163, 164, 179
border controls 124
economic policy co-ordination 133
economy 185, 188
financial regulation 101, 103, 104, 107, 188
Fiscal Compact 189
foreign policy 51
immigration 62, 122–3
military intervention in Libya 153–4, 165
national banks *107*, 108, *109*, 110
presidential election 86, 140, 144, 172
referendum on Constitutional Treaty 59
sovereign debt 22, 179
Franco–German relations 55, 69, 86, 88–90, 91, 97
Frankfurt Group 190
Frattini, Franco 122
free trade agreements 155, 166–7
EU–Japan 175
EU–Mercosur 172
EU–South Korea 167, 175
Frontex 122–5, 129
Füle, Štefan 152

G20 102, 105, 162, 173, 191
Gaddafi, Muammar 1, 154, 165
Gates, Robert 165
Geithner, Tim 173
Geneva Convention 118–19
Georgia 125, 154, 156
Georgieva, Kristalina 168
Gerardo Ruiz Zambrano v *Office national de l'emploi (ONEm)* 140
Germany 58, 70, 78, 91, 153, 164, 165, 179
  bonds risk premium 45, 60, 195
  border controls 124
  division of 49, 50
  economic policy co-ordination 133
  economy 180, 182, 183, 185, 202
  financial performance 47, 64
  financial regulation 101, 102, 103, 107, 188
  Fiscal Compact 189
  national banks *107*, 108, *109*, 110, 112
  national parliament 94–5
  unemployment 180
  unification of 50
global financial crisis 2, 132–3, 172
governance 85–98
  economic 85, 132–40
Greece 2, 101, 158, 164
  bail-outs 36, 60–1, 85, 87, 95, 189, 192
  economy 180, 182, 184, 186
  governance 85
  national parliament 94, 140
  referendums 95–6
  sovereign debt 21, 30, 31, 38, 53, 60–1, 69, 96, 108, 116, 178, 179, 190, 195
Grybauskaitė, Dalia 156

Hadžić, Goran 158
Herrmann, Joachim 123
Hollande, François 89
human rights 80, 155
humanitarian assistance 150, 154
Hungarian Presidency 3, 68–75, 76, 79, 82, 90, 93, 155
  cohesion policy 68, 70
  Danube Strategy (DRS) 70, 72
  energy policy 72
  enlargement 70
  migration 72
Hungary 64
  economic developments 202–3
  economic growth 196
  government debt 200
  inflation 197
  private sector financial balances 199
  public finances 199
  unemployment 196

Iceland 149, 156, 157, 159
immigration 54, 56, 62, 116
  Seasonal Workers Directive 119–20
India 166, 172
  relations with EU 170–1
inflation 8, 36, 40, 41–2, 180, *181*, 197–8, *198*
innovation triangle 68
integration 53–67, 77, 91, 97, 121, 144, 148
intergovernmentalism 86, 91, 105
internal market 60, 62, 78, 79, 99–115
  Alternative Investment Fund Managers Directive 114
  Capital Requirements Directive/Capital Requirements Regulation (CRDIV-CRR) 100, 105–7, 108, 109, 111, 113
  European Market Infrastructure Regulation (EMIR) 100, 101–5, 113
  Financial Conglomerates Directive (FiCOD) 106, 111
  Markets in Financial Instruments Directive (MiFID) 100, 113
  Markets in Financial Instruments Regulation (MiFIR) 100
  Organized Trading Facility (OTF) 100
internal security co-operation 127–8
  EU Organized Crime Threat Assessment (OCTA 2011) 127–8
  Europol 127
  JHA External Relations Trio Programme 128
International Criminal Tribunal for the former Yugoslavia (ICTY) 158
International Monetary Fund (IMF) 6, 7, 23, 29, 106–7, 110, 111, 159, 178, 182, 190, 191, 192, 204
  financial resources *24*
Iran 164, 169, 172, 174
Iraq 1, 50
  war in 60
Ireland
  bail-outs 36, 85, 189
  economy 185, 186
  integration 59–60
  national parliament 94
  referendum on Nice Treaty 59
  referendums 95–6
  sovereign debt 22, 30, 31, 60, 61, 62, 178, 195
Italy 2, 101
  economy 182, 185

immigration 62, 122–3
national parliament 94
sovereign debt 22, 25, 33–4, 36–8, 40, 42–6, *43*, *44*, *46*, 61, 63, 88, 96, 179, 190

Japan 58, 167, 171, 174
earthquake 72, 175, 195
foreign exchange reserves 23
relations with EU 175
sovereign debt 208
Jordan 1, 153
judicial co-operation 125–7
European Protection Order (EPO) 127
Hague Convention on the International Recovery of Child Support and Other Forms of Family Maintenance 125
Juncker, Jean-Claude 89, 97, 192
justice and home affairs (JHA) 116–31, 153
asylum policy 116–19
border and visa policy 122–5
Convention of the Hague Conference on Private International Law 116
Council 116, 128
criminal justice co-operation 116
European Court of Human Rights (ECtHR) 116, 119
European Court of Justice (ECJ) 55, 91, 92, 119, 132, 133, 138 n 39, 140–3, 144, 145, 174, 189
internal security co-operation 127–8
judicial co-operation 125–7
migration policy 116, 119–21
Stockholm Programme 128

Kazakhstan 169
Kirk, Ron 174
Kohl, Helmut 91
Kosovo 54, 62, 150, 157, 158–9
Kuwait 1
Kyrgyzstan 154, 169

Laeken Declaration 2, 59
Lagarde, Christine 190, 191, 192
Latvia
economic developments 203
economic growth 196
government debt 200
inflation 197
unemployment 196
laws and legal systems 132–46, 157–8
acquis Union 140–3
European Court of Justice (ECJ) 55, 91, 92, 119, 132, 133, 138 n 39, 140–3, 144, 145, 174, 189
excessive debt procedure (EDP) 34, 60, 133–4, 136–7
Fiscal Compact 2, 31, 34, 62, 85, 86, 89, 92, 94, 96, 132, 137–40, 144, 147
multilateral surveillance 133–7
Six Pack reforms 2, 34, 69, 72, 77, 79, 82, 85, 91, 92, 93–4, 96, 133–7, 139
Lehman Brothers 45
liberal intergovernmentalism 57
Liberia 170
Libya 1, 51, 72, 79, 117, 125, 147, 150, 151, 153–4, 164–5, 169, 174
Lisbon Treaty 68, 76, 77, 81, 82, 83, 94, 96, 120, 163, 168, 169, 186
foreign policy 148, 151, 152
proposed changes 85
standing European Council Presidency 89
Lithuania 111
economic developments 203–4
economic growth 196
government debt 200
inflation 197
private sector financial balances 199
unemployment 196
Luxembourg 188
Luxembourg Compromise 59

Maastricht Treaty 37, 47, 54, 64, 133
Macedonia 54, 157, 158
Macroeconomic Imbalance Procedure (MIP) 34
Malmström, Cecilia 117
Malta 117, 179
economy 186
markets 58
bond 1, 37, 40, 41
financial 39, 45, 179, 182, 184, 189, 191, 195, 200
labour 62
sovereign debt 53, 54, 60, 101
sub-prime mortgage 64
Maroni, Roberto 117, 122
Mauritania 125
Medvedev, Dmitry 169
Merkel, Angela 60, 78, 82, 88–90, 91, 92, 93, 95, 96, 97, 112, 183
Mladić, Ratko 158
Moldova 125, 154, 156
Montenegro 157, 158, 159

Monti, Mario 88, 179
Morocco 1, 125, 153, 167
Mozambique 168
M.S.S. v *Belgium and Greece* 116

national border controls 54
national central banks (NCBs) 7, 9–21, *14–16*, *19–20*, 25, 27–8, 29, 32, 37–8, 41
neofunctionalism 57
Netherlands 82, 164, 165
  economy 185
  Icesave dispute 157
  referendum on Constitutional Treaty 60
  sovereign debt 22
Nigeria 170
North Atlantic Treaty Organization (Nato) 59, 153–4, 158, 165
Norway 125

Obama, Barak 51, 173, 190
Orbán, Victor 70–1, 73
Organisation for Economic Co-operation and Development (OECD) 59, 65, 106–7, 111, 199
Organization for Security and Co-operation in Europe (OSCE) 59, 65
Osborne, George 191
over-the-counter derivatives (OTC) 99, 101, 102–3, 105, 113

Pakistan 170
Palestinian statehood 174
Papademos, Lucas 178
Papandreou, Georges 95–6, 178
peacekeeping operations 62
Pearson, Patrick 103
Poland 49, 64, 87
  economic developments 204
  economic growth 196
  financial regulation 102
  government debt 200
  private sector financial balances 199
Polish Presidency 3, 72–3, 76–84, 87, 93, 123, 155
  economic growth 78–9
  energy security, climate and defence 80–1
  eurozone crisis 77–8
  external relations 79–80
Portugal 91
  bail-outs 36, 189, 191
  economy 180, 182, 185, 186, 192
  national parliament 94
  sovereign debt 22, 30, 61, 96, 178, 179, 195
post-conflict diplomacy 62
Praet, Peter 183
Prodi, Romano 59
Putin, Vladimir 155, 169

Qatar 167

radical right-wing parties 64
redistribution 58
referendums 63, 95–6
  on Constitutional Treaty 59–60
  Croatian on accession 157
  Irish on Nice Treaty 59
Rehn, Olli 91, 93, 111, 187
Romania 72, 82, 157
  economic developments 204–5
  economic growth 196
  government debt 200
  inflation 197
  private sector financial balances 199
  unemployment 196
Rostowski, Jacek 77
Roussef, Dilma 172
Russia 65, 81, 149, 155, 166, 167, 172
  foreign policy 50, 51, 165
  presidential election 168–9
  relations with EU 168–9
  visa facilitation agreements 125

San Francisco Settlement 49
Sarkozy, Nicolas 62, 78, 82, 87, 89–90, 91, 93, 95, 97, 123, 183, 189
Saudi Arabia 167
Schengen agreement 54, 56, 62, 72, 82, 116, 117, 122–4, 157
  Schengen Information System (SIS II) 125
Schulz, Martin 93, 97
Securities Market Programme (SMP) 6, 25–6, 28–9, 33, 37, 182–3, 184, 191
Serbia 149, 150, 157, 158, 159
Shirley MacCarthy v *Secretary of State for the Home Department* 141, 143, 145
Sikorski, Radosław 78, 79
Singapore 166
single currency 1, 2, 3, 56, 69, 76, 150
single market 55, 91, 150
Slovakia 94, 111, 179
  economy 182, 185, 202

Slovenia 64, 157, 179
 economy 185
Smaghi, Lorenzo Bini 183
solidarity 4, 57–9, 117, 118
Somalia 169
Sørensen, Peter 159
South Korea 166
sovereign credit default swaps (CDS) 101
Soviet Union 50, 58, 65, 169
Spain
 border controls 124
 economy 185
 financial regulation 101, 108, 111
 national banks 112
 national parliament 94
 sovereign debt 22, 25, 33–4, 36–8, 40–1, 42, 61, 96, 179
Spanish–Belgian–Hungarian (SBH) team Presidency 68–70, 73
Sri Lanka 170
Stability and Growth Pact 31, 34, 133, 134, 144, 178, 185–7, 189, 192
 Six Pack reforms 2, 34, 69, 72, 77, 79, 82, 85, 91, 92, 93–4, 96, 133–7, 139, 178, 187–8, 192
Stark, Jürgen 183, 192
Steinbrück, Peer 60
Strauss Kahn, Dominique 190
Sudan 170
summits
 EU–Brazil 172
 EU–Japan 175
 EU–Latin America and Caribbean 173
 EU–Russia 169
 EU–US 173, 174
 European Council 86–92, 95, 96, 158–9
 G20 2009 Pittsburgh 102
 G20 2011 Cannes 173, 179, 190, 191, 192
supranationalism 55, 86, 91, 97
Sweden 80, 82, 165
 economic developments 205
 economic growth 196
 financial regulation 111, 113
 government debt 200
 inflation 197
 private sector financial balances 199
 public finances 199
 unemployment 196
Switzerland 78
Syria 1, 165, 169, 174

Tajikistan 169
Trans-Caspian Gas Pipeline System 81
Treaty on the Functioning of the European Union 38, 132, 138
Trichet, Jean-Claude 96–7, 179, 183, 185
Tunisia 1, 62, 117, 122, 125, 147, 154
Turkey 54, 149, 156, 157, 158, 172
Turkmenistan 81
Tusk, Donald 76, 77, 78, 83, 87, 88, 90
Tymoshenko, Yulia 80, 82, 155

Ukraine 80, 125, 147, 149, 154, 155–6
unemployment 56, 119, 121, 180, *181*, 196–7, *197*, 209
United Kingdom (UK) 86, 98, 163, 164
 economy 179, 195–6, 205–9
 EMU opt-outs 87, 189
 financial crisis 64
 financial regulation 101, 102, 103–4, 111, 112, 113
 Fiscal Compact 85, 147, 178, 190
 foreign exchange reserves 23
 foreign policy 51
 Icesave dispute 157
 military intervention in Libya 153–4, 165
 national banks *107*, 108, *109*, 109–10
 private sector financial balances 199
 public finances 199
 referendums 95–6
 residence permits 141–3
 sovereign debt 40–1
 unemployment 196
 wartime solidarity 58
United Nations 50
 UN Charter 50
 United Nations Office for the Co-ordination of Humanitarian Affairs (OCHA) 151
 United Nations Security Council 50, 153, 163, 165, 169
United States of America (USA) 78, 165, 171, 171
 economy 179, 183, 184, 207
 foreign exchange reserves 23, 104, 106
 foreign policy 4, 50, 51, 151, 163
 free trade agreement 167
 and IMF 7
 judicial co-operation 125
 relations with EU 173–5
 sovereign debt *45*, *208*
 sub-prime mortgage markets 64, 110
 wartime solidarity 58
Uzbekistan 79

Van Rompuy, Herman 53, 56, 69, 76, 77, 82, 83, 86, 87, 88, 89–90, 91, 94, 95, 97, 153, 171
Vanackere, Steven 187

Verhofstadt, Guy 89, 93
Vienna Settlement 49
visa liberalization 155
Visser, Robert 117

Weber, Axel 179, 183, 192
Weidmann, Jens 183
welfare state 58, 60, 62
West European Union 56
Western Balkans 54, 68, 70, 72, 128, 149, 150, 157, 158
World Bank 204
World Trade Organization (WTO) 104, 166, 167, 169, 173
World War I 49
World War II 4, 54, 58

Yemen 1

Zambrano judgment 142–3, 145

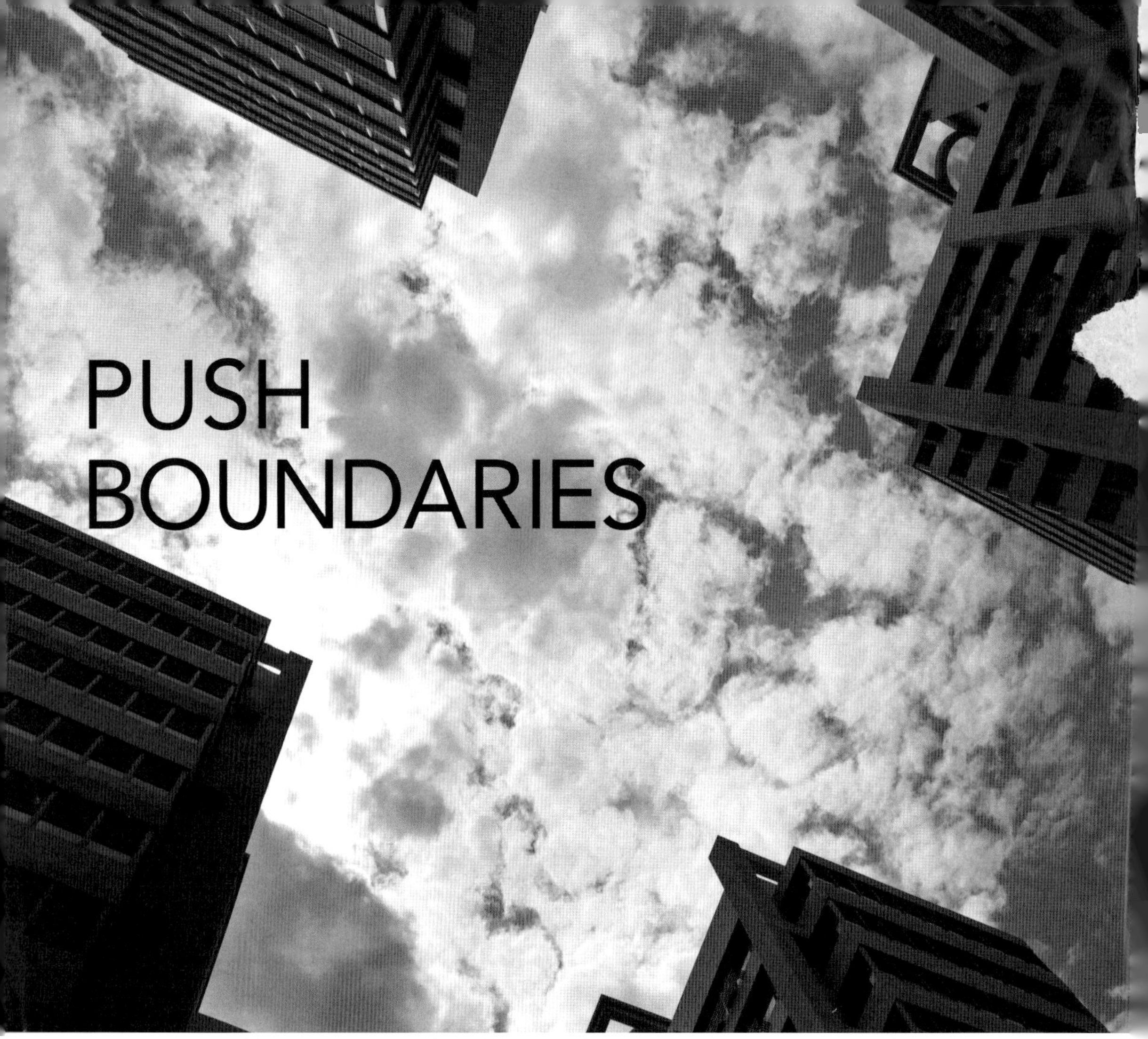